Intolerant Justice

Intolerant Justice

Conflict and Cooperation on Transnational Litigation

ASIF EFRAT

OXFORD
UNIVERSITY PRESS

OXFORD
UNIVERSITY PRESS

Oxford University Press is a department of the University of Oxford. It furthers the University's objective of excellence in research, scholarship, and education by publishing worldwide. Oxford is a registered trade mark of Oxford University Press in the UK and certain other countries.

Published in the United States of America by Oxford University Press
198 Madison Avenue, New York, NY 10016, United States of America.

Library of Congress Cataloging-in-Publication Data
Names: Efrat, Asif, author.
Title: Intolerant justice : conflict and cooperation on transnational litigation / Asif Efrat.
Description: New York, NY : Oxford University Press, [2023] |
Includes bibliographical references and index.
Identifiers: LCCN 2022024267 (print) | LCCN 2022024268 (ebook) |
ISBN 9780197658895 (hardback) | ISBN 9780197658918 (epub)
Subjects: LCSH: Exterritoriality. | Noncitizens—Legal status, laws, etc. | Universal jurisdiction. |
Criminal justice, Administration of—International cooperation. | Judgments, Foreign. |
Judicial assistance. | Conflict of laws.
Classification: LCC KZ3678 .E37 2022 (print) | LCC KZ3678 (ebook) |
DDC 341.4—dc23/eng/20220924
LC record available at https://lccn.loc.gov/2022024267
LC ebook record available at https://lccn.loc.gov/2022024268

DOI: 10.1093/oso/9780197658895.001.0001

1 3 5 7 9 8 6 4 2

Printed by Integrated Books International, United States of America

To Michael and Aviv

CONTENTS

ACKNOWLEDGMENTS

There is something both obvious and counterintuitive about cooperation among national legal systems. It is obvious, since such cooperation can do much good by facilitating crossborder economic transactions and aiding the fight against crime. But it is also counterintuitive, since law is quintessentially national: it represents *our* values, *our* way of life, *our* sovereignty—and all these might be compromised or threatened if we cooperate with foreign legal systems. I found this tension fascinating as a law student and, later, when working on a major case of extradition as a law clerk at the Israeli Supreme Court. My prior research on illicit trade led me, almost naturally, to put this tension at the center of a new research project that culminated in this book.

This project began with the case of child abduction, which I find particularly interesting: it shows how states manage to cooperate on a sensitive family matter. Abe Newman collaborated with me in the study of this case and, later, in the analysis of extradition and mutual legal assistance. Many of his ideas and insights can be found throughout the pages of this book, and I owe him a special debt of gratitude. Indeed, it was Abe who first suggested that this project result in a book!

Writing a theory is hard. I was fortunate to write the theoretical chapter of this book in the beautiful, serene environment of the European University Institute in Florence. My thanks go to Liav Orgad for hosting me there.

My own institution, Reichman University, also offered a wonderful setting in which to work on this book. I could not have completed this project without the encouragement and support of many wonderful colleagues, including Amnon Cavari, Boaz Ganor, Sivan Hirsch-Hoefler, Liza Ireni-Saban, Amichai Magen, Alex Mintz, Assaf Moghadam, and Daphné Richemond-Barak.

I received excellent research assistance from Yohan Zerbib. Guy Friedman helped with the statistical analysis, and Ruvik Danieli provided another pair of very helpful eyes.

At Oxford University Press, Dave McBride was a pleasure to work with, as always. I thank Dave for seeing the value of this book and leading the process of its publication. Three anonymous reviewers offered helpful comments, which allowed me to improve the manuscript. Bríd Nowlan's copyediting was helpful and thoughtful, and Sarah Ebel and Ganga Balaji ensured the smooth and professional production of the book.

Several articles laid the groundwork for Chapters 5, 6, and 9: "Deciding to Defer: The Importance of Fairness in Resolving Transnational Jurisdictional Conflicts" (with Abraham Newman), *International Organization* 70:2 (2016), 409–441; "Resisting Cooperation against Crime: Britain's Extradition Controversy, 2003–2015," *International Journal of Law, Crime and Justice* 52:1 (2018), 118–128; "Value-free Extradition? Human Rights and the Dilemma of Surrendering Wanted Persons to China" (with Marcello Tomasina), *Journal of Human Rights* 17:5 (2018), 605–621; and "Divulging Data: Domestic Determinants of International Information Sharing" (with Abraham Newman), *Review of International Organizations* 13:3 (2018), 395–419. I thank the publishers—respectively, Cambridge University Press, Elsevier, Taylor & Francis, and Springer—for the permission to use these materials.

This book is dedicated to my partner Michael and our daughter Aviv. Michael has been by my side throughout this project, and I am deeply grateful for his love and support. He is simply the best, in so many ways. Aviv became a part of our family as I was working on this book, and she has brought so much joy to my life. I hope that one day, when she is old enough to read this book, she will think it offers some insight into conflict and cooperation in the world. I also hope that Aviv—and her big siblings Tal and Yuly—will grow up in a world that sees much more cooperation than conflict.

SECTION I

INTRODUCING AND THEORIZING COOPERATION ON LITIGATION

1

Introduction

Let's begin this book with a little thought experiment.

Consider the following three scenarios:

1. You are studying toward a degree at a university located in a foreign country.
2. While traveling in that foreign country, you suddenly experience a medical emergency due to a car accident. You then go to the nearest hospital to get treatment.
3. You are charged with reckless driving that caused the car accident and expect to appear before a criminal court in the foreign country.

These three scenarios involve your interaction with foreign institutions of different types: respectively, foreign educational, medical, or judicial institutions. Which of these institutions are you most uncomfortable with? Which do you trust the least to treat you appropriately?

A reasonable guess is that studying at a university abroad raises little concern. You, the reader, may have indeed studied outside your home country. While people may appreciate their home country's educational system, they also recognize the benefits of studying at a university abroad, and many will happily attend one given the opportunity.[1]

Most of us will similarly be willing to receive medical service at a foreign hospital. Despite the intimate and sometimes invasive nature of medical treatment, we would typically agree to being examined and even operated on by doctors whose language we may not speak. We will simply assume or hope that they will deliver appropriate care.[2]

I would guess, however, that the third scenario made you, the reader, uncomfortable. Indeed, the thought of being criminally prosecuted before a foreign court will cause many of us to recoil. When it comes to standing before a foreign judge and being tried on the basis of foreign law, we will not typically assume or trust that justice will be delivered. On the contrary: we will doubt whether

Intolerant Justice. Asif Efrat, Oxford University Press. © Oxford University Press 2023.
DOI: 10.1093/oso/9780197658895.003.0001

foreign judges and foreign law will produce a fair outcome. Our strong preference would be to avoid a trial before a foreign court and, if necessary, to be tried by a court in our home country. Indeed, the prospect of a criminal trial before—and punishment from—legal institutions whose rules are unfamiliar could be terrifying.

This thought exercise demonstrates the strong attachment we typically feel toward our country's legal system—more than to some of the other systems that influence our lives. We may gladly acquire education in a foreign university; we may be willing to receive care in a foreign hospital; but we are deeply nervous about facing a foreign court. Indeed, we may seriously doubt whether the legal process and its outcome will meet our country's standards. This book examines the political ramifications of those doubts regarding foreign justice and how they might affect international cooperation among national legal systems. The need for such cooperation arises in a category of cases termed here *transnational litigation*: cases that come before domestic courts but are not purely domestic in nature. Rather, they involve foreign elements, and more than one country can claim legal authority over them. To handle a transnational case cooperatively, one legal system must cede its authority over the case to a foreign legal system. This effectively means that a local citizen could be subjected to foreign legal authority, raising a host of questions and concerns: Does the foreign legal system abide by the rule of law? Does it guarantee human rights? Will the foreign court grant our citizen the due process and fair treatment they would have enjoyed at home?

This book argues that the human disposition toward *ethnocentrism*—the tendency to denigrate out-groups and see them as inferior to the in-group—will often lead policymakers and other actors to answer these questions negatively. To the ethnocentric, a foreign legal system typically falls below the home country's standards and is unlikely to treat its citizens fairly. Understandably, such a view would make cooperation more difficult to establish. It would be harder to relinquish the jurisdiction over transnational cases to a foreign system; extraditing an alleged offender to stand trial abroad would seem unjust; and local enforcement of judgments issued by foreign courts could be perceived as an affront to legal sovereignty that contravenes fundamental norms. This book examines who expresses such views and how they frame them; and, on the other hand, who seeks to dispel these concerns and what arguments they use. In other words, the domestic political debate over transnational litigation stands at the center of the following pages. In contrast to some optimistic accounts of judicial globalization,[3] the account offered here shows that cooperation among legal systems could raise a heated controversy, fueled by fear and mistrust of foreign justice.

Scope of the Analysis: Defining Transnational Litigation

This book examines the domestic political tensions surrounding transnational litigation and cooperation with foreign legal systems. Demarcating the boundaries of the analysis requires us, first, to define what transnational litigation is. As Roger Cotterrell has observed, the realization that the law often spills out beyond the borders of the nation-state has led scholars to employ the term transnational law to indicate legal relations and norms that are not those of domestic law, on the one hand, but, on the other hand, do not clearly fall within the realm of international law. While widely invoked, however, the term transnational law is rarely defined with much precision.[4] Here we will seek to be more precise in defining the admittedly narrower concept of transnational *litigation*. For the purposes of this book, we consider transnational litigation to be a legal process before a domestic court involving a foreign element. That foreign element may take various forms. For example, the case before the court may revolve around events, activities, or situations that occurred in a foreign country; the case may involve foreign parties; or it may include another foreign legal element, such as the application of foreign law, the enforcement of judgments issued by foreign courts, or obtaining evidence from abroad.[5]

This definition is narrow in scope in that it focuses on formal legal processes before *domestic courts*. This excludes various other processes of dispute resolution before international courts[6] or private arbitration bodies.[7] At the same time, this definition is broad in that it includes both civil and criminal litigation. Analyses of transnational litigation, typically written by legal scholars, tend to focus on transnational *civil* litigation, from commercial disputes through tort claims to crossborder family matters.[8] Yet there is nothing in the concept of transnational litigation to limit its applicability to the civil realm. Criminal cases may also involve foreign defendants or arise from events that occurred outside the national territory.[9] This book therefore addresses the dilemmas surrounding civil as well as criminal litigation. In both the civil and criminal areas, the transnational legal process determines the legal responsibility of *private* actors (individual, collective, or corporate); and it does so on the basis of state-made legal sources: international treaties, national legislation, or case law.[10]

Systematic data on transnational litigation are scarce. This concept captures a large variety of legal processes, carried out by domestic legal authorities, and there is no single source to keep track and record data on relevant cases—within a single country, let alone across countries. One would generally expect to observe more transnational legal cases in the age of globalization, which is characterized by growing crossborder interaction.[11] Bits and pieces of existing data tend to support this expectation. Kaczmarek and Newman document an increase in the number of cases against companies that engage in corrupt conduct abroad during the 2000s.[12] The number of individuals extradited among EU members—transferred from one EU country to stand criminal trial in another—increased more than eightfold from 836 in 2005 to 6,976 in 2018.[13] Quintanilla and Whytock present a more complex picture of fewer civil cases involving foreigners before U.S. District Courts in the 1990s and 2000s, alongside an increasing number of cases seeking to enforce foreign judgments in the United States.[14]

But the significance of transnational litigation is not measured only in numbers of cases or in the immediate impact on the parties to the cases. Rather, transnational litigation carries broader ramifications for the certainty, stability, and efficiency of transnational exchange and for the conduct of transnational actors. For example, the ability to have a foreign judgment enforced against a party for breach of contract may offer reassurance that facilitates the signing of the contract; the prospect of criminal prosecution for one's actions abroad may deter companies from offering bribes to foreign officials.[15]

In this book, however, we focus on the *political* ramifications of transnational litigation. Indeed, transnational litigation carries major significance for governments, as it determines the boundaries of their spheres of influence and the allocation of governance authority among them. The ability to apply and enforce its laws in transnational cases expands the state's influence and allows it to shape transnational interactions in accordance with its policy goals and preferences; an inability to do so limits the reach and effectiveness of national rules.[16] Transnational litigation therefore raises a host of sensitive questions regarding sovereignty, statehood, national control, and interstate relations. The assertion of jurisdiction over actions that occur in a foreign territory might clash with the foreign state's own claim of jurisdiction; the enforcement of judgments issued by foreign courts could be seen as compliance with the orders of foreign sovereigns and as undermining local legal sovereignty;[17] and the (in)ability to have individuals extradited from abroad affects a government's capacity to maintain the rule of law and punish criminal conduct.

Our interest in the political aspects of transnational litigation prompts us to shift the focus of investigation from the courts to the political arena—a move that constitutes one of the primary innovations in this book as compared to existing analyses of transnational litigation. Works on transnational litigation typically focus on courts and how they handle or decide transnational cases.[18] The focus on courts seems obvious: if transnational litigation involves legal cases heard and decided by courts, then courts should stand at the heart of the analysis. Yet courts—and other actors involved in law enforcement, such as prosecutors or the police—do not handle transnational cases in a vacuum. They operate within a normative framework of national legislation and international agreements that guides their cooperative interaction with foreign legal systems. Indeed, transnational legal cases implicitly or explicitly raise dilemmas of cooperation with foreign legal systems: Should we exercise extraterritorial jurisdiction over a matter that occurred on foreign territory and comes under a foreign country's jurisdiction? Should we extradite this alleged offender pursuant to the foreign country's request to try them before its courts? Should we enforce a judgment issued by a foreign country's courts? Treaties and statutes can answer these questions in a more cooperative or less cooperative manner. They may facilitate greater cooperation with the foreign legal system by restraining local courts' extraterritorial jurisdiction, allowing extradition with limited conditions and requirements, and enabling easy enforcement of foreign-court judgments. Alternatively, treaties and legislation may allow courts to exercise broad extraterritorial jurisdiction, and they may establish conditions and requirements that make it harder to extradite wanted persons or enforce foreign judgments.

This book focuses on the rules and arrangements—domestic and international—crafted by political authorities for handling transnational litigation. It is these arrangements—treaties and statutes—that establish the basic parameters for interactions with foreign legal systems and set the fundamental rules for cooperation, long before any specific case reaches a judge.[19] In that sense, transnational litigation resembles other policy domains associated with globalization, such as immigration or trade, where treaties and statutes establish the scope and depth of international cooperation and the degree of openness to foreign influences.[20] Similarly, transnational-litigation arrangements determine the extent to which a country is (un)willing to limit its legal sovereignty and accept the exercise of legal authority by foreign countries. By examining these arrangements, we gain insight into the fundamental question of who has the authority to make and enforce rules and adjudicate disputes in a world characterized by multiple and overlapping jurisdictions.[21] In yet another similarity to the study of trade and immigration,[22] this book focuses on the *domestic political contestation* surrounding transnational litigation: the tensions, dilemmas, and controversies that transnational litigation raises, and how they play out in the domestic political arena. From this perspective, transnational litigation is not an arcane topic, of interest only to a small group of lawyers and judges. Rather, much like trade and immigration, it is an issue that can generate public interest and concern and become the topic of a lively, heated political debate. Politicians, bureaucrats, the media, nongovernmental organizations (NGOs), and members of the public may all participate in and fuel this debate, supporting or opposing cooperation with a foreign legal system. That political debate—and the rules for transnational litigation that it yields—stands at the center of this book.

Theoretical Approach and Argument

Transnational litigation involves an overlap and potential conflict of legal authority between multiple countries. As the legal case concerns foreign actors, or arises from events that happened in a foreign country, it potentially implicates the legal authority of more than one country. For the sake of the analysis, we will assume that two countries may exercise their authority over the case: a home country (where the case is actually being handled) and a foreign country (which may also exercise its authority over the case). Cooperation means that the home country abstains from or limits the exercise of its own legal authority and accepts—even facilitates—the foreign country's exercise of authority. For example, the home country may decline to exercise jurisdiction over a case and allow the foreign country to decide that case; it can abstain from prosecuting a person and, instead, extradite them to stand trial in a foreign country; it may decline to apply its own law to the case and, instead, apply foreign law; or it may enforce a judgment issued by a foreign court, rather than decide the case itself.

Engaging in cooperation on litigation carries important benefits: it provides certainty and stability for crossborder commercial relations, prevents conflicting decisions and a waste of legal resources, and avoids frictions and tensions among states.[23] Given such benefits, why resist cooperation? This is indeed the first question we ask in analyzing domestic political debates over transnational litigation. Why does cooperation with foreign legal systems often meet with objections and criticism? Such political resistance, however, is not uniform. Cooperation with certain foreign countries might indeed face fierce objections by home-country actors, while cooperation with other countries may raise little concern. Our second question is therefore: Why does a home country's willingness to cooperate vary across partner-countries? The third question we ask is: Why does the willingness to cooperate vary across domestic actors? Why are some domestic actors more favorable to the idea of cooperating with a foreign legal system, while others oppose it? And finally: How does the debate over cooperation play out? How do proponents and opponents of cooperation attempt, respectively, to mitigate or activate concerns about a foreign legal system and its exercise of authority?

To answer these questions, this book draws on the concept of ethnocentrism. Ethnocentrism is an individual disposition to divide society into an in-group—one's own group seen as superior—and an out-group that is different and inferior by comparison.[24] Such a worldview inspires solidarity, pride, trust, and favoritism toward in-groups, as opposed to hostility and denigration toward out-groups. Simply put, an ethnocentric outlook partitions the world into "us-against-them"—virtuous in-groups and nefarious out-groups—and it guides the perception, thought, and action of individuals independently of other social and political dispositions, such as partisanship or ideological identification. The ethnocentric puts their in-group at the center, rates and evaluates out-groups in comparison to the in-group, and typically finds that the out-groups fall short of the superior in-group, resulting in sentiments of mistrust and resentment toward out-groups.[25]

Various authors have sought to identify the causes of ethnocentrism: What inspires such a worldview, and why are some individuals more ethnocentric than others? Theories identify the origins of ethnocentrism in, among other things, feelings of fear and threat and the ability to find security with one's group;[26] an authoritarian personality;[27] a sense of self-esteem and need for superiority;[28] or ignorance regarding other groups and lack of contact with them.[29] This book, however, is not about the causes of ethnocentrism, but its *political consequences*. Several studies have explored some of these consequences. Donald Kinder and Cindy Kam's landmark study identifies ethnocentrism as an important driver of American public opinion. They find that ethnocentrism encourages American support for war and international confrontation, from the struggle against the Soviet Union to the fight against terrorism; and ethnocentrism also undercuts American support for assistance to foreign counties.[30] They further find that ethnocentric Americans tend to be more approving of discrimination against gays and less supportive of social-welfare programs.[31] While they cover a range of domestic and international issues, all these attitudes share a fundamental commonality: they reflect in-group pride and loyalty versus out-group hostility and denigration, or a general readiness to partition the world into allies and adversaries.

Studies that document a negative effect of ethnocentrism on attitudes toward crossborder exchange carry particular relevance for the subject matter of this book. A sizeable literature suggests that ethnocentrism might generate hostility toward immigrants, fostering a view of them as a threat to the local population and its values.[32] But it is not only the inflow of people that bothers the ethnocentric person. The inflow of goods—that is, trade—also exposes local society to foreign influences that may undermine its traditions and change its culture. Ethnocentric individuals have indeed been shown to view trade liberalization and economic integration as harmful.[33] Studies in international marketing also document a clear impact of ethnocentrism on consumer preferences. Ethnocentric consumers favor local over foreign products—reflecting their support for the domestic economy and their positive evaluation of the in-group.[34] Moving from goods to capital, U.S. states where ethnocentrism is rife have been shown to receive less foreign direct investment, likely because ethnocentrism is seen as creating an inhospitable environment for foreign businesses.[35]

Whereas existing studies examine the impact of ethnocentric sentiments on international *economic* exchange, this book applies the concept of ethnocentrism to the legal sphere and suggests that ethnocentrism fosters an aversion to foreign laws and foreign legal institutions. Indeed, transnational litigation presents a clear in-group vs. out-group setting that involves an interaction between the home legal system and a foreign legal system. In such a setting, the foreign legal system's exercise of authority could potentially be viewed as threatening the home country or its citizens. Such an ethnocentric view would reflect the law's central role in society and its cultural significance: the law as part of a country's social fabric, embodying local values, traditions, and way of life.[36] The law's close link with one's culture and values yields an attachment to the home legal system: a perception that one should be subject to the legal norms and institutions of the country of which one is a national.[37] This in-group bias is coupled with out-group negativity. Since it reflects the values, practices, and traditions of another country, the foreign legal system might be viewed by the ethnocentric person as incompatible with, and inferior to, the home system. This could fuel sentiments of mistrust or hostility toward the foreign system and a reluctance to accept its exercise of authority.

The prejudice against the foreign legal system is twofold. First, foreign legal authorities themselves may seem alien, untrustworthy, and even dangerous. An ethnocentric will not trust foreign legal institutions to handle a case fairly and will fear the biased or abusive treatment they might accord to the home-country citizen.[38] This concern is not aimed at a specific foreign country: it is the exercise of foreign legal authority in a case involving the home country that raises concern. Second, the foreign legal rules and procedures might be deemed inconsistent with and inferior to the home country's rules and procedures. This means that an ethnocentric conducts an implicit or explicit comparison between the laws of a *specific* foreign country and the home country's laws. In such a comparison, the ethnocentric may not expect full consistency between the two systems, but an expectation of compatibility does drive the comparison of fundamental procedural attributes and substantive norms. On the procedural side, the foreign system may be assessed on its conformity to the rule of law (e.g., the independence and impartiality of the courts);[39] respect for fair-trial rights (e.g., the presumption of innocence and the right to legal representation);[40] and any other procedural or institutional element that the home country deems fundamental (such as a jury in the United States[41]).[42] Foreign substantive rules may be evaluated on their conformity with fundamental values, such as human rights and legal equality.[43] Tending to denigrate out-groups, an ethnocentric will typically find that the foreign rules and procedures fall below those of the home country, as they insufficiently protect core values and principles.

Both types of concerns—the rejection of any foreign legal involvement in litigation relating to home-country actors or apprehension about specific foreign rules or procedures that seem unjust—yield a similar noncooperative preference: cooperation on litigation is viewed as posing a risk to the home country and its citizens and, as such, should be avoided. Some domestic actors are particularly likely to subscribe to this noncooperative preference and its underlying ethnocentric view. Among them are the government's political opponents, who may portray the government's willingness to cooperate as a dangerous surrender to a foreign legal system, which undermines local values and threatens the home country's citizens. Civil society actors may similarly hold concerns and reservations about legal cooperation. The home-country bias of journalists,[44] often exhibited during times of war or national crisis, may lead them to rally against the threat to local citizens and values. NGOs concerned for human rights might fear the human rights consequences of cooperation with a foreign legal system. Lawyers, steeped in local rules and procedures, may take pride in their legal system and reject foreign rules and procedures as wrong or inferior.[45]

By contrast, actors within the state apparatus typically view cooperation on litigation more favorably. Jurists who belong to the state—such as judges, prosecutors, and the justice-ministry bureaucracy—may support cooperation out of a concern for reciprocity or based on the principled belief that offenders should not escape responsibility by crossing national borders.[46] The ministry of foreign affairs and the ministry of defense may similarly support cooperation on litigation that could yield diplomatic or security benefits.[47]

As the political debate unfolds, actors will either seek to obstruct or weaken the cooperative efforts by activating and amplifying ethnocentric concerns about the foreign legal system; or they may seek to facilitate cooperation by allaying these concerns. In particular, actors will try to shape and manipulate policymakers' understanding of the gap separating the home and foreign legal systems. After all, it is difficult to measure or evaluate this gap in an objective, clear-cut manner. For example, if the home country holds jury trials and the foreign country does not, does this make the foreign trials unfair? Those opposing the cooperative efforts would answer in the affirmative. They will emphasize the differences between the two legal systems, exaggerate their significance, and present the foreign rules and procedures as inherently unfair or dangerous. Specifically, they would argue that a trial without a jury goes against notions of justice or undermines a fundamental right of the home-country citizen.[48] By contrast, actors who support cooperation will downplay the differences. They may argue that not every deviation from local standards is necessarily wrong, or they may reassure policymakers that, notwithstanding the gap between the home and foreign systems, adequate safeguards exist that will guarantee fair treatment by foreign legal authorities.[49] In the jury example, the actors in favor of cooperation will argue that the foreign criminal-justice process includes enough protections and safeguards to make a trial fair even in the absence of a jury.

Additional factors may influence the intensity of ethnocentric concerns and the degree of resistance to cooperation on litigation. If legal cooperation is presented as not only causing suffering and distress to the individual involved, but as having a negative impact on society as a whole—such as harming national security or undermining core social values—cooperation may encounter stronger resistance. The intensity of ethnocentric concerns may also vary with the identity of the individual concerned. The exercise of foreign legal authority over a citizen of the home country will likely raise more concern than the subjection of a foreigner to a foreign legal process.[50] Unpopular groups within the home country—for example, ethnic or religious minorities—may be more easily subjected to foreign legal processes. By contrast, the prospect of ill-treatment by foreign legal institutions will likely provoke significant concern when the individuals involved represent the state or act on its behalf, such as diplomats and soldiers.[51]

The theoretical framework described above is laid out in full in Chapter 2, where it is summarized by a set of propositions that appear throughout that chapter.

In closing this overview of the book's theoretical account, three important points deserve mention and clarification. First, this theoretical account addresses the concerns that transnational legal cooperation raises and how opponents and proponents of cooperation seek, respectively, to highlight or downplay them. It examines how differences between legal systems are interpreted by various actors, the arguments they adduce to support their views, and the likelihood of these arguments' gaining traction. In short, the theoretical focus is on the *dynamic of the domestic political debate* over transnational litigation, rather than the debate's outcome. Second, this book's focus on ethnocentrism does not imply that that is the only obstacle to cooperation on litigation. Cooperation between legal systems may face a variety of other, more familiar obstacles, from limited government capacity or resources[52] through the noncooperative preferences of domestic actors[53] to diplomatic frictions between governments.[54] By highlighting ethnocentrism this book advances our understanding of an underappreciated constraint on international cooperation. Third, while this book emphasizes ethnocentric sentiments as a key influence on transnational litigation, these sentiments do not necessarily trump all other influences and do not always obstruct cooperation. Whether cooperation is actually established and in what form also depends on the government's willingness and ability to counter and overcome the ethnocentric resistance. The ethnocentric criticism makes cooperation costly for the government, but the government may believe that the necessity or benefits of cooperation are compelling enough to outweigh the political costs. If the government holds the necessary political leverage, it may be able to overcome the ethnocentric resistance and establish cooperation.

Overview of the Empirical Cases

The political debate over transnational litigation stands at the heart of six qualitative empirical chapters that are grouped in three sections: jurisdiction, extradition, and foreign-judgment enforcement. Each section examines the challenges of cooperation on litigation from a different angle, but they all focus on the *political dynamic* of transnational litigation. This means that discussion of legal technicalities is kept to the minimum necessary for analyzing the politics of the law. The empirical analysis in the six chapters serves to illustrate and probe the plausibility of the propositions that summarize the key theoretical insights.

The jurisdiction section addresses the dilemma that arises when the home country's citizens, present in a foreign country, commit offenses there. Such a situation presents a jurisdictional overlap. The home country typically has jurisdiction over these individuals and may try them for their crimes abroad; but they also come under the foreign country's jurisdiction for the crimes committed on its territory against its citizens. Who will get to try these offenders?

Chapter 3 examines this dilemma in the context of the 1951 NATO Status of Forces Agreement (SOFA), which allocates jurisdiction over American troops who commit criminal offenses in the European countries that host them. That jurisdiction over the troops is divided between the United States and host countries was, in itself, a major innovation. Prior to 1945, military forces operating on foreign soil often enjoyed immunity from local jurisdiction under the "law of the flag" doctrine. Yet a growing sense of national sovereignty and pride in countries hosting U.S. forces after World War II made it difficult for the United States to demand that its troops abroad be subject exclusively to its criminal jurisdiction.[55] In the NATO SOFA the United States agreed that NATO members would exercise criminal jurisdiction over U.S. troops, especially those who committed off-duty offenses, from traffic accidents to bar fights to rape or murder of local citizens. Yet this sacrifice of jurisdiction over American troops sparked a fierce controversy when the NATO SOFA came before the U.S. Senate for ratification in 1953. Consistent with the theoretical expectation, supporters of the agreement came from the State Department, the Department of Defense, the Department of Justice, and the military. For them, the distribution of jurisdiction between the United States and host countries was fair, sensible, and appropriate. They suggested that an insistence on exclusive U.S. jurisdiction over the troops was unnecessary from a military standpoint, might antagonize allies, and could undermine an agreement that was vital to U.S. security. Importantly, they saw little reason to fear the legal differences between the United States and its allies which, they believed, had civilized standards of justice.

Opponents of the agreement in the Senate heavily disputed the latter claim. In ethnocentric fashion, they held up the American legal standards as the metric for the evaluation of foreign systems and highlighted the flaws that, in their view, existed in the legal systems of NATO allies: from trial without a jury through the absence of the presumption of innocence to cruel and unusual punishment. While defenders of the NATO SOFA sought to downplay these purported flaws as a misunderstanding or an exaggeration, opponents of the agreement insisted that U.S. troops before European courts would not enjoy a fair trial that met American standards and that the safeguards included in the NATO SOFA were insufficient. While its opponents ultimately failed to thwart the ratification of the NATO SOFA, their efforts give us insight into the tactics that may be employed to fuel ethnocentric concerns over transnational litigation: from framing U.S. troops as "boys" deserving of protection to citing letters from troops who denounced the agreement as a "sad travesty."

The chapter concludes by demonstrating that, to this day, the United States looks at foreign legal systems with suspicion and is often reluctant to submit U.S. troops to their jurisdiction.

While Chapter 3 deals with a population considered deserving of strong legal protection—soldiers—Chapter 4 examines the exact opposite: foreign fighters for the Islamic State—ISIS—returning to their home countries in Europe. The fall of the ISIS "caliphate" in 2018 ignited a debate about whether Europeans who fought for ISIS in Syria and Iraq should be allowed to return to their countries of origin and which court should try them for their crimes. It is the latter question that occupies us here, and we examine the debate as it unfolded in Britain. In that debate, the government was adamant that Britons who had joined ISIS should *not* stand trial before British courts. Rather, the government argued that they should be prosecuted "in the most appropriate jurisdiction"—outside Britain.[56] This reluctance of the government to exercise criminal jurisdiction over its own citizens—indeed, their abandonment to any foreign jurisdiction—stems from the view of the foreign fighters as a security threat, the moral revulsion from the atrocities they committed, and their belonging to a minority group—the Muslim community—that faced some prejudice in Britain. These three factors combined to effectively cast the foreign fighters as an out-group unworthy of British justice. This supports one of the book's theoretical insights, namely, that the intensity of ethnocentric concerns may vary with the identity of the actors subjected to foreign legal authority. While soldiers are seen as deserving of strong protections from foreign justice (the subject of Chapter 3), individuals who betrayed their country, such as foreign terrorist fighters, can be left to the mercy of courts in Syria or Iraq that lack due process.

The book's second empirical section examines international extradition: the surrender of alleged offenders to a foreign country for the purpose of criminal prosecution or punishment. A key tool for fighting crime, extradition raises ethnocentric concerns: Does the foreign country requesting the extradition meet the home country's standards of due process and human rights, and will the extradited person enjoy a fair legal process there? Chapter 5 examines how two countries considered to be human rights leaders—Australia and Canada—grappled with these questions as they contemplated the signing of an extradition treaty with China, a country with a poor human rights record and weak rule of law. In contrast to this book's other chapters, where the debate revolves around the subjection of the home country's citizens to a foreign legal process, in this case Australia and Canada faced the dilemma of sending *Chinese* citizens back to China to stand trial. Yet the political debate in both countries, which took place in 2016–2017, largely unfolded along the theoretically expected lines. In Australia, the strongest opposition to the extradition treaty came from the legal community. The Law Council, which represents the legal profession, raised a host of concerns regarding China's respect for human rights, the rule of law, and procedural fairness in criminal proceedings, doubting whether the extradition treaty was indeed in Australia's national interest. Australia's NGO community shared these doubts and questioned the effectiveness of the safeguards included in the proposed treaty. By contrast, defenders of the treaty from the Attorney-General's Department insisted that these safeguards do guarantee adequate human rights protection; furthermore, they argued that extradition relations, in fact, do not require equivalence between justice systems. Labor—the opposition party—rejected these arguments, demonstrating how political opponents may attack a government willing to cooperate on litigation.

In Canada, the political debate unfolded along similar lines, with critics of the planned extradition treaty emphasizing China's lower standards of justice and supporters arguing that extradition to China would actually push the latter closer to international legal standards. As in Australia, the extradition-treaty initiative provided ammunition for the opposition to attack the government and accuse it of hypocrisy or naivety. Yet, while in Australia it was the left-leaning Labor who opposed extradition to China, in Canada it was the right-wing Conservatives who led the charge against the extradition-treaty initiative. This demonstrates that legal ethnocentrism does not necessarily correlate with partisanship and is not limited to the right-wing side of the political spectrum, as one might intuitively expect.

Whereas hesitations and reservations about extradition to China seem understandable and natural, Chapter 6 examines a more surprising debate in Britain arising from concerns about extradition to democratic countries generally committed to human rights: the United States and European Union members. More specifically, critics targeted the 2003 U.S.-UK extradition treaty and the 2003 Extradition Act; the latter, among other reforms, implemented the European Arrest Warrant, a streamlined framework for extradition among EU members. The critics—in particular, conservative members of parliament, NGOs concerned with the rule of law and criminal justice, and certain media outlets—raised two types of concerns. First, they sought to impose or maintain barriers to extradition on the belief that British citizens deserve British justice and should be tried at home. This reflects a principled resistance to any foreign legal system exercising its authority over British citizens. Second, extradition critics aired a set of more specific complaints, noting perceived incompatibilities between British justice and foreign justice and expressing a belief in the superiority of the former over the latter. From concerns about the harshness of U.S. criminal justice to denunciations of human rights standards in certain EU countries, extradition critics exhibited ethnocentric thinking as they considered deviations from British legal standards to be indications of unfairness. The defenders of Britain's extradition arrangements criticized the ethnocentric tendency "in this country [to] think our system is best and, therefore, anybody who does anything differently has got it wrong."[57] This repudiation of ethnocentrism, and support for easier, faster extradition, came primarily from jurists in the state apparatus who prioritized the effectiveness of law enforcement over the protection of individuals from a possibly unfair legal process abroad. For them, cross-country differences in legal rules, procedures, and institutions amounted to normal variations among legal systems, which should not impede criminal-justice cooperation. Overall, the controversy over Britain's extradition arrangements, like the controversy over extradition to China, serves to demonstrate how different actors within a country may vary tremendously in their evaluation of the significance and implications of the differences among legal systems.

The book's third empirical section takes us from the area of criminal justice to the civil-justice territory. Specifically, it examines concerns regarding the enforcement of civil judgments issued by foreign courts. Giving local effect to foreign judgments serves the interests of legal certainty and stability and prevents re-litigation of disputes with possibly conflicting decisions. At the same time, these judgments are the products of foreign laws issued by foreign institutions, and, as such, they might offend local norms and values. Chapter 7 seeks to identify why American judgments often encounter obstacles to their enforcement in the courts of Continental Europe. The unwelcoming attitude toward U.S. judgments stems in large part from the European view of American civil justice as marred by significant unfairness. The chapter focuses on three expressions of perceived unfairness in U.S. law: punitive damages, pretrial discovery, and personal jurisdiction.

In tort cases, American courts may require offenders to pay damages to compensate plaintiffs for the harm they suffered; and they may also impose *punitive damages* on offenders to punish them for their outrageous behavior and to deter them and others from committing similar conduct in the future. These two goals of retribution and deterrence turn punitive damages into a quasi-penal remedy situated within a private-law domain. Whereas in the United States and in other common-law countries punitive damages are seen as a legitimate instrument that serves important purposes, civil-law countries in Europe consider punitive damages problematic and unfair. The civil law maintains a strict separation between the private law of torts and criminal law; tort damages that serve to punish blur the boundary between the two domains. Furthermore, the vagueness of the standards for determining the offender's liability for punitive damages, as well as the amount of damages, goes against the civil law's quest for certainty.

Broad pretrial discovery is another hallmark of U.S. civil justice that Continental Europeans abhor. In discovery, lawyers for the parties gather the facts of the case with minimal court supervision, and they may require the other party to make available any document that is relevant to their party's claim or defense. While this process is aimed at increasing trial fairness by preventing unfair surprises, it is also expensive and prone to abuse. For these reasons, it has come under criticism in the United States itself. But the reservations of Europeans about this process go deeper, since discovery reflects a legal culture and values that are antithetical to theirs. Assigning the task of evidence gathering to the parties reflects a mistrust of authority and a belief in litigant activism—in contrast to the more bureaucratic legal model of the civil law with its official responsibility for fact-finding and a limited role for the litigants. Furthermore, Europeans hold a more expansive notion of privacy than Americans. As evidence gathering entails a balance between finding the truth and protecting the privacy of litigants, Europeans assign greater weight to the protection of privacy.

The Europeans' quest for clarity, certainty, and predictability of legal rules leads them to reject the American notion of personal jurisdiction. In the civil law, jurisdiction builds on a limited number of bright-line rules that provide litigants with relatively certain knowledge as to where jurisdiction might exist. In the United States, by contrast, jurisdictional rules include broad, open-ended terms. For example, an American court may acquire jurisdiction over a nonresident of the state when that nonresident has sufficient "minimum contacts" with that state. Such rules, in the European view, are unclear and unfair. They may establish jurisdiction in the absence of a substantive connection between the actual claim and the forum state and give judges too much discretion in the application of the law.

The European wariness toward American judgments, and the resulting difficulty in enforcing American judgments in Europe, motivated the United States to initiate a global convention on the enforcement of foreign judgments. The chapter concludes with an examination of the challenges that this initiative faced from its onset in 1992 to the completion of a convention in 2019.

Chapter 8 also examines concerns about foreign judgments. This time, these are American concerns about libel judgments issued by British courts against American authors and publishers. These courts became attractive sites for suing Americans whose publications had little connection with Britain—a phenomenon labeled "libel tourism"—because of the plaintiff-friendly attitude of British defamation law. First and foremost, British law traditionally has placed on the defendant the burden of proving the truth of the defamatory statement—in contrast to the United States, where it is the plaintiff who has to prove that the statement is false. British libel judgments thus ran contrary to U.S. libel law and to the American commitment to free speech enshrined in the First Amendment. This British-American gap in protecting free speech, and its exploitation against American authors and publishers, prompted Congressional action. In 2010, Congress enacted the SPEECH Act,[58] which instructs a U.S. court to enforce a foreign libel judgment only if it determines that the foreign defamation law provided at least as much protection for freedom of speech and press in that case as would be provided by the First Amendment. This noncooperative measure—a legislative prohibition on enforcing foreign judgments that fail to meet American standards—followed the advocacy campaign of an American author who was sued in a London court by a Saudi billionaire whom she had described in her book as a financier of terrorism. This case demonstrates how a personal story of hardship can elicit ethnocentric concerns about foreign law, and how such concerns are magnified when the story is framed more broadly. Proponents of the legislation presented libel tourism as foreign interference with the cherished American right of free speech and also as a security threat, since it chilled the exposure and discussion of terrorism. Both Democratic and Republican lawmakers embraced these arguments, demonstrating that legal ethnocentrism may hold a bipartisan appeal.

The various case studies all offer support for a key theoretical insight: states prefer partners whose legal rules and institutions resemble their own. If the foreign legal system is judged to fall below the standards of the home system, cooperation might meet resistance among the home-country actors and will be more difficult to establish. Chapter 9 tests this proposition through a quantitative analysis that includes a large number of countries. The analysis shows that greater similarity in substantive legal rules or in legal procedures and institutions increases the likelihood of cooperation between two countries; as the legal gaps widen, the likelihood of cooperation diminishes. This finding, in the criminal domain, emerges from an analysis of mutual legal assistance treaties (MLATs): agreements that commit states to sharing evidence with their foreign partners to assist in the investigation or prosecution of transnational legal cases. Such evidence sharing, however, raises concerns of possible misuse or abuse of the information provided. The analysis here finds that states tend to lower this risk by being selective in their choice of MLAT partners. States that rank high on judicial independence are more likely to enter into MLATs with countries whose courts are similarly independent. Furthermore, states prefer MLAT partners that belong to the same legal tradition as themselves: civil, common, or Islamic law. Similarity of legal tradition or equivalence of judicial independence enhances the expectation that information will be used, distributed, and secured in a familiar manner, reducing the perceived risk of abuse.

Chapter 9 further shows that legal-system similarity fosters cooperation in the return of children wrongfully taken abroad by a parent—without the knowledge or consent of the left-behind parent and in violation of that parent's custody rights. The 1980 Convention on the Civil Aspects of International Child Abduction establishes a mechanism of automatic, expedited return of such abducted children to their country of origin. Yet this mechanism raises concerns: Will a partner country have the capacity and will to carry out the prompt legal process required for child return? And if a child is returned to a partner country and its courts have to rule on custody, will they do so fairly? In particular, will the mother—who, in most cases, is the parent taking the child abroad –receive equal legal treatment in the determination of custody? To assuage such concerns, states parties to the abduction convention can pick and choose the countries to which they are willing to return abducted children. We find that states prefer partners that are close to themselves in terms of the quality of the rule of law as well as women's rights and equality. This once again demonstrates the book's key point: the use of one's own standards as the metric for the evaluation of foreign legal systems and the tendency to cooperate with those who do not stray too far from these standards.

Why Examine These Cases?

Several considerations guided the choice of cases to be analyzed in this book. First, they cover both the criminal and civil legal domains. Among the qualitative sections, two—jurisdiction and extradition—examine criminal justice, and one—foreign judgments—focuses on civil litigation. The quantitative chapter similarly examines cooperation in criminal matters (MLATs) and in civil matters (return of abducted children). While discussions of legal fairness often focus on criminal proceedings, we found it important to include civil cases as well, since many transnational legal cases—especially those arising from crossborder commercial activity—are civil, rather than criminal. The inclusion of civil cases therefore allows us to better represent the universe of cases in the real world. Furthermore, civil litigation constitutes a *hard* case for our argument. One would expect greater concerns about fair treatment and a lesser willingness to cooperate with foreign legal systems in criminal proceedings, where the liberty—or even life—of a defendant is at stake. We might assume that differences between legal systems will matter less in civil litigation, which typically revolves around money, such as a compensation to be paid. Our analysis suggests, however, that states may exhibit serious concerns about cooperation with foreign justice even in the civil context. The existence of ethnocentric concerns and the difficulties of cooperation in both the criminal and civil domains give added force to our argument.

In selecting cases we also sought to ensure appropriate variation on both sides: that of the home countries that are considering cooperation and that of the foreign countries whose legal systems are the subject of evaluation and possible criticism. In terms of home countries, the case studies explore concerns and political conflicts about transnational litigation in the United States (Chapters 3 and 8), Britain (Chapters 4 and 6), Continental Europe (Chapter 7), as well as Australia and Canada (Chapter 5). As for the foreign countries, our analysis does include some "usual suspects." It is certainly unsurprising that criminal-justice cooperation with China or Iraq (Chapters 5 and 4, respectively) would provoke concerns, given their practice of the death penalty and lack of judicial independence, among other flaws.[59] It is much more surprising that the legal systems of Britain and Continental Europe would be the subject of criticism and that the idea of cooperating with them would raise contention. Yet this is exactly what Chapters 3, 6, and 8 demonstrate. And American readers may be surprised to learn that the U.S. legal system is considered by many outside the United States to be the epitome of injustice. As Chapters 6 and 7 show, U.S. criminal justice may be viewed by European countries as overly harsh and punitive, while certain elements of U.S. civil litigation offend Europeans' values and their sense of legal fairness. This demonstrates that concerns about foreign justice are far from limited to countries with a poor record regarding the rule of law and human rights. In the eyes of the ethnocentric, any deviation from local standards could be wrong and unfair. Even American or European justice might therefore be labeled unjust. The relative nature of legal ethnocentrism is further demonstrated in that countries may find themselves in the dual position of criticizing the legal system of a foreign country and being criticized by that same country. Consider the British reservations about the American penal system (Chapter 6) and the American denunciation of British libel law (Chapter 8). While the British consider their legal system superior to the American one, Americans believe it is their system that possesses the correct standards.

Finally, the diversity of cases this book examines allows us to offer a unified framework for analyzing a set of issues that thus far have been treated separately. Jurisdictional overlap and extraterritoriality; extradition; enforcement of foreign judgments; mutual assistance in criminal matters; and international child abduction—each of these has been studied as an issue unto itself.[60] This book seeks to tear down this separation and trace the common political logic that links these domains. All of them share certain fundamental similarities in the ethnocentric concerns that they trigger and the resulting challenges to international cooperation. By cutting across legal fields and doctrinal categories, as this book sets out to do, we can gain deeper insight into these challenges.

In terms of sources for the various case-studies, this book relies on records of parliamentary (or Congressional) debates as the primary source of information. Discussions among members of parliaments—and testimonies and evidence presented to them—give us a direct window into the views of the various actors and their arguments for or against cooperation on litigation. Some of these arguments are also made in the media, and media coverage thus provides another source of data, as do, where appropriate, NGO reports and secondary literature. In Chapter 8, the analysis relies, in part, on personal interviews we held with the participants in the legislative process that produced the SPEECH Act. All in all, the analysis relies on rich materials that allow us to paint a nuanced picture of the political debates over transnational litigation.

Placing This Book in the Broader Literature

An academic work forms part of a larger scholarly project. It builds on, and contributes to, existing works that examine similar and related issues. This section presents the larger scholarly context of this book—connecting it to four bodies of literature: political science studies of transnational litigation; the international law/international relations literature; works on judicial globalization and the transnational judicial dialogue; and the literature on domestic institutions and international cooperation.

Studies of Transnational Litigation

Legal scholars have long analyzed transnational litigation by identifying legal doctrine and tracing its development in the various areas of practice.[61] Political scientists, however, have largely overlooked transnational litigation. As the next subsection explains, the political science literature has focused on international law and international courts to the neglect of the litigation arising from the transnational activity of private actors. A few scholars have, however, empirically examined transnational litigation and made important progress in revealing its political logic.

Several of these scholars have examined extraterritoriality, that is, the application of a state's laws to activities or entities outside its boundaries, or to adjudicate disputes relating to such foreign activities or entities.[62] Christopher Whytock empirically analyzed issues relating to conflict-of-laws, that is, the body of law that guides courts in the application of legal authority in transnational private-law disputes, where another country may have a legitimate claim to assert its authority.[63] And sovereign immunity, which occasionally comes up in transnational litigation, has also received empirical analysis.[64] All these studies shed light—theoretically and empirically—on the dynamics of transnational litigation. This book, however, differs from these works in three important respects.

First, most existing works look at the practice of *courts* in transnational legal cases. They seek to explain why courts handle these cases the way they do. In that sense, these works address the politics of judicial decision-making. This book, by contrast, shifts the focus from judicial decisions to international agreements and legislation on transnational litigation. It moves away from the judicial arena and into the political arena, where cooperation with foreign legal systems is the subject of public debate. Key actors in this book include members of the legislature, bureaucrats, and civil-society organizations, rather than judges. This shift from the judicial to the political arena allows us to fill a gap in the courts-focused literature on transnational litigation.

Second, existing empirical works on transnational litigation typically examine a single domain, such as extraterritorial jurisdiction, the choice of law applicable to transnational disputes, or sovereign immunity. This book, however, offers a broader perspective by examining multiple issues together and revealing their joint political logic. While each domain of transnational litigation involves its own idiosyncratic influences, the different domains have much in common in terms of their underlying political dynamic. The preferences of actors, the arguments they make for or against cooperation with foreign legal systems, and the contours of the unfolding debate are similar across the different issues, and it is this fundamental political similarity that this book exposes.

Third, nearly all the works cited above examine transnational litigation from an American perspective. This book examines multiple national perspectives on transnational litigation: from the United States, Britain, Australia, Canada, and Continental Europe. It also offers a global statistical analysis of two transnational legal issues. The variety of national perspectives, and the use of both qualitative and quantitative methods, yield findings that are more robust and generalizable.

Studies of International Law

Moving beyond transnational litigation, this book is situated in the broader literature on international law and international relations (IL/IR), and it echoes that literature's focus on the domestic legal foundations of international law. In seeking to explain the role of international law and international courts in world politics, scholars have increasingly set their sights on domestic legal institutions and norms. Studies have explored how domestic legal rules affect states' entry into treaties;[65] how domestic law and courts may shape the implementation of international law within a country;[66] and how domestic legal actors may facilitate or hinder state compliance with international legal obligations.[67] International courts also build on domestic legal foundations. Domestic legal institutions have been shown to affect the design of international courts, their caseload, and the likelihood that a state will comply with their rulings.[68]

Placing domestic legal institutions and norms at the center of the analysis, this book provides further evidence for the important role of domestic law in world politics. As the same time, the scope of this book departs from the IL/IR literature in two important respects.

First, IL/IR scholarship overwhelmingly focuses on *public* international law and its regulation of state behavior in areas such as the use of force, trade, human rights, and the environment. Yet, as Whytock notes,[69] the field of IR is increasingly moving toward a broader paradigm of world politics that includes transnational relations, that is, crossborder interactions among private actors. Various works have explored the behavior of private actors, including their role in governing the global economy and establishing international rules.[70] This book embraces this more expansive notion of world politics, as the various chapters examine the regulation of private behavior: from the extradition of individuals to be tried and punished for their crimes, to the enforcement of foreign judgments rendered in lawsuits involving private parties; from the criminal conduct of soldiers acting in a private capacity for personal gain, to the return of children wrongfully taken abroad by their parents.

Second, IL/IR scholarship focuses on international agreements and international courts, with a bias toward those with a global membership. In this book, some of the chapters do not address any element of the international legal system. The SPEECH Act, for example, is a domestic U.S. law enacted by Congress. While applicable to transnational legal relations—crossborder libel cases—this law is entirely domestic and cannot be traced to any international legal rule or agreement. Furthermore, even when this book examines international agreements—such as the NATO SOFA, the Australia-China extradition treaty, and the child-abduction convention—it does so with a very different emphasis than the IL/IR literature. That literature highlights the *vertical* interaction between national legal systems and the international legal system: how domestic legal systems influence international law and vice versa. This book, by contrast, focuses on the *horizontal* interaction between national legal systems. States here do not evaluate international agreements or courts to decide whether to join or comply with them. Rather, they evaluate the legal systems of *other countries* to determine the desirability and appropriateness of cooperating with them. Our goal is to understand how states view and treat foreign legal systems, not how they perceive or engage with international agreements or courts.

Studies of Judicial Globalization

This book also speaks to the literature on judicial globalization, defined by Anne-Marie Slaughter as a "process of judicial interaction across, above and below borders, exchanging ideas and cooperating in cases involving national as much as international law."[71] Legal scholars have tended to focus on a specific type of interaction among courts: a transnational judicial dialogue, that is, judges' practice of using and citing external judicial decisions—issued by foreign or international courts—as an element of influence in the interpretation and application of the law.[72] Many works have documented this practice and explored its possible causes and implications.[73] To the extent that the decisions cited are those of courts in other countries, the judicial dialogue presents a horizontal interaction between legal systems—akin to the horizontal interactions studied in the book. Nonetheless, the interactions explored here differ from the judicial dialogue in two respects.

First, studies of the judicial dialogue focus on judges and courts and their engagement with foreign courts. In this book, as discussed above, the site of activity is the political arena, and the focus is on the views of a range of non-judicial actors that participate in the political debate over transnational litigation. Second, the practice of consulting and citing foreign rulings constitutes a rather shallow form of cooperation. Judges do not treat the foreign rulings they cite as authoritative or binding: they are free to cite whichever foreign decision in whatever manner fits their purpose. As Melissa Waters suggests, "courts engage in this comparative dialogue not out of a sense of legal obligation; foreign judicial decisions, of course, are not binding precedent." Instead, they are valuable resources to help clarify the issues at hand and to identify solutions to similar problems.[74] More meaningful expressions of crossborder legal interaction are those where countries limit their own legal sovereignty as they accept and facilitate the exercise of authority by foreign courts. Agreeing to grant jurisdiction over one's soldiers to foreign countries; extraditing persons to stand trial in foreign courts; enforcing decisions issued by foreign courts; sending children back to their country of origin, where custody will be decided: all these present deeper, more meaningful instances of cooperation than citing foreign rulings as sources of ideas, inspiration, or comparison.

Studies of Domestic Sources of Cooperation

Finally, this book joins studies that examine the impact of domestic institutions on international cooperation. These studies take either a monadic approach—looking at a country and its propensity to cooperate—or a dyadic approach that looks at the similarity of institutions between pairs of countries. The monadic studies have evolved from a focus on regime type—the cooperative tendency of democracies[75]—to examining a more fine-grained set of institutions that are directly involved in the cooperative effort. In particular, scholars have examined the impact of domestic legal institutions on the commitment to or violation of human rights treaties[76] and on memberships in international courts.[77] Dyadic studies have seen similar progress: from a focus on the regime types of dyad members as an influence on cooperation[78] to examining specific attributes of domestic institutions and how they affect the likelihood of cooperation between dyad members.[79]

This book joins the latter vein of the literature. It offers a dyadic analysis, in which the prospects of cooperation hinge on a relative evaluation of domestic institutions: How similar is the prospective partner to oneself? At the same time, this book goes beyond existing studies by developing a more comprehensive, nuanced account that captures the variation in preferences among domestic actors and explains the unfolding of the political debate over cooperation. The in-depth analysis of the political debate through multiple case studies, alongside the quantitative analysis, significantly enhances our understanding of how domestic institutions may facilitate or obstruct dyadic cooperation, and why cooperation may be sensitive or controversial.

Finally, and perhaps most importantly, this book contributes not only to the scholarly literature, but also to our understanding of contemporary reality. It provides insight into the legal frictions and tensions that accompany crossborder flows and interactions in the era of globalization. And it gives us a close look at the impact of out-group negativity, which has become so prevalent in international politics.[80] From Britain's withdrawal from the European Union to the protectionist trade policies of the United States under President Trump to the increasing anti-immigrant rhetoric of parties and politicians[81]—our world today is filled with prejudice against out-groups. A systematic examination of this prejudice in the legal arena allows us to better understand a powerful sentiment that will shape international politics in the years to come.

Notes

1. See OECD 2019, 228–244.
2. In fact, many people choose to travel to another country for the purpose of getting medical care—a phenomenon known as "medical tourism." See Connell 2011.
3. Slaughter 2000; Rosas 2007.
4. Cotterrell 2012, 501–502; Shaffer 2013, 4.
5. See Whytock 2011, 486; Bookman 2015, 1083–1084. The definition used here is closer to a functional, narrow conceptualization of transnational law—transnational law as the law addressing "transnational problems"—than to the broader sociolegal understanding of transnational law that focuses on the construction of legal norms and their migration across borders, regardless of whether they address transnational activities or purely domestic ones. Shaffer 2013, 5–8.
6. Alter, Helfer, and Madsen 2018.
7. Mattli 2001; Mattli and Diez 2014.
8. Teitz 1996; Lowenfeld 2002; Baumgartner 2004; McCaffrey and Main 2010.
9. Boister 2018a.
10. Cotterrell 2012, 501.
11. Whytock 2011, 495–496.
12. Kaczmarek and Newman 2011.
13. European Commission 2020.
14. Quintanilla and Whytock 2012, 36–37.
15. Jensen and Malesky 2018.
16. See Whytock 2009a, 76–83.
17. Wasserstein-Fassberg 2013, 254.
18. For example, Koh 2008; Dodge 2015.
19. Baumgartner 2004; Quintanilla and Whytock 2012.
20. Davis 2012; Peters 2019.
21. Raustiala 2009; Whytock 2009b.
22. Mansfield and Milner 2012; Hainmueller and Hangartner 2013.
23. Wallach 1986, 1504; Michaels 2009.
24. Jimenez-Guerrero, Gázquez-Abad, and Linares-Agüera 2014, 176.
25. LeVine and Campbell 1972; Kinder and Kam 2009; Bizumic 2019.
26. Sherif 1966; LeVine and Campbell 1972.
27. Adorno et al. 1950; Duckitt 2000; Altemeyer 2004.
28. Dollard 1937; Tajfel and Turner 1986.
29. Allport 1954; Stephan and Stephan 1984.
30. Kinder and Kam 2009, 103, 122.
31. Kinder and Kam 2009, 171, 186.
32. Sniderman et al. 2000; Hainmueller and Hiscox 2010; Valentino, Brader, and Jadrina 2013; Konitzer et al. 2019.
33. Margalit 2012; Mansfield and Mutz 2009 and 2013; Mutz and Kim 2017.
34. Shimp and Sharma 1987; Verlegh 2007; Zeugner-Roth, Zabkar, and Diamantopoulos 2015.
35. Andrews, Leblang, and Pandya 2018.
36. Silbey 1992; Mezey 2001, 46; Finnemore and Troope 2001, 743.
37. Baumgartner 2013, 976.
38. For example, Plachta 1999; Deen-Racsmany 2004.
39. Møller and Skaaning 2014; Versteeg and Ginsburg 2017.
40. See an enumeration of fair-trial rights in Article 14 of the International Covenant on Civil and Political Rights.
41. Abramson 2000; Jonakait 2003.
42. See, for example, assessments of the fairness of the trial of Saddam Hussein before an Iraqi court. Bassiouni and Hanna 2006; Doebbler 2007; Sissons and Bassin 2007.
43. See, for example, an assessment of the compliance of "foreign fighter" laws with human rights in Tayler 2016.

44. Murray et al. 2008; O'Reilly 2008.
45. Simmons 2009, 72–73.
46. Sadoff 2016; Boister 2018b.
47. Efrat 2012, 141, 190.
48. McKenzie 1958.
49. Illuminati 2013; Weissbrodt 2014.
50. Crepeau and Jimenez 2004.
51. Simmons 2017.
52. UNDP and UNODC 2016.
53. Efrat 2012.
54. Bergman and Lopez 2021.
55. Egan 2006.
56. Sabbagh 2020.
57. Select Committee on Extradition Law 2015b, 58.
58. Public Law 111-223—Securing the Protection of our Enduring and Established Constitutional Heritage Act or the SPEECH Act.
59. Trevaskes 2012; Pimentel and Anderson 2013.
60. For example, Baumgartner 2013; Ryngaert 2015; Sadoff 2016; Schuz 2013.
61. For example, Lutz 2007; McClean 2012; Bassiouni 2014.
62. Raustiala 2009; Putnam 2009 and 2016; Kaczmarek and Newman 2011.
63. Whytock 2009b and 2011.
64. Chilton and Whytock 2015; Verdier and Voeten 2015.
65. Simmons 2009; Haftel and Thompson 2013.
66. Verdier and Versteeg 2015; Aust and Nolte 2016.
67. Hillebrecht 2014; Lupu 2015; Crabtree and Nelson 2017.
68. Mitchell and Powell 2011; Alter, Hafner-Burton, and Helfer 2019.
69. Whytock 2018, 18.
70. Buthe and Mattli 2011; Green 2013; Cutler and Dietz 2017.
71. Slaughter 2000, 1104.
72. Müller 2017.
73. Gelter and Siems 2014; Law 2015; Andenas and Fairgrieve 2015a.
74. Waters 2005, 493–494.
75. Mansfield, Milner, and Rosendorff 2002; Leeds, Mattes, and Vogel 2009; Battig and Bernauer 2009.
76. Powell and Staton 2009; Simmons 2009; Lupu 2013.
77. Mitchell and Powell 2011; Powell 2015.
78. Siverson and Emmons 1991; Leeds 1999; Lai and Reiter 2000.
79. Powell 2010; Baccini 2014.
80. Bieber 2018; Snyder 2019.
81. Bump 2019; Santora 2019.

2

Theorizing Cooperation on Transnational Litigation

As firms, criminals, and ordinary individuals take advantage of international markets, mobility, technology, and communication, legal disputes—both criminal and civil—spill across national borders.[1] In transnational legal disputes, the conduct in question may have taken place in a foreign country, or some of the parties involved in the legal process before the court might be of foreign nationality: foreign private individuals, foreign corporations, or foreign governmental authorities. The foreign conduct or actors, in turn, may bring foreign legal elements into the local legal process, such as foreign legal rules, foreign judicial decisions, or legal evidence obtained abroad. All this poses challenges in a world of national legal systems based on the principle of territorial jurisdiction, which is part of a state's legal sovereignty.[2] Indeed, transnational litigation creates tension and conflict between the jurisdictional authorities of the states involved. In the strict sense, territorial jurisdiction is exclusive: only the state controlling the territory has the authority to regulate conduct occurring within that territory, adjudicate disputes arising from such conduct, and take enforcement action with respect to such conduct.[3] In transnational legal cases, however, the territorial state—the state on whose territory the relevant conduct took place or where the parties are present—may find its legal authority challenged, as it faces competing jurisdictional claims. Another state might wish to apply its laws to the case; the courts of another state might wish to hear and decide the case; or another state might seek to enforce its laws through the arrest, prosecution, or punishment of persons involved in the case or by obtaining evidence regarding the case.[4] For cooperation to occur, the territorial state needs to qualify its jurisdictional claim and allow the foreign country to exercise *its* authority over the matter. In other words, cooperation entails a limitation of one country's sovereign authority in favor of another's. Such a sacrifice of legal authority is not made lightly. It raises concerns for the fate of the individuals involved, who will

Intolerant Justice. Asif Efrat, Oxford University Press. © Oxford University Press 2023.
DOI: 10.1093/oso/9780197658895.003.0002

come under the authority of a foreign legal system. It might also raise broader concerns about the foreign impact on one's society or legal system. Such worries make cooperation on litigation controversial, possibly resulting in a rejection of the foreign legal system's authority and a refusal to cooperate with it.

This chapter offers a theoretical look at the politics of transnational litigation, focusing on the challenges to cooperation in this area. To be sure, legal scholarship has long identified some of these challenges, yet it has done so in a compartmentalized way, which separates the different areas of transnational litigation.[5] It has not offered a unified logic of common challenges and concerns across transnational legal issues. Furthermore, the legal literature—focused on the *law*—does little to identify the social roots of concerns over cooperation or the political dynamic they give rise to. The following theoretical account, by contrast, highlights the socio-psychological origins of negative sentiments toward foreign law and attributes them to the mental habit of ethnocentrism. Most importantly, the account here shifts the focus from the courts to the political arena. While it is courts that ultimately hear and decide transnational legal cases, they do so within a framework of national legislation and international treaties established in the political arena. In that arena, policymakers decide whether, and to what extent, to cooperate with other legal systems, and a variety of domestic actors seek to influence and shape that decision. These actors vary in their perceptions of foreign legal systems and the desirability and appropriateness of cooperation with them, and they make different arguments to press their case. This political debate surrounding transnational litigation stands at the heart of the following theoretical discussion.

What Is Cooperation on Litigation?

In a globalized world, complete sovereignty—full and exclusive control over one's territory and the exclusion of foreign authority from that territory—is a fiction or "organized hypocrisy."[6] Yet states often seek to maintain their sovereignty and to resist the influence or pressure of external actors, be they major powers, international organizations, international courts, or NGOs.[7] Transnational litigation raises similar concerns about foreign encroachment into the local legal system, since the authority to make legal rules, adjudicate disputes, and take enforcement measures constitutes a part of national sovereignty. States typically seek to keep this authority intact and exercise it to the fullest over their citizens and territory. Transnational legal disputes, however, pose a challenge to the state's legal authority, since they involve an overlap between the legal authority of multiple states. The resolution of transnational legal disputes may therefore require states to compromise their sovereignty by ceding all or part of their authority over a legal case to another country. Cooperative behavior is exhibited through a state's consent to restrain its own legal powers and to relinquish all or some of its authority over a case to a foreign legal system. The cooperating state accepts that the legal rules governing the case will be those of the foreign legal system; that the dispute will be heard and decided by a foreign court; or that foreign authorities will be taking enforcement action in the case. Noncooperation is manifested through the assertion of one's legal authority over the case and a refusal to turn authority over to a foreign legal system. Following are several examples.

Consider a situation in which a citizen of State A commits a criminal offense on the territory of State B. Where will this person face trial? The two states hold overlapping authorities. State A has legal authority over acts of its citizens abroad,[8] whereas state B has authority over acts committed on its territory. Both states are therefore entitled to exercise jurisdiction over the offender. Cooperation here may take one of two forms: State A's acceptance that its citizen will face trial in State B; or State B's acceptance that a person who committed an offense on its territory will stand trial before State A's courts. In both cooperative scenarios, one state limits its own legal authority in favor of a foreign country and opts not to conduct a criminal legal process that it is entitled to carry out. In a noncooperative scenario, both states seek to assert their authority over the case and try the offender.[9]

Extradition similarly implies a state's relinquishment of legal authority to try or punish an offender. In that case, State A seeks to prosecute or punish a person present on the territory of State B. State A claims authority over that person, since she committed an offense on its territory before fleeing to State B. State B possesses legal authority over that person by way of her presence on B's territory. If State B chooses to cooperate with State A's extradition request, it surrenders the wanted person to State A—giving up its legal authority over that person and allowing the exercise of State A's authority instead. With the wanted person under its control, State A can carry out the legal process of prosecution or punishment in accordance with its rules and practices. By contrast, a rejection of the extradition request by State B will prevent State A from exercising its legal authority. State B will maintain authority, allowing it to prosecute and punish the wanted person in its own legal system or, alternatively, refrain entirely from legal action.

When faced with a request to enforce a civil judgment issued by State A's court, State B must accept that a foreign legal system has already asserted its authority to adjudicate the case in accordance with its rules. By cooperating and enforcing the foreign judgment, State B affirms State A's exercise of adjudicative authority over the case. State B essentially cedes its own authority to adjudicate the case and merely exercises its enforcement authority—in the service of

State A. By contrast, State B's refusal to enforce the foreign judgment amounts to saying that it was inappropriate for State A to exercise its authority to adjudicate the case, that the rules applied to the dispute were themselves inappropriate, or that the foreign judgment is defective in some other way.[10]

A fourth example concerns the application of foreign law.[11] A party in a case before the court of State B may ask the court to decide the case in accordance with the laws of State A. The court may respond cooperatively and apply State A's laws, thereby ceding State B's prescriptive authority, that is, the authority to apply its own laws to the case. Alternatively, the court may insist that it is State B's laws that should govern the case.

In all the examples above, a legal system is asked to sacrifice some of its authority to handle and resolve a legal case. This sacrifice may be complete, as in the case of extradition. Once State B surrenders the wanted person, it typically loses any authority over the case: the wanted person will be tried and punished by State A in accordance with its laws.[12] In other cases, such as foreign-judgment enforcement and the application of foreign law, the cooperating state retains certain legal authority over the case and does not cede its authority entirely. Note also that cooperation may—but need not be—reciprocal. State B may cede its legal authority to State A and, in reverse cases, State A will restrain its legal authority in a reciprocal manner, allowing State B to assert its legal powers. Alternatively, cooperation could be one-sided: while State B chooses to accept State A's exercise of legal authority, State A may decline to relinquish its authority and insist on asserting it. Consider, for example, the common law-civil law divide on the extradition of one's nationals. Many countries—especially those belonging to the civil-law tradition—either prohibit the extradition of their nationals to stand trial abroad or allow it only under certain circumstances. By contrast, common-law countries typically do extradite their nationals.[13] This results in a lack of reciprocity: a common-law country will cooperate by handing over its citizens to stand trial in a civil-law country, while the latter may fail to cooperate as it refuses to surrender its own citizens. Indeed, the following empirical chapters examine several cases where one country fully cooperates while the other restricts cooperation or considers doing so.

A government's willingness to cooperate on litigation—or the absence of such willingness—carries immediate implications for the cases at stake and the exercise of legal authority over them. It is important to note, however, that the implications of (non)cooperation on litigation go beyond specific cases. They concern fundamental questions of global governance: Who governs and how is governance authority allocated among states? More specifically: Who prescribes the rules that control crossborder interactions? Which state has the authority to apply the rules and adjudicate the disputes resulting from these interactions? And who may take action to enforce its rules? Greater authority to prescribe, adjudicate, or enforce extends a state's sphere of influence, giving it the ability to shape crossborder interactions in a manner consistent with its preferences.[14] Why, then, would a state ever choose to cooperate on litigation, willingly ceding some of its legal authority to another country?

Why Cooperate on Transnational Litigation?

One can identify several possible rationales for the seemingly puzzling willingness of states to cooperate on transnational litigation and relinquish their legal authority in favor of a foreign legal system.

Considerable research looks upon international cooperation as a means to facilitate crossborder exchange and smooth any frictions that might hinder flows and interactions among states.[15] For example, the purpose of the international trade regime is to induce states to lower barriers to the crossborder movement of goods and services.[16] Bilateral investment treaties seek to provide investors with assurances of fair treatment and to secure their rights in order to encourage the investment of capital in foreign countries.[17] Similar concerns about legal frictions certainly motivate cooperation on litigation, since noncooperation might upset transnational relations and raise problems for private parties interacting across borders. Indeed, crossborder commercial relations require certainty and stability—and these are undermined if actors can evade litigation altogether or escape the enforcement of a judgment, or if a legal right that an actor has secured in one country vanishes in another country. Re-litigation of disputes in multiple countries with potentially conflicting decisions similarly does little to bring stability to crossborder exchange; rather, it leads to the waste of time, money, and judicial resources.[18] Cooperation on litigation provides a remedy: it can smooth the frictions arising from the overlap and conflict of legal authority and provide transnational actors with a more certain and secure legal foundation for their interaction. Such a foundation, in turn, may facilitate commerce and other types of transnational relations.[19]

This "mutual convenience" justification for cooperation dates back to the very early thinking about transnational litigation: the writing of seventeenth-century Dutch jurist Ulrich Huber. Following the 1648 Peace of Westphalia, Europe was divided into independent states possessing exclusive and absolute territorial sovereignty. Against this background, Huber put forth the doctrine of comity to suggest that rights acquired under the laws of one country could and should have an effect within the territory of another. The detrimental impact of absolute territorial jurisdiction on trade served as a key rationale for comity: "nothing could be more inconvenient to commerce and to international usage than that transactions valid by the law of one place should be rendered of no effect elsewhere on account of a difference in the law."[20] This rationale still holds true today, perhaps even more so than in the past. In an age of a global economy and growing crossborder commerce, the removal of legal hurdles to economic activity is ever more important.[21]

A second justification for cooperation on litigation is to maintain friendly international relations, since an overlap of authority between states might sow tensions and fuel conflicts. This is clearly evident in the case of conflicting claims over territory, which might lead to war.[22] Overlapping claims of *legal* authority may not cause bloodshed, but they can certainly generate political discord if one state rejects the other's claim of authority—for instance, by refusing to cede jurisdiction over a case, declining to extradite an offender, or failing to enforce a foreign judgment. At the symbolic level, such a rejection might be interpreted as an affront to a country's sovereignty and honor.[23] At the practical level, such a rejection might have problematic consequences, such as impunity for an offender whose extradition was refused. Controversy over transnational litigation thus holds the potential for creating unwanted friction in the relations among states.[24] By contrast, a willingness to cooperate will prevent legal matters from becoming a thorn in the relations between the two states and may even work to enhance their relations. In other words, states may be willing to sacrifice some of their legal authority to score foreign-policy gains.

Reciprocity serves as one of the primary engines of cooperation in international relations. Once hailed by Robert Keohane as "the most effective strategy for maintaining cooperation among egoists,"[25] reciprocity stands as the foundation of cooperation in various areas: from the laws of war through arms control to trade. Expecting a reciprocal response, states are willing to behave more humanely on the battlefield, reduce their level of arms, or lower barriers to trade.[26] Similarly, states may be willing to extend cooperation on transnational litigation in anticipation of reciprocal treatment. Such treatment may involve *specific* reciprocity,[27] that is, an exchange of equivalent value: if State B extradites a person to State A upon the latter's request, then State A will, in turn, surrender persons that State B requests. Alternatively, a cooperating country may expect *diffuse* reciprocity wherein the equivalence of the exchange is less precise. For example, if State B extradites a person to the requesting State A, A may provide B with law-enforcement assistance of some other kind or cooperate with A on a nonlegal matter. By contrast, B's refusal to cooperate in the present could make it harder for B to obtain A's cooperation down the road.

The inability or unwillingness of legal systems to handle certain problematic cases themselves may serve as another motivation for cooperation to pass the "hot potato." Consider the case of Joaquín Guzmán Loera, the notorious drug lord known as El Chapo. The Mexican government, which once sought to imprison El Chapo in Mexico, changed course after his Houdini-like escape in 2015, when his associates tunneled him out of Mexico's most secure prison. To avoid the embarrassment of another escape, the government extradited El Chapo to the United States in 2017.[28]

The four preceding rationales for cooperation all reflect a country's self-interest in facilitating crossborder exchange, maintaining friendly international relations, obtaining reciprocal benefits, and getting rid of inconvenient cases. The fifth rationale, by contrast, transcends self-interest and is of a more ideational or normative character: A state may value the rule of law and see it as its duty and responsibility to uphold it.[29] A belief in the rule of law implies respect for the exercise of legal authority, including that of a foreign country. It means that the law should have an effect even as it crosses borders. It also means identifying a shared interest among states in enforcing both civil and criminal law and ensuring legal accountability: making sure that contracts are fulfilled and that criminals are brought to justice. A state may be willing to cede some of its legal authority over a case if this sacrifice ultimately works to support and enhance the rule of law.[30]

Why *Not* Cooperate on Transnational Litigation? The Role of Ethnocentrism

Cooperation over transnational litigation may serve the need of individuals and corporations for legal certainty and allow governments to more effectively fight crime, support the rule of law, and contribute to friendly international relations. At the same time, such cooperation involves costs. Some of these costs fall on the private parties involved. For example, an extradited person facing criminal trial in a foreign country and a foreign language is likely to experience significant challenges not present in a domestic trial in one's home country. Our primary interest here, however, lies in the potential *political* costs that transnational litigation entails, as it involves the voluntary limitation of a country's legal authority and the acceptance of the exercise of foreign legal authority. As a result of cooperation, a foreign court might pass judgment on a country's citizens or firms, or on events that took place on its territory; its nationals might find themselves subject to foreign legal rules, procedures, or decisions, and they might receive punishment at the hands of foreign authorities. The prospect of foreign encroachment and the displacement of local legal authority fuels *ethnocentric* concerns.

The term "ethnocentrism" is made up of the word "ethnic," that is, relating to a group of people, and centrism, which means focused. The introduction of this term into the social science lexicon is attributed to sociologist William Graham

Sumner, who in 1906 defined it as the "view of things in which one's own group is the center of everything, and all others are scaled and rated with reference to it."[31] Indeed, the ethnocentric view of the world consists of a self-centered, self-important, and superior in-group—one's own group—with all others viewed as "out-groups."[32] Such an outlook inspires sentiments of attachment, solidarity, pride, and favoritism toward in-groups as opposed to hostility and denigration toward out-groups. As Donald Kinder and Cindy Kam note in their review of the concept of ethnocentrism:

> Ethnocentrism is a mental habit. It is a predisposition to divide the human world into in-groups and out-groups. It is a readiness to reduce society to us and them. Or rather, it is a readiness to reduce society to us *versus* them. This division of humankind into in-groups and out-groups is not innocuous. Members of in-groups (until they prove otherwise) are assumed to be virtuous: friendly, cooperative, trustworthy, safe, and more. Members of out-groups (until they prove otherwise) are assumed to be the opposite: unfriendly, uncooperative, unworthy of trust, dangerous, and more. Symbols and practices become objects of attachment and pride when they belong to the in-group and objects of condescension, disdain, and (in extreme cases) hatred when they belong to out-groups. Ethnocentrism constitutes a readiness to act in favor of in-groups and in opposition to out-groups.[33]

More loosely and succinctly, Kinder and Kam define ethnocentrism as "prejudice, broadly conceived,"[34] or as a "friend or foe" or "Us against Them" outlook: the tendency to parse the social world into two opposing camps of virtuous in-groups and nefarious out-groups.[35] A belief in the superiority of the in-group is key to this distinction: the ethnocentric views the in-group as better than or superior to out-groups on certain dimensions, such as morality, economy, development, military might, and so forth. Placing the in-group at the center, the ethnocentric also believes in the foremost importance of the in-group's interests and the need to pursue them regardless of the views or feelings of out-groups.[36] In another important expression of in-group self-centeredness, the ethnocentric tends to judge and rate out-groups in relation to the in-group: the in-group sets the "correct" or "appropriate" standard to which the out-group is compared.[37]

Much like Kinder and Kam in their analysis of the impact of ethnocentrism on American public opinion, the present study examines the *political consequences* of this mental tendency. Therefore, we will not delve deeply into the origins of ethnocentrism. Social psychologists and other scholars have, in fact, offered various explanations of the causes of ethnocentrism and how it arises. For Sumner himself, in-group solidarity and out-group hostility resulted from a realistic group conflict: an actual threat that one group poses to another.[38] By contrast, social identity theory proposes that ethnocentrism does not require an actual conflict of interest among groups. Rather, social categorizations and classifications highlight the similarities between people and their in-group while accentuating differences between themselves and various out-groups. One's need for a positive identity and self-esteem results in favoring the in-group—and hence the self.[39] A third theory attributes ethnocentrism to a certain type of individual personality: an authoritarian personality characterized by elements such as rigid loyalty to certain values and customs, a simplistic black-or-white worldview, strong condemnation of those who deviate from convention, submissiveness to authority, and preoccupation with power and strength.[40] A fourth theory identifies the source of ethnocentrism in the human tendency to form categories as a means to simplify a complex world. Being prone to simplify may also reflect ignorance and lack of knowledge about out-groups.[41]

Regardless of the root or cause of ethnocentrism, we know today that it constitutes a deep habit and a stable predisposition of individuals. The division of human society into virtuous in-groups and bad or dangerous out-groups is "a form of individual readiness that guides perception, thought, and action,"[42] and it is different from and unrelated to other social and political dispositions, such as partisanship or ideological identification.[43] In particular, ethnocentrism should be distinguished from other group-related constructs, such as xenophobia and nationalism. Xenophobia and ethnocentrism are similar in that they both involve a rejection of those who are different. Xenophobia, however, also involves a mix of fear and hatred toward the out-group, while ethnocentrism requires neither of those.[44] Nationalism resembles ethnocentrism in its expression of in-group superiority, but it includes other characteristics that are not a part of ethnocentrism, such as the emphasis on loyalty to the nation, homogeneity of the nation, and an uncritical acceptance of political authority.[45] Indeed, the concept of ethnocentrism captures the specific combination of the nationalist sentiment—the excessive valuation of one's own nation—and the denigration of out-groups that results from that sentiment.[46] According to Boris Bizumic and John Duckitt, "ethnocentrism can be seen as a more basic and fundamental (as well as much older) construct than its more recent manifestation and modification, nationalism."[47]

It is also important to emphasize that people vary in their tendency to divide the social world into in-groups and out-groups: some individuals are strongly ethnocentric, while others are more weakly so or not at all. Whether such differences are rooted in genetics, personality, or education,[48] they carry important implications for cooperation on litigation, since on their account individuals express different and opposing views with respect to foreign legal systems: While some may see a foreign legal system as fair, others might view the same system as violating fundamental notions of justice. Whereas the former may consider cooperation with that foreign system to be beneficial and desirable, the latter will reject cooperation as risky or harmful. These contrasting views fuel the political debates over transnational litigation that stand at the center of this book.

Ethnocentrism and Crossborder Exchange

As a first step toward understanding the effect of ethnocentrism on litigation, we turn to studies that examine ethnocentrism's impact on other types of transnational exchange. More specifically, these studies explain negative attitudes toward globalization as the product of ethnocentrism. They suggest that ethnocentric sentiments—apprehension and anxiety about foreign influences—intensify the view of global integration as harmful. From an ethnocentric viewpoint, inflows of people, goods, or capital might bring with them undesirable foreign intervention and the erosion of local traditions or values.

Consider immigration. While economic concerns about labor-market competition might inspire anti-immigrant sentiment,[49] a considerable body of literature suggests that ethnocentrism may also generate animosity toward immigrants. Ethnocentric sentiments foster the view of immigrants as a cultural threat and a menace to cherished local values and traditions, resulting in a preference for reducing the inflow of immigrants.[50]

Economic concerns have figured prominently as an explanation for negative views of trade. Various studies of individual attitudes toward trade explain the opposition to free trade as the product of self-interested concerns about one's labor market standing and earning prospects: People oppose economic integration because they fear it exposes them to the risks of lower income, job insecurity, or unemployment.[51] Yotam Margalit, however, identifies a different engine of popular apprehension about free trade and, more broadly, international economic integration: the perception of a sociocultural threat. In people's minds, international trade is not merely an economic exchange, but one that carries social and cultural consequences: increasing exposure to foreign influences, a shift toward a less traditionalist society, and possibly growing American cultural dominance.[52] People might therefore oppose economic integration because they see it as part of a larger process of change that affects things they care deeply about, such as the values and ideas that their children are exposed to, the traditions respected in their society, or their national and cultural identity. Importantly, the depth of concerns about foreign cultural influences varies among individuals. Margalit finds that individuals exhibiting greater apprehension about social and cultural openness are more likely to view trade liberalization and economic integration as harmful.[53]

In their study of individual attitudes toward trade, Edward Mansfield and Diana Mutz similarly find a notable effect of ethnocentric sentiments: free trade wins little support among people who think less of those who are racially or ethnically different from themselves. Such views, Mansfield and Mutz report, carry a much greater impact on trade preferences than economic self-interest.[54] They reach similar findings in a separate study of offshoring: the decision by a firm to locate a part of the production process abroad and thereby shift some jobs overseas. Attitudes toward offshoring, Mansfield and Mutz report, tend to be shaped by ethnocentrism and anti-foreign sentiment: there is little support for offshoring among individuals who exhibit prejudice toward groups unlike themselves. "[A]ttitudes are shaped less by the economic consequences of [offshoring] than by what offshoring implies about heightened interaction with and dependence on out-groups, foreign firms and foreign people."[55] A study by Mutz and Kim further reinforces the centrality of in-group favoritism—more specifically, intergroup competition—in shaping trade preferences: some Americans favor trade policies that not only benefit the United States but also occasion loss for the trading partner country, so that the United States obtains a greater relative advantage.[56]

Ethnocentrism has attracted much interest in the field of international marketing, and its impact on consumers' evaluations of products and purchase intentions has been documented in a large number of studies. These studies examine "consumer ethnocentrism," that is, the appropriateness and morality of buying foreign-made products versus purchasing locally made products. For an ethnocentric consumer, buying products from other countries is inappropriate, since it hurts the domestic economy and domestic employment. Rather, one should support domestic companies and workers through the purchase of domestic products.[57] Beyond the economic motivation of supporting one's domestic economy, recent works emphasize socio-psychological motivations of national identification as the basis for favoring domestic products. The need to maintain a positive evaluation of the self and the social groups one belongs to may lead individuals to be favorably biased toward the in-group and its members, products, and achievements.[58]

The above-cited studies demonstrated the impact of ethnocentrism on individual attitudes toward crossborder flows. But do ethnocentric sentiments translate into real-world impact? Andrews, Leblang, and Pandya[59] suggest that ethnocentrism might deter greenfield foreign direct investment, that is, the establishment of new production facilities by foreign companies. They find that U.S. states where ethnocentrism is rife receive less of those investments. A likely reason is that ethnocentrism creates an inhospitable climate for foreign investment by eroding the trust necessary to establish crossborder contractual relations and creating an aversion to the consumption of foreign products. Firms that seek to establish new production facilities prefer a friendly environment rather than one where foreigners face hostility.

Now that we have established that ethnocentrism might influence attitudes toward different types of crossborder exchange—from immigration to imported consumer products—a key question arises: Does the impact of ethnocentrism extend to the legal sphere as well? Does ethnocentrism create an aversion toward foreign laws and foreign legal authority, as it does for foreign people or foreign goods?

Ethnocentrism in the Legal Sphere

Ethnocentrism might indeed color and shape one's thinking about foreign law, since interaction with other countries' legal systems clearly presents an in-group vs. out-group setting. One's citizens and firms belong to the in-group; the foreign legal system belongs to the out-group, serving the interests and needs of out-group members and embodying their values. The foreign legal system and its encroachment into the local system may thus be viewed, from an ethnocentric perspective, as posing potential risks to the in-group and its legal order. This implies that foreign legal authority over one's citizens or firms should be rejected in favor of domestic legal authority.

Such an expectation of an in-group bias in the legal sphere, or legal ethnocentrism, comes from the central role that the law plays in one's society and culture—its embodiment of the country's sovereignty and its expression of the local values, customs, and way of life. The attachment to one's own national law goes back to nineteenth-century Europe where legal codes served as instruments of unification around which the nation could coalesce:

> The ideal of a cohesive nation state was implicit in the scope of a civil code. To be French, Dutch, German, or Italian meant, among other things, to live under the same regime of civil laws as one's countrymen, young and old, male and female, from birth until death. Often contained in a single volume, or at most two, a civil code defined what Benedict Anderson has denominated an "imagined community." Together with grammar books, maps, encyclopedias, newspapers, history primers, and other printed material, it served to establish and reify common culture, language, and law.[60]

To this day, the national law is perceived as an expression of the country's sovereignty and ideals, and as such, it enjoys an elevated status. Consider the following examples.

The French civil code is seen as expressing French culture, tradition, and consciousness. It serves as a political symbol as well, standing for French self-determination and sovereignty—fought for through revolution and the liberation from feudalism—and it is also an emblem of French democracy. Such veneration of the national code explains the shock and outrage of French scholars at the initiative to establish a European civil code in the early 2000s.[61] Americans similarly feel an attachment to the national constitution as *their* achievement and the product of their efforts. They view it as an expression of their national identity and an embodiment of the ideas of patriotism, freedom, and the rule of law.[62] In the Indian constitutional imagination, the constitution marks a sharp and decisive break with the past. Indians consider their constitution as belonging to *them*, identify it with the nation, and routinely call upon the memory of the constitution's founding.[63] In Gary Jacobsohn's conceptualization, constitutions acquire an identity: they represent a combination of political aspirations and commitments that express a nation's past, as well as the determination of those within the society who seek in some ways to transcend that past.[64] The view of the constitution as representing national history and values inspires attachment to this document and to other legal norms and institutions that are a part of the constitutional order.

Studies of law and culture shed further light on the importance of law and the national attachment to it. From this perspective, the law serves as a building block of culture, ingrained within society. It constitutes a broad social phenomenon embedded in the practices, beliefs, and traditions of societies,[65] part of the cultural processes that actively contribute to the composition of social relations.[66] Indeed, law and culture mutually influence each other: "law shapes individual and group identity, social practices as well as the meaning of cultural symbols, but all of these things (culture in its myriad manifestations) also shape law by changing what is socially desirable, politically feasible, legally legitimate."[67] The nexus of law and culture also accounts for how the law works. From a cultural perspective, the law typically operates by influencing modes of thought rather than by determining conduct in any specific case; it enters social practices by making law's concepts and commands seem perfectly natural and benign. Law is, in this sense, constitutive of culture.[68]

Yet it is not only scholars who realize that the law has a powerful presence in social and cultural life—that it is "an inseparable dimension of social relations."[69] The close link between the law and social norms is evident to the lay person as well. Hot-button issues—from the role of the church in public life to racial discrimination and privacy matters—are settled through law and the courts.[70] According to Ran Hirschl, the growth of courts' social and political role has intensified in recent years, becoming a worldwide trend. He identifies a growing reliance on judicial means for settling fundamental moral controversies and contentious political questions, thereby transforming national high courts into major political decision-making bodies.[71]

All this suggests a strong attachment of citizens to their national legal system.[72] Since the law is tightly linked to a country's values and traditions, and since it represents national sovereignty, individuals should have the privilege and the obligation to be subject to the legal norms and institutions of the country of which they are nationals.[73] This attachment to one's legal system could inspire suspicion of foreign legal systems. Foreign systems reflect the values, practices, and traditions of their respective countries, and may therefore be incompatible with, and inferior to, one's own.

It is also important to note that while the ethnocentric attachment is typically to the legal system of one's own country, an ethnocentric may also feel attached to a larger in-group. For example, the in-group may be the entire legal tradition to which the national legal system belongs. Thus, a lawyer immersed in the common law's method of legal reasoning and its set of norms and procedures might dismiss the civil law tradition as strange or inferior.[74] Alternatively, the ethnocentric may be attached to their own civilization. A Western lawyer might reject non-Western legal practices as inconsistent with fundamental views and values of the West. Legal systems outside the Western tradition might be deemed regressive, cruel, or barbaric.[75]

Let us now consider a few examples of legal ethnocentrism. One major historical case of ethnocentrism in the legal arena involved the system of extraterritoriality in the nineteenth and early twentieth centuries. That system operated in non-Western territories that were not subject to imperial control, especially China, Japan, and the Ottoman Empire.[76] Under extraterritoriality, citizens of the major powers—especially the United States and United Kingdom—were not subject to the laws and courts of the host country. Rather, they were tried by their own consular officials under their own country's laws, even when the case involved natives of the host country. The assumptions undergirding this system were the inherent superiority of Western culture and institutions and the need to protect them against the unjust and even barbaric laws of the host countries.[77]

The debate over the transnational judicial dialogue provides a vivid contemporary demonstration of legal ethnocentrism at work. Judicial dialogue is a practice whereby judges resort to foreign or international court decisions as a source of ideas and inspiration and cite such decisions, typically in constitutional interpretation.[78] By citing foreign rulings, judges can address gaps or ambiguity in local law, bolster and better justify their own decisions, or borrow legal solutions that have worked elsewhere.[79] Note that such practice differs from the various forms of transnational litigation examined in this book, since it does not involve a real cession of legal authority to a foreign legal system. In the judicial dialogue, the foreign case law merely possesses a persuasive quality: A court is free to choose whether to cite the foreign ruling and, if so, how to use it in its own decision. Nevertheless, the practice of citing foreign rulings has met with significant resentment in the United States. During the 2000s, Republicans in Congress introduced a series of bills requiring American courts to base their decisions on the laws of the United States alone and not on the laws or judicial opinions of any foreign country.[80] One of the proposed bills carried the title "American Justice for American Citizens Act"—connoting the strong link between a country's citizens and their legal system.[81]

In 2005, a heated public exchange occurred between U.S. Supreme Court Justices Antonin Scalia and Stephen Breyer over the citation of foreign rulings in the wake of the Supreme Court's 2003 decision in *Lawrence v. Texas*, which struck down a law criminalizing homosexual sodomy. In striking down the Texas law, the majority's opinion noted that "Other nations, too, have taken action consistent with an affirmation of the protected right of homosexual adults to engage in intimate, consensual conduct. . . . The right the petitioners seek in this case has been accepted as an integral part of human freedom in many other countries."[82] In the 2005 debate, Justice Breyer expressed support for the practice of citing foreign rulings. By contrast, Justice Scalia argued that an American judge should be applying the "standards of decency of *American* society—not the standards of decency of the world, not the standards of decency of other countries that don't have our background, that don't have our culture, that don't have our moral views."[83] This statement neatly captures the ethnocentric view of foreign legal systems: drawing a stark contrast between one's own system and the foreign system as having incompatible standards and practices, reflecting their different views and values.

We suggested earlier that the sense of legal incompatibility may arise when the foreign legal system belongs to a different civilization. The proliferation of anti-Sharia initiatives in the American states in the 2010s reflects an ethnocentric backlash against non-Western, religious-based law. Indeed, all sources of Islamic law, including the Koran and the Sunna, are closely tied to the Islamic faith. According to Islamic law, God is the sovereign and owns the land, and the state is supposed to administer it in accordance with God's laws and moral principles.[84] For the ethnocentric, the origin of Sharia in a non-Western religion turns it into a potential threat to a Western, secular legal system. The threat may intensify as the ethnocentric will likely focus on extreme versions of Islam, ignoring the diversity of this religion's interpretations and practices. The gross mischaracterization—indeed, demonization—of Islamic law is evident in the writings of the activists who fueled the anti-Sharia movement in the United States. According to these activists, Sharia is a totalitarian doctrine, and its basic tenets include the duty of every faithful Muslim to wage jihad against those who do not adhere to Sharia; a rejection of democracy and man-made laws, since

God is the source of law; the inferiority of women, including honor killing, female genital mutilation, and underage marriage of girls; brutal punishments, such as lashing and stoning to death; and a belief that Islam is superior to every other culture, faith, and government and that it is ordained by God to conquer and dominate them. Indeed, the goal of Muslims, according to this view, is for Sharia to apply globally, making Sharia a serious threat to the United States and to freedom worldwide.[85] The activists warned that Sharia was already influencing decisions in U.S. state courts, contrary to the Constitution and public policy[86]—a claim that others have shown to be misguided.[87]

Yet this warning and the inflated sense of threat triggered a wave of legislative initiatives to counter the impact of Sharia; according to one count, such bills were introduced in over 30 states between 2010 and 2013.[88] To avoid being invalidated on the grounds of discrimination against Muslims, these anti-Sharia measures were recast as bans on the use of foreign and international law by state courts, but the intent was clearly anti-Muslim.[89] While most of these measures never became law, they are important for our purposes here as they reflect legal ethnocentrism: "The very premise of foreign law bans, however, is that law that comes from outside the United States is something to be feared."[90] The anti-Sharia campaign successfully tapped into deep-seated suspicions about the influence of foreign laws on the U.S. legal system—suspicions that mounted since the foreign law in question had a non-Western, religious origin.

The Political Implications of Legal Ethnocentrism

The affinity for one's national legal system and the prejudice against foreign systems translates into two types of concerns over transnational litigation: *legal delegation* and *legal incongruity*.

Legal delegation relates to the locus of decision-making: the extent to which one's own legal institutions retain legal authority or transfer that authority to another country. From an ethnocentric point of view, relinquishing legal authority in favor of another legal system poses a problem. Foreign legal authorities, such as courts and prosecutors, seem alien, untrustworthy, hostile, even dangerous. As part of the out-group, foreign legal institutions cannot be trusted to handle a case fairly, and they surely cannot be trusted to accord fair treatment to a member of the in-group. Indeed, they might exhibit bias against one's citizens and perhaps even abuse them.

Such worries over the delegation of authority away from the nation-state to foreign legal systems mirror concerns about the transfer of legal authority to international courts. From the resistance to the International Criminal Court in the United States and Africa[91] to the backlash against the European Court of Human Rights and the Inter-American Court of Human Rights,[92] international courts often inspire suspicion or outright hostility. Critics argue that they undermine national sovereignty, promote agendas, interests, or values that are inimical to those of certain countries, or suffer from a bias against certain countries. In the context of transnational litigation, similar concerns may be leveraged against the transfer of authority to a foreign legal system. Such an act could be seen as neutering the decision-making authority of the state in favor of foreign institutions that might be hostile to it. Concerns about legal delegation thus inspire slogans such as "American Justice for American Citizens" (mentioned above) or "British Justice for British Citizens" (to be discussed in Chapter 6). These slogans convey a clear message: national legal institutions should adjudicate disputes involving local citizens, and the authority to handle and resolve these disputes should not be delegated to a foreign legal system—*any* foreign legal system. Indeed, legal-delegation concerns are not aimed at a specific foreign legal system and are not based on a specific evaluation of such a system. Rather, it is the very notion of delegating authority to a foreign system that is anathema to the legal ethnocentric.

A second set of sensitivities, which we term legal incongruity, rests not on the locus of authority, but on the legal process itself: the substantive rules applied or the institutional procedures and practices implemented. Persons holding ethnocentric sentiments will take pride in and feel attachment to their own country's substantive rules and norms as well as its legal procedures and institutions. By contrast, they will be suspicious of foreign rules and procedures and deem them incongruent with or inferior to those of their own country. In other words, ethnocentrism gives rise to a sense of legal absolutism, which envisions a hierarchical relationship between national legal systems. The home legal system is held up as "the best," and it serves as the metric and reference point: foreign legal systems are judged relative to the home system and are evaluated by its standards.[93] Given ethnocentrism's emphasis on in-group superiority, such a relative evaluation will often place the foreign system in a subordinate and inferior status to the home legal system. The foreign system's institutions and procedures could be seen as deficient, objectionable, unfair, or of poor quality, and its substantive rules might be viewed as inappropriate or as violating fundamental principles. In short, an ethnocentric view will magnify and emphasize the differences between the home legal system and the foreign system, resulting in a view of the latter as unjust.

The discussion above yields our first two propositions.

***Proposition 1*:** Transnational litigation raises concerns about the delegation of authority to a foreign legal system and about incongruities between the home and foreign legal systems. Political debates will emphasize the contrast and incompatibility between the home and foreign systems and the danger of surrendering legal authority to the latter. Debates will also reflect pride in one's rules and procedures and denigration of other legal systems.

Proposition 2: Actors tend to use their home legal system as the metric for the assessment of foreign legal systems. Deviation from local, familiar standards will be seen as evidence of the unfairness of the foreign system.

Which procedures and rules of the foreign legal system will be evaluated and compared to those of the home legal system? Obviously, one cannot expect full symmetry or complete consistency between the home and foreign systems. A comparison of the two is therefore likely to focus on substantive rules as well as institutional procedures and practices that are of a *fundamental* nature.

The fundamental procedures or practices of a legal system are typically subsumed under the notion of the rule of law (in its formal or "thin" conception[94]). These include issues such as clarity and stability of legal rules; access to the courts and timeliness of decisions; independence of the judiciary and safeguards against undue influence on the legal process in the form of political pressure or corruption; the capacity to enforce judicial decisions; and impartiality of the courts.[95] The latter carries particular importance in transnational litigation given the concern that the home country's citizens might face bias and prejudice before the foreign country's courts.[96]

Another set of key procedural elements are those known as "due process rights" or "fair trial rights." A well-known enumeration of these rights appears in Article 14 of the International Covenant on Civil and Political Rights (ICCPR). The ICCPR guarantees, among other things, the presumption of innocence; the right to legal assistance and representation of one's choosing; the right to be tried without undue delay; and the right to examine the witnesses against oneself. Due process may also require humane treatment of individuals, such as the nonuse of torture and reasonable detention conditions.[97]

Finally, a country may view as fundamental any specific feature of its legal procedure and institutions. Americans, for example, see an inextricable link between the jury system and the ideas of justice and democracy. The jury epitomizes democracy by placing power directly in the hands of citizens, and it supposedly delivers justice that expresses the conscience of the community.[98] Indeed, the jury is "celebrated for its contributions to American democracy, as a venue for citizen self-government."[99] In American eyes, juries are also seen as furthering a government of checks and balances and constraining the abuse of power; being better at determining disputed facts than other fact-finding means; and facilitating public acceptance of legal determinations. The jury system is thus woven deeply into the fabric of American society, firmly enshrined in state and federal constitutions, history, and traditions.[100] The centrality of juries in the American conception of justice influences the American view of foreign legal systems. For an American, a foreign system without juries might seem to be missing a crucial institution.[101] It might be deemed strange, unfair, or inferior to the U.S. justice system.

An ethnocentric view of foreign legal systems also involves a comparison and relative assessment of *substantive* legal rules. If there is a significant disparity in substantive legal rules between the home country and the foreign country, the home country cannot expect that its citizens or firms will receive fair treatment from the foreign legal system, and the exercise of authority by that system becomes harder to accept. To reach such a conclusion of legal incongruity, the two legal systems need not have completely different rules in every domain. Their comparison focuses on substantive rules and norms of a fundamental nature, such as human rights and legal equality. The foreign legal system will be viewed as unfair if it fails to adequately protect individual rights and liberties that are guaranteed by the home legal system, or if it discriminates against members of certain groups that receive equal treatment before the home legal system.[102] Another core norm concerns perceptions of appropriate punishment versus punishment that is severe, excessive, or cruel. For example, many countries consider the death penalty inhumane;[103] a very long prison sentence, in certain circumstances, might be seen as too harsh or unfair.[104]

Yet the evaluation of the foreign legal system and its comparison to the home legal system is hardly conducted as a methodical exercise in comparative law. Rather, it is prone to suffering from two types of biases: parochialism and an endowment effect.[105]

The assessment of the foreign legal rules or procedures could be parochial in that it rarely relies on in-depth, comprehensive knowledge of the foreign legal system. Indeed, a significant effort is required in order to gain a deep understanding of the logic behind legal rules or to fully comprehend how these rules operate and how they fit within the broader framework of the foreign legal system. In debates on transnational litigation, however, actors often lack the means, knowledge, patience, or interest to conduct a thorough legal analysis—one that places the foreign legal elements in their broader context and recognizes that rules and procedures in one system may take a different shape in another. Instead, an "easier" comparison is likely to look at the foreign legal elements in isolation, removed from their legal and cultural context. Such a superficial comparison would expect an equivalence between the home and foreign rules and procedures. When this expectation is not met, the foreign legal system might be seen as flawed.[106]

To borrow from behavioral economics, another shortcoming in the evaluation of foreign legal systems may be termed an endowment effect, that is, people's tendency to overestimate the value of what they possess.[107] In legal comparisons, this translates to an idealized view of the home legal system. The home legal system's rules and procedures are assumed to work perfectly or produce the best results; rarely is there a recognition that they might suffer from flaws and weaknesses or that their operation in practice might result in poor outcomes. The utopian image of the home legal system is juxtaposed next to the realities of the foreign system, and such a comparison naturally favors the former and makes the foreign system seem unjust or inferior. Whereas problems in the home legal system will be dismissed as mere aberrations and will not tarnish the positive view of that system, problems in the foreign system are deemed endemic and ingrained.[108]

The foregoing analysis identified two types of concerns about transnational litigation: legal delegation and legal incongruity. The two are distinct theoretically: legal-delegation concerns involve a rejection of any foreign legal authority, whereas legal-incongruity concerns aim at a specific legal system whose rules or procedures seem flawed or unfair. Yet the two sensitivities may be difficult to distinguish empirically. Both are rooted in a similar underlying sentiment of suspicion and mistrust toward foreign legal systems; both push in a similar direction of discouraging cooperation on transnational litigation. The exercise of authority by foreign legal institutions that seem alien or hostile could meet resistance; similarly, the application of legal procedures or substantive rules that are incompatible with one's own might trigger an angry response. As we move to examining the political tensions over transnational litigation, the key question is: Who would typically raise concerns about foreign legal systems and oppose cooperation with them? Who, by contrast, tends to exhibit support for such cooperation?

Resisting or Supporting Cooperation on Litigation

Understanding the political dynamic of transnational litigation requires us to examine how its benefits and costs play out in the domestic political arena. As described above, cooperation on litigation may deliver important rewards, from legal stability and a stronger rule of law to friendly international relations and reciprocal cooperation in the legal and nonlegal spheres. Certain actors may appreciate these benefits and support the cooperative arrangements that deliver them. But it is the costs of transnational litigation, perceived through an ethnocentric prism, that trigger and drive the political debates. Note that these costs may be actually realized or only anticipated. Cooperation on litigation may already be in effect, creating negative consequences for home-country litigants; alternatively, cooperation may only be proposed or planned, but some actors view it as threatening or harmful. Furthermore, the concerns could exaggerate the actual costs of litigation: the foreign legal system may treat home-country litigants better than cooperation critics believe. But it is the *perception* of costs that matters here, and it can generate political blowback against governments that could be accused of abandoning their citizens to the mercy of foreign courts or abrogating local values and principles.

Importantly, opponents of cooperation on litigation typically are more vocal than its supporters, as is often the case in other areas, such as trade. While consumers stand to benefit from free trade, they typically do not organize politically to influence trade policy due to collective-action problems or because they are uninformed about trade policy. This means that the political debate over trade is dominated by the small interest groups that trade openness might harm.[109] Similarly, those who stand to gain from cooperation on litigation may be unaware of the benefits or might feel that they are too uncertain or remote to merit political support. For instance, while the enforcement of foreign judgments aims to lay a stable legal foundation for commerce, many firms might fail to recognize its importance, let alone organize politically in its support.[110] While extradition promotes the public interest in bringing offenders to justice, few actors in society are likely to feel they have such a large and direct stake in this mechanism as to mobilize in its defense.[111] Whereas the benefits of cooperation on litigation may not be easily visible or appreciated, the actual or expected harm is more tangible and hence more likely to rally opponents in protest. Seeing a fellow citizen receive an unfair trial or a harsh sentence from a foreign court, or perceiving an affront to national values, could stir strong emotions that overshadow the benefits of cooperation.

Who, then, is likely to doubt and criticize cooperation on litigation?

First and foremost, cooperation on litigation, when supported by the government, provides excellent fodder for politicians who wish to criticize the government. Naturally, such critics often come from the opposition, but even politicians belonging to the ruling party may join the criticism of cooperation that they view as misguided. Political critics may portray cooperation as a dangerous surrender to a foreign legal system, which offends and undermines local laws, values, or public policy. At the same time, these critics would argue, such cooperation puts the home country's citizens or firms in danger, since their fate would be decided by foreign courts on the basis of legal rules and procedures that are unfair by local standards.[112] These criticisms will emphasize the differences between the home and foreign legal systems and their contrasting and incompatible approaches to the legal matter in question. A government willing to cooperate in the face of such gaps will be criticized as betraying local norms or as abdicating its responsibility to protect its citizens—all in order to curry favor with the foreign country and reap the diplomatic or economic gains of international cooperation. Indeed, critics might portray cooperation on litigation as a cynical ploy to improve the country's foreign relations at the expense of justice and national sovereignty.[113]

What motivates those politicians who denounce cooperation on litigation? The basic motivation we ascribe to politicians is their desire to win political support and enhance their political standing.[114] Attacking cooperation on litigation can advance these goals and increase politicians' popularity among concerned constituents. By rejecting cooperation, politicians can present themselves as guardians of the country's sovereignty and legal system and as protectors of local citizens against foreign injustice. Such an image can attract votes; it may also draw the support of commercial firms resisting transnational litigation.[115] But politicians' opposition to cooperation may reflect more than the cynical pursuit of political support: it may also stem from genuine concerns about foreign justice systems and cooperation with them.[116] Like any member of society, politicians may exhibit legal ethnocentrism: they may feel attachment to their country's legal norms and institutions; accordingly, they may reject foreign norms and institutions as inferior. In fact, politicians' ethnocentrism may be particularly strong: many of them see it as their mission to protect the state's norms and institutions. These sentiments, in turn, may fuel concerns about the implications of cooperation. For an ethnocentric politician, ceding authority to a foreign legal system could result in a sacrifice of sovereignty, undermining of the national legal system through foreign encroachment, betrayal of fundamental values, and the abandonment of local citizens who might fall victim to foreign injustice. And if politicians fail to naturally recognize such outcomes, other concerned actors may educate them and raise their awareness. As we discuss below, debates over transnational litigation involve a variety of actors who work to persuade policymakers to resist cooperation by pointing out the harms it might bring.[117]

Do political ideology and party affiliation matter here? One might, perhaps, expect ethnocentric attacks on cooperation to come from the right, since we more typically associate right-wing ideology with a sense of national superiority and denigration of out-groups.[118] Yet, as Kinder and Kam demonstrate, partisanship and ethnocentrism are distinct dispositions and not necessarily correlated.[119] Concerns about transnational litigation, therefore, are not limited to right-wing parties. In some cases, cooperation on litigation could threaten the fundamental human rights of individuals—values that left-wing politicians may care about. In such instances, it will be left-wing politicians who denounce cooperation as antithetical to national values.[120] It is also possible to envision scenarios that bring together right-wing and left-wing politicians in joint criticism of legal cooperation. When transnational litigation threatens values that enjoy broad political support from across the political spectrum, opposition to cooperation may transcend the left-right divide.

Proposition 3: Domestic political rivals may criticize the government's willingness to cooperate on litigation as an undermining of national values and a betrayal of the duty to protect one's citizens. Attacks on cooperation may come from both right-wing parties and left-wing parties.

Outside the political system, controversies over transnational litigation often attract the attention of actors in civil society, including the media, human rights NGOs, and the legal community.

Many studies have documented the home-country bias of journalists. During times of national crisis, and especially during military conflict, the media tends to exhibit loyalty to the country or nation. Displaying their loyalty, journalists often adopt the governmental framing of the crisis, avoid criticizing their government during the conflict, express solidarity with the national community, and ignore the other side ("the enemy"), its positions, and narratives.[121] Transnational litigation resembles national security crises in the Us-against-Them setup: it involves a clash between the home and foreign legal systems. Like military conflict, transnational litigation involves a foreign government that might treat the home country's citizens poorly or harm them if they come under its authority. Covering transnational litigation, the media may therefore express its loyalty to the home country and rally against the threat to local citizens and values. Media outlets may in fact whip up sentiment against cooperation by highlighting the travails of those who come under the authority of foreign legal norms or institutions.[122]

For NGOs concerned with human rights, the exercise of foreign legal authority over the home country's citizens could result in human rights violations. The foreign legal system might fail to respect due-process rights; it could engage in torture or other abusive treatment of individuals under its authority; and the punishment it imposes might be viewed as excessive or inhuman.[123] In such cases, NGOs will likely condemn and reject cooperation with the foreign system as a violation of human rights, contrary to national norms as well as international human rights standards. The latter carry particularly significant weight for *international* NGOs seeking to promote compliance with international human rights. In other words, the reference point for international NGOs may not only be the particular national legal system where they operate; rather, they evaluate foreign legal systems according to *international* legal standards: international human rights agreements as well as standards enforced by international courts that work to protect human rights, such as the European Court of Human Rights and the International Criminal Court. These NGOs thus tend to reprimand governments willing to cooperate with foreign legal systems that fail to meet international human rights standards.[124] Given their singular focus on human rights, we would expect NGOs to be less receptive to justifications of cooperation based on the need to enforce laws or hold people legally accountable. Rather, they typically will resist cooperation with a foreign legal system that, in their view, fails to uphold human rights norms. Alternatively, they may demand that cooperation be subject to human rights protections and safeguards—measures that might complicate or obstruct the establishment of cooperation.[125]

How do NGOs advocate against cooperation on litigation? As Margaret Keck and Kathryn Sikkink argue, NGO activists often seek to influence policy through the provision of information. They offer facts as well as testimonies—stories of people whose lives have been affected. Activists interpret those facts and testimonies in simple terms of right and wrong in order to enhance their persuasive power. By appealing to shared principles, they seek to transform the issue from a technical one, subject to consideration by "qualified" experts, to something that concerns a broader national or global constituency.[126] In controversies over transnational litigation, NGOs can certainly employ such information tactics. They may provide facts, as well as personal testimonies, on human rights abuse or unfair conduct by the foreign legal system. Through such information, they will seek to reframe transnational litigation as not an arcane professional matter of interest only to lawyers, but an issue that raises major human rights problems and should be of concern to a broad audience. In addition, NGOs may deploy what Keck and Sikkink label "accountability politics"—embarrassing governments by exposing the distance and tension between their rhetoric and practice.[127] Here, activists can point to the hypocrisy of a government's vowing to uphold human rights while at the same time cooperating with a foreign legal system that violates human rights.

Proposition 4: The media and NGOs are likely to voice concerns about foreign legal systems and to resist cooperation on litigation.

What role does the legal community play in debates on transnational litigation? Lawyers and jurists may not speak with one voice. On the one hand, some lawyers have a direct stake in these debates, as they represent individuals or firms who might come under the authority of a foreign legal system. These lawyers may seek to shield their clients from foreign legal authority. To that end, they will raise doubts and concerns about the delegation of authority to the foreign system and highlight substantive and procedural incongruities between the home and foreign systems—all of which, they would argue, result in the denial of fairness to home-country actors subjected to a foreign legal process. Such anti-cooperation views may draw support from lawyers or lawyer associations that are not directly involved with transnational litigation but are nevertheless alarmed about foreign encroachment into the local legal system. Trained in local rules and procedures and working with them on an everyday basis, lawyers may feel an attachment to—and pride in—their legal system and will seek to defend it against incompatible rules and procedures of a foreign origin.[128]

On the other hand, lawyers may appreciate the goals that cooperation on litigation serves: enhancing legal certainty, stability, and efficiency; securing compliance with legal rules and decisions; and, more broadly, strengthening the impact and effectiveness of the law and legal systems.[129] Jurists in the state's legal apparatus—such as judges, prosecutors, and the justice-ministry bureaucracy—should be particularly mindful and appreciative of these considerations and, accordingly, more prone to supporting cooperation.[130] Committed to the rule of law and effective law enforcement, these actors may more readily accept the exercise of foreign legal authority, based on the principled position that law should travel between countries and national borders should not allow actors to evade legal responsibility. Furthermore, judges and law-enforcement bureaucrats understand the reciprocal nature of cooperation. They realize that a refusal to cooperate with a foreign legal system could prompt the latter to respond in kind. Non-enforcement of a foreign country's judgments might result in the foreign system's refusal to enforce the home country's judgments; unwillingness to extradite criminal suspects to foreign countries could make it more difficult to have persons extradited from abroad or to obtain other forms of law-enforcement assistance.[131] More broadly, questioning and criticizing foreign rules and procedures exposes one to similar criticism from abroad. We might expect jurists in the state apparatus, who seek to avoid such undesirable outcomes for the state, to be less critical of foreign legal systems and more open to cooperating with them.

Proposition 5: Lawyers, attached to local legal rules and procedures, are likely to oppose cooperation on litigation. Jurists in the state apparatus, however, may support such cooperation, which facilitates effective law enforcement.

Other parts of the government might share the preference for cooperation on litigation. The ministry of foreign affairs, for example, is likely to appreciate the possible benefits of cooperation in improving diplomatic relations or trade and to care less about legal differences among countries and their consequences.[132] The ministry of defense will similarly favor the gains from legal cooperation in terms of strengthening security ties with foreign countries; concerns about legal delegation or legal incongruity carry less weight with security-minded officials.[133]

Proposition 6: Government ministries that are not justice-related, such as the ministry of foreign affairs and the ministry of defense, tend to support cooperation on litigation as a means to facilitate friendly international relations and obtain cooperation in other areas, such as trade or security.

Activation and Mitigation of Ethnocentrism

While this book examines political conflicts over transnational litigation, one must acknowledge that such conflicts are the exception rather than the rule. Cooperation on litigation occurs on an everyday basis without attracting much public attention or arousing controversies. The ethnocentrism that feeds concerns about cooperation with foreign legal systems is typically held at bay. Yet ethnocentric sentiments are not a constant: they may be weaker or stronger, varying across issues and partners. The prospects of cooperation are strongly linked to the ability of political actors to activate (or mitigate) ethnocentric sentiments and to stoke (or alleviate) concerns over legal delegation and legal incongruity. Since intense ethnocentric sentiments threaten to constrain cooperative efforts or derail them altogether, a key question arises: Under what conditions is ethnocentrism activated?[134]

Kinder and Kam identify sufficient public attention as a first precondition for the activation of ethnocentrism in the political process.[135] Such attention may result from media coverage of the legal case. When the media shines a spotlight on a case and brings it into public awareness, concerns about the exercise of foreign legal authority are more likely to arise.[136] Once the case is on people's minds, they are more likely to question the appropriateness of foreign legal rules or institutions and to worry about the fairness of the outcomes that they might produce. Such worries could be further intensified if the media coverage takes a critical tone that sows doubts about the foreign legal system's trustworthiness or its compatibility with the home country's norms.[137]

Yet it is not only the media that brings public attention to transnational litigation. Such attention may also result from the work of individuals, firms, or organizations that seek to be shielded from a foreign legal system. These actors—or others who sympathize with them—may launch an advocacy campaign to bring public attention to their plight; they may also engage in lobbying to persuade politicians that the exercise of foreign legal authority over them is unjust and should be thwarted. Such self-advocacy will emphasize personal stories about the poor treatment that one has suffered or might suffer in the course of the foreign legal process. This aims to convey the message that cooperation on litigation causes real-world damage and unjustifiable harm to home-country citizens who should be subject to their own legal system.[138]

Ethnocentric concerns about the foreign legal process may become further intensified if its effects are framed in broad terms, not only as causing injustice or harm to the individual that is directly involved, but also as having broader implications that are troubling or damaging for society. For example, the exercise of foreign legal authority may be presented as posing a security or economic threat that goes beyond the specific case in question, or the foreign legal process may be framed as threatening to undermine the home country's core values. The perception of such material or ideational threat may aggravate the concerns about the foreign legal system and galvanize resistance to cooperation.[139]

***Proposition** 7*: Broad framing of the negative effects of cooperation—emphasizing the harm not only to the individual involved in transnational litigation but to society—may intensify ethnocentric concerns.

The intensity of ethnocentric concerns will also vary with the identity of the person who might be subject to foreign legal authority. We would expect these concerns to focus primarily on citizens of the home country. As part of the in-group, home-country citizens should enjoy the protection of the home legal system and the full rights that this system accords. By contrast, noncitizens of the home country have a weaker claim to such protection. Since they are not an integral part of the local community, subjecting them to foreign legal authorities raises less of a problem. Indeed, many people presume that noncitizens do not deserve the same rights as citizens,[140] and they may not be deemed worthy of justice.[141] This perception makes it easier to subject noncitizens to foreign legal standards lower than those of the home country.

Yet it is not only the legal treatment of noncitizens that likely raises limited concern. Unpopular or despised groups with full citizenship in the home country may also meet with indifference when they come under the authority of a foreign legal system. Unpopular groups—such as religious or ethnic minorities—may themselves be seen as out-groups within the home country's population, and they often face discrimination before the home country's legal system.[142] We can expect their discrimination or abuse by the foreign legal system to trigger a relatively muted reaction. Conversely, ill-treatment by foreign legal institutions will provoke an outcry when the individuals concerned represent the state or are acting on its behalf. Diplomats are one example of a population deemed particularly worthy of protection from foreign justice.[143] The Vienna Convention on Diplomatic Relations stipulates that "A Diplomatic Agent shall enjoy immunity from the criminal jurisdiction of the receiving State."[144] Soldiers also act on behalf of their state, and they put their lives on the line for it. Soldiers may thus be seen as deserving certain privileges, including insulation from foreign justice.[145]

***Proposition** 8*: The intensity of ethnocentric concerns will vary with the identity of the individuals involved in the legal process. Concerns will be weaker regarding the fate of noncitizens or citizens that belong to unpopular groups. Concerns will be stronger when the foreign legal system exercises authority over citizens of importance to the home country, such as soldiers.

The activation of ethnocentric concerns also depends on the magnitude of the gap between the home and foreign legal systems. The greater the differences between the substantive rules or procedures of the two systems, the more threatening the foreign system seems. In some cases, these differences can be defined objectively. For example, if the foreign country exercises the death penalty and the home country does not, then a clear, significant gap exists between them. Yet in many cases, the assessment of the gap and its significance is far from clear-cut. If the home country uses the jury system and the foreign country does not, what does this difference imply for the fairness of trials? Are foreign courts less likely to reach just outcomes in the absence of juries?[146] If the foreign legal system resorts to plea bargains at a higher rate than the home system, does this necessarily compromise the quality of criminal justice and the rights of suspects?[147] Such questions do not have clear, straightforward answers. The assessment of the differences between legal systems is further complicated by significant uncertainty. It is rarely based on full, systematic information about the foreign legal rules and their effects or about the quality of legal institutions. For example, it is often difficult to assess the overall quality of prison conditions in the foreign country or the degree to which criminal investigations there involve coercion. The relevant information may be scarce or nonexistent. Anecdotes and general impressions may thus substitute for hard facts.[148]

These challenges of evaluation and assessment create fertile ground for actors seeking to shape and manipulate the understanding of the gap between the legal systems and its implications. Actors seeking to weaken or thwart cooperative efforts will emphasize the differences and exaggerate their significance. They will present the foreign rules and procedures as wrong and unfair, as an offense to local values and practices, or as a threat to the home country's citizens or legal system. Actors *supporting* cooperation will seek to diffuse these concerns and downplay the differences between the home and foreign legal systems. For example, they may argue that these differences should not be feared and that not every deviation from familiar local standards is necessarily wrong. They may also claim that one cannot expect perfect consistency between legal systems; or that seemingly large differences in legal rules carry little significance in practice, as the different rules yield similar outcomes. Another line of argument might point to safeguards included in legislation or treaties. For example, concerns about the death penalty may be assuaged by requiring the foreign country to provide assurances that persons extradited to it will not be executed.[149] Critics of cooperation may counter by doubting the credibility of these assurances and pointing to the difficulty of enforcing them.[150]

Proposition 9: Cooperation on litigation is more likely to meet domestic resistance the greater the differences between the home and foreign legal

> systems. Actors will seek to highlight or downplay these differences in accordance with their preference on cooperation. Actors favoring cooperation will minimize the differences as inconsequential and emphasize the existence of safeguards. By contrast, those opposing cooperation will portray the differences as large and significant; they will also dismiss safeguards as unreliable.

The above analysis sketched the contours of the domestic political debate on transnational litigation, highlighting ethnocentric sentiments as a key influence in this debate. Ethnocentrism, however, does not always prevail over other considerations: it is an important influence against cooperation, but not necessarily a decisive influence. Whether ethnocentrism will manage to scuttle cooperation may depend on two additional factors.

First, although the ethnocentric critics may seek to deter the government from cooperation, the government will also consider the benefits and importance of cooperation. If the cooperative endeavor carries significant benefits, the government may choose to cooperate on litigation in the face of the ethnocentric resistance. If the benefits are limited in importance, the government may opt to yield to the ethnocentric criticism and forgo cooperation.

Second, even if the government chooses to resist the ethnocentric sentiments and pursue cooperation, doing so may depend on its political leverage and ability to garner the necessary political support. If the government possesses the required leverage, it may be able to convince or pressure other actors into accepting cooperation despite their doubts. In other cases, the ethnocentric critics may be able to exercise veto power and block cooperation.[151]

Note, however, that this book does not focus on the final (non)cooperative outcome. Our primary goal is not to understand whether cooperation was eventually established, but rather to understand the debates and controversies surrounding cooperation between legal systems: the concerns and misgivings that cooperation skeptics hold—and how cooperation proponents seek to address and overcome them.

Conclusion

Cooperation on litigation raises a host of concerns. It might be viewed as posing a threat to national sovereignty, local law, local values, or local actors. The theoretical account offered here underscores the roles of both socio-psychological and institutional factors in activating or muting these concerns over transnational litigation and the handling of legal disputes by a foreign legal system. As for socio-psychological forces, we stress the importance of *ethnocentrism*: the tendency to divide human society into in-groups and out-groups. We argue that ethnocentrism fuels resistance to the delegation of decision-making to foreign courts or to the subjection of individuals to foreign rules and procedures deemed unjust by the home country's standards. At the same time, we expect micro-institutional differences between legal systems to mitigate or amplify the ethnocentric concerns over cooperation. Actors skeptical of cooperation may exploit legal differences between the home and foreign countries to arouse fears regarding delegation to foreign courts or legal asymmetries. Foreign judicial systems might be flagged by these actors as untrustworthy or as a Trojan Horse set to undermine fundamental domestic values. By contrast, similarities in domestic institutions and norms such as human rights, due process, or judicial independence may undermine ethnocentric concerns. By identifying these similarities and downplaying differences, proponents of cooperation may be able to diffuse the political threats to the cooperative efforts. The complementary logics of ethnocentrism and (dis)similarity in legal institutions form the core argument traced throughout this book.

The integration of socio-psychological forces and institutional elements into a single theoretical framework is analytically eclectic: it uses theoretical constructs embedded in different research traditions to build a complex argument that bears on the substantive problem of interest.[152] More specifically, the theoretical account presented here blends rationalist (institutional) and nonrationalist (psychological) elements. While various studies have identified the impact of domestic institutions on international cooperation, they have typically explained this impact in rationalist terms. Democracies' greater tendency to cooperate has been explained as the product of institutional obstacles to changing policy or of the government's need for public support to ensure its political survival.[153] Domestic legal institutions are thought to generate costs that might discourage governments from ratifying human rights treaties.[154] States, it is argued, seek to design international courts in a way that resembles their domestic legal systems to reduce uncertainty about international law.[155] The theory proposed here, however, suggests that concerns about litigation before foreign courts are not only, or even primarily, rationalist: the fundamental problem is not the financial or other material costs that foreign litigation entails. Rather, concerns arise from our innate tendency to divide the world into positive in-groups and negative out-groups and the placing of foreign legal systems in the out-group domain, which leads to their being viewed as unfair, dangerous, or failing to meet the in-group's standards. The injection of this nonrationalist element into the analysis affords us a deeper understanding of how institutional differences among countries matter and why they might hinder cooperation. Indeed, institutional differences in themselves have no clear, objective significance. It is political actors who either highlight and underscore those differences or, alternatively, downplay them.

The following chapters explore this last point: how different actors evaluate foreign legal systems and what significance they attach to the gaps between the home and foreign systems. The subjection of American troops to trials before the courts of European countries; the exercise of jurisdiction over British citizens who fought for ISIS in Iraq and Syria; extradition to China, the United States, or EU countries; and enforcement of civil judgments issued by American or British courts—all these cases of transnational litigation exhibit various interpretations of the differences between legal systems. Let us turn to exploring these competing views, their origins, and the implications for cooperation.

Notes

1. Baumgartner 2004; Putnam 2016.
2. Raustiala 2009; Farmer 2013.
3. Buxbaum 2009, 636.
4. This corresponds to the threefold distinction between types of jurisdiction: legislative/prescriptive jurisdiction; adjudicative jurisdiction; and enforcement jurisdiction. International Bar Association 2008, 7–8; Whytock 2009a, 76.
5. See generally Whytock 2009a, 69. Examples include Shearer 1971 (extradition); Plachta 1999 (extradition); Baumgartner 2004 (foreign judgments and taking of evidence); Wasserstein-Fassberg 2013 (foreign judgments).
6. Krasner 1999.
7. Carothers 2006; Christensen and Weinstein 2013; Usherwood and Startin 2013; Sandholtz, Bei, and Caldwell 2018; Voeten 2020.
8. This is known as the "active personality" principle of criminal jurisdiction. Ryngaert 2015, 104–105.
9. A state's unilateral choice to exercise extraterritorial jurisdiction in a civil case—that is, to decide a civil dispute concerning persons or events in a foreign country—serves as another example of noncooperation. See Putman 2016.
10. Whytock 2009a, 82–83.
11. Alexander 1975; Wasserstein-Fassberg 2013, chap. 3.
12. States may, however, extradite a person on the condition that they be returned to serve their punishment. See, for example, Israel's Extradition Law, Article 1A.
13. Plachta 1999; Efrat and Newman 2020.
14. Whytock 2009a, 72, 75–76.
15. Keohane 1984; Drezner 2001; Raustiala 2002.
16. Barton et al. 2006; Davis 2012.
17. Elkins, Guzman, and Simmons 2006; Haftel and Thompson 2018.
18. Wallach 1986, 1504; Michaels 2009.
19. Wasserstein-Fassberg 2013, 254.
20. Cited in Dodge 2015, 2086.
21. See Efrat 2016a and 2016b.
22. Hensel and Mitchell 2005; Toft 2014.
23. American Banana Co. v. United Fruit Co., 213 U.S. 347, 356 (1909).
24. Consider the case of Julian Assange, WikiLeaks founder, who evaded extradition to the United States during his seven-year asylum in the Ecuadoran embassy in London (2012–2019). Ecuador's sheltering of Assange negatively affected its relations with the United States. Sieff, Hernández, and Martinez 2019. An earlier example concerns Israel's 1999 turning down of the American request to extradite Samuel Sheinbein, an Israeli American who fled to Israel after committing a murder in Maryland. That refusal strained U.S.-Israel relations. Kraft 1999.

25. Keohane 1984, 214; Keohane 1986, 2.
26. Rhodes 1989; Weber 1991; Morrow 2007; Posner 2013.
27. Keohane 1986, 4.
28. Ahmed 2017.
29. Finnemore and Sikkink 1998, 903–904; Kelley 2007.
30. Bassiouni 2013, 489.
31. Sumner [1906] 2008, chap. I. See also Bizumic and Duckitt 2012, 889 (arguing that anthropologist William McGee was actually the first to use the term "ethnocentric" in print in English in 1900).
32. Jimenez-Guerrero, Gazquez-Abad, and Linares-Aguera 2014, 176.
33. Kinder and Kam 2009, 8. Emphasis in the original.
34. Kinder and Kam 2009, 52.
35. Kinder and Kam 2009, 42; Andrews, Leblang and Pandya 2018.
36. Bizumic and Duckitt 2012, 891, 893–894.
37. Balabanis, Mueller, and Melewar 2001, 159.
38. Sumner [1906] 2008. See also LeVine and Campbell 1972; Sherif 1966.
39. Tajfel and Turner 1979; Turner 1981; Turner et al. 1987; Kinder and Kam 2009, 20–21.
40. Adorno et al. 1950; Altemeyer 1998; Kinder and Kam 2009, 14.
41. Allport 1954; Neuberg and Newsom 1993.
42. Kinder and Kam 2009, 23, 66–68.
43. Kinder and Kam 2009, 58–61, 68.
44. Bizumic and Duckitt 2012, 899.
45. Blank and Schmidt 2003, 292, 305–306; Rosenblatt 1964.
46. Blank and Schmidt 2003, 294; De Figueiredo and Elkins 2003.
47. Bizumic and Duckitt 2012, 898.
48. Feldman 2003; Stenner 2005; Hello, Scheepers, and Sleegers 2006; Meeusen, Vroome, and Hooghe 2013.
49. Scheve and Slaughter 2001a; Mayda 2006; Ortega and Polavieja 2012. But see Hainmueller, Hiscox, and Margalit 2015 for evidence to the contrary.
50. Chandler and Tsai 2001; Dustann and Preston 2007; Hainmueller and Hiscox 2010; Ford 2011; Hainmueller and Hangartner 2013; Miller 2020.
51. Scheve and Slaughter 2001b; Mayda and Rodrik 2005; Rho and Tomz 2017.
52. Margalit 2012, 486–487.
53. Margalit 2012, 496.
54. Mansfield and Mutz 2009.
55. Mansfield and Mutz 2013, 572.
56. Mutz and Kim 2017.
57. Shimp and Sharma 1987; Jimenez-Guerrero, Gazquez-Abad, and Linares-Aguera 2014, 176.
58. Verlegh 2007; Zeugner-Roth, Zabkar, and Diamantopoulos 2015.
59. Andrews, Leblang, and Pandya 2018.
60. Jacobson 2002, 312.
61. Michaels 2012.
62. Klein 1995; Balkin 2013.
63. Choudhry 2013.
64. Jacobsohn 2010, 7.
65. Finnemore and Troope 2001, 743.
66. Silbey 1992, 41.
67. Mezey 2001, 46.
68. Sarat and Kearns 1998, 7.
69. Mautner 2011, 841.
70. Horowitz 1977; Toobin 2008; Rosenberg 2008; Tankard and Paluck 2017.
71. Hirschl 2008, 95, 112.
72. Demleitner 1999, 742.
73. Baumgartner 2013, 976.
74. Simmons 2009, 72.
75. Kollewijn 1951; Collier 1994.

76. Kayaoglu 2010; Cassel 2012.
77. Pletcher 2003.
78. Waters 2005; Goodwin-Gill and Lambert 2010; Gelter and Siems 2014; Law 2015; Novak 2020, chap. 3.
79. Markesinis and Fedtke 2006.
80. Seipp 2006, 1422–1424; Sperti 2013. See, for example, H.Res.446, 108th Cong. (introduced November 18, 2003); H.Res.97, 109th Cong. (introduced February 15, 2005); S.Res.92, 109th Cong. (introduced March 20, 2005); H.R.3052, 114th Cong. (introduced July 14, 2015).
81. H.R. 4118, 108th Cong. (introduced April 1, 2004).
82. *Lawrence v. Texas*, 539 U.S. 558, 576–577 (2003).
83. Scalia and Breyer 2005, 523, 526. Emphasis in the original.
84. Powell 2015 and 2020.
85. Center for Security Policy 2010, 6, 11–12, 23, 27–33, 78.
86. Center for Security Policy 2011.
87. Patel, Duss, and Toh 2013, 6; Volokh 2014.
88. Patel, Duss, and Toh 2013.
89. Patel, Duss, and Toh 2013, 34.
90. Patel, Duss, and Toh 2013, 3.
91. Kelley 2007; Mude 2017; Ssenyonjo 2018.
92. Madsen 2016; Voeten 2020, 416–417.
93. Efrat and Newman 2016, 2018b, and 2020.
94. Tamanaha 2004; Moller and Skaaning 2012.
95. Bedner 2010; Moller and Skaaning 2014; Versteeg and Ginsburg 2017.
96. See the debate on whether foreign litigants face xenophobia in American courts. Clermont and Eisenberg 1996 and 2007; Moore 2003; Bhattacharya, Galpin, and Haslem 2007.
97. Sadoff 2016.
98. Abramson 2000.
99. Lempert 2015, 829.
100. Jonakait 2003, xxiv.
101. See Brooks 2016.
102. For an example of an assessment of the compliance of national laws with human rights, see Tayler 2016. On violations of the principle of legal equality, see Miller 1996; Cho 1998; Tonry 2011.
103. Hammel 2010; Mathias 2013; Hood and Holye 2015.
104. Whitman 2003; Appleton and Grøver 2007; Ogletree and Sarat 2012; Kleinfeld 2016.
105. Mirabella 2012, 255.
106. See Clarke 2006 and Seidman and Seidman 2006 for an analogous discussion of superficial or "hasty" legal transplants, that is, the borrowing of foreign legal norms and institutions without considering their history and broader context.
107. Thaler 1980; Kahneman, Knetsch, and Thaler 1990 and 1991.
108. Demleitner 1999, 742; Mirabella 2012, 257.
109. Gilligan 1997; Rho and Tomz 2017.
110. Cf. Efrat 2016a, 318.
111. Consider the case of Anne Sacoolas, the wife of a U.S. government employee stationed in the UK. Driving on the wrong side of the road, Sacoolas hit and killed a young local man in 2019. She then fled the UK back to the United States. The State Department rejected the UK's request for her extradition (Peltier 2020). According to a public opinion poll, nearly two thirds of Americans supported Sacoolas's extradition, but this support received little public expression (Smith 2020).
112. Baumgartner 2004; Joint Standing Committee on Treaties 2016d.
113. Efrat 2012, 141. An analogous argument has been made with regard to human rights treaties, namely, that states join these treaties in order to reap rewards such as greater aid or foreign investment. See Nielsen and Simmons 2015 for an overview and empirical analysis of this argument.
114. Bueno de Mesquita et al. 2003.

115. Baumgartner 2003, 114.
116. Cf. Kelley 2007, 577.
117. On NGO advocacy, see Carpenter et al. 2014; Hall, Schmitz, and Dedmon 2020.
118. Mudde 1995, 209–210; de Figueiredo and Elkins 2003; Wodak 2015, chap. 4; Bergmann 2017.
119. Kinder and Kam 2009, 59; Kam and Kinder 2012.
120. McFarland and Mathews 2005; Hertel, Scruggs, and Heidkamp 2009, 451.
121. Ginosar 2015, 292. See, for example, Murray et al. 2008; O'Reilly 2008.
122. See, for example, journalistic criticism of the U.S. government's willingness to subject American troops serving abroad to the jurisdiction of foreign courts. 99 *Congressional Record* 8780–8781 (1953). Samples of journalistic criticism of Britain's extradition arrangements include Slack and Seamark 2009; Pearson 2012.
123. Dugard and Van den Wyngaert 1998, 195–205; Sadoff 2016, chap. 7.
124. On international NGOs' criticism of human rights violations, see, for example, Murdie and Davis 2012; Peterson, Murdie, and Asal 2018.
125. On NGOs' demands for protections and safeguards in the context of international economic agreements, see He and Murphy 2007; Murphy 2010.
126. Keck and Sikkink 1998.
127. Keck and Sikkink 1998.
128. Nomi 2006; Simmons 2009, 72–73.
129. For example, Michaels 2009; Sadoff 2016; Boister 2018a.
130. Boister 2018b.
131. Feller 1975; Elbalti 2017.
132. Government Accountability Office 2006, 35; Apodaca 2006; Efrat 2012, 141, 190.
133. This would be consistent with the limited impact of human rights considerations on the allocation of military aid and on arms exports. See Apodaca and Stohl 1999; Blanton 2005; Erickson 2013.
134. Kinder and Kam 2009, 35–36.
135. Kinder and Kam 2009, 39.
136. On the contribution of media coverage to public awareness, see Sampei and Aoyagi-Usui 2009; Gollust et al. 2013; Williams and Schoonvelde 2018.
137. For an analysis of how the news media may shape domestic audiences' view of foreign countries, see Fung, Yan, and Akin 2018.
138. For similar examples of self-advocacy (e.g., advocacy by victims of human rights abuse; healthcare advocacy by patients) see Grover 2005; Funk et al. 2006; Hagan and Donovan 2013.
139. As analogies, consider the framing of criminal offenses as causing harm not only to the direct victims but to society at large. The prohibition on drug use is based on the framing of drugs as an evil that harms the individual user as well as society as a whole—for example, by fueling crime. Taylor 2008; Hughes, Lancaster, and Spicer 2011. To galvanize action against human trafficking, this practice is similarly framed not only as an abuse of victims, but as a problem of crime and as a source of profit for criminal groups. Simmons, Lloyd, and Stewart 2018.
140. Cole 2003, 369. On the legal treatment of foreigners, see Gurowitz 2006; Ugelvik 2017.
141. Crepeau and Jimenez 2004, 623.
142. Stolzenberg, D'Alessio, and Eitle 2013; Spohn 2015; Schleutker 2019.
143. Frey and Frey 1999.
144. Vienna Convention on Diplomatic Relations, Article 31(1).
145. Egan 2006.
146. Brooks 2016.
147. For arguments that question the fairness of plea bargains, see Savitsky 2012; Rakoff 2014.
148. For an analogous discussion of the quality of information in measuring human rights, see Fariss 2014 and 2018.
149. Kendall and Siracusa 2013.
150. For analogous arguments questioning the enforceability of international commitments, see Fuhrman 2012, chap. 9; Posner 2014.

151. Mansfield, Milner, and Pevehouse 2007; Bang, Hovi, and Sprinz 2012; Allee and Elsig 2017.
152. Sil and Katzenstein 2010.
153. Martin 2000; Battig and Bernauer 2009.
154. Simmons 2009, 71–75.
155. Mitchell and Powell 2011.

SECTION II

JURISDICTION

3

Should American Troops Face Foreign Courts?

Debating the NATO Status of Forces Agreement

A global military presence has long been crucial to the power projection and longevity of great powers. Seventeenth-century powers—Britain, France, Spain, Portugal, and the Netherlands—saw worldwide bases as critical for building their colonial empires. The United States embarked on the establishment of a global network of military bases as it was thrust into both the European and Pacific theaters in World War II. Whereas in 1938 the United States had only a handful of military bases beyond its continental boundaries, by the end of the war it had constructed some 4,000 military bases and facilities around the world, becoming the largest overseas military power. This global network then became an important element of protection against the Soviet Union as well as a pillar in the securing of the world's communication and trade sea lanes.[1] After the end of the Cold War, the number of U.S. bases decreased. As of 2017, the United States maintained 514 military sites in 45 foreign countries.[2] Yet overseas bases remain the cornerstone of American global dominance and military superiority. They function as "force multipliers" that allow the United States to project power worldwide. Indeed, overseas U.S. bases perform a variety of strategic and geopolitical roles: from deterring aggression and strengthening alliances to providing global logistics networks and facilitating smooth resource flows; from supplying intelligence and securing access to critical territories to creating a stable environment that encourages trade and investment.[3] Yet, for all their importance in preventing conflict and facilitating interdependence, overseas U.S. bases raise inherent tensions, as they involve the presence of one nation's military on another nation's territory. This type of worldwide military presence is historically unique. While empires used to deploy military forces in their colonies, the United States has stationed its soldiers in sovereign, independent countries.[4]

Intolerant Justice. Asif Efrat, Oxford University Press. © Oxford University Press 2023.
DOI: 10.1093/oso/9780197658895.003.0003

The peacetime presence of U.S. troops abroad gives rise to transnational litigation when American troops commit crimes against local citizens in base-hosting countries: from minor offenses such as assault, disorderly conduct, and traffic offenses to serious crimes such as murder, manslaughter, rape, and robbery. Indeed, U.S. troops have committed many such crimes. Between 1954 and 1970—a time period for which systematic data exist—legal authorities in host countries filed a total of 361,487 criminal cases against U.S. personnel, primarily American troops (more than 90% of cases), as well as civilian employees of the military and dependents.[5] These cases present an overlap between the legal authority of the United States over its troops and the authority of host countries to try offenders who commit crimes on their national territory against local citizens. Cooperation on the part of the United States means that U.S. authorities will cede some of their jurisdiction over troops, who may then find themselves under the host country's jurisdiction. For the host country to cooperate, it has to accept that certain crimes committed on its territory against its citizens will fall under U.S. jurisdiction and will not be tried in local courts. Cooperation requires both the United States and the host country to give up some of their legal authority, and this compromise raises concerns on both sides.

The concerns on the host country's side have been well documented and analyzed in the literature, especially that dealing with local responses to the U.S. military presence in East Asia.[6] The efforts of U.S. authorities to shield American troops from trial before local courts have occasionally stirred angry protests in host countries aggrieved by the affront to their sovereignty and a sense of injustice. Host-country publics and governments resent the implication that their judicial systems fail to meet standards of fairness and the possibility that serious offenses against their nationals will be adjudicated by the U.S. legal system—especially when the American offender is unlikely to face vigorous prosecution or, indeed, any prosecution by U.S. authorities.[7] Calls for revising the jurisdictional arrangements concerning U.S. troops—to make them more equitable toward host countries—have ensued.[8]

While we have a good understanding of the host-country perspective on sharing jurisdiction over U.S. troops, the same cannot be said about the American side. We know little about the domestic debate within the United States over the subjection of U.S. troops abroad to foreign jurisdiction. The following analysis examines the domestic American debate over the 1951 NATO Status of Forces Agreement (SOFA): the agreement established to regulate the U.S. military presence on the territory of its NATO allies and the first treaty in which the United States granted host countries certain jurisdictional authority over American troops. Before delving into the political debate, however, a brief introduction to SOFA is in order.

Status-of-Forces Agreements in a Nutshell

Since the emergence of the territorial state, states have claimed jurisdiction over people and conduct within their territory. A sovereign state was seen as having exclusive jurisdiction to punish offenses against its laws within its borders—and such territorial jurisdiction extended to foreigners.[9] An important exception to this rule concerned foreign military forces present on one's territory. Prior to 1945, visiting military forces often enjoyed immunity from local jurisdiction under what became known as "the law of the flag" doctrine. Under this doctrine, a military force operating on foreign soil is not subject to the territorial sovereign. Rather, it exercises an exclusive right of jurisdiction over its members.[10] Without full authority to punish offenders within his unit, so went the reasoning, the commander might soon lose control: his "forces would cease to be an army and would become a mob."[11] The law-of-the-flag doctrine governed U.S. foreign and military policy for nearly 150 years and was given formal expression in international agreements. During World Wars I and II, the United States negotiated agreements with host countries granting American authorities exclusive jurisdiction over U.S. service members. When an American soldier committed an offense, only U.S. authorities had the right to prosecute.[12]

Following World War II, law-of-the-flag-theory began to crumble. Nations slated to host foreign military forces increasingly asserted their sovereignty, and the principle of absolute immunity for foreign troops came under attack. The growing sense of national sovereignty and pride in countries hosting U.S. forces made it difficult for the United States to keep insisting that its troops abroad be subject exclusively to its criminal jurisdiction.[13] Such insistence became even more difficult to sustain given the nature of U.S. troop deployment in NATO countries: the near-permanent stationing of forces during peacetime. Forgoing jurisdiction, which may be acceptable during war, becomes less palatable for host countries after hostilities cease.[14] The NATO SOFA, signed by NATO members in June 1951 as a complement to the 1949 NATO Treaty, marked the American recognition of the need to relinquish some jurisdictional authority over U.S. troops in favor of the host country. At the same time, the agreement required host countries to compromise their territorial sovereignty and accept limits on their right to punish foreigners who commit crimes within their borders. A key purpose of the NATO SOFA was therefore to allocate criminal jurisdiction over U.S. troops between the United States and the host,[15] and it is Article VII of the agreement that lays out the allocation of jurisdiction.

Article VII gives the United States (referred to as the "sending State") exclusive jurisdiction over U.S. military personnel for crimes recognized by American laws but not recognized by the laws of the host country. Conversely, the host country enjoys exclusive jurisdiction over U.S. service members, civilian components, and dependents for crimes recognized by its laws but not recognized by the laws of the United States. More importantly, however, Article VII addresses concurrent jurisdiction: when the act in question comes within the criminal or disciplinary jurisdiction of both the United States as well as the host state. In these cases, either the United States or the host state will hold the primary right to exercise jurisdiction—that is, the right to prosecute first—depending on the nature of the alleged crime. The United States has primary jurisdiction over offenses against its property or security, or where the perpetrator and victim are both citizens of the United States (e.g., an offense committed by a U.S. soldier against another U.S. soldier). The United States also enjoys primary jurisdiction over acts conducted or omitted in the performance of official duty.[16] In all other cases, the host country has the primary right to exercise jurisdiction. Practically speaking, these are offenses which are civilian in nature and committed while off duty, ranging from traffic offenses to bar fights to rape and murder. Troops who commit such offenses act in their private capacity, and not on behalf of the U.S. military, and may thus face trial before the host-country courts. Yet Article VII also establishes the option of *waiving* the primary right to exercise jurisdiction in concurrent cases. The country holding the primary right in a specific case must give "sympathetic consideration" to a request from the other country for a waiver of its right if the other country considers such a waiver to be particularly important.[17]

In addition to allocating jurisdiction, Article VII establishes procedural safeguards for U.S. personnel tried by host countries. Paragraph 9 lays out these safeguards, including a prompt and speedy trial, the right to have legal representation, the right to have an interpreter, and the right to communicate with a representative of the U.S. government.[18] The inclusion of these safeguards in the NATO SOFA reflects the American concern for the proper treatment of U.S. troops in foreign courts—a concern that fueled the Congressional debate over the ratification of the agreement, as we will see below.

The NATO SOFA is of particular importance due to its groundbreaking nature as an international agreement that departs from law-of-the-flag doctrine and formalizes the cession of authority over American troops to host countries. Yet it is also significant for its broad membership. While other SOFAs concluded by the United States subsequently typically took a bilateral form, the NATO SOFA is a multilateral agreement linking the United States and its NATO allies.[19] Furthermore, the NATO SOFA's shared-jurisdiction framework has served as the paradigm and blueprint for other U.S. SOFAs worldwide.[20] It is also important to note that the NATO SOFA—as well as subsequent SOFAs[21]—is not limited to the issue of criminal jurisdiction. These agreements typically address a variety of matters concerning the stationing of U.S. troops in foreign territory, including freedom of movement of U.S. personnel, taxation, applicability of local labor and environmental laws, civil liability for damage to property, and access to the electromagnetic spectrum.[22] Yet the most important provisions of SOFAs, to this day, are those that limit the exposure of U.S. troops to the jurisdiction of host countries. A 2015 report by the Department of State's International Security Advisory Board explains:

> SOFAs serve a number of important U.S. interests, key among them being protection of U.S. military personnel from being subject to unfair criminal or civil justice systems. This is important not only to protect the rights of U.S. service members and to vindicate the United States' interest in exercising disciplinary jurisdiction over U.S. uniformed personnel, but also because U.S. willingness to deploy forces overseas—and public support for such deployments—could suffer significant setbacks if U.S. personnel were at risk of being tried in an inherently unfair system, or at any rate, in one that departs fundamentally from U.S. concepts of basic procedural fairness.[23]

But at the time international agreements are entered into, their effects and consequences may be difficult to foresee,[24] and this uncertainty clearly shaped the reception of the NATO SOFA as it came up for ratification by the U.S. Senate. The agreement aimed to shield U.S. military personnel from unfair investigation, trial, sentencing, or imprisonment by host countries that might not share the American legal philosophy or procedures.[25] It meant to ensure that U.S. service members accused of crimes would be treated fairly and in a manner consistent with U.S. constitutional protections.[26] Yet, it remained uncertain whether the agreement could actually accomplish these goals. Given the precedential nature of the NATO SOFA, many doubted whether it would indeed ensure fair legal treatment of American troops, as the following analysis reveals.

The Debate over the Ratification of the NATO SOFA

In June 1952, President Truman transmitted the NATO SOFA to the Senate in anticipation of receiving its advice and consent. A State Department report accompanying the agreement explained that it guaranteed adequate legal protection to the armed forces, while at the same time recognizing the peacetime rights and responsibilities of the civilian authorities in the host countries. The

Senate was asked to give favorable consideration to the agreement as it was essential to the development of an integrated force under NATO.[27]

This book's theoretical framework, laid out in Chapter 2, suggests that the executive branch will typically approve of cooperation on litigation, often with little regard for the quality of the partner country's legal system. For the ministry of foreign affairs or ministry of defense, diplomatic or security ties trump concerns over legal standards (Proposition 6). This expectation receives strong support here, as members of the executive branch, from the president down, explained the SOFA's importance and benefits, highlighted practical considerations in support of the SOFA, and urged senators to ratify the agreement despite their doubts and misgivings about surrendering U.S. troops to foreign criminal jurisdiction. President Eisenhower—who occupied the White House when the ratification debate was being held in 1953—drew on his personal experience as a senior military commander in explaining the need for ratification:

> In my judgment, failure of the United States to ratify these agreements could seriously affect the security of the United States, for such failure could result in undermining the entire United States military position in Europe.
>
> I can certainly appreciate the concern of those who fear that these agreements might subject American soldiers overseas to systems of criminal justice foreign to our own traditions. I do not share such fears, however, because of the many years' experience I have had in command of American troops overseas. That experience convinces me that our friends abroad will continue to cooperate, as they have in the past, in turning over those charged with offenses against their laws to our own military courts for trial.
>
> Ratification of these agreements[28] would be a great forward step toward cementing the mutual security effort among the nations of the free world, and I earnestly hope that they will be ratified by the United States without reservations that would require their renegotiation.[29]

Eisenhower essentially makes two arguments here: U.S. troops charged with crimes would likely be turned over to U.S. authorities and would not, in fact, stand trial before host countries' courts; and ratification of the SOFA would enhance American security. Other senior officers who participated in the SOFA debate echoed the latter argument. They emphasized the SOFA's importance for the operation of American forces overseas and for the U.S. position in and leadership of NATO, expressing little concern over the subjection of U.S. troops to the criminal jurisdiction of NATO members. According to Omar Bradley, Chairman of the Joint Chiefs of Staff:

> The effectiveness of our forces stationed in the NATO countries and the effectiveness of the entire NATO military organization is closely related to this treaty . . .
>
> I discussed this matter with the three service chiefs just last week and they were unanimous in the opinion that it is very important that this agreement be approved at an early date. Failure to approve it would not only be a blow to our own defense effort and the NATO defense effort, but would seriously hamper our negotiations for operating rights in the NATO countries and would be a setback in our efforts to provide for both the operating effectiveness and the wellbeing of American forces in Europe.
>
> We all believe that this agreement is eminently satisfactory and is the best arrangement we can make with our allies when you consider the important issues of sovereignty which are involved . . .
>
> All these factors convince us that ratification of the NATO Status of Forces Agreement at this session of Congress is of great importance to our national defense.[30]

Admiral Arthur W. Radford, who would soon succeed Bradley as chairman of the Joint Chiefs of Staff, underscored the agreement's military importance and warned of the implications of a failure to ratify it:

> This agreement is essential to the welfare of United States military personnel stationed in the NATO countries. Furthermore, it plays a very important part in the development of our military plans, for it eliminates many of the barriers to the building of an effective defense organization.
>
> In my judgment, this agreement represents a sensible and practical balancing of the various interests involved. Any serious modification of its principles would create a grave risk that the agreement would fail. Such failure could have serious effects on both the United States military position and the United States military personnel in Europe.[31]

General Matthew Ridgway, Supreme Allied Commander Europe, similarly endorsed the SOFA as a satisfactory compromise:

> The status of forces agreement does not fully satisfy all that the United States or any other country might desire. It does, however, represent the best common denominator of conflicting national requirements which could be agreed upon by the NATO nations. Particularly, considering that it is a reconciliation on a multilateral basis of diverse national

views, its terms appear appropriate and acceptable. It is in that respect a noteworthy achievement and evidence of the NATO cooperative effort. From the point of view of my responsibility as the United States commander of United States Forces in the area, I support its ratification. Without ratification, that spirit of mutual trust and confidence, so vital to NATO's success, would sustain a very damaging blow.[32]

The Department of Defense shared the military's concerns about a possible failure to ratify the SOFA. Secretary of Defense Charles Wilson suggested that the NATO SOFA is "simply a fair way of working out the human problems that exist when the nationals of one country are present in another country for peaceful purposes."[33] For him, agreements relating to NATO—including the SOFA—were "another step forward in our program to protect the security of our country."[34] Assistant Secretary of Defense Frank C. Nash warned that the alternative to the SOFA would be far worse for American troops and their rights:

> If the agreement should fail, our forces would be left where they are now—covered in some countries by special or temporary arrangements and treated in others in accordance with the individual country's views of what is customary and appropriate. These arrangements and these views vary tremendously from country to country and are subject to change. I am convinced that further efforts to crystallize them either by bilateral agreements or by the negotiation of some other multilateral agreement would not be as advantageous to our forces as the rights and privileges which we will receive under the NATO Status of Forces Agreement.
>
> It is the position of the Department of Defense that the NATO Status of Forces Agreement is workable and practical and provides the essential framework in which status problems can be readily solved.[35]

State Department representatives made a similar point: the SOFA is the best possible arrangement for the distribution of jurisdiction over U.S. troops. It was certainly better, they argued, than the then-existing patchwork of interim jurisdictional arrangements between the United States and host countries.[36] The interim arrangements rested, in large part, on the goodwill of partner countries and their willingness to avoid placing U.S. troops on trial upon the request of American authorities: "we have been working out our problems solely by reason of the cooperative spirit of the other countries and their authorities." By contrast, the SOFA "would clarify, codify, and authorize on a firm legal basis the treatment which has been extended to us solely on the basis of grace and good will" and would allow U.S. military authorities and host-country authorities to cooperate "in resolving problems on a mutually satisfactory basis." In addition, a permanent agreement would serve as evidence of the good-faith partnership of NATO. "The sincere good faith and willingness of the United States to cooperate on a reasonable basis of equality could be questioned if other formulas are to be followed."[37]

The State Department rejected another alternative to the SOFA: exclusive American jurisdiction over U.S. troops in accordance with the traditional law-of-the-flag doctrine. Undersecretary of State Walter Bedell Smith made a strong case against exclusive jurisdiction or extraterritoriality of U.S. law:

> First: The United States Government as a matter of policy does not seek extraterritoriality anywhere in the world. To do so, in this case, when there is neither necessity nor desirability, would give a foundation to critics of our policy, at home and abroad, on the score that we are indirectly seeking imperialistic aggrandizement and attempting to subject other nations to our activities . . .
>
> Second: The concept of exclusive jurisdiction strikes at the very essence of the North Atlantic Treaty Organization. NATO is a coalition of sovereign powers, freely banded together in a common effort. [Exclusive jurisdiction over U.S. troops] would in effect vitiate article VII of the agreement and indicate that local sovereignty was to be sacrificed for military necessity. As I have indicated above, there is no such military necessity. To foreign eyes, whether friendly or not, this could appear an unwarranted attempt to use the stationing of forces abroad in a common defense effort as a means to secure an extension of the authority of the United States in the territory of its sovereign allies. Inasmuch as we are dealing here with countries of common cultural bonds united together in the North Atlantic Community, all of whom have advanced and fully civilized systems of law, it is apparent that the implied affront would strike at the common spirit and morale of the North Atlantic Treaty Organization.[38]

Note the key points in Smith's statement: exclusive jurisdiction over U.S. troops was unnecessary from a military point of view (to this he attested as a former senior military officer himself); and, furthermore, it would be harmful in that it would antagonize allies and create unnecessary tensions. To buttress his view, Smith downplayed the differences between the U.S. and European legal systems—a key tactic used by proponents of legal cooperation. According to Smith, the legal systems of NATO members were all "advanced and fully civilized," and there was no reason to reject their jurisdiction over U.S. troops. Contrarily, if the United States had jurisdiction over offending troops, host countries might worry that they would be treated leniently. According to Herman Phleger, the State Department legal advisor, "if any American soldier off duty commits a crime in the receiving country, and our military authorities immediately take possession of him and try him, if the people of the receiving state think that he has not been properly tried or punished, it creates a public relation there which is not advantageous."[39]

Overall, the representatives of the U.S. military, the Department of Defense, and the Department of State sought to reassure senators contemplating the ratification of the NATO SOFA. While not a perfect agreement, they argued, it was a satisfying compromise and the best arrangement possible, with an important role to play in the U.S.-European joint security effort. Most importantly, they showed little concern about subjecting U.S. troops to foreign jurisdiction. The Department of Justice (DOJ) showed a similar attitude, as we will now see.

Department of Justice

According to the theoretical framework (Proposition 5), the justice bureaucracy will generally support cooperation on litigation out of concern for reciprocity and effective law enforcement. This argument clearly finds support in the NATO SOFA debate.

The DOJ was tasked, first, with clarifying the legal status of military forces stationed on foreign territory. SOFA opponents in the Senate argued that international law gave foreign forces immunity from the jurisdiction of host states; the SOFA—which granted no such immunity—violated international law, according to this thinking.[40] In a lengthy memorandum,[41] the DOJ presented a thin conception of immunity of foreign forces, arguing that law-of-the-flag did not reflect a binding legal norm: "it is the opinion of the Department of Justice that this status-of-forces agreement violates no principle of international law. We also say that there is no foundation for the contention that under international law friendly foreign forces are immune from the criminal jurisdiction of the host state for crimes committed therein."[42] According to the DOJ, "the only immunity for which there is any substantial support is for an offense committed in the line of duty, although even this is questionable."[43] This led the department to a second conclusion. Since the NATO SOFA gave the United States primary jurisdiction over both line-of-duty offenses and other offenses, the United States actually enjoyed more extensive jurisdiction through the SOFA than it would have in the absence of that agreement.[44] The SOFA "affords the members of the United States forces more protection from local criminal jurisdiction than they reasonably could expect under the so-called rules of international law."[45]

As a third finding, the DOJ concluded that the SOFA was more favorable to the United States and gave it more jurisdiction over its forces than interim bilateral agreements with host countries.[46] This comported with the views of the Department of Defense and the Department of State, described above.

The DOJ's final conclusion was that "the treaty gives to the members of our forces when they are to be tried in the courts of the receiving state adequate safeguards in accordance with civilized standards of justice."[47] By so concluding, the department responded to the litany of concerns about the inadequate standards of justice in NATO countries: "it has been intimated as well as expressly stated that if the treaty were ratified, the members of our forces and the civilian components would not have protection of civilized standards of justice."[48] Recognizing that this was a crucial question in the debate, the department sought to dispel such concerns by pointing to the language of the treaty itself and, specifically, to paragraph 9 of Article VII, which "provides certain safeguards, so that if the local law of that country didn't meet with what we would consider in this country civilized standards of justice, they must apply them under this treaty."[49] According to Attorney General Herbert Brownell, "that language [of paragraph 9] makes it clearer than I could by any interpretation of my own that this treaty provides what we might term standards of civilized conduct, civilized standards of justice, regardless of the country wherein the trial might take place."[50] While acknowledging that the treaty's safeguards were not foolproof, Brownell suggested that they were adequate for protecting U.S. troops, and that the United States "ought to try them, and if we find there are some weaknesses which develop . . . later on we can improve these provisions, but these are the basic safeguards."[51] Consistent with the theoretical framework (Proposition 9), we see how an actor supporting legal cooperation emphasizes the existence of safeguards and trusts that they will guarantee "civilized standards of justice." The belief in the adequacy of treaty safeguards is, in fact, not unique to the U.S. justice bureaucracy. We will encounter a similar attitude on the part of the Australian justice bureaucracy in Chapter 5.

Senatorial Defenders of the SOFA

The Senate Committee on Foreign Relations expressed a cooperative position in its report on the NATO SOFA and the two other NATO-related agreements submitted for ratification.[52] While "anxious to insure a fair trial and to protect the rights of our troops in every way possible,"[53] the committee rejected the idea of exclusive criminal jurisdiction over U.S. forces out of consideration for the sensitivities of host-country populations:

> Exclusive criminal jurisdiction . . . creates difficult problems. In the eyes of the local population, it sets Americans apart as a special, privileged class, and this fact acts as a constant irritant. If American courts martial return verdicts of acquittal, or if they impose sentences which seem lenient to the aggrieved parties, they are open to charges of favoritism. If, on the other hand—as has sometimes happened—they impose sentences substantially greater than those provided by local law for the same crime, they can be accused of flouting local customs and sensibilities. Regardless of how fair and just American courts-martial may be, the existence of exclusive criminal jurisdiction seems to the other country to be an infringement of its sovereignty.[54]

The committee also suggested that a U.S. demand for complete jurisdiction over its troops abroad would be illegitimate on the grounds of reciprocity: "The committee would not look with favor upon a complete surrender of criminal jurisdiction over foreign troops in the United States to a foreign power. The committee therefore believes that the United States should not expect such a surrender by a foreign power over United States troops on its soil."[55]

By contrast, the committee approved of the division of jurisdiction under the SOFA and emphasized that "the American on trial in a foreign court will have all the rights to which a citizen of the country in question is entitled," such as the right to a prompt and speedy trial and to representation by counsel. The committee was "convinced that there are adequate safeguards in the agreement so that there need be no concern."[56] Accordingly, the Committee on Foreign Relations concluded that prompt ratification was in the national interest.[57]

In the Senate debate that followed, proponents of the agreement made similar arguments. Consistent with the theoretical framework (Proposition 9), they downplayed concerns about foreign justice systems, expressed confidence in the SOFA's safeguards, and dismissed alternatives to the SOFA.

Chairman of the Foreign Relations Committee Alexander Wiley (R-WI) emphasized the goal of "mak[ing] sure that our boys who commit offenses in foreign lands receive a fair trial with due regard for proper legal safeguards and the rights of the individual"—specifically, ensuring that "American servicemen who may be tried in foreign courts are accorded all the essential rights which they would receive under the Constitution of the United States." Wiley was indeed satisfied that "a number of these rights are spelled out in the treaty itself. Others are provided for in the laws of the other NATO countries." Thus, according to Wiley, the compromise that the agreement established was "quite satisfactory," and one could not find "any other adequate solution to this thorny problem." In particular, maintaining exclusive criminal jurisdiction over U.S. troops abroad was "wholly impractical, because the other countries simply will not agree to it."

Most importantly, Wiley expressed confidence in foreign justice systems and saw no reason to fear them: "We must keep in mind that the systems of law and justice which prevail in the other NATO countries are very well advanced. Indeed, most of them are older than our own. Thus far, our experience with these countries with respect to this problem has been good. Under the new agreements I am confident it will be even better."[58]

Senator William Knowland (R-CA) similarly sought to downplay the legal differences between the United States and NATO countries: "Certainly France, Great Britain, Belgium, and Italy cannot be considered to be backward or barbaric countries";[59] "These are civilized nations with which we are dealing. They are some of the greatest civilized nations on the face of the earth. They are not going to mistreat our men."[60] Knowland did acknowledge that the laws and legal procedures of NATO countries are different than those of the United States, and even that their protection of the individual is not comparable to the protection afforded U.S. citizens. "But each of those countries has a system of justice which each of them considers to be a civilized system of justice."[61] In case American troops nevertheless suffered mistreatment, mechanisms for redress did exist, and the U.S. government would address the matter vigorously, even at the presidential level: "From what I know of the President of the United States, I am absolutely certain that if he had a single case called to his attention in which he felt an American was being mistreated, he would use the full power of the Government of the United States in taking it up with the head of the other state, to make sure that the situation did not continue. If any nation should be so foolish as to deliberately flout or try to antagonize the people of the United States, in the final end result, of course, the President and the Congress would have the right to withdraw our troops from those countries. The treaty is necessary and it is desirable."[62]

Proponents of the NATO SOFA also argued that U.S. troops had already been facing foreign justice systems, and that their experience suggested little reason for concern. According to Senator Leverett Saltonstall (R-MA), Department of Defense "records do not reveal any instances of cruel or unusual punishment inflicted upon an American serviceman as the result of a sentence imposed by a court of a country with which arrangements respecting the exercise of concurrent jurisdiction have been entered into. There have been no reports to responsible American authorities of mistreatment of any American prisoner imprisoned by such a country."[63]

Senator Wiley similarly argued that "The treaty does not turn over American servicemen to foreign courts. American servicemen are already being tried by foreign courts. The treaty will give them more rights than they now have."[64] He denounced opponents of the SOFA who now "raise the question, well, we cannot permit any of our boys under any circumstances to be tried by any court of that land. We cannot permit it," although such trials had been taking place under existing agreements. "It is being done every day. . . . But no, immediately they raise a great big smoke screen, get the country agitated, get folks writing into my office telling me what an SOB I am because I am permitting some of my boys to be crucified under the jurisprudence of some of the other states. It is perfectly ridiculous."[65]

Senatorial Critics of the SOFA

In ethnocentric fashion, opponents of the SOFA held up American legal standards as the metric for the assessment of foreign justice systems and highlighted the ways in which these systems differ from the American one. In their view, any deviation from U.S. legal practices meant a denial of justice for the troops.

Jury

Given the centrality of the jury to the American legal process, critics of the NATO SOFA were quick to note that typically trials in European courts did not involve a jury.[66] They expressed concern about subjecting American troops to trial without a jury.[67] Senator Everett Dirksen (R-IL) complained that in the SOFA:

> There is no assurance of the right to a trial by jury [among the safeguards of Article VII, Paragraph 9]. Yet, if one will examine the first 10 amendments to the Constitution of the United States he will find set forth therein, in the sixth amendment, that there shall be the right of trial by jury in a criminal case, and a right to have compulsory process for witnesses, as well as representation by counsel. Nothing like that is guaranteed to our troops abroad by this instrument. So the effect of it is to subject an American sovereign, in the person of an American soldier, to the mercies and to the limitations of a foreign court.[68]

SOFA supporters sought to assuage the concern about juries. Robert Haydock, counsel for foreign and military affairs in the Department of Defense, argued that civil-law countries "do not utilize a trial by jury, but they do have many of the safeguards that we have."[69] Senator H. Alexander Smith (R-NJ) suggested that a jury in this context would provide little benefit to American troops, and might even harm them: "I am not sure that a jury trial there would mean as much as it would here. It would not be a jury of peers; it might even be a jury of a hostile population."[70] Therefore, "an American national tried before a foreign jury would be in a disadvantageous position."[71]

Presumption of Innocence

Several senators identified the presumption of innocence as a key guarantee of fairness in the American legal system—and one that, in their view, was missing from European legal systems and not guaranteed by the NATO SOFA.[72] According to Senator Homer Ferguson (R-MI), the presumption of innocence is a key legal safeguard—"really the fundamental of them all"—but it stood as "the vital point of the difference between a trial here and in some of these other countries." In those countries "there is no presumption of innocence . . . a man has to prove himself innocent instead of the state proving him guilty. . . . This would violate the very fundamentals of American criminal justice. Do you think that is right?"[73] Senator Dirksen similarly protested that the presumption of innocence—"one of the cardinal principles of American jurisprudence"—was absent from the safeguards included in paragraph 9 of Article VII.[74] Senator Knowland expressed a similar concern on this point: "Under these circumstances we are subjecting [Americans] to an entirely different legal system where they are presumed to be guilty rather than innocent. I think we have made a very basic change in the protection we afford our nationals."[75]

Supporters of the SOFA—representing diplomatic or security interests—sought to downplay this alleged difference between the U.S. and foreign systems. One line of argument rejected the expectation of equivalence between legal systems as unreasonable. According to Secretary of Defense Wilson, "we cannot force these partners of ours to accept our system completely."[76] Wilson also suggested that the difference between the legal systems was more rhetorical than real, since civil-law countries, in practice, had come to embrace the idea of a presumption of innocence, and the problem was therefore nonexistent: "[W]e do not seem to have had cases where innocent people have been proved guilty in France because they could not prove their innocence. We do not seem to have tangled with that one."[77] Herman Phleger, the State Department's legal adviser, explained that the concern was rooted in a misunderstanding. "The fact is that in civil-law countries the presumption of innocence does prevail and always has." As in the United States, a person accused of crime is presumed to be innocent until they have been convicted. The difference lies in the evidentiary threshold or standard of proof for establishing guilt. In the civil law, guilt is proven by a preponderance of evidence. "They do not apply the rule of evaluating evidence, as we do, that it must be beyond a reasonable doubt."[78]

The critics, however, did not find these responses satisfying. For Senator Ferguson, the difference in the burden of proof was very significant.[79] Senator Patrick McCarran (D-NV) argued that the lower burden of proof in civil-law systems effectively undermined the presumption of innocence. This presumption becomes "only a technicality, for there is no requirement that guilt must be proved beyond reasonable doubt. . . . It is only necessary to show that he could be guilty."[80]

This exchange demonstrates one of the pitfalls of comparing legal systems: parochialism. As described in Chapter 2, comparisons are often hasty and superficial, deficient in their understanding of the foreign legal system or outright mistaken. Furthermore, a superficial comparison will likely expect equivalence between the home and foreign norms and procedures. In the current case, Phleger was wrong to characterize the standard of proof in civil-law countries as a preponderance of evidence. In civil-law systems, the standard for criminal cases is high and close to the common-law standard.[81] The critical senators, on their part, expected European countries to have the exact same standard as prevails in the United States and would not settle for anything less than "beyond reasonable doubt." They considered any standard but the one familiar to them to be unfair.

Public Trial

Senators were also concerned that U.S. service members might not get an open, public trial.[82] Senator Ferguson argued that the NATO SOFA should have provided for a public trial "such as we in America have always provided in criminal cases, in order that our citizens may be assured that a fair trial is being held."[83] Phleger, the State Department's legal adviser, pointed out that this concern was unfounded: "the ordinary rules of jurisprudence of these countries do not call for secret trials" and "are very similar to our own."[84] Expressing confidence in the procedural safeguards of the SOFA's Article VII, Phleger also assured senators that American troops on trial were guaranteed the right to communicate with a representative of the U.S. government and to have them present at the trial, unless the court rules provided otherwise.[85] He further reminded the senators that they could be setting the bar too high, since U.S. military justice itself may not live up to the idea of an open trial: "Our courts-martial procedures may be closed also."[86] This demonstrates the "endowment effect" identified in Chapter 2, that is, the idealized view of the home legal system, which overlooks or minimizes its flaws. Critics of the SOFA demanded public trials for U.S. troops in NATO countries, all but ignoring the fact that the American system of military justice reserves the right to hold closed trials.

Punishment

SOFA critics in the Senate expressed concern about the severity of punishment that, in their view, might be imposed on U.S. troops in European courts. Senator McCarran warned of

> convictions of offenses which carry in some cases extreme penalties. For instance, in France a person convicted of manslaughter—not murder, but manslaughter—can be put to death or sentenced to imprisonment at hard labor for life. It would not be too difficult to imagine a conviction for manslaughter, under French law, on the basis of circumstances which in the United States would not give rise to a conviction even for involuntary homicide.... In France it would be possible for a man to be convicted of rape and sentenced to hard labor for 20 years on the basis of conduct which might be held only adultery, at worst, in a court of the United States. In France a man can be sentenced to 5 years in prison for petty larceny.[87]

Along similar lines, Senator John Bricker (R-OH) claimed that "there has been cruel and unusual punishment inflicted already upon some of the boys from our forces" and argued that a "protection against cruel and unusual punishment ought to be written into a treaty."[88]

Phleger, the State Department's legal adviser, explained that the senators' desire to regulate criminal punishment abroad was unrealistic: "Well, I do not think you expect a sovereign to yield up his right to determine what the punishment for offenses is."[89] Furthermore, he argued that the concern about severe punishments was exaggerated, since European countries did not impose the death penalty, and "in most instances the sentences and penalties are less in the European countries than they are in our own."[90] Responding to a concern about the disparity of punishments between NATO countries, Senator Walter George (D-GA) pointed out that "it is impossible, of course, to secure uniformity of punishment [across Europe] because it does not exist in the courts of our 48 States."[91] Once again, this exchange demonstrates the endowment effect: critics compared European justice to an idealized U.S. legal system, ignoring the reality of the harshness of American criminal justice, its use of the death penalty, and the variation in penal policy across the U.S. states.[92]

Prejudice against Americans

As Chapter 2 has suggested, transnational litigation raises concerns about a possible bias of foreign legal authorities against the home country's citizens.

Several senators indeed expressed alarm about a possible anti-American bias in European communities and European courts: "a very decided prejudice and antipathy toward the American forces in the countries where they are located."[93]

Senator Robert Hendrickson (R-NJ) based his concern on his own experience as a soldier:

> we for a long time occupied many of the countries in question, and troops of occupation, as I happen to know, having been one of them, are not particularly popular. They grow more unpopular as the years pass. I have great concern about having our troops tried by foreign courts in the countries where we have troops of occupation, for the reason that the prejudice which may exist is only natural and instinctive. That phase of the matter gives me great concern.[94]

Senator Russell Long (D-LA) warned of host-country hostility and prejudice against American troops, arguing that the SOFA's safeguards would do little to help U.S. troops before a court that was biased against them:

> In most places the fact is that there is a strong prejudice against the presence of American troops.
>
> The prejudice is much greater in many other places, including France, and it may be still worse in other places. Here we are being asked to surrender to foreign powers the right to see that our men are tried under our own laws and by our own courts.
>
> Anyone knows that in all communities where prejudice runs high against our men some of those young men have told of civilians spitting on them . . . In those areas we know that when those men come into conflict with foreign nationals and they are tried before a foreign judge and a foreign jury, in a foreign court, our men stand very little chance. We might as well face that fact.[95]

Non-Western Legal Systems

While cooperation with foreign legal systems generally raises concerns, not all foreign systems are treated equally. According to the theoretical framework (Proposition 2), we should expect a differential attitude: foreign legal systems perceived as similar to the home legal system will be seen as legitimate partners; the greater the dissimilarity between the home and foreign systems—especially when the foreign system belongs to a different legal tradition or civilization—the greater the concern about cooperation.

This expectation receives strong support in the Senate debate over the NATO SOFA. While generally concerned about subjecting American troops to the jurisdiction of NATO allies, participants in the debate seemed more comfortable with the legal system of one specific NATO ally: the UK. Since the American legal system originated from the British legal system, and given the continued resemblance between the two common-law systems, debate participants felt reassured that UK justice met American standards. Secretary of Defense Wilson explicitly suggested that he was not concerned "about the countries which have the same common-law background as we."[96] By contrast, debate participants felt far less comfortable with non-Western legal systems: those of Japan and Middle Eastern countries. In the Senators' minds, these systems were remote from and alien to U.S. conceptions of justice, and the prospect of possibly subjecting U.S. service members to their jurisdiction provoked even greater concern than did the Western legal systems of NATO members. Senator Smith warned that "the Japanese criminal code was very different from our Anglo-Saxon one."[97] Senator Bricker wondered: "What friendly nation has a criminal law and procedure more unlike our own than Japan or Turkey?"[98] Some senators, in fact, worried that Middle Eastern courts might punish American troops by cutting off their hands.[99]

Viewing Japanese and Middle Eastern justice as far removed from American conceptions of justice, senators expressed concerns that the NATO SOFA might constitute a model and precedent for status-of-forces agreements with non-European partners. They thought that agreements with these countries should *not* follow the terms of the NATO SOFA but establish more limited foreign jurisdiction over U.S. troops. In fact, at the time of the NATO SOFA debate, Japan had received the promise of a SOFA similar to the NATO SOFA,[100] fueling a concern that the United States would have to extend the same terms to Middle Eastern countries. "Is General Smith[101] going to tell countries of the Middle East that they are not genteel, or that their system of justice is inferior to that of the NATO countries? I think not. The Middle East is too important to be thrown into the arms of the Communists. . . . The probability is that rather than alienate [foreign countries'] friendship we would subject American boys to their criminal jurisdiction no matter how bizarre or inhuman by our standards."[102]

Inadequacy of Safeguards

The crossnational variation in legal standards poses a threat to cooperation on transnational litigation: for the ethnocentric, such variation suggests that the foreign legal system will not deliver justice. Safeguards and guarantees of fair treatment offer a means of overcoming this obstacle. But not everyone will be satisfied. The theoretical framework suggests that cooperation proponents tend to treat the safeguards as plausible assurances of fair treatment; by contrast, cooperation opponents might question the value of these safeguards, suggesting that they are insufficient or unreliable (Proposition 9). Such a divide was indeed on full display in the NATO SOFA debate, as actors differed in their assessment of the guarantees afforded by paragraph 9 of Article VII of the SOFA. Assistant Secretary of Defense Frank Nash was content with these guarantees: They "add up to just about what this man would get if he were being tried in a military court."[103] Senator McCarran, by contrast, argued that American troops abroad should enjoy the full menu of U.S. constitutional rights. Recognizing that the SOFA's Article VII did guarantee certain rights, he nevertheless maintained that these protections were inadequate:

> I think the constitutional guaranties should follow our boys in uniform wherever they are sent under the American flag, even in the territory of a friendly country, and I oppose this treaty because it would deny them those constitutional guaranties.
>
> There is a provision in this treaty, designed to guarantee certain rights to an American national who is prosecuted under the jurisdiction of a foreign country [Article VII(9)]. If you read this list of "guaranteed rights" rapidly, Mr. President, it looks like a pretty good list. But as soon as you start to analyze it, it becomes apparent that some of the most important guarantees under our own Bill of Rights have been omitted from this list.[104]

Specifically, McCarran argued that the SOFA lacked protections against self-incrimination, cruel and unusual punishment, unreasonable searches and seizures, double jeopardy, excessive bail and fines, and laws that abridge the freedom of speech or the right of free assembly. The right to appeal a decision or to be tried by a jury was also not guaranteed, according to McCarran. All of those rights "are rights enumerated and protected in the first 10 amendments of our Constitution; but every one of them is being waived, under the terms of this treaty, with respect to American soldiers who may find themselves charged with an offense under the laws of a foreign country."[105]

Senator Dirksen was similarly dissatisfied with the guarantees provided by paragraph 9 which, in his view, failed to fully live up to U.S. standards. He demanded an equivalence of legal protections for troops at home and abroad:

> Every American citizen and every American soldier is a symbol of American sovereignty when we send him abroad; and, unless we protect him, we demean and degrade the very sovereignty he represents. . . . he is entitled to the same protection abroad that he gets at home.

> Would he get that protection under this proposal? I do not believe so. . . . [An American soldier] may be in Indochina, he may be in Japan, in France, or in Korea; but while he is in uniform, he is still an American; and if he has a guaranty here [in the United States], how can we, under the organic law upon which this country is founded, barter away that guaranty, that right? I, for one, will not do so.[106]

The quotes from the two senators represent quintessential ethnocentrism: a citizen of the home country should enjoy the protection of the home country's standards everywhere, even when he is on foreign territory. He remains a member of the in-group wherever he goes and should always be accorded the full rights of in-group members; without guarantees of such rights, the home-country citizen should not come under the authority of the foreign legal system. This rigid viewpoint rejects any deviation from the home-country standards and fails to recognize the possibility of legitimate variation in criminal-justice rights and protections across countries.

The Framing of Anti-SOFA Arguments

An appropriate framing may activate ethnocentric sentiments and amplify the concern about cooperation with foreign legal systems. In the NATO SOFA debate, opponents of the agreement repeatedly referred to American troops as "boys" rather than what they actually were: armed men. Their being framed as "boys" was aimed at strengthening the empathy toward the troops by portraying them as young, innocent, vulnerable, and in need of protection.[107] Furthermore, the "boys" were owed such protection, it was argued, since their subjection to foreign jurisdiction was involuntary: it was the U.S. government that had drafted them and deployed them in Europe.

Senator McCarran, for example, argued that "no boy in uniform going across the water should go there without having the Constitution follow him. The flag follows him. His law should follow him."[108] Senator Long suggested that "if we are anxious to protect the rights of American citizens and to protect the rights of our American boys, whom we insist on sending overseas involuntarily, we should instruct our negotiators . . . that they should see to it that the rights of our citizens are protected in foreign lands."[109] Senator Smith did "not know of any case where we have yielded jurisdiction over our boys abroad to foreign criminal codes, to foreign penalties, to foreign courts. . . . We do not submit our boys to the jurisdiction of other courts."[110]

Another sympathy-inducing framing associated American troops with freedom. Senator Dirksen suggested that "it would be pretty difficult for me to reconcile any action approving the agreement without a reservation when

I think of the young Americans abroad. After all, are they not crusaders for liberty? Are they not defenders of the cause of freedom?"[111]

Senator Bricker's Efforts against the SOFA

Among the critics of the SOFA's Article VII, Senator Bricker stood out as the most adamant and vociferous.[112] The analysis above has already identified some of his criticisms, but the current section zooms in on his arguments and his attempt to undermine the SOFA by adding a reservation.

Bricker harshly assailed the NATO SOFA, denouncing it as "one of the worst [agreements] I have ever seen." Article VII, according to Bricker, "reflects a callous disregard of the rights of American armed forces personnel,"[113] based on a misguided internationalist sentiment: "the American GI was completely forgotten in the pursuit of global abstractions."[114] Furthermore, he argued that the Committee on Foreign Relations' decision to report favorably on the agreement was based on false and misleading representations of government witnesses. Specifically, he attacked the State Department for suggesting that U.S. troops should not enjoy immunity from foreign jurisdiction. In Bricker's mind, "The rule of international law . . . is that troops of a friendly nation stationed within the territory of another are not subject to the local laws of the other country, but are subject only to their own country's laws and regulations for the government of the armed services."[115] This exclusive-jurisdiction rule, Bricker argued, was substantively justified on foreign-policy grounds: "Foreign interference with American military justice and American interference with foreign judicial action is not conducive to friendly foreign relations. Nothing is more likely to tear the North Atlantic alliance apart than article VII of the proposed treaty."[116] Furthermore, immunity from foreign justice was required "to maintain morale in the military services."[117]

Such immunity was also necessary, Bricker argued, since Americans had higher legal standards than Europeans:

> So long as Americans insist on a higher standard of civil and political rights than their neighbors, they will, to that extent, seem to stand alone as a special, privileged class. The contrast would not be so great, of course, if Americans were willing to accept European concepts of freedom. Even in trials before courts-martial, Americans are guaranteed the presumption of innocence; protected against cruel and inhuman punishment; convicted only on proof of guilt beyond a reasonable doubt; granted the privilege against self-incrimination; and granted the rights to various appeals, even up to the President of the United States.

None of these safeguards for American forces are guaranteed by the Status of Forces Treaty.[118]

To the suggestion of Senator Theodore Green (D-RI) that NATO countries "have legal systems similar to our own" and could be trusted not to impose unusual punishments, Bricker responded: "I don't know that the systems are similar to our own. . . . cruel and unusual punishment, according to our standards, may be inflicted in some of the NATO countries that are even subject to this treaty."[119] This exchange demonstrates how individuals may significantly diverge in their assessment of the similarities or differences between legal systems. Legal systems that look similar to one person may seem dangerously different to another.

In support of his position, Bricker submitted newspaper articles and editorials as well as letters sent to him. He sought to demonstrate that his concerns about the legal mistreatment of American troops were borne out by actual experience and were shared by others. Obviously, Bricker picked those pieces consistent with his anti-SOFA view. Yet this sample does indicate that the SOFA raised serious concerns not only among elected representatives. Some members of the media held strong sentiments against the SOFA, as did certain U.S. service members and their families.

Following are some examples of journalistic criticisms of the SOFA, cited by Bricker:

- *The Tablet*, June 6, 1953: "Such an agreement as the trial of American Government employees in foreign courts without regard for their constitutional rights is dangerous, particularly when some courts, like those in parts of France, Italy, and elsewhere, are Communist-controlled."[120]
- Influential columnist Victor Riesel complained about the mistreatment of American troops and air-base construction workers in Europe where "[t]he phrase 'lousy Americans' is standard jargon" and "[o]n the streets the men are ignored and treated as pariahs." By his account, Americans "couldn't win a popularity contest in a race with a locust swarm in any country. No one really knows why—but one thing is certain. We're disliked. We're resented. Some psychiatrist will have to explain why."[121]
- "Due Process Denied," *Washington Times-Herald*, June 8, 1953: This editorial agreed with "Bricker's denunciation of these illegal trials, in which Americans are denied the protection of due process guaranteed them by the Constitution" and claimed that the senator managed to substantiate his allegation that "European procedure is radically different from that of American courts of law." Furthermore, "American forces in Europe are widely unpopular with the national populations to whose defense they have been assigned, and . . . Europeans with a phobia against the United States are often eager

to frame them and convict them. This is especially true in France and some other countries where the Communist element represents a formidable proportion of the population."[122] The editorial concluded that "the European trials of Americans do not differ in essence from what we did in Nuremberg to the enemy. The only distinction is that in these cases our supposed allies are seizing the occasion to use their courts to vent their spite and hostility on us."[123]

Note the common theme running through these excerpts: perceived hostility in Europe toward the United States and American troops. This clearly reflects an ethnocentric mindset, which views the out-groups as hostile to the in-group. Ethnocentrism also comes out in the following letters sent to Bricker by U.S. service members and dependents:

- An Army officer in East Asia: "Bravo for your strong stand against allowing foreign governments to have criminal jurisdiction over American troops stationed abroad. It would indeed be a sad travesty to deprive American troops overseas of the protection of the Government and Constitution many have given their lives to defend."[124]
- The wife of an American soldier serving in France: "I am a foreign war bride and have seen how other courts operate. Our soldiers could be very easy rooked into a crime by maybe a communistic or anti-American group and then be tried by a communistic or anti-American-inclined judge."[125]
- A resident of Cincinnati, Ohio: "Congress should take immediate action to forbid the further turning over of our service personnel to foreign nations for trial by backward and even barbaric nations."[126]
- A retired brigadier general: "It is illogical and unreasonable and can only represent another effort to place the rights and lives of American citizens under foreign control. Service personnel have no choice in their foreign assignments but do have an inalienable right to the protection of our Constitution. Is this to be denied them by the Congress of the United States?"[127]
- A service pastor in Europe: "It is inconceivable that American servicemen would be accorded just and fair trials as we understand these terms in the United States. In spite of the fact that American servicemen have gone thousands of miles from their homes on missions of liberation from tyranny . . . their overseas friends still think they are overpaid and pampered."[128]
- A U.S. Army officer: "I heartily agree with your important distinction between American citizens who go abroad voluntarily for reasons of business or pleasure, and a member of the military, or his dependents, who are stationed abroad by virtue of military orders. Certainly those in the latter category are entitled to the full protection and safeguards granted them under our

Constitution—particularly when the systems of jurisprudence, as practiced in these foreign countries, are so diametrically opposed to ours."[129]

- The wife of an American soldier stationed in French Morocco: "The French Government both in France and in French Morocco . . . discriminate against Americans both individually and collectively in every possible manner . . . It is a matter of record that French courts invariably assess maximum fines and punishments against Americans."[130]
- A civilian employee of the Air Force in West Germany: "I wish to applaud your stand opposing the treaty which would cause American civilians and soldiers to be tried in foreign civil courts and under foreign laws. This would certainly be an unfair and unjust way of handling the matter. Many foreign nations have laws that bear no semblance whatever to the American laws on the same subject."[131]
- A resident of Ohio: "It is good to know that someone is looking out for us. Knowing what we do, none of us want to come under Japanese police jurisdiction. They haven't forgotten the licking we gave them. With the ill-feeling toward us, it is not right to put us under the Jap police."[132]

These letters conveyed two types of concern, consistent with the theoretical framework. First, they exhibit concern about the delegation of legal authority over U.S. troops to foreign authorities and institutions that might be biased against them. Host-countries are seen here as hostile environments for U.S. troops: resentful of the foreign military presence, driven by memories of their defeat by the United States, or influenced by communism. The upshot is that legal institutions in these countries would be unfair toward Americans. Second, the letters show concern about legal incongruity: a sense that legal norms in host countries significantly differ from those of the United States and should not apply to an American soldier involuntarily stationed abroad. Rather, that soldier should enjoy the protection of American law and the U.S. Constitution.

The Bricker Reservation

Viewing foreign legal systems as inferior to American justice, Senator Bricker proposed to ratify the NATO SOFA subject to a reservation that would establish exclusive American jurisdiction over U.S. troops abroad.[133] Such a reservation would have overridden the division of jurisdiction laid out in Article VII, dealing a blow to the entire agreement.

While some senators expressed support for the proposed reservation,[134] other participants in the Congressional debate repudiated the reservation. For U.S. government agencies, it threatened to undermine a desirable and important agreement. Since the article on criminal jurisdiction is one of the key provisions of the SOFA, the Department of Defense argued, the adoption of the reservation would be tantamount to rejecting the agreement. This would leave U.S. troops worse off, "covered in some countries by special or temporary arrangements and treated in others in accordance with the individual country's views of what is customary and appropriate."[135] The State Department pointed out that NATO allies would refuse to allow the U.S. exclusive jurisdiction over the troops. Furthermore, since the SOFA is reciprocal, the United States would have to grant NATO members exclusive jurisdiction over their forces deployed in the United States. Such a sacrifice of the sovereign rights of the U.S. states and the federal government was a price not worth paying, the department suggested.[136]

Several senators similarly expressed their objection to the reservation. Senator Smith suggested that it falsely assumed that the United States would relinquish exclusive jurisdiction under the SOFA when, in fact, it did not have exclusive jurisdiction in NATO countries in the first place. Furthermore, "The evidence does not indicate that American troops have been discriminated against or unfairly treated in foreign courts."[137] Senator Wiley rejected Bricker's demand for troop immunity from foreign jurisdiction as inconsistent with international law.[138] He defended the SOFA's criminal-jurisdiction arrangement as a "satisfactory solution of the problem."[139]

Despite Bricker's plea "to see that the flag of the United States follows the members of our Armed Forces . . . wherever they may be sent,"[140] his proposed reservation was defeated 27 to 53.[141] However, the Senate did go some distance toward addressing the concerns of Bricker and fellow opponents of the SOFA. Upon the recommendation of the Foreign Relations Committee, a statement was attached to the Senate's advice and consent to the NATO SOFA on July 15, 1953. This was meant as an additional step—beyond the guarantees of Article VII—to ensure that U.S. troops tried in foreign courts would be accorded all the essential rights that they would receive under the U.S. Constitution.[142]

More specifically, the statement prescribed two procedures aimed at ensuring that U.S. personnel tried in the courts of NATO countries would receive fair trials according to U.S. standards. First, when a person subject to U.S. military jurisdiction is to be tried by a host country, the military commander is required to examine the laws of that country, with particular reference to the procedural safeguards of the U.S. Constitution. If he determines that the accused will not be adequately protected due to the absence of such safeguards, he is directed to request the host country to waive its jurisdiction and allow the United States to exercise jurisdiction in that case. If the request is refused, the military commander is to request diplomatic intervention by the State Department. Second, an official American representative will attend every trial of U.S. troops in foreign courts and report any failure to comply with the procedural safeguards of paragraph 9 of Article VII.[143]

This statement failed to satisfy Senator Bricker. He argued that the first procedure placed the United States in the humiliating position of having to beg for the release of an American soldier who was unlikely to get a fair trial. The second procedure, in his view, was "spineless" and "meaningless," since paragraph 9 of Article VII did not prohibit secret trials. This meant that host countries could prevent a U.S. representative from attending the trial of an American soldier.[144] Bricker's repudiation of these guarantees once again demonstrates that opponents of cooperation on litigation have little faith in assurances of fair treatment.

Debating the Revision of the NATO SOFA

Even ratification of the SOFA did not bring an end to the controversy surrounding this agreement. During 1955–1957, the House of Representatives considered several resolutions demanding that the SOFA be revised so that host countries would cease to exercise criminal jurisdiction over American troops stationed within their boundaries. Under some of the proposed resolutions, failure to obtain such a revision should prompt the president to renounce the NATO SOFA and all other agreements with similar provisions.[145] The drafters of the resolutions rehashed the arguments made by the opponents of the SOFA during the ratification debate: that the SOFA's criminal-justice provisions abrogated the basic constitutional rights of American soldiers serving on foreign soil; that they lacked fundamental protections such as public trial, trial by jury, presumption of innocence, right to bail, and right of appeal; and that they were inconsistent with the international legal principle requiring that armed forces be subject to the exclusive jurisdiction of their own country.[146] The argument regarding host countries' hostility toward American troops also reappeared: "Why should we abandon our standards of living, our constitutional rights and guaranties merely to appease and seek favor of our allies? We are told there is a feeling of hostility toward us in many countries . . . Then, why should we force our men into foreign courts to be tried in a hostile atmosphere, before hostile courts, without the humane rules of procedure set forth in our Constitution and laws?"[147]

During the debate over ratification of the SOFA, proponents of the agreement argued that subjecting U.S. troops to foreign jurisdiction raised little concern. During the revision debate, they could support their arguments with evidence based on the actual experience of implementing the agreement. The security-oriented actors—representatives of the Department of Defense or the U.S. military—indeed cited the positive experience with the SOFA's operation in practice. The agreement, they argued, "has been working out very satisfactorily."[148]

> First, we obtain . . . a very high percentage of waivers from the receiving or host nation in favor of our own jurisdiction. Our figures show that foreign NATO nations, since the beginning of 1954, have either dropped charges or waived their jurisdiction in about 70 percent of the cases subject to their jurisdiction.
>
> Second, only a very small percentage of the cases which are finally subject to foreign jurisdiction end up with a sentence in foreign jails—only about 1 percent.
>
> Third, our commanders and judge advocates in the field, with a few exceptions which we will discuss later, have reported that the application of the treaty has not had a detrimental effect on either the mission or the morale of the forces.[149]

Secretary of Defense Wilson sought to dispel alarming rumors "about the quality of justice dispensed in foreign courts. It has been said that our troops are subjected to cruel and unusual punishment, to maiming and flogging. There is simply no truth in these rumors. There have been no such cases."[150] He expressed alarm about the far-reaching strategic consequences of renouncing the SOFA in case of a failure to secure exclusive U.S. jurisdiction. Without an agreement to govern issues relating to the presence of American troops, "the situation of our forces becomes chaotic and potentially unmanageable." Furthermore, without a SOFA, foreign governments "would probably insist on the withdrawal of these troops," and the United States would lose its base-operating rights on the host's territory. "What could be more self-defeating to the basic national security interests of the United States than such a step?" The practical effect of the proposed revision would be "the withdrawal of United States forces from all over the world and reliance upon a Fortress America concept for the defense of the continental United States."[151]

Much like Secretary Wilson, General Alfred Gruenther, Supreme Allied Commander Europe, argued that "there is simply no basis for the charges which are sometime made that our people are being subjected to unfair trials or that they are being imprisoned under conditions so primitive or medieval as to shock the sensibilities." Indeed, "the places of incarceration themselves compare favorably with those of most institutions in the United States." He also warned that renunciation of the SOFA by the United States or insistence on a major revision "would so undermine the spirit of the alliance as to cause its serious deterioration with the gravest consequences to the essential security of our country. . . . While all the other NATO countries are agreed that their soldiers will receive fair hearings in the courts of the others, the United States would be alone in maintaining that its people can only be tried by United States courts. We would thus seem to place ourselves in a unique category. I can assure you no alliance can efficiently and successfully function if one of the partners thus sets itself apart from the others."[152]

General Lauris Norstad, who succeeded Gruenther as Supreme Allied Commander Europe, emphasized that host countries are *sovereign* countries and lauded their fairness toward U.S. personnel: "host nations are in general reluctant to take over jurisdiction. . . . in those cases where they do, they lean far over backward to be fair and cooperate. They are sincere about the alliance, and in fact grateful to the United States for the contribution we are making to the collective defense. They lean so far over backward that they are far more lenient with serious crimes than we would be in the United States courts. They are far easier with our people than we would be ourselves." Indeed, sentences imposed on U.S. troops in foreign courts "are by and large lighter than sentences adjudged in the United States civil and military courts for similar offenses." Renunciation of the SOFA, Norstad warned, "would be an act of irresponsibility."[153]

The State Department agreed that the SOFA worked well and should not be revised. "There was not a single case in which there was a basis for the United States to protest that the safeguards assured by the Status of Forces Agreement for a fair trial were not met, or that there was any other unfairness. There has not been a single instance of cruel or unusual punishment." In fact, "[s]ome commanders apparently feel that the local courts have actually been too lenient on American offenders."[154] In any event, a demand for exclusive U.S. jurisdiction was impractical: "[E]ven those nations most friendly to the United States and its objectives are unwilling to grant full extraterritorial rights. . . . if we were to insist upon full extraterritorial rights for the members of our Armed Forces stationed abroad, we would be unable to station our forces abroad."[155]

The positive experience with the actual operation of the SOFA and the SOFA's strategic necessity left supporters of the agreement's revision unpersuaded:

> Our Defense Department is hard put at times to minimize the actual effect of this treaty upon our soldiers abroad, and to try to make everything look good and fair and just and reasonable. The Department . . . stress[es] the fact that foreign courts waived their jurisdiction in many of these cases, and that where foreign courts retained jurisdiction, what seems to be a comparatively small number were sentenced to confinement. They also say that some of these sentences were suspended. . . . I do not care if this number seems to be only a few of those who were first arrested and charged with offense. . . . As long as only one American soldier can be subjected to the criminal jurisdiction of a foreign court, without the constitutional safeguards which he is told by the United States Courts-Martial Manual go with him, then this treaty is wrong and should be modified.[156]

A majority of the House Committee on Foreign Affairs ultimately recommended renegotiating "new arrangements with our allies which will not involve the surrender of criminal jurisdiction over United States military personnel." The committee chastised U.S. military and diplomatic officials for being "more concerned with public opinion in the nations in which the personnel of the United States armed forces are located than with public opinion in the United States."[157] A minority of members repudiated the criticisms of the SOFA as "based upon misrepresentation of the facts, through ignorance, or otherwise." They emphasized that there had not been a single case "where it is claimed that an American serviceman believed to be innocent has been imprisoned by a foreign court. . . . Neither has any case of mutilation, flogging, or any other cruel, unusual, or excessive punishment been cited."[158]

Yet the NATO SOFA was ultimately neither renegotiated nor renounced, and in the following years it reaffirmed the positive impressions of the military, the Department of Defense and the State Department with the SOFA's operation and effect. In 1955, the Senate Committee on Armed Services established a Subcommittee to Review Operation of Article VII of the NATO Status of Forces Treaty.[159] The subcommittee's annual review was based on information provided by the Department of Defense and the Army Judge Advocate General, the latter being tasked with monitoring foreign jurisdictional arrangements over American servicemen in all the services.[160] Based on this information, the subcommittee concluded every year—through 1970, the last year reviewed—that "generally the criminal jurisdictional arrangements regarding United States troops abroad have operated satisfactorily and have not adversely affected during the reporting period the morale and discipline of our forces, nor have they had a detrimental effect on the accomplishment of our military missions in the various countries."[161]

The NATO SOFA Ratification and Revision Debates: Conclusion

The case of the NATO SOFA provides strong support for this book's general argument and the specific theoretical propositions derived from it. Ethnocentrism clearly fueled the opposition to the agreement at the ratification stage and, later, triggered impassioned calls for the renegotiation or rejection of the agreement. The political debate focused on the supposed incompatibilities between the American and European legal systems, consistent with Proposition 1.

Opponents of the agreement were loath to place American citizens under the jurisdiction of European courts. They expressed concern about the delegation of judicial authority to courts that were supposedly biased and untrustworthy or exhibited substantive and procedural incongruities with U.S. courts. Indeed, critics argued that the punishments meted out by European courts were too harsh by American standards, while the procedural safeguards—due-process protections—were weak or nonexistent as compared to those afforded under the U.S. Constitution. Their strong objections to the SOFA were replete with pride in American law, denigration of "inferior" foreign legal systems, and concerns about a perceived European hostility toward Americans—all quintessentially ethnocentric. So entrenched were these views, so adamant the criticism of the agreement, that the SOFA opponents did not relent even in the face of evidence to the contrary. The primary stakeholders—the military and the Department of Defense—did confirm that the agreement was working satisfactorily and that American troops suffered no abuse or injustice in foreign courts; but the critics remained undaunted. The persistence and intensity of their concerns owed much to the identity of the individuals who would face foreign justice: troops. Indeed, under the SOFA, foreign authorities would primarily prosecute American troops for offenses committed in their *private* capacity for personal gain or advantage. Yet even for those crimes, SOFA critics believed, troops were entitled to be held accountable in an American court, with the same legal protections they would have enjoyed at home. The belief that they should enjoy immunity from foreign law reflected the view of troops as symbols of American sovereignty. Sent abroad by the state and risking their lives for the state, they should not be left to the mercy of foreign courts.

Proponents of the SOFA challenged these views and mounted a strong defense of the agreement. As expected theoretically, support for the agreement came from actors mindful of the diplomatic or security benefits of cooperation: the military, the Department of Defense, and the State Department. These actors recognized the importance of the SOFA for NATO and for the U.S. military presence in Europe; they exhibited concern about the likely negative response of host countries to American insistence on exclusive jurisdiction; and, from their point of view, there was little in the actual experience with foreign courts to warrant concern. The DOJ, consistent with the theoretical expectation, rejected the demand for exclusive jurisdiction of U.S. troops and expressed trust in the "civilized standards of justice" that, in its view, prevailed in foreign courts. This downplaying of differences between the home and foreign legal systems—suggesting that they all share civilized legal standards—is a common tactic in the hands of actors supporting cooperation, as is the emphasis on safeguards and the belief in their effectiveness. Indeed, faith in paragraph 9 of Article VII and the protections it afforded ran as a common theme through the arguments of SOFA supporters.

While cooperation on litigation can be fodder for an opposition seeking to attack the government, this was not the case here. The SOFA was negotiated and signed under a Democratic administration; but during the SOFA ratification debate of 1953 it was a Republican administration that held power. Nevertheless, the most prominent opponents of the agreement—first and foremost, Senator Bricker—were Republican. And yet, opposition to the SOFA was no partisan matter. Twelve Democratic senators joined 15 Republicans in voting for Bricker's reservation[162] to extend exclusive jurisdiction over U.S. troops. This demonstrates that ethnocentrism may be embraced by politicians across the political spectrum, not just by those on the right, consistent with Proposition 3.

The NATO SOFA debate in Congress, which took place in the 1950s, presents an early episode of contention over transnational litigation. This allows us the benefit of assessing persistence or change over time. Have the ethnocentric concerns raised during the debate persisted? Or have they dissipated over time in light of the positive experience acquired in the actual working of the NATO SOFA and similar jurisdictional arrangements with other countries?

The Persistence of Ethnocentric Concerns

The establishment of cooperation is often shrouded with uncertainty about its consequences. States typically enter into international agreements hoping to reap gains, but they fear that these gains may not materialize or that the cooperative efforts could even produce negative outcomes. However, over time, as the parties learn about the actual working and effects of the agreement, they may find the agreement satisfactory.[163] One might have expected to observe such a dynamic with the status-of-forces agreements. During the NATO SOFA ratification debate, it was still unclear how foreign legal authorities would treat U.S. troops. Under such uncertainty, some members of Congress believed that the troops might suffer unfair or abusive treatment and would be denied fundamental rights guaranteed by the U.S. Constitution. Yet the close monitoring of foreign jurisdictional arrangements over the years revealed that foreign legal systems, by and large, have treated American troops fairly.[164] The long satisfactory experience should have eased the concerns about subjecting U.S. troops to foreign justice. This, however, has not happened. U.S. authorities still have little faith in the fairness of foreign trials, and they seek to minimize the exposure of U.S. troops to foreign justice systems.

Department of Defense Directive 5525.1 clearly reflects this attitude. The directive was issued to implement the Senate's statement accompanying the consent to the ratification of the NATO SOFA; it has been revised over the years and was reissued in 2019 as DoD Instruction 5525.01. According to the instruction, if the laws of a host country suggest that an American soldier will not obtain a fair trial there, yet local authorities insist on holding a trial, U.S. military authorities may press a request for a waiver through diplomatic channels. The instruction further requires that U.S. observers attend trials of soldiers before foreign courts and prepare formal reports on their fairness.[165] Importantly, the instruction recognizes that one cannot expect full equivalence between U.S. and foreign law. "A trial will not be considered unfair merely because it is not conducted in a manner identical to trials held in the United States."[166] However, as a guide to identifying unfair trials, the instruction lists 17 fundamental safeguards of a fair trial in federal U.S. courts. These require, among other things, that the accused be present at the trial; be tried by an impartial court; have a public trial where the burden of proof is on the government; and have the assistance of a defense counsel.[167] In addition to guaranteeing the fairness of trials in accordance with U.S. standards, the instruction requires U.S. authorities to ensure that U.S. personnel held in foreign prisons enjoy "all the rights, privileges, and protections of personnel confined in U.S. military facilities."[168] The takeaway point here is the persistence of the American ethnocentric attitude. From the NATO SOFA ratification debate in 1953 to the present, American authorities have used the U.S. legal system as the metric for measuring foreign legal systems and assessing their fairness. Their basic position has remained unaltered: before foreign courts or in foreign prisons, U.S. personnel should enjoy rights and safeguards similar to those they would have in the American legal system.

Yet American authorities have not merely tried to ensure that foreign legal systems treat U.S. personnel fairly. Rather, their goal—from the 1950s to this day—has been to prevent foreign systems from exercising jurisdiction over U.S. personnel in the first place.[169] Specifically, U.S. authorities have often sought to label offenses as related to "official duty," and thus subject to American jurisdiction.[170] Alternatively, they have asked local authorities to waive their jurisdiction. Waiver requests are supposed to be submitted in cases of particular importance, yet in practice the United States considers every case in which an American soldier may be tried by a foreign court to be of particular importance and typically requests a waiver in cases of concurrent jurisdiction. The American practice of pushing for waivers is, in fact, reflected in DoD Instruction 5525.01, which establishes the goal of maximizing U.S. jurisdiction over troops to the extent permissible under applicable SOFAs.[171] In some cases, the United States has even been able to negotiate a supplemental bilateral agreement with host countries whereby the host will automatically waive its jurisdiction over U.S. personnel back to the United States. By contrast, the United States itself almost never waives its primary jurisdiction.[172]

These practices have indeed allowed U.S. authorities to secure jurisdiction over the majority of criminal cases involving American troops.[173] During the period 1954–1970—the height of the Cold War—foreign legal authorities filed 361,487 criminal cases against U.S. personnel—primarily American troops, but also including civilian employees of the military and dependents. Of this total, only 121,717 criminal cases—one third—reached trial before host-country courts. In the majority of cases, the foreign authorities granted a waiver or dismissed the case without an official waiver.[174] For the post–Cold War period we lack precise, comprehensive data on waivers, but the anecdotal data we do have confirm that host countries have kept waiving their jurisdiction in the great majority of cases. From 1989 to 2005, U.S. authorities secured jurisdiction in 98% of criminal cases involving American personnel in Spain. Spain denied only 18 out of 1,066 requests for a waiver of its jurisdiction over that period.[175] In South Korea, opposition to the U.S. presence intensified in the 1990s and concerns over crimes committed by U.S. personnel grew stronger, resulting in a slight decline of the waiver rate: from 99% in 1990 to 95% in 2002. Even with this decline, Korean authorities continued to relinquish their jurisdiction in the vast majority of cases involving U.S. personnel.[176]

This does not mean, of course, that U.S. authorities have always gotten their way. In some cases over the years, host countries have insisted on exercising jurisdiction and/or pre-trial custody, especially when the conduct in question was particularly egregious, or when the hosts' authorities were not assured that a waiver would lead to vigorous prosecution before a U.S. court martial.[177] Yet, overall, U.S. authorities typically request—and receive—waivers of foreign jurisdiction, as they have since the onset of status-of-forces arrangements in the 1950s. Concerns about subjecting U.S. troops to foreign jurisdiction have apparently not eased, and in fact may even have grown stronger. According to a 2015 report of the State Department's International Security Advisory Board, in concluding new SOFAs, U.S. authorities often aim for arrangements that go beyond the NATO SOFA model of jurisdiction that is shared between the United States and the host. Indeed, their goal is to establish *exclusive* American jurisdiction over troops.[178] This amounts to a reversal of the view that foreign justice systems should legitimately exercise some degree of jurisdiction over U.S. troops. Senator Bricker would surely have approved.

Military officers have, at times, publicly expressed their concerns about and criticism of foreign legal systems. Writing in 2008, a judge advocate in the U.S. Navy warned that:

> the U.S. government should be extremely reluctant to subject any U.S. service members to the Iraq criminal justice system without significant caveats. . . . the Iraqi legal system is vastly different from the U.S. system in terms of the fundamental protections given the accused, the lack of an adversarial process and the authority and professionalism

> of the judiciary. In addition, corruption, religious influence, bias against foreigners, ignorance or disdain for the rule of law amongst judges, and significant security threats are all attendant in day-to-day activities of the Iraqi courts. Unfortunately, it is a system that would be anathema to the average U.S. citizen's perception of justice.[179]

Another military legal officer was scathing in his criticism of the Japanese legal system where, he argued, prosecutors hold near-absolute power, harsh investigatory methods are employed, and the use of the accused's confession as key evidence eliminates the presumption of innocence.[180] He therefore contended that "The Japanese system . . . is structurally deficient and incompatible with the American idea of due process and an individual's right to defend themselves."[181]

In the course of the present analysis I do not seek to evaluate whether such criticisms have merit. A cursory glance will reveal that the U.S. military is, indeed, far from alone in expressing strong misgivings about Japanese criminal justice. Human rights NGOs and the international media have similarly denounced certain elements of Japan's criminal justice system, especially the practice of pre-indictment detention: a period of up to 23 days during which suspects come under pressure to confess their alleged crimes, as they are questioned without the presence of a lawyer and cannot request bail.[182] Iraq's courts have also attracted their share of criticism.[183] But the broader point is that the U.S. military persists in its suspicious attitude toward foreign legal systems and seeks to minimize their jurisdiction over American troops. Decades of experience with foreign jurisdictional arrangements have apparently not assuaged the ethnocentric concerns raised by opponents of the NATO SOFA back in 1953. Justice systems abroad are still seen as incompatible with or inferior to American justice and hence as unqualified to try American troops.

Notes

1. Gresh 2015.
2. Department of Defense 2017, 7.
3. Desch 1992; Posen 2003.
4. Calder 2007, 7–9; Schmidt 2014.
5. Efrat 2022a and 2022b.
6. Yeo 2011; Kawato 2015.
7. Lee 2003, 216; Flynn 2012; International Security Advisory Board 2015, 17 fn12.
8. Jung and Hwang 2003; Lee 2003; Gao 2009.
9. Erickson 1994, 138.
10. Egan 2006, 295; Voetelink 2015, 32.
11. King 1942, 548.
12. U.S. Senate 1953c, 41–43; Lepper 1994, 171; Erickson 1994, 139.
13. Lepper 1994, 171; Egan 2006, 296.

14. Egan 2006, 297.
15. Egan 2006, 297–298.
16. The NATO SOFA does not include a definition of official duty, allowing U.S. authorities to construe this term broadly to maximize their jurisdiction over U.S. troops. Lepper 1994, 175–176.
17. NATO SOFA, Article VII, Paragraph 3. See Egan 2006, 299–302.
18. NATO SOFA, Article VII, Paragraph 9.
19. Gao 2009, 595–596. Beyond NATO members, additional countries are subject to the provisions of the NATO SOFA through their participation in the NATO Partnership for Peace (PfP) program. Mason 2012, 18; International Security Advisory Board 2015, 27.
20. Lepper 1994, 172; Gher 2002, 236; Egan 2006, 298; International Security Advisory Board 2015, 18.
21. No exact count of SOFAs exists. Estimates put the number of agreements at more than 100. Cooley 2008, 33; Mason 2012,1; International Security Advisory Board 2015, 11–12.
22. Cooley 2008, 33; International Security Advisory Board 2015, 19–20.
23. International Security Advisory Board 2015, 1–2.
24. Koremenos 2005.
25. Egan 2006, 304; Cha 2010, 501–502.
26. International Security Advisory Board 2015, 16–17.
27. U.S. President 1952, 2, 4.
28. The president refers to the NATO SOFA and to an additional NATO agreement that was then before the Senate: the Protocol on the Status of International Military Headquarters set up pursuant to the North Atlantic Treaty.
29. 99 Congressional Record 8779 (1953). Message dated July 14, 1953. The president wrote the message to Senator William Knowland in response to the latter's query.
30. 99 Congressional Record 8770 (1953).
31. 99 Congressional Record 8779 (1953).
32. Cited in 99 Congressional Record 8777 (1953). See also the statements of Admiral Robert Carney (Commander of NATO's Allied Forces Southern Europe) in 99 Congressional Record 8770–8771 (1953); General Lauris Norstad (Commander in Chief of Allied Air Forces Central Europe and of the United States Air Forces in Europe) in 99 Congressional Record 8770 (1953).
33. U.S. Senate 1953a, 15.
34. U.S. Senate 1953a, 11.
35. 99 Congressional Record 8774 (1953).
36. U.S. Senate 1953a, 28.
37. U.S. Senate 1953b, 13. See also U.S. Senate 1953a, 26–27 (Joseph J. Wolf, Bureau of Regional European Affairs, Department of State).
38. 99 Congressional Record 8777 (1953).
39. U.S. Senate 1953a, 56.
40. U.S. Senate 1953c, 3.
41. U.S. Senate 1953c, 38–56.
42. U.S. Senate 1953c, 77.
43. U.S. Senate 1953c, 38.
44. U.S. Senate 1953c, 38–39.
45. U.S. Senate 1953c, 73.
46. U.S. Senate 1953c, 39, 75–76, 77.
47. U.S. Senate 1953c, 68.
48. U.S. Senate 1953c, 69.
49. U.S. Senate 1953c, 69.
50. U.S. Senate 1953c, 70.
51. U.S. Senate 1953c, 78.
52. Agreement on the Status of the North Atlantic Treaty Organization, National Representatives and International Staff (1951); Protocol on the Status of International Military Headquarters set up pursuant to the North Atlantic Treaty (1952).
53. U.S. Senate 1953b, 11.

54. U.S. 1953b, 11–12.
55. U.S. 1953b, 11.
56. U.S. 1953b, 12.
57. U.S. 1953b, 19.
58. 99 Congressional Record 8730 (1953).
59. 99 Congressional Record 8738 (1953).
60. 99 Congressional Record 8779 (1953).
61. 99 Congressional Record 8738 (1953).
62. 99 Congressional Record 8779 (1953).
63. 99 Congressional Record 8771 (1953).
64. 99 Congressional Record 8730 (1953).
65. U.S. Senate 1953d, 3–4.
66. U.S. Senate 1953c, 78.
67. U.S. Senate 1953a, 18–19.
68. 99 Congressional Record 8773 (1953).
69. U.S. Senate 1953a, 18.
70. U.S. Senate 1953a, 31.
71. U.S. Senate 1953c, 78.
72. On the historically shaky status of the presumption of innocence in the civil law, see Quintard-Morénas 2010.
73. U.S. Senate 1953a, 19–20.
74. 99 Congressional Record 8773 (1953).
75. U.S. Senate 1953a, 21.
76. U.S. Senate 1953a, 21.
77. U.S. Senate 1953a, 21–22.
78. U.S. Senate 1953a, 43–44.
79. U.S. Senate 1953a, 44.
80. 99 Congressional Record 8733 (1953).
81. See Ploscowe 1945, 380; Clermont and Sherwin 2002, 246; Engel 2009.
82. U.S. Senate 1953d, 9.
83. U.S. Senate 1953a, 57.
84. U.S. Senate 1953a, 57–58. This assertion was supported by a State Department memo citing the relevant legislative provisions of NATO members that generally require a public trial. U.S. Senate 1953a, 58–59.
85. U.S. Senate 1953a, 55, 57.
86. U.S. Senate 1953a, 55.
87. 99 Congressional Record 8733 (1953).
88. U.S. Senate 1953c, 81–82. See also U.S. Senate 1953a, 59.
89. U.S. Senate 1953a, 59.
90. U.S. Senate 1953a, 59–60.
91. U.S. Senate 1953a, 49. See Secretary Wilson making a similar argument in U.S. Senate 1953a, 16.
92. For a critical discussion of the U.S. justice system, see Stuntz 2011; Garland 2012.
93. U.S. Senate 1953c, 82 (Senator Bricker).
94. 99 Congressional Record 8738 (1953).
95. 99 Congressional Record 8778 (1953).
96. U.S. Senate 1953a, 21.
97. U.S. Senate 1953a, 30.
98. 99 Congressional Record 8747 (1953).
99. U.S. Senate 1953a, 50; U.S. Senate 1953c, 81; 99 Congressional Record 8779 (1953).
100. U.S. Senate 1953a, 5,15, 30; 1953c, 81.
101. Walter Bedell Smith, undersecretary of state at the time of the SOFA ratification debate and a retired general.
102. U.S. Senate 1953c, 7 (Senator Bricker).
103. U.S. Senate 1953a, 20.
104. 99 Congressional Record 8732 (1953).

105. 99 Congressional Record 8732 (1953).
106. 99 Congressional Record 8773 (1953).
107. On the framing of soldiers as boys, see Israeli and Rosman-Stollman 2015.
108. 99 Congressional Record 8734 (1953).
109. 99 Congressional Record 8779 (1953).
110. U.S. Senate 1953a, 30. See also 99 Congressional Record 4671 (1953) (Senator Bricker emphasizing the involuntary presence of U.S. troops in Europe).
111. 99 Congressional Record 8773 (1953).
112. Senator Bricker's fight against the NATO SOFA coincided with his efforts to pass a constitutional amendment that would limit the impact of international law on the U.S. legal system. The 1953 version of his proposed amendment declared that a treaty provision which conflicts with the Constitution will have no effect and that treaties must be incorporated through legislation to become effective in the United States. The proposed amendment also limited the president's power to sign executive agreements with foreign powers (Dean 1953). Bricker persisted in his efforts to enact the amendment through 1957, but ultimately failed.
113. U.S. Senate 1953c, 3.
114. U.S. Senate 1953c, 6.
115. U.S. Senate 1953c, 3, 40.
116. 99 Congressional Record 8746 (1953).
117. 99 Congressional Record 8747 (1953).
118. U.S. Senate 1953c, 7.
119. U.S. Senate 1953c, 82–83.
120. 99 Congressional Record 8780 (1953).
121. 99 Congressional Record 8781 (1953).
122. 99 Congressional Record 8781 (1953).
123. 99 Congressional Record 8781 (1953).
124. U.S. Senate 1953c, 59.
125. U.S. Senate 1953c, 59–60.
126. U.S. Senate 1953c, 60.
127. U.S. Senate 1953c, 60.
128. U.S. Senate 1953c, 60.
129. U.S. Senate 1953c, 61.
130. U.S. Senate 1953c, 61.
131. U.S. Senate 1953c, 59.
132. U.S. Senate 1953c, 59.
133. U.S. Senate 1953c, 1.
134. For example, Senator McCarran committed to voting against ratification of the SOFA unless the Bricker reservation was accepted.
135. 99 Congressional Record 8774 (1953).
136. 99 Congressional Record 8776–8777 (1953).
137. 99 Congressional Record 8770 (1953).
138. 99 Congressional Record 8774 (1953).
139. 99 Congressional Record 8776 (1953).
140. 99 Congressional Record 8782 (1953).
141. 99 Congressional Record 8782 (1953).
142. 99 Congressional Record 8730 (1953).
143. Levie 1958. See the full text of the NATO SOFA, including the Senate's statement, in 4 UST 1792; T.I.A.S. 2846.
144. 99 Congressional Record 8747–8748 (1953).
145. U.S. House of Representatives 1955, 1, 10, 243.
146. U.S. House of Representatives 1955, 2, 5.
147. U.S. House of Representatives 1955, 10 (Representative Frank Bow (R-OH)).
148. U.S. House of Representatives 1955, 171 (Wilber Brucker, general counsel, Department of Defense).
149. U.S. House of Representatives 1955, 171.

150. U.S. House of Representatives 1957, 13.
151. U.S. House of Representatives 1957, 10–11. See also U.S. House of Representatives 1955, 238–239.
152. U.S. House of Representatives 1957, 13–14.
153. U.S. House of Representatives 1957, 15–16.
154. U.S. House of Representatives 1955, 166.
155. U.S. House of Representatives 1957, 21.
156. U.S. House of Representatives 1955, 8 (Representative Frank Bow (R-OH)).
157. U.S. House of Representatives 1957, 2–3.
158. U.S. House of Representatives 1957, 27.
159. In fact, the subcommittee's mandate extended beyond the NATO SOFA to include arrangements with other countries regarding criminal jurisdiction over U.S. troops stationed in those countries. U.S. Senate 1955a, 1–2, 5–6; U.S. Senate 1955b, 2.
160. U.S. Senate 1955a, 1.
161. U.S. Senate 1958, 2. See a similar finding in U.S. Senate 1968, 2.
162. 99 Congressional Record 8782 (1953).
163. Koremenos 2001.
164. See note 161.
165. DoD Instruction 5525.01, Foreign Criminal and Civil Jurisdiction, effective May 31, 2019, sections 4.2, 4.4.
166. DoD Instruction 5525.01, paragraphs 4.2.b.(1); 4.4.e.(2).
167. DoD Instruction 5525.01, Section 5. See also Cha 2010, 503; Flynn 2012, 14–16.
168. DoD Instruction 5525.01, paragraph 4.7.a(2).
169. Jung and Hwang 2003, 1128–1129; International Security Advisory Board 2015, 5, 17, 50.
170. Gao 2009, 597–598.
171. DoD Instruction 5525.01, paragraphs 1.2.b.(1), 4.2., 4.2.c.(1).
172. Levie 1958, 324; Cooley 2008, 44; International Security Advisory Board 2015, 18–19; Gao 2009, 599–600.
173. International Security Advisory Board 2015, 18–19.
174. Efrat 2022a and 2022b.
175. Cooley 2008, 83–84.
176. Cooley 2008, 120–123.
177. International Security Advisory Board 2015, 17–18.
178. International Security Advisory Board 2015, 17–19, 36, 51.
179. Wexler 2008, 85–86.
180. Stone 2006, 238–239.
181. Stone 2006, 238.
182. Human Rights Watch 2019; Adams 2019; Wingfield-Hayes 2019.
183. Human Rights Watch 2013; UNAMI and OHCHR 2020.

4

Exercising Jurisdiction over "Bad Apples"

Who Should Try ISIS Foreign Fighters?

The Islamic State of Iraq and Syria—known as the Islamic State, ISIS, or Daesh—is a terrorist organization that follows a fundamentalist, jihadist doctrine of Sunni Islam. The organization won global attention in 2014, when it took over parts of western Iraq and eastern Syria. In the large territory it held, containing roughly 8 million people, ISIS enforced a strict interpretation of Sharia law. In that territory, ISIS also committed grave abuses of international human rights law, international criminal law, and international humanitarian law—acts that may constitute war crimes, crimes against humanity, and genocide.[1] The group became particularly notorious for its videos of beheadings and other gruesome executions of both soldiers and civilians, as well as its destruction of cultural sites.[2]

This "success" drew flows of "foreign fighters" who left their home countries and flocked to Iraq and Syria to join the Islamic State, both before and after the group proclaimed itself a worldwide caliphate in June 2014. A 2018 estimate put the number of foreign affiliates of ISIS at 41,490; men constituted 75% of that count; women and minors roughly 25%.[3] The age of the men and women typically ranged from 20 to 30 years. In terms of national origin, nearly half of the foreign affiliates (18,852) came from the Middle East and North Africa, the rest arriving from various regions of the world. Most relevant for the present analysis, 5,904 ISIS affiliates originated from Western Europe, including 1,910 from France, 960 from Germany, and 850 from the UK.[4] Strong levels of radicalization, as well as the will to build and live in a pious Islamic caliphate, motivated these men, women, and youth to leave their respective countries for Syria and Iraq. However, the inflow of

Intolerant Justice. Asif Efrat, Oxford University Press. © Oxford University Press 2023.
DOI: 10.1093/oso/9780197658895.003.0004

individuals who joined the caliphate was soon accompanied by an outflow of returnees who made their way back to their home countries for multiple reasons: some did not agree with everything ISIS was doing; some had no qualms about their own role or ISIS tactics, but decided to move on; and some were forced out by circumstances, such as loss of territory, or were captured and sent back to their home countries.[5]

The terror attacks that ISIS perpetrated—in Paris in November 2015,[6] in Brussels in March 2016,[7] and elsewhere—clearly demonstrated the risk that its recruits potentially posed upon their return to their home countries.[8] The debate over the treatment of the ISIS fighters—and whether to allow their return—intensified in 2019 in the wake of the caliphate's collapse, which threatened to generate a large outflow of returnees and put their home countries under pressure.[9] After the fall of ISIS, many of its affiliates ended up in prisons and camps controlled by the Syrian Democratic Forces (SDF), a Kurdish-led militia in northeastern Syria that is backed by the United States.[10] The SDF called on foreign governments to repatriate their citizens who had joined ISIS.[11] The United States made a similar plea: "The United States calls upon other nations to repatriate and prosecute their citizens detained by the SDF and commends the continued efforts of the SDF to return these foreign terrorist fighters to their countries of origin."[12]

This chapter analyzes the debate over the legal treatment of returning ISIS fighters. Note that the issue of repatriation itself is examined here briefly, as it is incidental to the primary question of concern to us: Who should exercise criminal jurisdiction over the former fighters for their offenses in the service of ISIS? Should they stand trial before their home-country courts or be prosecuted in another venue? We examine how one of the fighters' home countries—Britain—has grappled with these questions. Note that, while this book focuses on cooperation among legal systems, the British foreign-fighters debate did not revolve around "cooperation with a foreign legal system" as such: no foreign country expressed a desire to put the foreign fighters on trial. "Cooperation" here means a reluctance to prosecute ISIS fighters of British origin in the UK and willingness to have them tried by another legal system. The following analysis examines the arguments made by those willing to "cooperate" and cede jurisdiction over the foreign fighters, as well as the views of those who favored their prosecution in UK courts. The analysis mostly focuses on the debate that took place during 2019 following the defeat of ISIS, but also centers on the legal fate of the *men* who joined ISIS, since men were those who typically committed crimes on behalf of ISIS and continued to pose a potential terrorist threat.

Repatriation: Should British ISIS Fighters Come Home?

According to estimates by the British government, approximately 900 British citizens traveled to Syria or Iraq to join ISIS. By early 2019, roughly 20% of those individuals had been killed on the battlefield, 40%—or 360 individuals—had returned to the UK, and another 40% still remained in the region.[13] According to the government, those who returned posed a relatively low risk. They had been questioned and investigated; some joined deradicalization programs or received mental-health support.[14] A small number of the returning fighters—only about 40—faced prosecution in British courts.[15] The government provided little information about these prosecutions and their outcomes.[16]

But the thornier problem—the one that fueled the public debate over the foreign fighters—concerned British members of ISIS who were still in the Middle East at the time of ISIS' defeat. Those were seen as the most devoted to radical Islam and the most dangerous.[17] Participants in the debate considered them a grave threat to national security. According to Conservative Prime Minister Theresa May, "anyone who has travelled to Syria not only puts themselves in considerable danger but potentially poses a serious national security risk."[18] Home Secretary Sajid Javid (Conservative) maintained that "many of those individuals remain active and very dangerous, and we are continuing to work with our allies to see what we can do to maintain our national security."[19] According to Member of Parliament (MP) Diane Abbott (Labour), "Returning foreign fighters are a real threat to our security. That is a genuine terrorist threat."[20]

But beyond the threat to security, participants in the debate over the foreign fighters expressed alarm and outrage over the fighters' offense to British values. They were seen as individuals who had committed heinous acts and betrayed their country. Victoria Atkins (Conservative), the parliamentary under secretary of state at the Home Office, showed concern about the security threat that the fighters posed alongside moral revulsion at their actions:

> We know that those who remain in the conflict zone include some of the most dangerous, who choose to stay to fight, to raise families or otherwise to support Daesh. *They turned their back on this country to support a group that butchered and beheaded innocent civilians, including British citizens.* Those individuals pose a greater threat to the UK than those who returned earlier in the conflict. They will have become desensitised to violence and may have received combat training and intense indoctrination. They will have had the opportunity to expand their terrorist

network. Where they pose any threat to this country we will do everything in our power to prevent their return.[21]

Home Secretary Javid similarly expressed moral disgust with the fighters: "Whatever role they took in the so-called caliphate, they all supported a terrorist organisation and, in doing so, have shown that they hate our country and the values we stand for. This is a death cult that enslaved and raped thousands of Yazidi girls and that celebrated attacks on our shores, including the tragic Manchester bombing, which targeted young girls."[22] Javid further added that "In many cases, the people who left Britain knew exactly what they were doing. They were full of hate for our country and hate for our values. They went out there to murder, to rape, to support rape and to commit many violent and vile acts. We can absolutely imagine why hardly anyone among the British public would have any sympathy for them."[23]

Various other speakers, from across the political spectrum, also expressed their revulsion at the ISIS fighters. MP Stephen Metcalfe (Conservative) argued that the fighters had "joined an organisation whose aims are to destroy the values that we hold dear."[24] MP Kevin Foster (Conservative) revealed that he had "little sympathy for those who headed out to the middle east—to Syria and Iraq—to support a form of medieval barbarism that sought to enslave an entire people and who committed genocide while they were [at it] as well."[25] MP John Woodcock (Independent, formerly Labour) thought "It is abhorrent for anyone who claims to be British, who was born here and who has benefited from the manifest advantages that our country and society offer our citizens, to declare themselves effectively in opposition to everything that the UK stands for."[26] Others characterized the fighters' actions as "abhorrent crimes" or "the most barbaric crimes."[27]

Against this background, we can understand why the British government was reluctant to see the ISIS fighters return home.[28] One measure used to keep the fighters out was revoking their British citizenship. In light of the international prohibition on leaving a person stateless,[29] Britain could only take away the citizenship of individuals who held another citizenship. Home Secretary Javid suggested that the removal of citizenship was sometimes necessary "to protect the national security and citizens of this country."[30] He took pride in stripping more than 100 "dangerous dual nationals" of their British citizenship.[31] Javid even suggested that "many members of the British Muslim community do not want foreign terrorist fighters to return to this country, because they fear both the precedent that that will set for future potential foreign fighters and the radicalism of vulnerable young British Muslims by those returning foreign fighters."[32] Defense Secretary Gavin Williamson (Conservative) was even more adamant: "I do not believe that any terrorist, whether they come from this country or any other, should ever be allowed back into this country"; "We should do everything we can do to destroy and eliminate that threat," including killing the terrorists: "A dead terrorist can't cause any harm to Britain."[33] Rory Stewart (Conservative), the minister for international development, expressed similar sentiments. He suggested that the "only way" to deal with British fighters for ISIS was "in almost every case" to kill them, since they had moved away from any allegiance to Britain and posed a serious danger to UK security.[34]

Williamson's and Stewart's blunt statements seem to have captured the mood of the British public. According to a nationally representative public opinion poll, carried out in November 2017, roughly three quarters (77%) of UK adults thought that the government should prevent Britons who had joined ISIS from returning to Britain: 42% expressed a preference for stripping them of citizenship, while 35% thought they should be treated as enemy combatants and legitimate targets to be attacked. Only one in nine respondents (11%) believed that ISIS fighters should be brought back to Britain, to be either sentenced or rehabilitated.[35]

A 2018 e-petition submitted to Parliament expressed a similar public sentiment, calling upon policymakers to ban all ISIS members from returning to the UK. "By banning all returning ISIS members and by removing their citizenship and passports it would help keep the UK safe from terrorists and their actions. . . . It would also send a message to others that membership of a terrorist organisation will not be tolerated."[36] That petition garnered some 600,000 signatures. According to MP Luke Hall (Conservative), the petition "is representative of a concern raised by many people that, in recent years, our democracies have taken too lax an attitude in dealing with extremism, allowing people the freedom to act in unacceptable ways that contravene traditional British values."[37]

Yet support for the government's policy of preventing the return of ISIS fighters was not unanimous. That policy did draw some condemnation, primarily, but not exclusively, from the left. Critics argued that, notwithstanding the danger they posed, ISIS fighters of British origin were Britain's problem to deal with. MP Mark Garnier (Conservative) asked pointedly: "should we not be setting an example in how we take responsibility for people we consider to be a threat not just to British citizens, but to the world in general?"[38] MP John Woodcock (Independent, formerly Labour) argued that individuals radicalized in Britain were a problem that British society had created, and they were "our problem to sort out. How is it acceptable for the Government to deport the problem to another country?"[39] MP Gavin Newlands (Scottish National Party) maintained that "The UK must meet its international obligations, allow the return of its citizens and ensure that they face the full consequences of their actions. If we do not take responsibility for that, on whose shoulders should it fall? . . . Our position is clear: the UK bears responsibility for all its citizens, and the actions of the Home

Secretary are to be condemned. It is time for Daesh members to come back to the UK and face justice."[40] Even General Lord Richard Dannatt, former head of the British Army, argued that "If there are . . . a large number of foreign fighters in captivity in Syria who originate from countries like the UK, then they are our citizens and we have a responsibility to act responsibly towards them. That means they have got to come back to this country."[41]

The controversy surrounding the repatriation of ISIS fighters shaped the related debate concerning their legal treatment and the appropriate venue for their prosecution. A government and a public that did not wish to see ISIS fighters return to the UK naturally had little interest in prosecuting them before a UK court.

Where Should ISIS Fighters Face Trial?

To be sure, government representatives emphasized that returning ISIS fighters *may* face prosecution in a UK court. Home Secretary Javid suggested that "Individuals who manage to return will be questioned, investigated and, potentially, prosecuted."[42] Prime Minister May said the same.[43] Ben Wallace (Conservative), then minister for security and economic crime, argued that the British government was "using a range of tools to disrupt and diminish that threat [posed by returning fighters], including prosecution under the full range of existing counter-terrorism legislation."[44] But while claiming to seek justice in its treatment of the fighters,[45] the government maintained that actually achieving justice in a UK court might prove difficult.

More specifically, the government cited two primary obstacles to a successful criminal prosecution of ISIS fighters. According to Home Secretary Javid, "one challenge is having the right laws in place," that is, having appropriate legal standards applicable to the crimes committed by the fighters: terrorist-related criminal offenses that carry significant prison sentences. The second challenge was "collecting battlefield evidence. These individuals are returning from a war zone. Collecting evidence in the battlefield is incredibly difficult."[46] Javid argued that the government was working to meet both challenges. Regarding the first, "We are constantly considering what further improvements can be made, and what further tools can be introduced to prosecute returning foreign fighters."[47] One example was a new criminal offense established by the Counter-Terrorism and Border Security Act 2019: entering or remaining in a designated area (an area outside the UK that the UK government prohibits its citizens and residents from entering or remaining in, for the purpose of protection against terrorism).[48] The act also established an offense of recklessly expressing support for a proscribed organization[49] and made some updates to the UK's terrorism laws, including extending the maximum sentence for the encouragement of terrorism from 7 to 15 years.[50]

Regarding the evidence-collection challenge, Home Secretary Javid argued that "we have done, and continue to do, a lot of work through the MOD [Ministry of Defence] and with our defence allies and Five Eyes partners [Australia, Canada, New Zealand, and the United States] to try collect more such evidence, so that we can use it in the courts for more successful prosecutions."[51]

This supposed interest in prosecuting the returning fighters in Britain is difficult to reconcile with the government's reluctance to allow the repatriation of the fighters. Indeed, other statements of government officials indicated little interest in holding UK prosecutions. To the contrary, the government preferred *not* to try the fighters in UK courts. Defense Secretary Ben Wallace[52] said bluntly that the fighters should not be brought back to the UK for prosecution because they were dangerous "diehards" and the chances of convicting them were low.[53] Others more subtly suggested that justice should best be pursued in the area where ISIS crimes were committed, that is, outside the UK. Home Secretary Javid explained that "we will seek to work with our allies to make sure, first of all, that justice can be done in the region, but if that cannot be done, we will look to work with our allies on other means."[54] The Foreign Office similarly said that anyone who has fought for or supported ISIS should face justice "in the most appropriate jurisdiction, which will often be in the region where their offences have been committed."[55] According to Victoria Atkins of the Home Office, "Those who have fought for or supported Daesh, whatever their nationality, should wherever possible face justice for their crimes in the most appropriate jurisdiction. Sometimes that is in the region where their offences have been committed."[56]

Three things stand out with respect to these statements. First, they are vague and nonspecific. Exactly which court in the region will try the fighters? An Iraqi court? A court established in Syria by the SDF militia? An international tribunal to be located in the region? The British government did not say.[57] Second, these statements showed little concern about the standards of justice to be applied by the court trying the fighters. *The Guardian* quoted a Foreign Office spokesperson as saying that "Any internationally supported justice mechanism [for ISIS fighters] must respect human rights and the rule of law as well as ensure fair trials and due process."[58] But overall, the British government made little attempt to ensure that the fighters would receive fair trials. Its primary concern was to avoid holding these trials in British courts. This is a far cry from the U.S. government's extensive efforts to guarantee fair trials for American troops abroad, as described in Chapter 3. Third, the government maintained its refusal to prosecute the ISIS fighters in the face of U.S. pressure. The Trump administration pressured the UK government, and other European governments, to repatriate their nationals who had joined ISIS and try them at home. The Trump administration was likely not motivated by a firm belief in the rule of law, but by a concern that the continued concentration of ISIS fighters in the Middle East would lead to a resurgence of terrorism.[59] That the UK repudiated the pressure of the United States—its close ally—shows how reluctant it was to put the fighters on trial in the UK.

The UK government's position reflected both security concerns about ISIS fighters as well as a moral revulsion at their actions. As they posed a danger to public safety, and given the heinous crimes they had committed, they were not seen as deserving of a trial before a UK court. Instead, they should face trial outside the UK—even if such trial did not meet due-process standards.

This position of the government, however, faced domestic criticism. Several MPs insisted that returning ISIS fighters, as UK citizens, deserved to have their day in a British court. Their arguments echoed those made by opponents of the NATO SOFA, as described in the previous chapter. MP Nick Thomas-Symonds (Labour) claimed that "anyone returning to this country as a UK citizen should expect to face justice for their actions, in a legal process in which our police, our prosecutors and our courts will take into account the individual circumstances of each case."[60] MP Diane Abbott (Labour) argued that "if [the fighters] are British they are Britain's responsibility and should be subject to the British criminal justice system."[61] According to MP Luke Hall (Conservative), "If someone is born, raised and radicalised in Britain, it ought to be the British Government's responsibility to hold them to account for their actions. They should be tried in front of a British jury by British judges, and held accountable to the standards required of our great legal system."[62] MP John Woodcock (Independent, formerly Labour) identified the instrumental value of prosecutions in the UK: "finding a way properly to prosecute them for any evil acts they might have done . . . would be the deterrent effect to stop future generations going over."[63] Some MPs expressed dissatisfaction with the low prosecution rate among fighters who had already returned (roughly 40 of 360 returnees) and called upon the government to improve it. "I say to the Home Secretary that [the existing rate] is simply not enough."[64]

Parliamentary critics did acknowledge the difficulties of prosecuting the foreign fighters based on existing UK law. They proposed revisiting and updating the provisions of the Treason Act "to ensure that these appalling activities receive suitable and just punishment."[65] They also proposed the application of the designated-area offense retroactively, that is, the prosecution of individuals who joined ISIS in Iraq and Syria prior to the offense's coming into force in 2019. The government, however, believed that "in line with normal judicial principles," the offense could not apply retroactively.[66] For the critics, this showed that the government was being disingenuous. The Home Secretary "talks about doing whatever it takes to bring people to justice, so why is he not making the very valuable designated area offence, for which many of us campaigned, retrospective?"[67] Indeed, "The failure to prosecute, or the apparent unwillingness to countenance such radical measures to hold them to account, leads people to lose faith in our judicial system."[68]

The Times identified another disingenuity in the government's position—specifically, the argument that ISIS fighters should face trial outside the UK, close to where they committed their crimes. The newspaper pointed out that, in fact, no such realistic option existed. Having the Kurdish-led militia—the SDF—try British ISIS fighters was clearly a bad idea. In one camp in northern Syria, where ISIS fighters were held under SDF supervision, conditions "are more reminiscent of a concentration camp than a prison. There are no proper medical facilities nor any legal process."[69] *The Times* further ruled out the option of trying ISIS fighters in Iraqi courts. Those courts could only exercise jurisdiction over crimes that were committed on their country's own territory, but not in Syria; and if they did exercise jurisdiction, they might impose the death penalty. Nor did *The Times* expect the establishment of an international court to try foreign ISIS fighters, since Russia would likely block any tribunal from prosecuting war crimes in Syria, to defend the Assad regime.[70] In the absence of a viable non-UK option for prosecuting ISIS fighters, the newspaper called upon the British government to "take the lead in bringing home all its citizens, male and female, to face justice. . . . If the West is to succeed in the battle of ideas against radical Islam, it needs to have the confidence to live up to its ideals, no matter how politically uncomfortable."[71]

Families of ISIS victims echoed the demand for UK trials. Dragana Haines, the widow of David Haines, an aid worker whom ISIS beheaded in 2014, argued that "Those men committed vicious crimes against British citizens, and if for nothing else, that is the reason they should be put through trial in the UK."[72]

To be fair to the British government, one has to acknowledge that the prosecution of ISIS fighters in UK courts indeed carried some risks. If the fighters were to be tried by British courts, they could walk free due to a lack of evidence necessary for conviction. Alternatively, they could be convicted of lesser crimes that do not carry heavy prison sentences, such as membership in a terrorist organization. Even if the fighters were to end up behind bars, they could still cause harm by radicalizing other inmates and passing on their knowledge of firearms and explosives. And ultimately the fighters would find themselves free—after serving a prison sentence or much sooner (if they were not prosecuted or convicted). They might return to engaging in terrorism, thereby triggering a public backlash.[73]

While these are all valid concerns, the government's reluctance to make a real effort to put ISIS fighters on trial nonetheless suggests some other motivations at work. One is public opinion. As we have seen, the British public largely opposed the repatriation of the foreign fighters. If the government were to have brought the fighters back and prosecuted them, the public might have disapproved. But a second likely motivation was the government's belief that ISIS fighters were simply not entitled to a fair trial—in the UK or elsewhere. Given the heinous crimes they had committed, they were seen as having forfeited their right to face trial before British courts—and the right to due process and humane treatment more broadly. The following section provides another example of that attitude: the government's willingness to assist a U.S. legal process that would have led to the imposition of the death penalty on ISIS fighters.

U.S. Prosecution and Death-Penalty Concerns

El Shafee Elsheikh and Alexanda Kotey were half of an ISIS cell of four Britons who handled Western hostages and whose British accents won them the nickname "The Beatles." The group was known for its brutality and bore responsibility for the beheading of at least 27 hostages. Whereas the leader of this group—Mohamed Emwazi, often referred to as Jihadi John—was killed in a U.S. drone strike in late 2015, Kotey and Elsheikh were captured in Syria in January 2018 by the U.S.-backed Kurdish militia. They were prohibited from returning to the UK, since the UK government had stripped them of their British citizenship. The United States wanted to put the two on trial; however, in order to do so, U.S. authorities needed evidence gathered by Britain's law enforcement, including the backgrounds of the two ISIS fighters, their associations, path of radicalization, movements, and activities. In exchange for providing the evidence, British officials initially asked the United States for assurances that it would not seek the death penalty if the two were convicted. Yet the Trump administration refused to grant these assurances, arguing that the British government, which itself declined to prosecute the two ISIS fighters, should not place restrictions on the United States. The British government ultimately gave in to the American demand and decided to provide the evidence without receiving the death-penalty assurances, partly because it feared the possible alternative: that the Trump administration might send the two former Britons to the U.S. military prison at Guantánamo Bay, Cuba.[74]

In Parliament, the government's decision to assist U.S. authorities came under attack, with critics demanding that the UK honor its commitment to the abolition of the death penalty.[75] MP Chi Onwurah (Labour) argued that "Many of these fighters seek to undermine our democratic values by the most evil and despicable of means. Does the Minister [for Security and Economic Crime] understand the essential importance of not outsourcing our moral and ethical base by helping in the execution of the death penalty, against those democratic values?"[76] According to MP Afzal Khan (Labour), "The Labour party makes it absolutely clear that those who commit abhorrent crimes should face the full force of the law, but in bringing people to justice we should never sacrifice the very values that those who wish us harm seek to attack."[77] MP Patrick Grady (SNP) shared these sentiments: "no matter how heinous and barbaric the alleged crimes are—and they are—if individuals are brought to justice, they should be not subject to the death penalty."[78] The British legal community joined the critics. One experienced human rights barrister argued that the UK "cannot be complicit with the death penalty. As with the absolute prohibition on torture, there are no exceptions."[79]

Ben Wallace, then minister for security and economic crime, sought to defend the decision to assist U.S. authorities in prosecuting the two ISIS fighters. He argued that the exceptional circumstances of the case, and the lack of better options, led the government to forgo the death-penalty assurances. The two jihadists, Wallace argued, could not face trial in the UK: there was no "magic wand to get people miraculously into a UK court or provide evidence that matches the statute book that we happen to have." Ultimately, "the rights of those individuals detained are better served by a judicial trial in the United States [where] they have a better chance of proper representation in a court of law than if they were left in detention by non-state actors [the SDF] in a war zone in north Syria, sent to Guantanamo Bay—something that the Government oppose fully—or allowed to go back into the battlefield and wreak murder and death in the same way that they have been accused of doing in the past." Given the unappealing options, the government, "charged with keeping people safe and trying to deliver justice for the victims," felt that there were compelling reasons not to seek death-penalty assurances when sharing the evidence for a criminal trial in the United States. Wallace also reminded the critics that the two individuals in question had committed heinous crimes, including torture and beheading. He further argued that the United States has an independent judiciary and a strong rule of law, and the sharing of evidence with such a legal system was therefore reasonable.[80]

Yet the UK Supreme Court thought otherwise. In March 2020, by a unanimous judgment, seven justices of the court ruled that the government's decision to assist U.S. authorities without death-penalty assurances was unlawful.[81] This decision left U.S. authorities little choice: in August 2020, Attorney General William Barr committed to not seeking the death penalty against Kotey and Elsheikh. With these assurances, the UK transferred the evidentiary material to the United States, paving the way for the duo's trial.[82]

This debate vividly demonstrates Proposition 8: the intensity of concern about mistreatment at the hands of a foreign legal system may vary with the identity of the actors expected to suffer such mistreatment. We have seen in the previous chapter that a government may go to great lengths to ensure proper legal treatment for its soldiers and protect them from cruel punishment. But when it comes to individuals who joined a foreign terrorist organization and committed horrific crimes, a government may be far less insistent on ensuring fair legal treatment and may be willing to sacrifice even fundamental principles, such as opposition to the death penalty.

Conclusion

The case of the British foreign fighters shows us a government willing to "cooperate" by relinquishing jurisdiction over its citizens, although this constitutes cooperation with a twist. In Chapter 2, we argued that states generally seek to exercise their legal authority over their citizens or their territory. They may be willing to cede their legal authority in favor of another country to maintain good relations with that country, to obtain reciprocal cooperation, or to ensure that offenders are held accountable and do not evade the law. Chapter 3 demonstrated this dynamic. The United States clearly wished to exercise full jurisdiction over its troops abroad, yet realized the necessity of sacrificing some of its legal authority to legitimize the American presence in host countries. Despite that recognition, the United States sought to minimize the cession of its jurisdiction by maximizing the number of waivers from foreign jurisdiction. In other words, the American cooperation with hosts' legal systems was reluctant. In the case of the ISIS foreign fighters, by contrast, the cession of British legal authority was anything but reluctant. Indeed, the British government showed little interest in exercising its own jurisdiction over the fighters and held no reservations or compunction about subjecting them to foreign jurisdiction. And the willingness to have these British citizens tried in Middle Eastern countries had little to do with maintaining good relations with those countries or obtaining their reciprocal cooperation. Nor did the willingness to subject British citizens to foreign justice stem from a principled commitment to the rule of law and the punishment of offenders. Rather, a perceived security threat presumably posed by the former fighters made the government reluctant to allow their return to the UK and their trial by British courts. The security concerns were reinforced by the sense that the foreign fighters were not entitled—from a moral standpoint—to be tried in Britain. Given their heinous actions, they no longer deserved the protection of the British legal system and maybe not even a fair legal process, even outside the UK.

All this means that the British government exhibited little of the ethnocentric concerns that stand at the center of this book. We argued in Chapter 2 that ethnocentrism generates concerns about foreign justice and creates a bias in favor of the home legal system. At the same time, we suggested that not everyone may be seen as deserving of the protection of the home legal system. Local citizens who are unpopular—due to their ethnicity or religion—may be perceived as belonging to an out-group, and their legal treatment at the hands of foreign authorities will raise little concern. The Britons who fought for ISIS are Muslims, and the dilemma regarding their legal treatment arose during a period of increasing anti-Muslim sentiment in Britain, possibly related to a spate of terrorist attacks in the UK in 2017.[83] A 2019 report by the NGO "HOPE not hate" found that "Muslims are seen as uniquely different from the majority British public." According to the report, 35% of Britons believe that Islam poses a threat to the British way of life, the number rising to 49% among Conservative voters.[84] Such prejudice against Muslims, coupled with the atrocities that the foreign fighters committed, made it easier for the government and the public to view them as belonging to an out-group and to ignore the perils they might face under foreign jurisdiction.

But not everyone shared these sentiments. Consistent with Proposition 3, MPs from Labour—the leftist opposition party—criticized the government's refusal to prosecute the fighters in a UK court. They argued that, notwithstanding the horrible crimes they had committed, Britain bears responsibility for ISIS fighters and should hold them accountable through its criminal-justice system. Also consistent with Proposition 3, criticism of the government's policy was not entirely limited to one side of the political spectrum. Some Conservative MPs shared the view that British foreign fighters should face trial in the UK. Consistent with Proposition 5, lawyers—the guardians of local legal norms—condemned the government's willingness to assist U.S. authorities as a betrayal of the commitment to the abolition of the death penalty.

In closing our analysis, it is important to note that Britain was not alone in refusing to exercise jurisdiction over its citizens who had fought for ISIS. Other European governments held a similar position.[85] France, for example, steadfastly opposed the repatriation of the French foreign fighters held in Syria in the aftermath of the collapse of ISIS.[86] France's foreign minister Jean-Yves Le Drian declared that the fighters "should be brought to justice close to [the place of] the crimes they committed."[87] In May 2019, an Iraqi court convicted seven Frenchmen of the offense of joining the Islamic State and sentenced them to death by hanging. The seven trials were held over only four days. In response, the French Foreign Ministry said that "France respects the Iraqi authorities' sovereignty," but added that "France is opposed, on principle, to the death penalty, anytime and anywhere."[88] Laurent Nuñez, the junior interior minister, argued that Iraq "is a sovereign state that dispenses justice. We have no reason to oppose having these individuals judged there."[89] According to the *New York Times*, "France, a country that prides itself as a champion of human rights and opponent of the death penalty, essentially outsourced the judicial process to Iraq. . . . France, which has sometimes refused to return foreigners to face justice in countries that use torture and the death penalty, has turned its citizens over to a legal system in which due process rights are significantly weaker and the death penalty is common."[90] In France, as in Britain, individuals of Muslim origin who had committed heinous terrorist acts were not seen as deserving of fair legal treatment and due process. A strong sense of anger and moral revulsion resulted in the evaporation of the ethnocentric concerns that would typically accompany the prosecution of one's citizens in foreign courts.

Notes

1. First report of the Special Adviser and Head of the United Nations Investigative Team to Promote Accountability for Crimes Committed by Da'esh/Islamic State in Iraq and the Levant. S/2018/1031, 16 November 2018.
2. Callimachi 2014; Curry 2015.
3. The count of minors includes over 700 infants who were born in the ISIS caliphate. The rest included young children that were brought to the caliphate by their parents and ideologically motivated teenagers who came on their own.
4. Cook and Vale 2018, 17.
5. Barrett 2017, 18–19.
6. Nossiter, Breeden, and Bennhold 2015.
7. Rubin, Breeden, and Raghavan 2016.
8. Hoffman and Furlan 2020, 6–11.
9. Chulov 2019.
10. Berger 2019. See Jenkins 2019, 11, for estimates of the number of ISIS fighters held by the SDF.
11. Hall 2020.
12. El Deeb and Lee 2019.
13. HC Deb 18 February 2019, c1194.
14. HC Deb 18 February 2019, cc1205–1206; HC Deb 18 March 2019, c259WH; Dearden 2019.
15. HC Deb 11 March 2019, c52; HC Deb 18 March 2019, c246WH.
16. HC Deb 18 March 2019, cc251WH, 260WH; Dearden 2019.
17. HC Deb 11 March 2019, c45.
18. HC Deb 20 February 2019, c1464.
19. HC Deb 11 March 2019, c54.
20. HC Deb 18 March 2019, c257WH.
21. HC Deb 18 March 2019, c259WH. Emphasis added.
22. HC Deb 18 February 2019, c1193. Javid is referring to the bombing in the Manchester Arena following a concert by singer Ariana Grande on May 22, 2017.
23. HC Deb 18 February 2019, c1203.
24. HC Deb 18 February 2019, c1206.
25. HC Deb 18 February 2019, cc1203–1204.
26. HC Deb 18 March 2019, c249WH.
27. HC Deb 11 October 2018, c294 (MP Azal Khan (Labour)); HC Deb 18 February 2019, c1196 (MP Michael Fallon (Conservative)).
28. Hamilton and Simpson 2018; Sabbagh 2020.
29. See 1961 Convention on the Reduction of Statelessness, Article 8(1): "A Contracting State shall not deprive a person of its nationality if such deprivation would render him stateless."
30. HC Deb 11 March 2019, c55.

31. HC Deb 18 February 2019, c1193.
32. HC Deb 11 March 2019, c51.
33. Quoted in Elgot 2017.
34. Quoted in BBC 2017.
35. The poll was conducted by Opinium Research, 27–30 November 2017. The full results are available from the author.
36. E-petition 231521. See https://petition.parliament.uk/archived/petitions/231521.
37. HC Deb 18 March 2019, c246WH.
38. HC Deb 11 March 2019, c55.
39. HC Deb 18 March 2019, c249WH.
40. HC Deb 18 March 2019, cc253WH, 255WH.
41. Cited in Mason 2019.
42. HC Deb 18 February 2019, c1193.
43. HC Deb 20 February 2019, c1464.
44. HC Deb 11 October 2018, c291.
45. HC Deb 11 October 2018, c296.
46. HC Deb 11 March 2019, c53; see also Dearden 2019.
47. HC Deb 11 March 2019, c51.
48. Counter-Terrorism and Border Security Act 2019, Part 1, Chapter 1, Section 4.
49. Counter-Terrorism and Border Security Act 2019, Part 1 Chapter 1 Section 1.
50. Counter-Terrorism and Border Security Act 2019, Part 1 Chapter 2 Section 7.
51. HC Deb 11 March 2019, c53.
52. Wallace was minister for security and economic crime from 2016 to 2019. He became secretary of state for defense in July 2019.
53. Courea and Swinford 2019.
54. HC Deb 18 February 2019, c1204.
55. Sabbagh 2020. See also Fisher 2019 (citing Downing 10).
56. HC Deb 18 March 2019, c260WH.
57. Spencer 2019.
58. Sabbagh 2020.
59. Fisher 2019; Fredericks 2019; Sabbagh 2019.
60. HC Deb 18 February 2019, c1195.
61. HC Deb 18 March 2019, c257WH.
62. HC Deb 18 March 2019, c247WH.
63. HC Deb 18 March 2019, c250WH.
64. HC Deb 11 March 2019, c52 (MP Philip Hollobone (Conservative)); see also HC Deb 18 March 2019, cc246WH, 248WH (MP Luke Hall (Conservative)).
65. HC Deb 20 February 2019, c1464 (MP Philip Hollobone (Conservative)). See also HC Deb 18 February 2019, c1198 (MP Julian Lewis (Conservative)); HC Deb 18 March 2019, cc251WH-252WH (MP John Woodcock (Independent, formerly Labour)). See also Ekins et al. 2018; Schraer 2018. The Treason Act 1351 is still in force. It includes offenses such as levying war against the sovereign in the realm, or adhering to the sovereign's enemies, giving them aid and comfort, in the realm. Yet the Treason Act has lain dormant since 1945. The last person to be prosecuted (and later executed) for treason in the UK was William Joyce, a member of the British Union of Fascists who fled the UK to Germany in 1939 and served as a Nazi propaganda broadcaster to the UK.
66. HC Deb 18 March 2019, c261WH.
67. HC Deb 18 February 2019, c1201 (MP John Woodcock).
68. HC Deb 18 March 2019, c251WH (MP John Woodcock).
69. The Times 2019.
70. Prosecution of the ISIS fighters before the International Criminal Court was also not feasible. ICC 2015.
71. The Times 2019. See also Boyes 2019.
72. Hamilton and Simpson 2018.
73. Maher 2019; Sabbagh 2019.
74. Goldman, Schmitt, and Savage 2018; Savage and Goldman 2019 and 2020.

75. The UK held its last execution in 1964. In 1969, capital punishment was abolished for murder; in 1998, it was abolished for the few remaining offenses to which it applied. In 1999, the UK joined the Second Optional Protocol to the International Covenant on Civil and Political Rights, Aiming at the Abolition of the Death Penalty; in 2004, the 13th protocol of the European Convention on Human Rights—requiring the abolition of the death penalty in all circumstances—came into force for the UK.
76. HC Deb 11 October 2018, c298.
77. HC Deb 11 October 2018, c294.
78. HC Deb 11 October 2018, c295.
79. The Times 2018; Dodd and Elgot 2018.
80. HC Deb 11 October 2018, cc293–295, 298.
81. Bowcott 2020. See *Elgizouli v Secretary of State for the Home Department* [2020] UKSC 10, judgment of 25 March 2020.
82. Savage 2020.
83. Casciani 2018.
84. HOPE not hate 2019, 22. According to another study, 25.9% of the British public holds negative feelings toward Muslims. Jones and Unsworth 2022.
85. Boyes 2019.
86. Onishi and Peltier 2019.
87. Spencer 2019.
88. Rubin 2019a.
89. Rubin 2019b.
90. Rubin 2019a.

SECTION III

EXTRADITION

5

The Dilemma of Extradition to China

Criminal justice potentially raises serious human rights concerns. From lack of due process through harsh interrogation techniques to excessive punishment and poor prison conditions—the criminal justice process is prone to abuses that may affect the life, liberty, and physical integrity of individuals.[1] In the previous section, we saw how these concerns play out in the context of a jurisdictional overlap between countries. The current chapter moves us into a different realm in which these concerns often arise: international extradition. A key tool of cooperation against crime, extradition places an individual in the hands of a foreign legal system whose commitment to human rights may be weaker than one's own. A country that respects human rights might find itself surrendering a person to a country that uses torture or the death penalty or lacks due process.

But how exactly do states think about human rights in policymaking on extradition? How do they assess the human rights record of the extradition-requesting country and how do they balance that record against other concerns, such as the desire to maintain friendly diplomatic relations? China's determined pursuit of extradition treaties with Western democratic countries brings these questions into sharp relief. By entering such treaties and helping China's anti-corruption campaign, these countries could boost their relations with a major power and an important trade partner. Yet this would come at a heavy price: agreeing to surrender a person to a legal system where human rights violations are pervasive and a fair trial is unlikely. How states handle this dilemma can teach us much about how cooperation between legal systems is established—or why it might fail.

We focus our analysis on two countries that have a strong human rights record: Australia and Canada.[2] A variety of actors in each country—including human rights groups, lawyers, the media, and certain politicians—maintained that extradition to China could not be reconciled with respect for human rights and had to be avoided. Yet the Australian and Canadian governments thought otherwise, arguing that an extradition relationship in no way required

Intolerant Justice. Asif Efrat, Oxford University Press. © Oxford University Press 2023.
DOI: 10.1093/oso/9780197658895.003.0005

equivalence between justice systems and Chinese assurances could be trusted. In 2016, the Australian government sought to ratify an extradition treaty with China, whereas the Canadian government announced its intention to begin negotiations over such a treaty. The domestic political debate over these initiatives sheds light on how differences between legal systems are interpreted by different actors. This debate also demonstrates that transnational litigation can be extremely contentious domestically, making cooperation difficult or even impossible.

Human Rights in the Extradition Process

Extradition is a central instrument of international cooperation in the suppression of crime. It prevents criminals from escaping justice by fleeing to a foreign country and facilitates the punishment of criminal conduct. At the heart of the extradition process stands an individual—a person whose surrender to a foreign country is requested in order for them to be criminally prosecuted or punished. Given the far-reaching implications of this process for the person whose extradition is requested, extradition treaties have traditionally included a set of safeguards. The political-offense exception allows states to refuse extradition when the purpose is to prosecute someone for a politically motivated crime; the principle of specialty guarantees that the extradited person will only be tried for the crime for which they were extradited; and the requirement of double criminality—namely, that the acts charged are criminalized by the laws of both countries involved in an extradition—ensures respect for the principle of *nullum crimen sine lege*.[3] Yet overall, respect for human rights used to play only a modest role in the traditional paradigm of extradition. The aforementioned rules and requirements, in fact, do not serve only—or even primarily—to secure the rights of the individual; they protect the interests of states as well. The political-offense rule, for example, allows the state from which extradition is requested to avoid becoming embroiled in a political dispute in the requesting state. Furthermore, other practices and procedures favor the requesting state and prevent the individual from invoking human rights concerns as a bar to extradition. Key among these is the rule of noninquiry, which forestalls the requested person from supplying evidence to show that they might face discrimination, an unfair legal process, or inhuman treatment in the requesting state. Indeed, this rule is not absolute and may not be followed in egregious cases.[4] Yet by and large, "[t]he assumption that the requesting state will give the fugitive a fair trial according to its laws underlies the whole theory and practice of extradition."[5] Such an assumption tilts extradition proceedings in favor of upholding the extradition request, and it reflects the primary interests and motivations underlying the traditional model of extradition: fighting crime; and facilitating friendly international relations, based on respect for state sovereignty. Respect for human rights occupies a much smaller role in this model.[6]

Yet the traditional model of extradition has been modified since the late 1980s, incorporating human rights as a central concern. Harbingers of this change appeared as early as the 1950s. The 1957 European Convention on Extradition allows extradition to be refused if the requesting state retains the death penalty and fails to provide assurances that this penalty will not be imposed if the person is extradited.[7] That same convention also bars extradition if the request "has been made for the purpose of prosecuting or punishing a person on account of his race, religion, nationality or political opinion, or [if] that person's position may be prejudiced for any of these reasons."[8] Yet it is the European Court of Human Rights' decision in the case of *Soering v. United Kingdom*[9] that is heralded as the human rights turn for extradition. In its 1989 decision, the court ruled that the extradition of a person who would be put on death row in the United States, taking into account the conditions and length of detention prior to execution, constituted inhuman or degrading treatment, in violation of Article 3 of the European Convention on Human Rights. The court further determined that the requested state would bear responsibility if it extradited the person despite the foreseeable rights violation.

Following *Soering*, human rights concerns have received growing emphasis in various treaties as well as in extradition legislation and case law. Examples abound. Article 3(f) of the 1990 UN Model Treaty on Extradition prohibits extradition if the person whose extradition is requested would be subjected in the requesting state to torture or inhuman treatment or if that person would not receive the minimum guarantees in criminal proceedings, as contained in Article 14 of the International Covenant on Civil and Political Rights (ICCPR). Article 19(2) of The Charter of Fundamental Rights of the European Union prohibits extradition if there is a serious risk that the person "would be subjected to the death penalty, torture or other inhuman or degrading treatment or punishment." Section 21 of Britain's Extradition Act, as amended in 2003, expressly links extradition to human rights: the judge is required to decide whether the requested person's extradition would be consistent with the European Convention on Human Rights within the meaning of the Human Rights Act 1998. Drawing on legislative provisions, constitutional safeguards, or general notions of fairness and justice, courts in various countries have considered human rights claims in extradition proceedings and at times refused to grant extradition on these grounds.[10]

Which human rights concerns might serve to block extradition? As extradition subjects the requested person to a criminal trial or punishment by a foreign legal system, it potentially threatens a variety of human rights. We may broadly distinguish between three sets of rights concerns.[11]

A common concern is that the extradited person might experience torture or some other kind of abusive treatment, such as harsh interrogation techniques, corporal punishment, or poor detention conditions. The aforementioned *Soering* case belongs in this category, as do other cases in which extradition was challenged on the grounds of detention conditions or execution methods.[12] Indeed, the Convention against Torture explicitly prohibits the extradition of a person to a country where they might be subjected to torture.[13]

Another concern that frequently arises is that the extradited person will not receive a fair trial. As noted above, the UN Model Treaty on Extradition requires the requesting state to provide minimum guarantees in criminal proceedings as stipulated by the ICCPR's Article 14. These include, among others, a fair and public hearing by an independent and impartial tribunal; a presumption of innocence; adequate time and facilities for the preparation of one's defense; a trial without undue delay; no compulsion to testify against oneself or to confess guilt; and a right to appeal the conviction and sentence. Also in this category of unfair trials are cases in which the prosecution or court in the requesting state might discriminate against the requested person or prejudge them on the basis of their race, nationality, or other factors.

The third set of concerns revolves around the excessive nature of the punishment. Most countries of the world have abolished the death penalty; and they tend to include provisions in their domestic legislation, as well as in international agreements they negotiate, to bar extradition to countries where the death penalty might be imposed—unless the requesting state provides assurances that such punishment will not be implemented.[14] Some countries also consider a life sentence to be excessive punishment. The Inter-American Convention on Extradition, for example, prohibits extradition if the death penalty, life imprisonment, or a degrading punishment might be imposed.[15]

As the following analysis will detail, the Chinese criminal justice system raises all three sets of concerns: abusive treatment, including the use of torture; unfair trials; and the death penalty. Should these concerns prevent the extradition of wanted persons to China? How should they be weighed against the competing interests that push in favor of extradition: the suppression of crime, as well as maintaining friendly international relations with a rising great power?[16] We turn to examining two countries' struggle with this dilemma.

China's Pursuit of Extradition Treaties with Western Countries

Chinese efforts to conclude extradition treaties with Western democracies began in the mid-2000s as part of the country's large-scale anti-corruption campaign. This campaign cracked down on government officials, executives of state-owned companies, high-ranking military officers, and other officeholders suspected of corruption. Some of them sought refuge abroad, prompting efforts by the Chinese government to seek their return—efforts which significantly intensified under President Xi Jinping and came to be known as Operation Fox Hunt. In some cases, the return of the wanted persons could be arranged on the basis of an extradition treaty. Beginning in 1993, China signed a set of extradition treaties with various countries, especially in the developing world, and could now use them to have persons surrendered from places such as Cambodia, Indonesia, and Uganda. Many of the wanted individuals, however, fled to Western countries, with the United States, Canada, and Australia the three most popular destinations.[17]

Western countries previously had refused to enter into extradition treaties with China, citing concerns about human rights violations and the unfairness of the Chinese justice system.[18] In the absence of extradition treaties, the Chinese government resorted to other instruments to bring about the return of wanted persons from these countries. "Persuasion"—in fact, coercion—served as a primary tool. Chinese agents entered the United States, Canada, and Australia, undercover, where they targeted wanted individuals with intimidation tactics, including threats to harm the person's family in China, and offered incentives, such as a promise of leniency if the person returned to China. Many of the wanted persons ultimately agreed to return to China "voluntarily."[19] Ad hoc extradition or deportation can also serve as alternatives to an extradition treaty. By handling individual surrenders on a case-by-case basis, the United States and Canada could exercise more control over the terms of the person's return and receive assurances regarding their treatment, without establishing a legal commitment to extradite.[20] One of the most notable cases of a non-treaty surrender of a wanted person involved Lai Changxing, the leader of a major smuggling ring, who was at the top of China's most-wanted list. Canada deported him in 2011, following several years of legal proceedings, after China promised that he would not be executed.[21] He was sentenced to life imprisonment.

The Chinese government recognized, however, that its anti-corruption campaign required a more efficient, streamlined, and reliable process of surrender from developed countries: "a global extradition net" of extradition treaties "to bring back corrupt officials who have fled abroad."[22] The first Western country to join this net was Spain.[23] Its extradition treaty with China was signed in November 2005 and entered into force in April 2007. In January 2007, China signed extradition treaties with France and Portugal. Whereas the treaty with Portugal came into force in July 2009, the one with France only entered into force in July 2015. The extradition treaty between China and Australia was signed in September 2007, but has not come into effect as of this writing. In

October 2010, China signed an extradition treaty with Italy, which entered into force in December 2015. In September 2016, Canada agreed to begin negotiating an extradition treaty with China, but no such treaty has been signed to date. Belgium signed an extradition treaty with China in 2018 and ratified it the following year.

Of the various countries with which China has sought to conclude an extradition treaty, we focus on Australia and Canada: two primary destinations for the individuals sought by the Chinese government. Furthermore, the two countries are committed to promoting human rights and the rule of law worldwide. Both countries have participated in and contributed to the international human rights regime since its inception in the aftermath of World War II, and their active involvement with the regime continues to this day.[24] This record should make Australia and Canada interesting sites for examining this book's argument: given their longstanding commitment to human rights, it would be difficult for these countries to accept criminal-justice cooperation with a country that is a flagrant violator of human rights. And indeed, the prospect of extradition to China created tensions and raised concerns in both countries. Each of the following case studies lays out the arguments made by the opponents of an extradition treaty with China, followed by the justifications that treaty defenders offered. Our goal is to provide a rich and nuanced picture of the domestic political conflict over extradition and to examine its consistency with this book's theoretical propositions.

Australia

As one of the primary destinations for the persons sought by Chinese authorities, Australia ranked high on China's priorities for an extradition treaty. Australia's expected benefits from the treaty were largely indirect: the treaty was supposed to enhance and improve Australia's relations with a major trade partner and a rising great power in Australia's neighborhood. It was also hoped that a commitment to return wanted persons to China would motivate Chinese authorities to stem the flow of illegal drugs from southern China to Australia.[25] Yet China's poor human rights record raised deep concerns, resulting in a considerable delay in the ratification of the extradition treaty by Australia. The treaty was signed on September 6, 2007, when the Liberals held power in Australia. It was quickly ratified by China's parliament—the National People's Congress—on April 24, 2008. Yet Australia's Labor government, which came to power in December 2007, shelved the treaty, and it was the Liberal government of Malcolm Turnbull that resurrected it and began the process of bringing it into force. The extradition treaty with China was tabled in Parliament on March 2, 2016, and brought before the Joint Standing Committee on Treaties for consideration.[26] A heated debate ensued, in the press and in Parliament.

The theoretical framework (Proposition 5) suggests that lawyers, attached to local legal rules and procedures, may resist cooperation on litigation. Consistent with this expectation, the staunchest opposition to the extradition treaty came from Australia's legal community, with lawyers accusing the government of attempting "to appease China, to gift it with a right of extradition and to abandon any citizen to the fate of a criminal justice system that lacks the most basic protections"[27]—an act of "supine compliance" motivated by the importance of the Chinese market for Australia.[28] The Law Council of Australia, which represents the legal profession at the national level, expressed the profession's collective view. In a scathing report, and before the Joint Standing Committee on Treaties, the Law Council highlighted the gap between Australia's commitment to the protection of human rights and the rampant violation of rights in China. While recognizing the need for an effective extradition regime, the Law Council emphasized that "Australia must adhere to fundamental rule of law principles and remain compliant with its international human rights obligations." The council, in fact, argued that ensuring respect for human rights in the administration of justice was a matter of national interest—to be balanced against the interest in enforcing laws and bringing criminals to justice. While suggesting that it did not oppose an extradition treaty between Australia and China per se, the council expressed serious concerns about China's respect for human rights, the rule of law, and procedural fairness in criminal proceedings, "rais[ing] questions about whether the proposed Treaty is indeed in Australia's national interest."[29]

The Law Council's litany of concerns included corruption within the Chinese judiciary; political interference, prejudgment, and bias in trials; denial of procedural fairness (due process), such as preventing challenges to evidence by not providing it to defendants; physical abuse of prisoners; the use of torture to extract confessions; and poor prison conditions. Of particular concern for the council was the ill-treatment of the legal profession in China, including denial of access to suspects for lawyers, detention and interrogation of lawyers, and revocation of lawyers' licenses. The council therefore concluded that a ratification of the extradition treaty "will be likely to expose a person extradited to denial of the right to a fair trial in China" and urged nonratification "in the absence of sufficiently robust protections to the right to a fair trial." The council particularly highlighted a safeguard that is often included in Australia's extradition treaties: the ability to refuse an extradition if it is unjust or oppressive—providing grounds for the refusal of extradition due to the denial of a fair trial. Yet the words "unjust or oppressive" were omitted from the Australia-China treaty.[30]

The Law Council also criticized the treaty's no-evidence approach, which means that an extradition request needs to be supported by a statement of the offense and the applicable penalty alongside a statement setting out the requested person's alleged conduct, but does not require evidence—such as witness statements—to prove the alleged offense. Such an approach, the council argued, was appropriate for rule-of-law democracies. "However, where there are very substantial concerns about the rule of law and the ability of a State to afford those charged with a criminal offence a right to a fair trial then the adoption of the 'no evidence rule' is very likely to compromise the human rights of an extradited person."[31]

Given these concerns, the Law Council made a set of recommendations, including several proposed treaty amendments and the establishment of a monitoring requirement to ensure that the extradited person is not subjected to the death penalty or torture. The council also highlighted the fact that China was not a member of the ICCPR and called on Australia to only ratify the extradition treaty subject to China ratifying the ICCPR or, at least, to encourage Chinese ratification of the ICCPR.[32] To further buttress its argument, the Council pointed out that most Western countries had been unwilling to enter into bilateral extradition treaties with China.[33]

Consistent with the theoretical framework (Proposition 4), the NGO community—especially Amnesty International Australia—joined the legal community's criticism and condemnation of the proposed treaty. While acknowledging that the treaty contained human rights safeguards—including the refusal of extradition due to the possible imposition of the death penalty or the use of torture—Amnesty questioned the effectiveness of these safeguards (consistent with Proposition 9). One cause of concern for Amnesty was the secrecy that shrouds executions in China. According to Amnesty, China likely executes thousands of people every year—including for economic crimes—yet very little information about these executions was available. This would undermine any Chinese assurances regarding the non-imposition of the death penalty on extradited persons: "How would Australia monitor to ensure the Chinese government is upholding its undertaking? . . . Without this transparency, diplomatic assurances regarding the death penalty may not be reliable, effective, and enforceable." Amnesty also invoked Australia's opposition to the death penalty and its advocacy for the abolition of that penalty worldwide: "[T]his treaty's ratification could undermine Australia's unequivocal opposition to the death penalty."[34]

Amnesty further questioned the effectiveness of the treaty's bar against extradition due to the possibility of torture or abusive treatment. Given the high prevalence of torture and other ill-treatment in the Chinese legal system, Amnesty argued, it would be extremely difficult to ensure that extradited persons were not mistreated, and any assurances from the Chinese government would be insufficient. Other attributes of China's legal system also raised Amnesty's concern: a non-independent judiciary; the inability to access legal counsel, especially in politically sensitive cases; and forced "confessions"—all these, as per Amnesty, cast doubt on the likelihood of a fair trial for the extradited person.[35]

The theoretical framework (Proposition 5) has posited that jurists in the state apparatus, seeking to facilitate crossborder law enforcement, may *support* cooperation on litigation. Consistent with this expectation, the Attorney-General's Department (AGD) set out to defend the proposed treaty with China and push for its ratification. This push began with the department's National Interest Analysis (NIA), which explained why Australia should bring the treaty into effect. According to the NIA, the treaty would promote Australia's ability to combat domestic and international crime through a responsive, streamlined extradition system; specifically, it would facilitate closer cooperation between law-enforcement authorities in China and Australia and assist their efforts to bring criminals to justice. The NIA further highlighted the treaty's consistency with Australia's domestic extradition arrangements under the Extradition Act and the "range of human rights safeguards" that the treaty included: extradition must be refused if the extradited person might be subjected to torture or other inhuman treatment; if the extradition is sought for a political offense or for prosecuting the person on account of their religion or political opinion; or if the offense for which extradition is sought carries the death penalty—unless the requesting state promises that the death penalty will not be implemented. These safeguards, according to the NIA, were consistent with Australia's international human rights law obligations. Also consistent with international standards, the NIA maintained, was the treaty's adoption of the no-evidence rule for extradition requests: such a simplified evidentiary approach conformed to the UN Model Treaty on Extradition and to other extradition treaties that Australia had signed,[36] and a more rigorous evidentiary standard was unnecessary.[37]

Before the Joint Standing Committee on Treaties, representatives of the AGD emphasized that the treaty did not provide an automatic process for extradition and continued to insist that its safeguards guaranteed adequate human rights protection (consistent with Proposition 9). In particular, they argued that the treaty, in conjunction with the Extradition Act, did provide a basis for refusing extradition if the extradited person might not receive a fair trial—for example, through the exercise of authority under the act to refuse an extradition based on any relevant circumstances.[38] Furthermore, the Australian government could require Chinese authorities to provide fair-trial assurances on a case-by-case basis. AGD representatives indeed expressed confidence in the credibility of Chinese assurances not to carry out the death penalty or use torture, if such concerns arose in specific cases. Whereas the Law Council warned that such assurances were not enforceable—indeed, "a joke"—the AGD insisted that noncompliance would carry consequences and would negatively affect anti-crime cooperation between the two countries as well as the broader bilateral relationship. "It would be quite extraordinary if a country were to breach an undertaking that it had made on a government-to-government basis."[39]

Overall, the AGD maintained that human rights concerns did receive considerable weight in extradition decisions and that "extradition relationships in no way require equivalence between justice systems . . . there is no requirement that another country apply the same standards as Australia." Herein the AGD expressed its view on what is the primary bone of contention in transnational-litigation controversies: Does cooperation on litigation require similarity of legal standards and practices between the partners? Or can legal systems cooperate irrespective of the differences between them? An actor that tends to favor cooperation, the AGD supported the latter position. And it did not stand alone. In its defense of the proposed treaty with China, the AGD received support from the Department of Foreign Affairs and Trade (consistent with Proposition 6).[40] Foreign-affairs ministries, as we have already seen in Chapter 3, appreciate the diplomatic gains that legal cooperation may yield and are less sensitive to dissimilarities in legal standards among partners.

In the course of two parliamentary hearings on the treaty, members of the Joint Standing Committee on Treaties made comments and asked questions that reflected the conflicting incentives: crime suppression versus human rights protection. MP Brett Whiteley (Liberal) expressed discomfort with a position that placed human rights above the need to fight crime and might result in the harboring of criminals:

> The price we pay is to provide safe haven indefinitely to someone who we are 90 percent sure has committed a crime. Because they are going to be subjected to the death penalty or whatever it might be from the list you have given us, we will just provide protection and haven and we will not agree to extraditions. It is a pretty high price to pay for our community.[41]

Other committee members, however, expressed concern about extradition to a country that did not observe the rule of law and did not guarantee a fair trial, where executions are shrouded in secrecy: "[H]ow could we as a government be assured that . . . [the death penalty] will not in fact be carried out and hidden from us?"[42] MP Michael Danby (Labor) asked pointedly:

> When did we change, from the system of never extraditing people or having arrangements with countries that had these peculiar judicial systems, to the belief that our principal ethical attitude ought to be that we are determined not to allow people to evade justice by being in another

> jurisdiction? . . . Are you saying now that Australia takes a value-free attitude towards a country like China, where, if they say they are not going to execute the person, we do not make any judgment about their whole judicial system before we contemplate making such an arrangement, such a treaty with them?[43]

The committee's report, submitted in December 2016, demonstrated a similar duality, emphasizing that "Australia does not wish to become a safe haven" for criminals, but also that cooperation against crime should not come at the expense of human rights. Given the lack of transparency in the Chinese legal system and its use of the death penalty and torture, the committee found the treaty's grounds for refusing extradition insufficient and argued that "more needs to be done to take into consideration the conditions existing within the [Chinese] system as a whole in order to strengthen the protection of individual human rights." To that effect, the committee made a set of recommendations. It recommended that extradition decisions should take into account governmental and nongovernmental reports on human rights and the rule of law in China's criminal justice system; that undertakings to provide a fair and open trial should be routinely included in agreements to surrender an individual to China; and that the Australian government should enhance its monitoring of the welfare of individuals post-extradition. Subject to these recommendations, the committee expressed support for the treaty and recommended its ratification.[44]

The members of the committee from Labor—the opposition party—did not join the latter recommendation. In a dissenting report, they argued that Australia's legislative framework for extradition provided inadequate human rights protection—and that these general concerns took on particular potency in the context of the treaty with China. In particular, the dissenting members emphasized the treaty's omission of an important safeguard: the ability to refuse an extradition request that is unjust or oppressive. They agreed with the Law Council that this omission cast doubt on the ability to refuse extradition due to fair-trial concerns. Whereas the AGD's defense of the treaty highlighted the assurances that China may be asked to provide in the extradition process, the dissenting Labor members argued that "Australia has a moral obligation to protect the human rights of extradited persons beyond simply accepting the undertakings of countries making extradition requests." In light of these doubts and concerns, they recommended that ratification of the treaty be delayed until after a review of Australia's extradition arrangements to ensure adequate protection of the rule of law and human rights.[45]

The government accepted some of the committee's recommendations while rejecting the dissenting report's call for a review of the country's extradition arrangements prior to ratification of the treaty.[46] In March 2017, preparing to ratify the treaty, the government tabled in Parliament the regulations required to bring the treaty into effect—only to meet an unexpected revolt. The Labor party and the Greens refused to back the treaty, and several members of the Liberal party—the ruling party—threatened to withhold their support as well. Another prominent Liberal voice—former Prime Minister Tony Abbott—argued against the treaty: "In my judgment, China's legal system has to evolve further before the Australian government and people could be confident that those before it would receive justice according to law."[47] This backlash against the treaty was inspired, at least partly, by the case of Chongyi Feng which took place at the same time. A Chinese-born professor working at an Australian university and critical of China, Feng was held and questioned by Chinese authorities on a trip there—reinforcing doubts about China's legal system.[48] Ultimately, the government had to cancel the parliamentary vote and withdraw the treaty, while vowing to continue working on ratification.[49] Foreign Minister Julie Bishop came out forcefully in defense of the treaty and denounced ratification opponents. She argued that "It is in Australia's national interest to ensure that we can send back to China those who have committed crimes, subject to the significant safeguards that we have in place."[50] Yet, as of this writing, Australia has failed to ratify its extradition treaty with China, and the treaty has not gone into effect.

Using their own human rights standards as a metric, Australians found the Chinese legal system inadequate and thus an inappropriate partner for extradition relations. A similar dynamic scuttled a proposed extradition treaty between China and Canada at an even earlier phase: before the treaty even came into existence.

Canada

While Canada had occasionally cooperated on a case-by-case basis with China's efforts to repatriate suspects,[51] Beijing sought to replace such ad hoc cooperation with a formal extradition agreement. In September 2016, shortly after Canadian Prime Minister Justin Trudeau's visit to Beijing, Canada and China agreed to begin negotiations over a bilateral extradition treaty.[52] The news about the intended treaty met with wariness and skepticism in Canada, generating a barrage of criticism from human rights advocates, lawyers, academics, the media, and politicians outside the ruling Liberal party. The points made by the critics echoed those raised by their Australian counterparts. It was argued that China is "a country where trials are politicized, confessions are secured through torture, defence lawyers are harassed and detained, and the death penalty is applied for a wide variety of crimes"—including white-collar crimes. In the absence of due process and fair-trial rights, "Defendants in China have no opportunity to challenge the 'evidence' against them. The Canadian government, or a Canadian judge, would be similarly unable to evaluate the evidence behind an extradition request. By negotiating a treaty, the Canadian government is indicating a willingness to take Chinese prosecutors at their word."[53] It was also argued that persons requested by China may actually be political dissidents, rather than criminals.[54]

In another similarity to the Australian debate, Canadian critics doubted the effectiveness of Canadian monitoring of extradited persons. Canadian authorities, they suggested, would lack the capacity to monitor transferred suspects to make sure they were not abused or executed.[55] Critics also suggested that Chinese assurances were not credible and should not be believed: after all, China had ratified the Convention against Torture yet continued to engage in torture.[56] One commentator claimed that "[s]ince the rule of law in China is a sham," Chinese promises not to carry out the death penalty "would hardly be worth a red yuan."[57] Ultimately, argued a prominent lawyer, Canada could not accept the Chinese justice system as fair "when it is manifestly not so."[58] The popular newspaper *The Globe and Mail* declared: "Our courts and government could find themselves regularly asked to ship offenders across the Pacific to the care of a legal system that does not meet our standards."[59]

Critics also repudiated the argument that an extradition treaty would motivate China to improve its human rights practices: "Prime Minister Justin Trudeau is naive if he thinks an extradition treaty with China could respect human rights. He is even more naive if he thinks that, by negotiating such a treaty, he can exert a positive influence on China—somehow forcing police, prosecutors and judges there to comply with international norms."[60] Furthermore, the result would be to betray Canada's own ideals and commitments. According to Amnesty International Canada, "It's impossible to imagine how you would have an extradition treaty that would line up with Canada's obligations to not send people to face the death penalty."[61] Conservative MP Jason Kenney argued that an extradition treaty with China would breach the Canadian Charter of Rights and Freedoms and give a seal of approval to China's judicial system where executions, torture, and political imprisonment were rife—in violation of Canada's belief in the rule of law and human rights.[62] By entering into an extradition treaty, Canada would damage its reputation as a defender of human rights and "ensnare [itself] in the controversial workings of an audacious Chinese global dragnet."[63] It would strengthen China's hand, while failing to protect Canadian interests and values.[64]

Critics also questioned the benefits that Canada would reap from the treaty, arguing that it would primarily benefit China.[65] Conservative MP Rona Ambrose, leader of the opposition, called the government's approach "shockingly naive" and exhorted Liberal Prime Minister Trudeau: "Canadians expect the prime minister to act in our national interest. What possible benefit to Canada would an extradition [treaty] with China provide us?"[66] Others charged that an extradition treaty with China would not serve to enhance Canadian law enforcement. Instead, it aimed to achieve quite different goals. At the immediate level, critics argued, Canada had promised the extradition treaty as a quid pro quo in exchange for the release of a Canadian missionary who had been jailed in China on trumped-up spying charges (this was denied by the Canadian government).[67] More broadly, the treaty was a bargaining chip for trade access: "China will promise to open up its markets to our goods and services to a larger extent than they are open now."[68]

Treaty opponents pointed to peer countries—the United States, Britain, Australia, and New Zealand—which had not established extradition treaties with China. According to the popular daily *The Star*, "All these countries prize judicial independence and the rule of law, and aren't prepared to turn Chinese citizens accused of economic or political crimes over to the vagaries of that country's legal system." The Canadian government should follow these countries, or run "the risk of making Canada complicit in the worst aspects of China's inconsistent, politicized and often brutal judicial system."[69] According to Human Rights Watch, a treaty with Canada would provide China with "a veneer of legality for fundamentally abusive tactics. Beijing will then also be able to say to other governments, 'Canada signed one, why won't you.' "[70]

Defenders of the treaty made several arguments. The Ministry of Foreign Affairs said that the promotion and protection of human rights were a priority in Canada's relationship with China and that the extradition discussions emphasized Canada's high standards.[71] Prime Minister Trudeau similarly highlighted Canada's "extremely high standards on extradition treaties," which the treaty with China would maintain, as well as the "very, very rigorous process that conforms with the expectations and the values of Canadians." He suggested that a fugitive facing the death penalty would not be extradited to China.[72]

Treaty supporters also pointed out that Canada had extradition treaties with other countries that practice the death penalty, including the United States, as well as countries whose human rights record was weaker than Canada's. They noted that other rule-of-law countries, including France and Spain, had signed an extradition treaty with China.[73]

Another line of argument highlighted the treaty's benefits for Canada. At the broader level, Prime Minister Trudeau emphasized, the extradition treaty was meant to be a part of a high-level security dialogue that would enhance Canada's relations with China.[74] Other benefits included the establishment of a firm and transparent legal framework to deal with China's surrender requests—a move that could facilitate Canadian-Chinese cooperation in other areas; preventing Canada from serving as a safe haven for corrupt Chinese officials and laundered money; and sending a message of Canadian commitment to the rule of law and the fight against corruption. Whereas critics argued that the treaty would do little to raise China's human rights standards, supporters argued that "it will have helped nudge China closer to international judicial standards" and "move [China] into the international law arena."[75] They suggested that it was better to engage with China on the basis of Canadian interests and values, rather than "decrying the Chinese system, but doing nothing about it."[76]

Given the political controversy, however, the Canadian government hesitated to formally begin discussions on the treaty. In early April 2017, Canada's ambassador to China declared that "We are a long, long way from negotiations, let alone agreeing to such an agreement."[77] It is possible that Australia's repudiation of its treaty with China in March 2017 gave Canada pause. As *The Globe and Mail* declared, "Australia's stern rebuke to China serves as a warning to Canada and other Western countries about the merits of co-operating with an autocratic regime whose judicial system condones torture and is susceptible to political interference."[78]

Conclusion

What does the dilemma of extradition to China tell us about the politics of transnational litigation? For a start, the pair of cases examined here show how contentious that politics can be. While transnational legal issues might seem arcane and technical, at times they generate fierce controversy and fuel a heated public debate. In fact, the Australian and Canadian controversies seem tame compared to a far more contentious conflict over extradition to China, and one that captured global attention: the struggle over Hong Kong's extradition bill. In February 2019, the government of Hong Kong proposed a bill to amend Hong Kong's extradition legislation in a way that would allow extradition to China on a case-by-case basis (thus reversing a ban on extradition to the Chinese mainland). The introduction of the legislative proposal met heavy criticism from a variety of domestic groups. Hong Kong's business community, legal community, and human rights organizations expressed concerns about significant differences in trial fairness and human rights between Hong Kong and mainland China and about the potential use of extradition as a tool to intimidate and silence critics of China.[79] These concerns ultimately inspired a series of mass marches during the summer of 2019. Hundreds of thousands of Hong Kong residents came out against the bill in huge protests that sometimes escalated into clashes with the police.[80] These protests bore fruit. On September 4, the Hong Kong government announced the withdrawal of the proposed extradition bill.[81] In Hong Kong, as in Australia and Canada, the incompatibility between the local legal system and China's system was too great for domestic constituencies to tolerate.

The controversy over Hong Kong gave Australia and Canada another opportunity to demonstrate their commitment to human rights as trumping the surrender of criminal suspects to China. On June 30, 2020, China imposed on Hong Kong a new national security law aimed at stamping out opposition to the ruling Communist Party in the former British colony. Indeed, the vaguely worded offenses that the law included—separatism, subversion, terrorism, and collusion with foreign countries—can easily be used to target anti-China activists. The law also gave Beijing broad authority to intervene in Hong Kong's legal system and opened the way for defendants in important cases to stand trial before courts in mainland China.[82] As the legal systems of Hong Kong and China became more closely intertwined, Canada and Australia responded swiftly by suspending their extradition treaties with Hong Kong (the Australia-Hong Kong and Canada-Hong Kong treaties were signed in 1993, prior to the 1997 transfer of the territory from Britain to China).[83]

The Australian and Canadian debates over extradition to China demonstrate several of this book's propositions. At the center of those debates stood the incongruity in values and legal practices between the home systems of Australia and Canada on the one hand and the foreign Chinese system on the other. That incongruity was seen as potentially endangering those individuals who might come under China's jurisdiction following their extradition (consistent with Proposition 1). Note that these individuals are primarily *Chinese nationals*, rather than Australians or Canadians. This serves as an important corrective to this book's theory, which focuses on concerns for one's own nationals under foreign legal authority and has suggested that concerns will be weaker as regards noncitizens (Proposition 8). The current case demonstrates that legal ethnocentrism does not arise only from the subjection of local citizens to foreign law. Matters involving foreign nationals may also fuel ethnocentric sentiments of attachment to one's legal system and denunciation of a foreign system. Legal ethnocentrism, in other words, is not necessarily about the protection of local citizens from foreign law; it is also about protecting local law and values from foreign law and preventing the latter from tainting or undermining the former. In both Australia and Canada, extradition-treaty opponents expressed concern that the surrender of fugitives to China would betray their country's values and commitments, making it, in effect, complicit in rights violation. Throughout the debates in both countries, the metric for assessing the Chinese legal system was human rights as understood and practiced in the West, rather than China's interpretation and application of human rights (consistent with Proposition 2).[84]

The variation in preferences among domestic actors generally conforms to the theoretical expectations. In both Australia and Canada, the ministry of foreign affairs—tasked with fostering friendly international relations—supported the establishment of a treaty that would enhance relations with China (consistent with Proposition 6). In Australia, the AGD—responsible for law enforcement—threw its support behind a treaty that was supposed to improve the country's ability to tackle domestic and international crime (Proposition 5). NGOs, as expected, came out strongly against the proposed treaties, questioning whether any person surrendered to China would receive a fair trial and warning that such a surrender might violate Australia's and Canada's international human rights obligations (Proposition 4). Australia's Law Council, representing the legal profession and protective of local legal norms and practices, similarly abhorred the violation of rule-of-law and human rights principles that extradition to China entails: "The rule of law which is fundamental here in Australia is not understood in the same way in China"[85] (Proposition 5). And the opposition parties, both in Australia and Canada, also made the case against the proposed treaties, charging that the government was trying to curry favor with China at the price of undermining fundamental values (Proposition 3). Indeed, the proposed treaties provided ammunition for the opposition to criticize the government and accuse it of hypocrisy or naivety. Importantly, left- and right-wing parties stood on opposite sides of the divide in the two cases. In Australia, it was the right-wing government led by the Liberals that sought to ratify the extradition treaty against Labor's opposition. In Canada, however, it was the right-wing Conservatives who led the charge against a left-leaning government that contemplated the negotiation of an extradition treaty with China. This demonstrates that legal ethnocentrism does *not* necessarily correlate with partisanship and is not limited to the right-wing side of the political spectrum. Leftist politicians may also denounce cooperation on litigation that, in their view, undermines national values and practices.

Proponents and opponents of extradition to China differed on certain key points. Opponents emphasized China's lower standards of justice and argued that an association with them would inevitably taint the home legal system and undermine its own values, such as the commitment to the abolition of the death penalty. Proponents, by contrast, argued that extradition to China need not compromise the home system's commitment to human rights and may, in fact, serve to narrow the gap between the two systems, since it would push China closer to international legal standards. Another key disagreement concerned the credibility of Chinese assurances. Whereas extradition proponents argued that such assurances and safeguards would protect the rights of individuals surrendered to China, opponents dismissed them as unenforceable and meaningless (Proposition 9). Note the striking similarity to the debate over the NATO SOFA's fair-trial guarantees, as described in Chapter 3.

What was the impact of the broader political climate on the extradition controversy? It seems quite clear that the Australian and Canadian governments saw the extradition treaties as a means to enhance their relations and engagement with a rising China. They expected to reap trade and other benefits by delivering the fugitives that China wanted to lay its hands on. It is harder, however, to pinpoint whether opposition to the treaty was motivated by concerns over the rise of China. Both Australia and Canada have reasons to worry about China's growing power and influence, since both countries belong in the U.S.-led camp of Western democracies and are military allies of the United States.[86] The growing economic dependence of these countries on China has also caused alarm.[87] Furthermore, both countries, Australia in particular, have been facing Chinese efforts to influence and interfere in their domestic political arenas.[88] Such concerns may indeed have amplified the objections to criminal-justice cooperation with China. But these objections, at their core, were fueled by a commitment to the fundamental values of the local legal system and reluctance to sell them out for the sake of foreign-policy gains.

This chapter has demonstrated the critical importance of domestic politics in shaping extradition policy: governments that sought to enter extradition treaties came under a barrage of domestic criticism which ultimately thwarted them from achieving their goal. This is consistent with this book's emphasis of the domestic contention underlying international cooperation on litigation. This domestic focus, however, contrasts with much of the existing analysis of international extradition, which overlooks domestic politics.[89] The following chapter shows that a domestic-politics frame centered on ethnocentric sentiments is also useful for understanding the controversial evolution of Britain's extradition policy.

Notes

1. Emmerson, Ashworth, and MacDonald 2012.
2. For example, in the 2021 *Freedom in the World Report*, Freedom House gave Australia an overall score of 97/100 for its human rights record; Canada received a score of 98/100.
3. Sadoff 2016, chaps. 5, 7.
4. Dugard and Van den Wyngaert 1998, 188–191.
5. Argentina v. Mellino, [1987] 1 S.C.R. 536, 554–555 (Canadian Supreme Court).
6. Dugard and Van den Wyngaert 1998, 189; de Felipe and Martín 2012, 590.
7. European Convention on Extradition, Article 11.
8. European Convention on Extradition, Article 3(2).
9. 161 Eur. Ct. H.R. (ser. A) (1989).
10. For example, Magee v. O'Dea [1994] 1 I.R. 500 (Ireland, H. Ct); Norris v. United States of America [2010] UKSC 9.
11. Dugard and Van den Wyngaert 1998, 195–205; Sadoff 2016, chap. 7.
12. For example, Ng v. Canada, Communication No. 469/1991, U.N. Doc. CCPR/C/49/D/469/1991 (1994) (Human Rights Committee).
13. Convention against Torture and Other Cruel, Inhuman, or Degrading Treatment or Punishment, Article 3(1).

14. Sadoff 2016, 307. See, for example, Israel's Extradition Law, Article 16; Extradition Treaty between the Government of the United States of America and the Government of the United Kingdom (2003), Article 7.
15. Inter-American Convention on Extradition, Article 9.
16. de Felipe and Martín 2012, 590.
17. China Daily 2006; Wee 2014.
18. Bloom 2008.
19. Vanderklippe 2016; Lipkowitz 2019, 454–455.
20. Bloom 2008, 199–202; Choo 2018.
21. Wee 2011.
22. China Daily 2006. See Lipkowitz 2019, 455–457.
23. The extradition treaty with Spain was preceded by extradition treaties with three Eastern European countries: Bulgaria, Romania, and Lithuania.
24. For example, Australia served on the UN Human Rights Council during 2018–2020. For an overview of Australia's approach to international human rights, see Department of Foreign Affairs and Trade n.d. Canada is involved in a variety of international human rights initiatives, including in the areas of gender equality, freedom of religion, LGBT rights, and persons with disabilities (Government of Canada 2020).
25. Smyth 2016.
26. Wen 2016; Joint Standing Committee on Treaties 2016c, 19.
27. Lennox 2017.
28. Patterson 2017.
29. Law Council of Australia 2016, 3–4.
30. Law Council of Australia 2016, 3, 6–10, 11–13.
31. Law Council of Australia 2016, 18.
32. Law Council of Australia 2016, 27–29.
33. Byrnes 2016.
34. Amnesty International Australia 2016. On Australia's international strategy for the abolition of the death penalty, see Department of Foreign Affairs and Trade 2018.
35. Amnesty International Australia 2016.
36. Attorney-General's Department 2016.
37. Joint Standing Committee on Treaties 2016a, 13 and 2016b, 5.
38. Extradition Act, Section 22(3)(f).
39. Joint Standing Committee on Treaties 2016a, 8, 12–16 and 2016b, 3, 6, 8, 14, 16–17.
40. Joint Standing Committee on Treaties 2016a, 14 and 2016b, 8, 10.
41. Joint Standing Committee on Treaties 2016a, 10.
42. Joint Standing Committee on Treaties 2016b, 16 (MP Andrew Wallace (Liberal)).
43. Joint Standing Committee on Treaties 2016b, 8–9.
44. Joint Standing Committee on Treaties 2016c, 35–36, 38–39.
45. Joint Standing Committee on Treaties 2016d, Art. 1.6, 1.8–1.14, 1.19–1.21, 1.27.
46. Callick 2017.
47. Murphy 2017a, b.
48. Riordan 2017.
49. Murphy 2017a, b.
50. Cave 2017.
51. Zhao 2016, 115–117.
52. Levin 2016.
53. Byers 2016; Fife 2016; Tremonti 2016 (interviewing political science professor and former diplomat Charles Burton).
54. Capaln 2016.
55. Byers 2016; Fife 2016; Tremonti 2016; *The Star* Editorial 2016.
56. Byers 2016; Tremonti 2016; Vanderklippe 2016.
57. Caplan 2016.
58. Chase and Fife 2016 (lawyer David Matas).
59. *Globe and Mail* Editorial 2016.
60. Byers 2016.

61. Russell 2016.
62. Chase and Fife 2016; Kupfer 2016.
63. Byers 2016; Vanderklippe 2016.
64. Levin 2016.
65. *Globe and Mail* Editorial 2016.
66. Kupfer 2016.
67. Fife 2016; *The Star* Editorial 2016; Levin 2016.
68. Tremonti 2016.
69. *The Star* Editorial 2016; Kupfer 2016.
70. Levin 2016.
71. Levin 2016.
72. Kupfer 2016; *The Star* Editorial 2016; Vanderklippe 2016; Chase and Fife 2016.
73. Duhaime 2016; Stephens 2016.
74. Chase and Fife 2016; Kupfer 2016.
75. Stephens 2016; Tremonti 2016; Vanderklippe 2016.
76. Stephens 2016.
77. Vanderklippe 2017.
78. Chase, Fife, and Vanderklippe 2017.
79. Hong Kong Bar Association 2019; Creery 2019; Justice Centre Hong Kong 2019; Lam 2019; Law Society of Hong Kong 2019.
80. Ives and May 2019; Griffiths, Regan, and Cheung 2019.
81. Ramzy and Yu 2019.
82. Hernández 2020.
83. Kuo 2020; Ramzy 2020.
84. On the Chinese understanding of human rights, see Civic 1995.
85. Dziedzic 2016 (citing president of the Law Council of Australia Stuart Clark).
86. Thayer 2011; Manicom and O'Neil 2012; Tow and Envall 2015.
87. Laurenceson and Zhou 2019.
88. Diamond and Schell 2019; Cave 2019.
89. Magnuson 2012, 839.

6

Extradition Reconsidered

The British Debate

After the reform of the Extradition Act in 2003 and the signing of a new extradition treaty with the United States that same year, international extradition fueled a long and intense public debate in Britain. The analysis of this controversy serves to reinforce some of the points that the debate on extradition to China demonstrated: doubts regarding the fairness of cooperation on litigation in light of a perceived gap between the home and foreign legal systems and wide variation across actors in their assessment of the magnitude and implications of that gap. At the same time, the present analysis shows that concerns about extradition may arise irrespective of the identity of the specific partner and their legal standards: it is the very act of surrendering legal authority to a foreign system that might generate resentment. While the debate about China raised a problem of legal incongruity vis-à-vis a specific country—China's norms and practices were deemed inconsistent with human rights and the rule of law—the British debate exhibits specific concerns about justice in the United States and the European Union, alongside a broader concern about legal delegation: a sense that no foreign legal institution can be trusted with the authority to prosecute British citizens.

The British extradition debate also serves as a hard case for this book's arguments on the role of ethnocentrism in transnational litigation. First, Britain is an unlikely setting for a controversy regarding extradition, since it is a country that generally adheres to the rule of law, with a long history of extradition relations dating back to the late eighteenth century. In fact, Britain has traditionally shown a stronger commitment to the idea of extradition than most European countries. Whereas the civil-law countries of Europe have typically restricted or prohibited the extradition of their citizens, Britain has surrendered its own citizens.[1] Given Britain's longstanding support for extradition, one would not have expected extradition policy to trigger an intense political debate and public

Intolerant Justice. Asif Efrat, Oxford University Press. © Oxford University Press 2023.
DOI: 10.1093/oso/9780197658895.003.0006

outcry. Yet the 2003 reform of the Extradition Act to implement the European Arrest Warrant (EAW), alongside the new extradition treaty with the United States, spawned a heated public debate that lasted until 2015, encompassing several official inquiries, numerous parliamentary discussions, acts of public protest, and extensive media coverage. Second, the identity of the partner countries makes the controversy unlikely. It is not difficult to understand why extradition to China—a non-Western, authoritarian country that violates human rights—was anathema to many in Australia and Canada. It is harder to envision extradition concerns arising with regard to Western, democratic, rule-of-law countries such as the United States and EU member states. Such concerns are particularly surprising in the U.S.-UK dyad. Both rooted in the common law, the British and American justice systems are in many respects similar, and they share various concepts, principles, and procedures. Indeed, American law evolved from English law.[2] If we would ever expect cooperation on litigation to flow smoothly, it is between Britain and the United States. This chapter will show, however, that this is far from the case. In fact, the U.S.-UK extradition treaty met significant public concern and criticism. Critics charged that American justice standards fall below Britain's legal standards and that this gap should inspire great caution in the extradition of British nationals. Indeed, legal systems that look quite similar to an outside observer can seem remarkably different to an ethnocentric insider.

Britain's Extradition Debate: Four Controversies

At the center of the controversy stood the Extradition Act 2003, which was passed to modernize and streamline the way in which extradition requests submitted to Britain are processed. This reform arose from concerns about the complexity of then-existing extradition arrangements and the delay they caused, which rendered them inadequate as crime had become increasingly global.[3] The establishment of the European Arrest Warrant in 2002 and the need to incorporate it into British law provided another trigger for the 2003 reform.

The EAW creates a fast-track procedure for extradition between EU members, based on the principle of mutual recognition of judicial decisions—a principle that requires that a decision made by a judicial authority in one member state receive full and direct effect throughout the EU.[4] This means that, under the EAW, national judicial authorities must accept a foreign warrant—a request for the arrest and surrender of a person submitted through a standard form—without inquiring into the underlying facts and circumstances and should execute it within strict time limits. The EAW also removes various barriers to extradition and limits the grounds for refusal. Notably, it lacks a human rights safeguard: human rights violations are not included among the mandatory or optional grounds for the non-execution of the EAW.[5] The EAW also limits political involvement in extradition. Traditionally, the executive branch possesses the authority to block extradition ordered by the courts. The EAW's system of surrender, however, relies on courts alone, with minimal formality and no involvement of the executive branch. Furthermore, the EAW removes the nationality exception. While most civil-law countries of Europe restrict or prohibit the extradition of their own citizens,[6] the EAW requires EU members to surrender their citizens.[7]

The 2003 Extradition Act established a new extradition regime for Britain. Part 1 of the act implements the EAW and lays out a simplified procedure for dealing with extradition to Category 1 territories—in effect, EU member states. Part 2 of the act deals with extradition to Category 2 territories—countries outside the EU with which Britain has extradition arrangements—and simplifies the extradition process to those as well. One of those Category 2 countries is the United States, with which Britain signed a new extradition treaty in 2003. Criticism of that treaty and of the Extradition Act began during the act's legislative process and escalated over time, fueled by a growing number of high-profile, controversial cases of extradition. Amid rising public concern, in October 2010 the government appointed a panel, chaired by Sir Scott Baker, to review Britain's extradition arrangements (hereinafter the Baker Panel). The panel's mandate, defined by the government, laid out the four main points of contention. Two of those points reflected concerns about legal delegation: the very idea of transferring the authority to try British nationals to foreign courts. The two other points demonstrated concerns about legal incongruity: worries about the legal rules, procedures, and institutions of specific partners.

The first issue was an initiative to establish a "forum bar" as a barrier to extradition. Such a bar would allow a judge to refuse extradition if the alleged offence took place in Britain and Britain is determined to be the appropriate forum, that is the right place for a trial. Such a safeguard reflects a preference for trying British citizens at home and a reluctance to have them tried by a foreign judicial system.

The second issue concerned the home secretary's role. Whereas previously the home secretary had enjoyed significant discretion to block extradition, the 2003 act eliminated most of that authority. Indeed, one of the act's purposes was to increase the judiciary's role in the extradition process at the expense of the executive branch.[8] Critics, however, called for maintaining the home secretary's authority as a check on judicial power and a means to limit the delegation of legal authority over UK nationals to foreign courts.

The third set of concerns related to specific judicial systems—those of EU members—which, it was argued, were incongruous with British standards.

Critics suggested that in certain EU countries prison conditions were poor and the right to a fair trial was not fully guaranteed, casting doubt on the EAW's fairness (note that the British debate over extradition examined here took place before Britain left the EAW on December 31, 2020). The fourth set of concerns similarly revolved around a specific justice system: that of the United States. From the extensive use of plea bargains to broad extraterritorial jurisdiction—critics deplored American standards of justice as low, making extradition to the United States unjust.[9]

The debates around these four points of contention show a clear fault line. Consistent with Proposition 5, the strongest support for Britain's existing extradition arrangements came from the law-enforcement community. Members of that community—police, prosecutors, and judges—are responsible for the day-to-day operation of the extradition process. As such, they have firsthand experience with the challenges and dilemmas of extradition, and they recognize the value and effectiveness of extradition as a crime-fighting tool. Their mission—enforcing the law and bringing offenders to justice—leads members of the law-enforcement community to support swift, efficient extradition, even in the face of varying standards of justice across countries.[10] The following analysis contrasts this pro-extradition position with a view that is far more apprehensive about the liberalization of extradition arrangements and the removal of protections and safeguards. Proponents of this skeptical view included politicians (especially from the right), the media, members of the public, as well as three NGOs concerned with human rights in the justice system: Liberty, JUSTICE, and Fair Trials International.

The contrast between the two camps can be clearly seen by comparing the Baker Panel with the three other official inquiries into Britain's extradition arrangements. Chaired by a former judge and consisting of two additional lawyers, the Baker Panel expressed the law-enforcement view: it sounded strong support for extradition, dismissed concerns about the unfairness of extradition arrangements, and opposed the introduction of additional safeguards, which would have made extradition more difficult. Unfairness concerns and demands for safeguards received a more favorable hearing from the three *political* bodies—parliamentary committees—that examined the subject: the House of Lords and House of Commons Joint Committee on Human Rights (reported June 2011); the House of Commons Home Affairs Committee (reported March 2012); and the House of Lords Select Committee on Extradition Law (reported February 2015).

The following analysis highlights the gulf between those seeking to facilitate extradition and those seeking to constrain it, as manifested in the four key dilemmas in Britain's extradition debate: the forum bar, the role of the executive branch, the EAW, and the U.S.-UK extradition treaty.

Forum Bar

In cases where a person committed the alleged offense in Britain, a forum bar would prevent extradition if it is contrary to the interests of justice for the person to be tried in the requesting foreign country. In such cases, the judge may determine that the appropriate venue for the trial is a British court, rather than a foreign court.[11] A forum bar is thus a potentially important safeguard that might prove a major constraint in extradition proceedings. The 2003 act, however, lacked a forum bar. Calls for introducing such a safeguard followed several high-profile, controversial cases in which the United States asked for the extradition of British citizens who had committed the alleged offense on British soil. One case was that of the "NatWest Three"—three British businessmen, involved in dealings with the American corporation *Enron,* who were extradited to the United States in 2006 to be charged with defrauding a British bank they were employed by in London.[12] A second case concerned Gary McKinnon who in 2001–2002 gained unauthorized access from a home computer in London to U.S. government computers, including those of the army, navy, air force, Department of Defense, and NASA. The United States requested McKinnon's extradition in 2004, and British courts found him extraditable. Yet in the face of intensifying public pressure, and after it was revealed that McKinnon suffered from Asperger's syndrome, the home secretary declined to order his extradition in 2012, citing incompatibility with human rights.[13] For critics, these and other cases epitomized the injustice of Britain's extradition system. They argued that British citizens who engaged in criminal conduct in Britain should not be extradited. If they are tried at all, they should be tried in Britain.

Pro-extradition View

A forum bar provides grounds for refusing extradition, especially of British citizens. The law-enforcement position, as expressed by the jurist-based Baker Panel, repudiated the forum bar in favor of speedy, effective extradition proceedings that serve to fight crime. According to the panel, a forum bar was unnecessary, as there was no evidence that any injustice was being caused by existing arrangements. Furthermore, panel members argued that a forum bar would be a step backward from the achievements of the 2003 act. It would complicate and slow down the extradition process, add to the cost of the proceedings without any corresponding benefit, and transfer decision-making on the appropriate forum for a trial to the courts, which are less equipped to deal with this issue than prosecutors. "The forum bar would require a detailed investigation of the circumstances of the particular case, this would be a source of delay and undermine international cooperation in the fight against crime."[14]

Members of the Baker Panel recognized that concerns about extradition stemmed from the desire to protect local citizens: nationality "is actually one of the issues that lies at the heart of many people's misgivings about the extradition system."[15] Yet the panel explicitly rejected the sentiment that a British national should preferably be tried in Britain rather than abroad. An obligation to prosecute citizens locally rather than extradite them, the panel reasoned, interferes with the principle of prosecutorial discretion, and it does not serve the public interest in having effective extradition procedures: when the crime affects another country and can be effectively tried there, there is no reason to insist on a local trial. The panel's report approvingly cited a nineteenth century commentator who argued that "The refusal to surrender citizens must, therefore, be regarded as resting upon sentimental considerations and an exaggerated notion of the protection which is due by a state to its subjects."[16]

The Crown Prosecution Service echoed the concern that a forum bar might complicate extradition proceedings and "will ultimately place the extradition courts in what may be an undesirable position: deciding in which jurisdictions prosecutions should occur."[17] According to extradition judges at the Westminster Magistrates' Courts, a forum bar would generate unnecessary litigation, resulting in a delay in extradition hearings.[18] The Association of Chief Police Officers argued that a forum bar would "frustrate the extradition process" and would not "serve the long-terms interests of mutual legal assistance and law enforcement relationships internationally."[19] Overall, and consistent with Proposition 5, we find the law-enforcement apparatus repudiating the forum bar as a threat to criminal-justice cooperation.

Extradition-Skeptic View

Supporters of a forum bar argued that a person should preferably be tried in Britain rather than be put "on a plane in chains to the far side of the world to be locked up in prison."[20] These supporters included politicians, NGOs, members of the public, and the parliamentary committees that examined Britain's extradition arrangements. They made a variety of fairness-based claims as to why courts should have the discretion to bar extradition on the grounds that a trial is more appropriate in Britain. Some of the arguments raised issues such as the transparency of decision-making on forum and courts' ability to take into account all relevant considerations. The House of Commons Home Affairs Committee, for example, criticized the making of forum decisions "by prosecutors, behind closed doors, without the accused having any opportunity to make representations." Instead, the principles of human rights, democracy, and the rule of law require that forum decisions be taken by a judge in an open court, allowing the defendant an opportunity to present their case.[21] Other arguments concerned the onerous burden of a trial abroad: separation of the extradited person from family, friends, and a support network, as well as lack of familiarity with the foreign country's laws and language. By creating a presumption in favor of a trial in Britain, argued several NGOs, a person would be able to avoid the "lengthy trauma of extradition" and go through a shorter judicial process.[22]

But other arguments in favor of a forum bar reflected concerns about legal delegation: a reluctance to see British nationals tried by foreign courts in accordance with foreign laws. MP Dominic Raab (Conservative) argued that lawmakers are charged "with the duty of preserving British standards of justice and . . . have the ultimate responsibility for protecting our citizens." MP Charlie Elphicke (Conservative) suggested that "people in this country should be tried by their peers."[23] As leader of the opposition, David Cameron (Conservative) declared in 2009 that "it should still mean something to be a British citizen—with the full protection of the British parliament, rather than the British government trying to send you off to a foreign court."[24] MP Dominic Grieve (Conservative) criticized the government's willingness to easily extradite British citizens as combining "an extraordinary internationalism and an attitude that state borders are rather archaic with a reluctance to stand up for their own. That is troubling, as it undermines public confidence in the state, and will ultimately, and corrosively, undermine public confidence in the criminal justice system."[25]

E-mails sent by British citizens to the Baker Panel similarly reflected a public sentiment of concern about the delegation of criminal-justice authority to foreign legal systems. One citizen argued that "If we allow America or any other country to demand extradition of British people for supposed crimes they have committed in Britain, we are betraying them and our own legal system. When are our politicians going to start looking after us?" Another citizen demanded "British courts for British people."[26] The slogan "British Justice for British Citizens" served as a rallying cry for opponents of the existing extradition arrangements and appeared in the public campaigns they waged. In 2011, a petition carrying nearly 150,000 signatures called on the government not to extradite a British citizen named Babar Ahmad to the United States, where he was accused of supporting terrorism, and instead "put him on trial in the UK and support British Justice for British Citizens."[27] In 2012, a public meeting was organized in London by the families of four men whose extradition was requested by the United States. In front of a screen bearing the slogan "British justice for British citizens," speakers urged the crowd to step up the campaign to revise the Extradition Act.[28]

The government ultimately heeded the calls for a forum bar. In May 2012, Home Secretary Theresa May announced her intention to introduce a forum bar to address the perceived lack of transparency in the extradition process and to restore public and parliamentary confidence in extradition arrangements.[29] The forum bar, as incorporated into the Extradition Act in 2013, allows courts to bar extradition if a substantial measure of the criminal activity took place in Britain and considerations of justice—such as the location of witnesses and the offender's connections with Britain—suggest that extradition should not take place. Yet if British prosecuting authorities produce a certificate to the effect that they would not prosecute the person in Britain, extradition may not be barred. The NGOs criticized this formulation of the forum bar as lacking teeth and skewed in favor of extradition, since it allows courts to consider only specific considerations of justice and grants veto power to the prosecuting authorities.[30]

Overall, the dispute over the forum bar shows how contentious legal delegation can be. Through extradition, a home country delegates the authority to try and punish offenders to a foreign legal system. Certain actors, expressing a law-enforcement perspective, had no qualms about such a transfer of authority, which they saw as a necessary component of the efforts against crime. Limits on delegation, in their view, would lead to an unnecessary and unjustified disruption of cooperation. Yet on the other side, a variety of actors expressed serious misgivings about the delegation of authority to try British nationals. For them, such delegation undermines the duty to protect one's nationals and should therefore be curbed.

The Role of the Executive Branch in Extradition

Extradition was traditionally an act of sovereignty, with the final word left to the executive branch. Under Britain's previous extradition legislation, the home secretary could ultimately decide not to order a person's surrender, based on any relevant circumstances. The 2003 reform of the Extradition Act aimed, among other goals, to limit the executive branch's role in the extradition process and to increase the role of the judiciary in order to speed up the process and "remove any perception that [extradition] decisions are taken for political reasons or influenced by political considerations."[31] Following the reform, the home secretary had no involvement in extradition under the EAW (to Category 1 countries). In extradition to Category 2 countries, the home secretary could consider a narrow range of issues that involve limited discretion and could also consider human rights concerns that arose after the extradition procedures had been completed.[32] This latter authority sparked controversy, since it allowed the home secretary to block extradition after it had been approved by a court. Law-enforcement representatives, seeking to facilitate extradition, called for further curtailing of the executive branch's involvement in the extradition process. By contrast, NGOs and politicians skeptical of extradition saw an important role for the executive branch as a check on judicial power. For them, the executive branch's authority to block extradition, like the forum bar, served to constrain the delegation of legal authority to foreign systems, thereby protecting British nationals.

Pro-extradition View

The jurist-based Baker Panel gave considerable weight to ensuring effective extradition procedures and saw little reason for concern about having foreign countries try British citizens.[33] Accordingly, the panel suggested that the home secretary's involvement in the process of extradition be further limited: courts, rather than the home secretary, should decide human rights issues arising at the end of the extradition process. According to the panel, this would allow courts to have full control over the extradition process, speed up this process that is prone to significant delays, and make it transparently nonpolitical.[34] For Scott Baker, the panel's chair, speeding up extradition by reducing the involvement of the executive branch would be "consistent with the way that extradition has been moving over past years. Whereas it started by being an entirely political decision, it has now moved much more into the courts."[35]

Other law-enforcement actors similarly favored a reduced role for the home secretary and emphasized the need for extradition to be a judicial process. Extradition judges, represented by the Chief Magistrate's Office, argued that the judicial process of extradition already contained safeguards against injustice and that the home secretary's involvement could lead to unnecessary delays and costs.[36] The Crown Prosecution Service suggested that less executive branch involvement would increase the speed of extradition and reduce its complexity, without any perceptible diminution of the protections afforded to persons requested for extradition.[37]

Extradition-Skeptic View

Actors concerned about the delegation of authority to try British nationals advocated a meaningful role for the home secretary in the extradition process. For the NGOs, such a role was one way to reverse what, in their view, had become an automatic process that rubber-stamped foreign countries' requests. Liberty, in particular, argued that while a judge is best placed to consider the facts of an extradition case, the home secretary's discretion serves as an important safeguard "to ensure that any extradition which would be unjust is stopped notwithstanding earlier court findings."[38]

Members of Parliament similarly argued against nullifying the home secretary's authority and rejected the view of extradition as wholly judicial in nature. MP Sir Menzies Campbell (Liberal Democrats) argued that such a view "fails to understand the nature of extradition . . . Extradition is diplomatic in the first instance. It becomes judicial and ultimately it is political."[39] MP Dominic Grieve (Conservative) indicated that people had written to him to say that the home secretary should exercise the discretion not to extradite—unaware that the 2003 reform had eliminated that once-broad discretion.[40] He summarized the public mood that, in his view, is contrary to the prevailing trend toward simpler, speedier extradition:

> [A]s there has been a progressive move towards removing the Executive from the decision-making process . . . the public's demand, interestingly enough, is the other way. They want Executive intervention when they feel that in some way that would cure some perceived unfairness.[41]

Whereas the jurist-based Baker Panel sought to further curtail the home secretary's authority, Parliament's Joint Committee on Human Rights did not support any changes.[42] Yet in 2013 the Extradition Act was amended to remove human rights matters from consideration by the home secretary, consistent with the Baker Panel's recommendation. Home Secretary May accepted the Baker Panel's reasoning that this would facilitate the management of extradition cases without undue delay and, she argued, it would also relieve political pressures.[43] Indeed, it is possible that the home secretary decided to reduce her involvement in extradition matters following the intense pressure that she faced to block Gary McKinnon's extradition.[44]

European Arrest Warrant

The EAW streamlines extradition among members of the EU, and it was in force for the UK until December 31, 2020. For critics, "[f]ast-track extradition purely on the basis of administrative convenience and efficiency is justice denied."[45] The critics raised multiple concerns regarding legal incongruity, that is, discrepancies between the legal rules and practices of Britain and those of EU partners. One such concern related to double criminality—a traditional safeguard in extradition. This requirement states that a person can be extradited to a foreign country only if the alleged conduct is also criminalized in the extraditing country. The EAW, however, dispensed with the requirement to verify double criminality for 32 broadly defined offenses, including murder, terrorism, and corruption, as well as racism and xenophobia. Critics argued that this opened the door to abuses of justice in cases where an extradition is requested for an alleged offense that is not a crime in Britain. The House of Commons Home Affairs Committee expressed concern "about the erosion of the safeguard of 'dual criminality' . . . and the ill-defined nature of the 32 categories of offence which will be exempt from the dual criminality requirement."[46] The NGO Liberty argued that "While at first blush there seems no problem with extraditing someone for 'murder,' we might think differently if another country's laws define murder as including abortion."[47] Yet the Baker Panel, representing the law-enforcement view, saw little reason for concern and concluded that there were no difficulties arising in practice from the abolition of the double-criminality rule. The panel clearly prioritized cooperation against crime and dismissed the crossnational variation in legal standards:

> While we accept that harmonisation of the criminal law within the European Union has not taken place, and that significant differences exist in the Member States' substantive criminal law, the trend should be towards even greater cooperation in the suppression of crime. This is in the public interest and reinforces the rule of law: it is not in the interests of good order both within a State and internationally for crime to go unpunished as a result of movement across borders.[48]

The controversy regarding double criminality captures a fundamental dilemma in cooperation on litigation: Must cooperating partners have similar legal rules and practices? Or can cooperation take place irrespective of legal differences? We have seen the U.S. Congress grapple with this question in the NATO SOFA debates, and the participants in the Australian debate on extradition to China disagreed vehemently on this issue. In Britain's extradition debate, the question of legal incongruity and its significance is again front and center—with some actors requiring a concordance of legal standards and others considering such a requirement as an unnecessary, even damaging, barrier to cooperation. The debate over criminal-justice rights across the EU—and their compatibility with British standards—provides another demonstration of this controversy. Critics argued that, in some EU countries, prison conditions were poor: cells could be overcrowded or filthy, and prisoners might be subject to mistreatment by prison personnel or other prisoners. In addition, it was suggested that some EU member states failed to guarantee the right to a fair trial; for example, by holding the extradited person in a long pretrial detention or by admitting evidence that has been inappropriately obtained.[49]

The Baker Panel dismissed these human rights concerns as exaggerated given "the climate of mutual confidence among the like-minded Member States of the European Union, and given their democratic institutions and their expressed commitment to uphold the rights and freedoms contained in the European Convention on Human Rights." Therefore, the panel argued, it is appropriate "to begin with an assumption that surrender to another Member State of the European Union would not involve a violation of human rights." While acknowledging that "[t]rust and public confidence in overseas legal systems is not to be taken for granted," the panel believed that "at the heart of the principle [of mutual recognition] is the idea that Member States should not fear the differences between their legal systems, and that these differences are not a sufficient basis to justify a refusal to cooperate." The panel thus concluded that the Extradition Act—which requires that extradition be consistent with the European Convention on Human Rights[50]—provides adequate protection against rights violations in EU countries.[51] The panel's chair, Scott Baker, argued that criticism of the EAW stems from ethnocentrism—a tendency "in this country [to] think our system is best and, therefore, anybody who does anything differently has got it wrong."[52]

The Crown Prosecution Service, representing a law-enforcement viewpoint, similarly argued that "the practical alternatives to reliance on the good faith and integrity of requesting States are limited."[53] Indeed, the service suggested that "the introduction of the EAW has improved extradition arrangements between members of the European Union and increased crossborder co-operation."[54] Scotland's prosecution service—the Crown Office and Procurator Fiscal Service—similarly suggested that the "introduction and operation of the EAW has undoubtedly led to a far swifter and more efficient system of surrender of fugitives from one EU Member State to another."[55] According to the Association of Chief Police Officers, the EAW had brought benefits to the police: "[I]t's a faster, more efficient way of doing business."[56] Indeed, the EAW had become an "essential weapon" for the police.[57] The Law Society of England and Wales noted the EAW's "significant achievements . . . in speeding up the extradition process," and argued that "[m]utual trust requires the acceptance of differences between Member States."[58]

These views express a recognition of the importance of the EAW and an acceptance of its underlying mutual-trust presumption: the notion that EU member states trust each other's justice systems, since they all share a commitment to democracy, human rights, and the rule of law.[59] Mutual trust stands at the heart of the European Union's criminal-justice policy and justifies its core principle of mutual recognition:[60] member states should give full effect to judicial decisions made in other member states, since they all sufficiently trust each other. Indeed, the Framework Decision establishing the EAW explicitly states that this mechanism is "based on a high level of confidence between Member States."[61] Extradition supporters expressed such confidence, unmoved by claims of variation in human rights protection across the EU. Extradition skeptics, by contrast, expressed much greater suspicion of European justice systems, and were reluctant to trust that they adhere to adequate standards of human rights and legal fairness. They were concerned that "British citizens [might] be whisked away to face trial . . . in countries with lower standards of justice than in Britain"[62] and that "All traditional British beliefs in protecting the liberties of the subject have been thrown out of the window."[63] Parliament's Joint Committee on Human Rights shared the concerns regarding a human rights gap between Britain and certain EU members:

> It is important, however, to balance the need to return alleged offenders to the country in which the crime took place with the need to respect the rights of those requested for extradition. In our Report we highlight a number of areas where we believe the protection of rights for these persons is significantly below the standard which a UK citizen should expect. This is in part due to the introduction of a streamlined extradition process in the Extradition Act 2003, including the European Arrest Warrant, and the varying human rights protections within the European Union.[64]

Others were more blunt. Baroness Ludford (Liberal Democrats) argued that "Varying criminal justice procedures and standards across the EU have meant some of those surrendered under the EAW suffer unfair treatment and breaches of their human rights."[65] According to the right-wing UK Independence Party (UKIP), "the automatic judicial surrender under the EAW is based on the assumption that the rights of the suspect would be protected anywhere in the EU just as well as they are protected in the UK. This is demonstrably not the case: the human rights record of most EU members is significantly poorer than our own."[66]

The NGOs participating in the debate argued that the existing human rights safeguard in the Extradition Act[67] was ineffective. They suggested that British courts had been, in practice, unwilling to exercise that safeguard for fear of failing the concept of extradition based on mutual recognition. This, the NGOs maintained, created a danger that human rights would become theoretical and illusory. Both Fair Trials International and JUSTICE therefore proposed that the human rights safeguard be amended to enhance its effect. In addition, Fair Trials suggested that the EU should build the mutual trust necessary for the EAW by working to create minimum defense-rights standards across Europe. According to this organization, the "operation of the arrest warrant has very much served to show the different standards of criminal justice across Europe, with significant human implications." Given this variation, Fair Trials in effect rejected the mutual-trust presumption, arguing that trust must be actively fostered rather than assumed.[68] The London Criminal Courts Solicitors' Association similarly suggested that mutual trust was undermined by member states' routine breaches of the European Convention on Human Rights.[69]

For some politicians, the case of Andrew Symeou demonstrated how the EAW's goal of speed and efficiency might result in the denial of justice. Symeou, a British citizen, was surrendered to Greece in 2009, where he spent a year in squalid prison conditions, only to be acquitted of manslaughter. According to MP Dominic Raab (Conservative), this experience showed that the assumption of the adequacy of justice standards across Europe was "a sham and a fraud." For him, it was "naive at best and reckless at worst" to believe that over time and with effort, the justice systems and prison conditions across Europe would get better, as EAW proponents suggested. For MP Nick de Bois (Conservative), the Symeou case demonstrated that the EAW was a tick-box exercise that sacrificed the fundamental rights of individuals on the altar of expediency and process.[70]

Overall, the EAW controversy demonstrates a clear divide. Certain actors, mindful of the EAW's contribution to law enforcement, refused to let the incongruity in human rights standards jeopardize that contribution. They maintained that any variation in human rights protections across the EU should not obstruct the surrender of wanted persons. Other actors, however, expressed wariness of European justice systems and a reluctance to trust them. For them, an assumption that EAW surrenders are consistent with human rights was untenable. Rather, they believed that Britain's extradition arrangements should protect British nationals from the lower standards of justice that, in their view, prevailed abroad. Once again, as already seen in Chapters 3 and 5, we observe highly divergent views among actors regarding the magnitude of the gaps between legal systems and their implications for cooperation.

U.S.-UK Extradition Treaty

The United States and Britain signed a new extradition treaty in March 2003, replacing an earlier treaty that had been in effect since 1972. At the heart of the controversy over the treaty stood the differential evidentiary burden borne by the two countries: the treaty required Britain to submit sufficient evidence to establish *probable cause* when requesting extradition from the United States; American extradition requests from Britain, by contrast, had to meet the *reasonable-suspicion* standard, as per the 2003 Extradition Act.[71] How significant is the difference between the two evidentiary standards? Does it constitute an unwarranted imbalance? Opinions diverged mightily. Critics argued that the treaty was unequal—it required less of the United States and caused injustice to British citizens, who might be extradited on the basis of little or no evidence. This criticism came from politicians and NGOs who claimed unfairness and demanded better safeguards for British citizens. MP Boris Johnson (Conservative) argued that

"[A] British national can be supramagnetically suctioned to America without any scrutiny of the evidence . . . whereas the Americans would never allow that to happen to any of their nationals. That is the fundamental problem. We are failing to protect our nationals."[72] Jago Russell of the NGO Fair Trials argued that "You don't need to look very hard at the treaty to see that there's a safeguard in that treaty that exists if there is an extradition from the United States but doesn't exist the other way round, and that, quite rightly, strikes a chord with the British public and seems to be unjust."[73] The *Daily Mail* also lent its support to the evidentiary-imbalance argument: "Crucially, the U.S. can demand a Briton's extradition without having to provide any evidence while Britain has to prove its case in a U.S. court." According to the newspaper, this resulted in an asymmetry in the number of persons extradited: "Courts in the UK are approving an astonishing 89 per cent of U.S. extradition requests. By comparison, only seven in ten requests to the Americans by the British authorities are granted." This meant that "[t]he odds are stacked overwhelmingly against any British citizens wanted by the Americans for extradition."[74] According to a Muslim civil society activist, through the "lopsided" treaty, "Our proud judiciary was now reduced to being, in effect, a rubber-stamping institution for the US."[75]

This latter quote suggests that concerns about the treaty's imbalance were amplified by a broader view critical of the inequality inherent in the relations between the UK and the United States. Such a sentiment of resentment also appeared in the parliamentary debate. MP David Winnick (Labour) expressed "concern that there is a growing feeling in Britain, even among people who would not view themselves as anti-American, that in our relationship with the US we are not getting the balance and equality that we should. People feel that what the US wants, we concede without too much difficulty, and without going properly through all the ramifications."[76] The extradition treaty was denounced as "just another example of the obeisance of the Government when it comes to the United States of America";[77] an "unfair" treaty whose signing was an act of "supine acquiescence" that failed to protect the interests of British citizens.[78]

These arguments critical of the treaty resonated with two of the political bodies that scrutinized Britain's extradition arrangements. The House of Commons Home Affairs Committee recognized that

> there is a body of respectable legal opinion which suggests that there is little or no distinction in practice between the "probable cause" and "reasonable suspicion" tests. Nevertheless, the imbalance in the wording of the Treaty, which sets a test for extradition from the US but not from the UK, has created the widespread impression of unfairness within the public consciousness and, at a more practical level, gives US citizens the right to a hearing to establish "probable cause" that is

> denied to UK citizens. . . . The Committee therefore recommends that the Government seek to re-negotiate the US-UK Extradition Treaty to specify that the information requirements be the same in both jurisdictions.[79]

The Joint Committee on Human Rights similarly recommended a renegotiation of the treaty to increase the burden of proof required for the extradition of British citizens to the United States.[80] Other actors, however, dismissed the notion of an improper evidentiary imbalance and saw no reason to insist on symmetry of standards. One of those was Prime Minister Tony Blair: "[I]t is not true that the United States has a different evidential burden from this country. The probable cause, which is the burden that the United States places on countries that want to extradite from the United States, is analogous to what we now provide under the Extradition Act 2003. It is not correct to say that the United States has been given preferential treatment or that the arrangements in respect of evidence are not reciprocal."[81] Actors representing the law-enforcement community shared Blair's view. The solicitor-general argued that "Exact reciprocity between two legal systems is almost impossible to achieve . . . although the approaches are not entirely equivalent, they are broadly so, in a rough and ready manner."[82] Baroness Scotland, minister of state for the criminal justice system at the Home Office, went further, arguing that "Complete reciprocity has never been a feature of our extradition arrangements."[83] The judge-led Baker Panel concluded that the difference between the probable-cause test and the reasonable-suspicion test had no significance: under both tests, it is necessary to demonstrate an objective basis for suspecting legal wrongdoing.[84] The panel therefore rejected the charge of imbalance between the evidentiary tests and concluded that a broad symmetry did exist between them.[85] Extradition judges at the Westminster Magistrates' Courts similarly concluded that "[t]he difference is academic and semantic."[86]

Yet the cat was out of the bag. Underlying the criticism of the treaty was not "the minutiae of the treaty agreement," but "a lack of public confidence in the US criminal justice system."[87] Both the Baker Panel and the House of Lords Select Committee on Extradition Law observed that many of the witnesses before them focused, in fact, on "aspects of the US justice system which they felt made extradition inappropriate or unjust."[88] Such criticisms came from politicians and NGOs, whose thinking demonstrated ethnocentrism at work: they measured the U.S. legal system by British standards and found it to be flawed. One criticism concerned the long prison sentences that American courts often mete out. MP Dominic Grieve (Conservative) observed that "[t]here is a lack of public confidence in the US criminal justice system . . . there are perceptions in this country that the US criminal justice system can be harsh and its penal policy can be harsh, and its sentencing policy can appear disproportionate by European and British standards."[89] Another concern was the high frequency of prosecutions ending in plea bargains. While plea bargains occur in the British legal system as well, it was argued that the American system obtains these deals excessively and under pressure: the prosecutor makes it clear that if the person chooses to go to trial and is convicted, they will face the maximum applicable sentence. By contrast, a plea bargain will result in a lighter sentence. In extradition cases, the promised deal may include another important benefit: the possibility of a transfer back to the home country to serve the sentence.[90] Ultimately, suggested MP David Davies (Conservative), the great power of American prosecutors to negotiate plea deals under the threat of a harsh sentence might result in unjust outcomes, including innocent people possibly being forced to make guilty pleas.[91] Thus, "the almost certain consequences of extradition to the US are a plea bargain and consequent conviction. The current system not only permits but also encourages aggressive US prosecutors to seek the extradition of people who may never have set foot in America, safe in the knowledge that conviction is all but assured, irrespective of the merits of the case."[92]

Various other features of the U.S. legal system raised concerns. One of them was the harsh conditions in American prisons. MP Douglas Hogg (Conservative), for example, argued that U.S. prisons are "ghastly . . . an affront to civilization."[93] *The Week* magazine reported that Chris Tappin, a retired British businessman extradited to the United States in 2012, was held in "a remote prison in the desert," where inmates suffer abuse and humiliating treatment.[94] The U.S. practice of electing judges was also seen as antithetical to the British notion of justice.[95] Lord Hart of Chilton expressed a concern that judges seek to enhance their election prospects through stiff sentencing.[96] Another source of concern was the fact that the United States consists of 50 different state jurisdictions plus the federal jurisdiction, and that standards of justice are not uniform across jurisdictions.[97] Critics further highlighted the harshness of pretrial conditions in the United States: lengthy periods of pretrial detention as well as a refusal of bail.[98]

The issue of personal jurisdiction drew particularly sharp criticism, with critics denouncing the "overzealousness of US prosecutors" and the "exorbitant extraterritorial jurisdiction" that is oftentimes based on a very tenuous connection with the United States.[99] "It appears to be very easy to engage the jurisdiction of the U.S. courts without ever entering the country, since activity on the internet, including sending and receiving e-mails, can involve the use of communications systems based in the United States, as can the use of the U.S. banking system."[100] According to Liberty's Isabella Sankey, the United States might claim jurisdiction based on a connection "as small as a computer being used with a US server."[101] This was seen in the case of Babar Ahmad—accused by the United States of providing support for terrorism through a website he operated in Britain. U.S. authorities claimed jurisdiction because one of the servers hosting the website was located in the United States. Such a broad view of jurisdiction was inappropriate, critics argued, and dangerous, given the punitive nature of the U.S. legal system.[102] GC100, an association of representing general counsel of companies, similarly denounced the "harshness of the US system"—especially the "aggressive use of the criminal law and process" to regulate business.[103]

The parliamentary bodies of inquiry and the NGOs concluded that the harshness of U.S. criminal justice caused public concern and a loss of confidence in Britain's extradition arrangements with the United States.[104] The jurist-based Baker Panel dismissed these concerns and expressed trust in the U.S. justice system:

> [T]he history of extradition between the United States and the United Kingdom provides no basis for concluding that individuals returned to that jurisdiction are generally not treated fairly.... [T]he United States is a rights-based democracy where accused persons have protections provided by the Constitution to ensure that they are able to participate effectively in a criminal trial process that is conducted fairly: extradition from the United Kingdom to the United States takes place against the background of this protection.[105]

Lord Brown of Eaton-under-Heywood, former justice of the UK Supreme Court, similarly argued that extradition proceedings, based on mutual trust, must accommodate legal and cultural differences between legal systems. "Naturally, we think that our own criminal justice system is best, but we cannot insist on all other countries following the same procedures."[106] This is a direct repudiation of the ethnocentric sentiments that fuel resistance to extradition.

Other actors expressing a law-enforcement perspective offered several responses to the argument concerning the overly broad U.S. jurisdiction. Scott Baker suggested that U.S. jurisdiction "is not as exorbitant as some people think. These days, with the internet and so forth, the tentacles of countries have to spread much wider than they previously did."[107] Anand Doobay, another member of the Baker Panel, argued that the broad American view of jurisdiction was just different from the British view. While British authorities would prefer to not prosecute cases that involve minimal contact with Britain, their American counterparts do pursue cases that have little U.S. contact. "[T]hat is simply that they are taking a decision that we would not take ourselves."[108] A representative of the Crown Prosecution Service suggested that American prosecutors were better funded than their British counterparts and could more easily handle expensive multi-jurisdictional cases.[109]

A former official of the U.S. Department of Justice, who testified before the House of Lords Select Committee, emphasized that the evaluation of legal incongruity is in the eyes of the beholder, using one's own standards as the metric and reference point. Whereas American criminal justice may seem unjust to Britons, an American would criticize certain aspects of UK law:

> courts in the United Kingdom routinely admit evidence that would violate our fourth amendment, and hearsay evidence that would violate our sixth amendment. Defendants in the United Kingdom do not have the protections of the United States' fifth amendment. This is not to say that your justice system in the United Kingdom is not fair; we believe that it is. The mutual respect for one another's justice systems is really the foundation that underlies the extradition treaty, and I think that is important to remember.[110]

Overall, the debate over the U.S.-UK treaty demonstrates two opposing attitudes to legal (in)congruity and its implications for cooperation on litigation. For one camp, exact compatibility of legal standards and practices is an unrealistic demand that will unnecessarily obstruct cooperation. For the other—ethnocentric—camp, legal congruity is an essential requirement of fairness. Given the gaps between American and British criminal justice, a British person extradited to the United States would not enjoy a fair legal process, and the risk of injustice should militate against their extradition.

Conclusion

Britain had long used extradition as a conventional instrument of law enforcement, employed to prevent criminals from escaping justice by crossing borders. That this instrument generated such political controversy is therefore surprising, and the surprise is even greater in light of the controversy's focus on EU countries and the United States. In the case of China examined in the previous chapter, the concerns over extradition are perhaps predictable given the gap between the Australian and Canadian systems—Western, common-law legal systems operating in a democratic environment—and the Chinese system—a non-Western, civil-law system that serves as an arm of a nondemocratic, repressive government. In the present case, however, the gap between the home and foreign system seems much smaller. The home system (UK) is a Western legal system in a democratic country committed to the rule of law and human rights; the same applies to the foreign legal systems of the United States and EU countries. The UK and U.S. systems even belong to the same common-law legal tradition.

These significant similarities should have made extradition from the UK to the United States or EU countries straightforward and noncontroversial. Yet, as this chapter has demonstrated, this was far from the case. For extradition critics in the UK, the American justice system, and some of the European justice systems, fell far below British standards, making extradition to these destinations dangerous and unjust.

The debate largely unfolded along the theoretically expected lines. It revolved around the extradition of British *citizens*, as demonstrated by the slogan "British Justice for British Citizens" (consistent with Proposition 8). British citizens constitute roughly half the persons extradited from the UK to the United States;[111] they are but a small fraction of the persons that the UK surrenders to EU members. Indeed, the vast majority of persons surrendered through the EAW were non-UK nationals.[112] Yet extradition critics apparently had little concern about sending non-nationals to stand trial outside the UK. It was the plight of a trial abroad for UK citizens that fueled the debate, coupled with the argument that Parliament has the duty to protect its citizens.[113] For critics, foreign criminal justice departs in many ways from British standards and practices; such deviations, in the ethnocentric mind, make foreign justice unfair. Throughout the debate, critics emphasized what they perceived as the incompatibility of British and foreign justice and the superiority of the former over the latter. Indeed, foreign legal systems were described using blunt and even derogatory language, such as U.S. prisons being "an affront to civilization" or a "hellhole."[114] Critics, however, did not limit their objections to the American or European legal systems. Indeed, the entire notion of delegating the authority to prosecute, try, and punish UK citizens seemed unfair to them, and they sought to limit that delegation through a forum bar or through the executive branch's authority to block extradition.

Where did the criticism of extradition come from? Among politicians, it was Conservative members of Parliament who led the charge against Britain's extradition arrangements. They began to voice their concerns when they were in the opposition, but persisted in their criticism even after becoming the ruling party in 2010. After all, the targets of their attacks—the 2003 Extradition Act and the 2003 U.S.-UK treaty—were crafted by the Labour government led by Tony Blair. Surprisingly, Labour politicians themselves took a back seat and did not put up a strong defense of the arrangements that their own government had established. It should be remembered that the establishment of these arrangements took place in the aftermath of the terrorist attacks of September 11, 2001—a seminal event that created strong pressure for enhanced law-enforcement cooperation. Yet the public mood on extradition seemed to have shifted. Amid growing public concern about the unfairness of extradition, Labour politicians may have been reluctant to defend unpopular arrangements that made extradition easier.

Consistent with Proposition 4, criticism of the UK's extradition arrangements also came from the NGO community, which prioritized the protection of human rights over the effectiveness of fighting crime or maintaining friendly international relations:

> [O]ur traditions of criminal justice standards in this country are something to be proud of yet, instead of requiring those same standards to be met by other countries, we have given away a lot of the procedural protections that we would require here in our own law. We think this may be for well intentioned reasons, because we want to have good diplomatic relations with other countries, and we understand that extradition is in the interests of everybody, but we think that there are basic first principles that must be returned to.[115]

Consistent with Proposition 4, the media also heaped its often-unsparing criticism. Newspaper coverage stoked controversy by focusing on persons subject to extradition and their travails, fostering the notion that extradition of British citizens is inherently unjust. Consider, for example, the media reaction to the handling of the American request to extradite Gary McKinnon. A columnist for *The Telegraph* denounced that request as a "heavy-handed and shameful disgrace." She wrote: "US authorities had been caught napping in the sensitive period after 9/11, and I reckon someone had to pay the price for wounded pride. Instead of an evil megalomaniac bent on world domination, they picked on Gary." The columnist praised the home secretary for employing her authority to block McKinnon's extradition and lamented the curtailment of that authority in the 2003 Extradition Act: "Unfortunately, thanks to New Labour, our Home Secretary no longer has the ability to protect Britons from unfair extradition."[116] The *Daily Mail,* in fact, took credit for the decision not to extradite McKinnon. In 2009, the newspaper launched the *Affront to British Justice* campaign, with extensive, critical coverage aimed at preventing McKinnon's surrender to American authorities. According to the newspaper, "[t]he campaign had attracted widespread political support and celebrities had also added their voices in the fight to keep [McKinnon] in the UK," resulting in a "victory": the decision to refuse McKinnon's extradition.[117]

What role did the legal community play in the debate? As expected, associations of lawyers who may be fighting the extradition of their clients—such as the London Criminal Courts Solicitors' Association—favored more restrictive extradition arrangements. Consistent with Proposition 5, the strongest support for easier, faster extradition came from jurists in the state apparatus, first and foremost, the judge-led Baker Panel. These actors focused on ensuring the effectiveness of law enforcement rather than protecting individuals from an unfair legal process abroad. In fact, they repudiated the ethnocentric view that sees unfairness in any inconsistency between the home and foreign legal practices. For them, such inconsistencies—far from posing dangers to extradited persons—present a normal variation among legal systems, which should not impede the punishment of crime. This demonstrates one of this book's key points: different actors vary in their interpretation of cross-country legal differences and in the assessment of their importance and implications. The divergent conclusions of the committees that examined Britain's extradition arrangements further demonstrate this point. Parliament's Joint Committee on Human Rights suggested that Britain's extradition arrangements leaned too heavily toward facilitating extradition and provided inadequate human rights protection;[118] looking at the same arrangements, the government-appointed Baker panel concluded that they did provide appropriate protection against human rights violations.[119]

In February 2020, the British government announced—against the warnings of law-enforcement officials—that it would not be seeking to participate in the EAW after completing its departure from the EU at the end of the year.[120] On December 31 of that year, Britain left the EAW framework. Yet, a day earlier Britain and the EU had concluded the Trade and Cooperation Agreement, which establishes extradition arrangements similar to those of the EAW.[121] Extradition critics thus did not get their wish to stop fast-track surrenders to EU countries. But perhaps their most significant achievement is that they managed to shake Britain's once-robust commitment to international cooperation on criminal justice and undermine public confidence in extradition. The notion that Britain should protect its citizens by not extraditing them; the view that crossnational variation in legal standards and practices can justify the avoidance of extradition—that such ideas received considerable support in a country traditionally committed to law-enforcement cooperation is testimony to the appeal of legal ethnocentrism.

Notes

1. Shearer 1971, 97–110; Plachta 1999.
2. Del-Bove and Francoz-Terminal 2015.
3. Home Office 2011, 69–70.
4. Plachta 2003.
5. Council Framework Decision of 13 June 2002 on the European arrest warrant and the surrender procedures between member states (2002/584/JHA), Articles 3 and 4. Other provisions of this decision do refer to rights protection; see Article 1(3) and recitals 12 and 13 of the Preamble.
6. Efrat and Newman 2020.
7. Home Office 2011, 91, 100.
8. Home Office 2011, 285–286.
9. Home Office 2011, 8.

10. See also Boister 2018b.
11. Home Office 2011, 208.
12. Clark and Truscott 2007.
13. Burns 2009; Cowell and Burns 2012.
14. Home Office 2011, 227–230.
15. Select Committee on Extradition Law 2015b, 54.
16. Home Office 2011, 222, 227–228.
17. Home Office 2012, written representation.
18. Home Office 2012, written representation.
19. Home Office 2012, written representation.
20. Select Committee on Extradition Law 2015b, 104 (David Bermingham, who had been extradited to the United States).
21. Home Affairs Committee 2012, 11.
22. Select Committee on Extradition Law 2015b, 747, 751.
23. HC Deb 24 November 2011, cc153WH, 172WH.
24. Cited in Drury 2009.
25. HC Deb 12 July 2006, c1419.
26. Home Office 2012, public views.
27. https://petition.parliament.uk/archived/petitions/885.
28. http://www.statewatch.org/news/2012/may/03-uk-extradition-treaty.html.
29. HC Deb 16 October 2012, c165.
30. Select Committee on Extradition Law 2015a, 47–49.
31. Select Committee on Extradition Law 2015b, 632.
32. The primary responsibility to consider human rights issues during the extradition process falls to the courts.
33. Home Office 2011, 8.
34. Home Office 2011, 291–292.
35. Select Committee on Extradition Law 2015b, 71.
36. Select Committee on Extradition Law 2015b, 246.
37. Select Committee on Extradition Law 2015b, 314, 325.
38. Joint Committee on Human Rights 2011a, 25 and 2011b, 118.
39. HC Deb 24 November 2011, c167WH.
40. HC Deb 12 July 2006, c1421.
41. Home Affairs Committee 2012, Ev 66–67.
42. Joint Committee on Human Rights 2011a, 54.
43. Select Committee on Extradition Law 2015b, 631–632, 873.
44. Rozenberg 2012.
45. Coles 2009.
46. Home Affairs Committee 2002, 5.
47. Coles 2009.
48. Home Office 2011, 188–189.
49. Joint Committee on Human Rights 2011b, 188–193.
50. Sections 21 and 87 of the Extradition Act 2003.
51. Home Office 2011, 137–138, 193.
52. Select Committee on Extradition Law 2015b, 58.
53. Select Committee on Extradition Law 2015b, 322.
54. Select Committee on Extradition Law 2015b, 314.
55. Home Office 2012, written representation.
56. Home Office 2012, oral evidence.
57. Home Affairs Committee 2013, 6.
58. Home Office 2012, written representation.
59. Efrat 2019.
60. Janssens 2013.
61. Recital 10 of the Framework Decision establishing the European Arrest Warrant.
62. Prince 2009.
63. Booker 2009.

64. Joint Committee on Human Rights 2011a, 7.
65. Select Committee on Extradition Law 2015b, 767.
66. Home Office, 2012, public consultation.
67. Sections 21 and 87 of the Extradition Act 2003.
68. Home Office 2011, 130–131; Select Committee on Extradition Law 2015b, 886.
69. Home Office 2012, written representation.
70. HC Deb 24 November 2011, cc148WH-149WH, 183WH.
71. The U.S.-UK treaty itself does not specify the evidentiary test for American extradition requests to Britain.
72. HC Deb 12 July 2006, c1432.
73. Home Affairs Committee 2012, 6.
74. Slack and Seamark 2009.
75. Bunglawala 2006.
76. HC Deb 12 July 2006, c1424.
77. HC Deb 12 July 2006, c1438 (MP George Galloway (Respect Party)).
78. HC Deb 12 July 2006, cc1445–1446 (MP David Heath (Liberal Democrats)).
79. Home Affairs Committee 2012, 7.
80. Joint Committee on Human Rights 2011a, 52.
81. HC Deb 5 July 2006, c807.
82. HC Deb 12 July 2006, c1412.
83. HL Deb 16 December 2003, c1063.
84. Home Office 2011, 242.
85. Home Office 2011, 242.
86. Home Office 2012, written representation.
87. Home Affairs Committee 2012, Ev 60.
88. Home Office 2011, 254; Select Committee on Extradition Law 2015a, 99.
89. Home Affairs Committee 2012, Ev 60.
90. Home Affairs Committee 2012, Ev 33–34, 39; Select Committee on Extradition Law 2015a, 100.
91. HC Deb 16 October 2012, c171.
92. Select Committee on Extradition Law 2015b, 77 (Statement of David Bermingham).
93. HC Deb 12 July 2006, c1440.
94. Edwards 2012.
95. Select Committee on Extradition Law 2015a, 103.
96. Select Committee on Extradition Law 2015b, 63.
97. HC Deb 12 July 2006, c1445; HL Deb 16 December 2003, c1066. Texas in particular was identified as a state where justice standards are suspect: "my understanding is that Texan juries are simple: people from Texas get a good hearing, but if people are not from Texas, it is a bit more hit and miss." HC Deb 24 November 2011, c172WH (MP Charlie Elphicke (Conservative)).
98. Select Committee on Extradition Law 2015a, 106.
99. Home Affairs Committee 2012, 11 (citing lawyer Julian Knowles).
100. Home Affairs Committee 2012, 11.
101. Select Committee on Extradition Law 2015b, 238.
102. Select Committee on Extradition Law 2015b, 37.
103. Home Office 2012, written representation.
104. Home Affairs Committee 2012, 12; Select Committee on Extradition Law 2015a, 106–107; Select Committee on Extradition Law 2015b, 226.
105. Home Office 2011, 252.
106. HL Deb 16 September 2015, c269.
107. Home Affairs Committee 2012, Ev 29.
108. Select Committee on Extradition Law 2015b, 64.
109. Select Committee on Extradition Law 2015b, 370.
110. Select Committee on Extradition Law 2015b, 680.
111. Select Committee on Extradition Law 2015a, 97.

112. During the period 2010–2016, the UK surrendered 7,945 individuals to various EU members under the EAW. Only 277 of those (3.5%) were British citizens. Source: National Crime Agency.
113. Select Committee on Extradition Law 2015b, 80. See, for example, the argument that "the extradition treaty and its enactment through the Extradition Act 2003 is manifestly unfair to British citizens" (MP Nick Clegg (Liberal Democrats)). HC Deb 12 July 2006, c1396.
114. HC Deb 12 July 2006, c1440; Select Committee on Extradition Law 2015b, 80, 108.
115. Select Committee on Extradition Law 2015b, 226–227 (Isabella Sankey of Liberty).
116. Pearson 2012.
117. Seamark, Slack, and Evans 2012.
118. Joint Committee on Human Rights 2011a, 3.
119. Home Office 2011, 318.
120. Grierson, Rankin, and O'Carroll 2020.
121. Trade and Cooperation Agreement between the European Union and the European Atomic Energy Community, of the one part, and the United Kingdom of Great Britain and Northern Ireland, of the other part, Part Three, Title VII.

SECTION IV

ENFORCEMENT OF FOREIGN JUDGMENTS

7

Judgments, Jurisdiction, and Juries

Challenges to the Enforcement of U.S. Court Rulings in Europe

This chapter examines the challenges to establishing cooperation on litigation in the context of civil justice, focusing on conflicting perceptions of legal fairness in the United States and Continental Europe. While Americans recognize certain flaws in their civil justice system,[1] Europeans are said to fear American courts like medieval torture chambers.[2] From the expansive U.S. conception of jurisdiction through broad discovery to punitive damages, Europeans abhor some key features of American civil justice. The conflicting perceptions of legal fairness often prove an obstacle to the enforcement of foreign-court judgments.

A note regarding terminology: This chapter uses the term *civil justice* to refer to noncriminal branches of the law, such as contracts and torts. The term *civil law* indicates the legal tradition to which the justice systems of Continental Europe belong.

The Enforcement of Foreign Judgments: An Introduction

In the age of globalization, the growing crossborder movement of people, goods, and information often results in transnational legal disputes that involve civil legal claims between individuals or firms of different nationalities: the plaintiff comes from one country, whereas the defendant resides in another. In many cases, such disputes are decided by a court outside the defendant's home country. The successful plaintiff will therefore request the enforcement of the judgment in the defendant's country, where the defendant's assets are likely located. The requested country faces a dilemma: on the one hand, refusing to enforce the foreign judgment will undermine the plaintiff's rights and legitimate

Intolerant Justice. Asif Efrat, Oxford University Press. © Oxford University Press 2023.
DOI: 10.1093/oso/9780197658895.003.0007

expectations following the judgment. More broadly, such a refusal runs contrary to the public interest in maintaining transnational legal certainty and avoiding repeated litigation and conflicting decisions. Transnational legal certainty, in turn, serves as an important foundation of crossborder personal and commercial relationships.[3] On the other hand, a foreign judgment raises suspicions and concerns in the country requested to enforce it. The judgment is a product of processes and arrangements that express foreign values and are carried out by foreign institutions. It is, in fact, an exercise of the legal powers of a foreign sovereign. By enforcing the foreign judgment, the defendant's home country defers to the foreign sovereign: It accepts the exercise of legal authority by the foreign legal system and gives it local effect. Enforcement of foreign judgments can thus be seen as compliance with the orders of a foreign sovereign and as undermining local sovereignty. Beyond sovereignty costs, the enforcement of foreign judgments poses threats to the local law and legal system. This is the case, for example, if the foreign judgment conflicts with the policy or values enshrined in the enforcing country's laws, if it conflicts with a preexisting judgment issued by local courts, or if it addresses a matter that the local legal system views as being within its exclusive authority. Furthermore, by agreeing to enforce foreign judgments, a country may encourage foreigners to bring lawsuits against its own citizens or firms in foreign courts. Such lawsuits place a burden on defendants who then have to litigate before a foreign court, away from home.[4]

How did the civil-law countries of Europe handle this dilemma? The territoriality principle—suggesting that national law applies within national boundaries and has no effect beyond them—colors much of Continental Europe's thinking about transnational litigation. This principle grew out of the notion of national sovereignty—a concept that gained popularity with the wave of nationalism that swept through Europe during the late eighteenth and early nineteenth centuries. In application to foreign judgments, the territoriality principle inspired the view of a judgment as the order of a sovereign, limited in its impact to the territory of that sovereign: It has no effect beyond the rendering country's territory, and other countries have no obligation to enforce it. Beyond protecting one's sovereignty, the refusal to enforce foreign judgments also meant protecting one's citizens, allowing them to evade the consequences of foreign rulings.[5] This reflected the view that individuals should have the privilege of being subject to the laws and procedures of their own country.[6]

Over time, European countries came to recognize the problematic results of their nonenforcement approach: judicial inefficiency, obstacles to international commerce, and a burden for private litigants seeking the enforcement of judgments in their favor abroad. In the face of such problems, some European countries—such as the Nordic countries and the Netherlands—stuck to their territorialist views, refusing to enforce foreign judgments in the absence of a treaty with the judgment-rendering country providing for reciprocal enforcement of judgments.[7] Other European countries, however, moved away from the nonenforcement position, each establishing its own regime for the enforcement of foreign judgments: a set of conditions and requirements for giving local effect to foreign judgments in a way that lessens any threat the foreign ruling might pose to the local sovereign and legal order. Notwithstanding some crossnational differences, the primary requirements are: that the foreign judgment be final; that it be based on a proper exercise of personal jurisdiction, proper service of the document initiating the lawsuit, and proceedings that are fair; that it not violate the enforcing country's public policy, not be based on fraud, and not be inconsistent with previous proceedings or decisions involving the same cause of action between the same parties.[8] Many European countries also required reciprocity and conditioned enforcement on equivalent treatment from the country that renders the judgment: they agreed to honor judgments from a foreign country only if that country would enforce their own judgments in similar circumstances. In the absence of a treaty guaranteeing reciprocity, the party requesting enforcement typically bears the burden of proving to the court that the foreign country will enforce that court's judgments in a reciprocal manner. The insistence on reciprocity stems from the deeply held European concern for legal sovereignty and a wariness of foreign legal systems: the enforcement of a foreign judgment is a sacrifice of sovereignty, which can be justified as the price for inducing foreign courts to give effect to the home country's judgments.[9]

Over time, some European countries further softened their approach and came to accord more favorable treatment to foreign judgments.[10] Furthermore, European countries made great strides in facilitating judgment enforcement among themselves. EU regulations[11] seek to "simplify the formalities with a view to rapid and simple recognition and enforcement of judgments from Member States," the objective being "free movement of judgments in civil and commercial matters."[12] But while the enforcement of judgments within the EU has become nearly automatic,[13] judgments from the United States are enforced under the same regime as judgments from less-important countries, with which no special relationship exists. Sovereignty concerns still play a role here,[14] and the basic attitude toward foreign judgments is suspicious rather than welcoming.

What kind of treatment do foreign judgments receive across the Atlantic? Unlike in Europe, the American approach to foreign judgments was not shaped by sovereignty concerns and did not stem from a territorialist view. Instead, its early inspiration came from the doctrine of comity, developed by seventeenth-century Dutch jurist Ulrich Huber. While taking the territorialist view of sovereignty as his point of departure, Huber also recognized the problems created by limiting the force of the law to the national territory. The solution he devised was *comity*: a sovereign will give effect to foreign laws and rights, while maintaining the discretion to deny such an effect to the extent necessary to protect itself or its citizens.[15] Building on the principle of comity, the U.S. Supreme Court laid the foundation for foreign-judgment enforcement in a seminal 1895 decision in *Hilton v. Guyot*[16]—a case involving a French judgment against American citizens. The court argued for "the recognition which one nation allows within its territory to the legislative, executive or judicial acts of another nation"[17] and determined that federal courts should usually enforce foreign judgments that meet certain requirements, such as the foreign court having jurisdiction, as well as reciprocity: U.S. courts will only enforce judgments of countries that grant enforcement to American judgments.[18]

The *Hilton* decision established a strong rhetorical position in favor of giving effect to foreign judgments alongside uniform standards for enforcement. In the following years, the enforcement of foreign judgments became a matter of state law: state courts kept relying on the *Hilton* criteria and, in fact, liberalized them further by abandoning the reciprocity requirement—that same requirement that expressed the sovereignty-based view of foreign judgments in Continental Europe.[19] In the absence of U.S. legislation governing enforcement, however, reciprocity-minded European courts were not satisfied that their judgments would be enforced in American courts.[20] The frequent refusal to enforce U.S. judgments prompted an American attempt to codify the most prevalent common-law rules governing enforcement. In 1962, the Uniform Law Commission (ULC)—a body that proposes legislation to bring clarity and stability to critical areas of state law—promulgated the Uniform Foreign Money-Judgments Recognition Act (hereinafter the 1962 Act). This model law established a streamlined legislative framework for enforcement in order to make it absolutely clear that judgments from the courts of other countries would be recognized and enforced in U.S. courts. This, it was hoped, would satisfy foreign courts requiring reciprocity and encourage them to enforce U.S. judgments.[21] Following in the footsteps of *Hilton*, the act begins with a general presumption that a foreign judgment is enforceable, subject to a set of mandatory and discretionary exceptions.[22] The majority of American states enacted the 1962 Act or an updated 2005 version[23] that has a similar pro-enforcement spirit. Other states retained their common-law-based friendly approach to foreign judgments, reflected in the Restatement (Third) of Foreign Relations Law,[24] which closely resembles the approach of the 1962 Act.

Whereas the United States takes a liberal, favorable approach to foreign judgments, the European attitude toward non-EU judgments is more circumspect, characterized by concerns for the protection of national sovereignty, the domestic legal order, and a country's citizens. These concerns mount when the enforcement of a U.S. judgment is requested. Various attributes of American civil justice offend European notions of legal fairness and are far removed from the

European understanding of how a civil trial should unfold. As a result, American judgments often do not fare well in European courts, which may refuse to enforce them.[25] We analyze the European-American tensions over foreign judgments in two stages. First, we examine the sources of these tensions: why American legal norms and practices might draw a negative reaction in Europe. This demonstrates this book's key point: one's own values and norms are used as a yardstick for measuring foreign legal systems and such an ethnocentric view might hinder cooperation on litigation. Second, we analyze the efforts to bridge the gaps between the American and European practices of judgment enforcement through a global convention—and explain why such a convention was so difficult to establish.

European Uneasiness with American Civil Justice

From a European standpoint, litigation in the United States is extremely costly, highly unpredictable, and characterized by significant unfairness.[26] Various elements of the American civil justice system offend European sensibilities. Europeans, for instance, harbor a deep mistrust of the U.S. jury system. The epitome of justice in American eyes, the jury is viewed by European critics as "more of a drama than a due process of law to find the truth and to give a fair judgment."[27] The possible prejudice of juries also raises concerns. Europeans commonly believe that U.S. jurors, even if carefully selected, will usually sympathize with the U.S. plaintiffs rather than with the foreign defendants.[28] Indeed, foreign corporations involved in U.S. litigation often express concerns about the susceptibility of the American jury to xenophobic bias.[29] Additional misgivings concern the power of American judges, including their power to sanction, which is breathtaking from a European perspective; the seeming flexibility of American law and the frequent use of interest-balancing tests; the relative rarity of full trials and the high frequency of settlements that are based on the negotiating capability of the attorneys; a rule of costs that requires each party to bear its own costs and expenses—forcing the defendant to pay their attorney even if the claim lacked merit; the imposition of seemingly absolute liability in product liability cases; the availability of class actions; the idea of contingency fees, which the lawyer charges for their services only if the lawsuit is successful; and a seemingly low threshold for finding causation.[30] In the following, we focus on three other components of civil litigation—punitive damages, pretrial discovery, and personal jurisdiction—and explain why the American and European views of them have traditionally diverged. Note the use of the word "traditionally." Over time, especially since the 1980s, changes in U.S. litigation have moderated the differences between American and European civil justice. This chapter, however, focuses on *perceptions* of American litigation—perceptions still inspired by the deep legal chasm that once existed between Europe and America despite its recent narrowing. As this book has emphasized, cooperation is shaped by one's subjective assessment of the foreign legal system, even if such assessment departs from or distorts the legal reality. It is the European perception of U.S. civil justice—however inaccurate or outmoded—that impedes cooperation on litigation and that will be examined here.

Punitive Damages

The American law of damages raises alarm in Continental Europe. Europeans tend to express concern over jury awards, which they deem excessive, up to many times more than what would be awarded elsewhere.[31] Yet it is the notion of punitive damages that Europeans find particularly distasteful. In the United States, the law of damages rests on two distinct pillars: compensation and punishment. Compensatory damages aim to compensate the plaintiff (the victim of the tort) for the harm they suffered or to replace something they have lost because of the wrongful act. By awarding such damages, the court aims to put the victim back where they would have been if the defendant had not committed the wrongful act. Punitive damages, on the other hand, aim at punishment and deterrence. By awarding them, in addition to and apart from the compensatory damages, the court seeks to punish the offender for their outrageous behavior and to deter them and others from engaging in similar conduct in the future. Whereas compensatory damages are equal to the loss suffered by the individual victim, punitive damages reflect the outrageous nature of the offender's conduct and their having caused damage through behavior that is reckless, conscious, willful, or otherwise deserving of retribution.[32]

Punitive damages are a common-law institution, dating back to eighteenth century English law. They are awarded in countries such as Britain, Canada, Australia, New Zealand, and the United States, although these countries vary considerably as regards the goals that punitive damages serve, the actions in which they may be awarded, the considerations in determining the amount of damages, and what constitutes an excessive award.[33] Of all common-law countries, the United States makes the most extensive use of punitive damages. Such damages are allowed in the vast majority of American states in actions involving torts, contracts, property, admiralty, and family law.[34] Juries traditionally enjoy broad discretion in determining the amount of damages. Once it is decided that the conduct justifies the award of punitive damages, the jury determines the amount, taking into account the gravity of the wrong and the need to deter similar conduct. The jury's determination is then subject to review by the trial judge and appellate courts.[35]

Awarded as damages to a plaintiff in a private lawsuit, punitive damages are quasi-criminal in nature, standing halfway between civil and criminal law. They are, in fact, a penal remedy situated within a private-law domain.[36] This penal nature is reflected in the goals that courts typically cite when awarding punitive damages. The first is punishment and retribution: the most fundamental purpose of criminal law. Since the wrongdoer injured another person through wanton misconduct, they should suffer punishment that restores the metaphoric scales of justice thrown out of balance by the offense. The retributive interest belongs to the victim but also to society, since the wrongdoer broke the reciprocal security pact among law-abiding members of society.[37] A second oft-cited rationale of punitive damages, also from the realm of criminal law, is deterrence: preventing similar misconduct in the future. Punitive damages help to deter misconduct by sensationalizing and publicizing the apprehension and punishment of offenders found guilty of egregious behavior. The awards, in essence, inform potential offenders that flagrant legal violations are subject to punishment in amounts exceeding the victim's actual loss and that the punishment, while not certain, is likely enough to take the apparent profitability out of the contemplated act.[38]

Beyond the key goals of retribution and deterrence, punitive damages serve an educational purpose. They educate the individual offender and society at large about the existence and importance of legally protected rights and societal standards of conduct, underscoring the condemnation that attaches to severe violation of these standards.[39] Punitive damages also encourage and facilitate law enforcement. The promise of a windfall may motivate reluctant victims to pursue their claims and enforce legal rules.[40] Furthermore, punitive damages may be used for compensation purposes, filling gaps in the compensatory award. They can help the plaintiff pay attorney fees as well as reimburse the plaintiff for losses that cannot be proven or measured.[41] Some, in fact, suggest that punitive damages relieve the pressure on the criminal justice system.[42]

Whereas in the common-law world punitive damages can serve important and useful purposes, civil-law countries hold a diametrically opposed view, considering this instrument to be unfair and repugnant. The most fundamental criticism concerns the confusion of private and criminal law. In the Continental mind, the private law of torts and contracts is completely separate from criminal law. Each legal domain is unique unto itself, and there should be no overlap of functions between the different fields of law. Whereas the purpose of criminal law is to punish and deter, tort law seeks to compensate injured persons for wrongfully inflicted harm. The idea of punitive damages—punishment within a private-law framework—is thus anathema to Continental thinking, in which "[t]he idea of punishment is outside of the private law."[43] In this view, criminal law is better suited to realizing the goals of retribution and deterrence that punitive damages aim to achieve.[44] Furthermore, punitive damages are seen as unfair to both the defendant and the plaintiff. While punitive damages resemble criminal fines, defendants do not enjoy the due-process safeguards of criminal procedure, such as a higher burden of proof.[45] The plaintiff, by contrast, receives an underserved windfall.[46] Another cause for concern is the vagueness of the standards for determining the defendant's liability for punitive damages as well as the amount of damages.[47] Such vagueness, it is argued, allows juries to award punitive damages improperly or excessively; it defies the requirement of legal certainty and violates the principle that punishment should be laid down by law.[48]

Yet the common law-civil law split on punitive damages reflects more than just conflicting approaches to that specific question. This sharp divergence stems from the fundamentally different values and attitudes underlying the two traditions. The civil law is characterized by a formalist, positivist, and legalistic approach that maintains a strict separation between legal and nonlegal norms as well as a separation between different legal domains.[49] In this tradition, the private law-public law distinction carries great weight, and the pragmatic considerations in support of punitive damages fail to undermine this formalist thinking. Furthermore, in the civil-law tradition certainty "has come to be a kind of supreme value, an unquestioned dogma, a fundamental goal."[50] The vague standards for awarding punitive damages conflict with the civil law's pursuit of certainty and leave broad discretion to the judge and jury, contrary to the civil law's quest to limit judicial discretion.[51] By contrast, the idea of punitive damages matches the common-law's thinking, which is more pragmatic and prefers substantive considerations and policy arguments to formalist rules and distinctions. While in common-law systems lawyers respect the private law-public law separation, they refuse to consider it a decisive barrier to punitive damages. For them, the practical utility of such damages—such as deterring conduct that may not be deterred through compensatory awards—carries greater weight.[52]

Let us consider the treatment of punitive damages in Germany, which influenced other civil-law countries. Until the nineteenth century, Germany lacked a uniform approach to punitive damages, and they were quite common in some Germans states. During the nineteenth century, however, influential legal scholars expressed opposition to the idea of intermingling damages with punishment. They argued instead for a strict separation of damages in civil justice and punishment in criminal justice, and their argument prevailed. The 1900 German Civil Code established a purely compensatory law of damages, on the view that damage awards serve exclusively to restore the losses caused by the wrongful act, while punishment belongs to criminal law.[53] Consistent with the code, German courts restricted damages to compensation and rejected the notion of punitive damages throughout the twentieth century, and this view came to shape their attitude to the enforcement of U.S. punitive damage awards.[54] U.S. punitive damages had already come under heavy criticism from German legal scholars, who considered them a violation of German public policy.[55] In 1992, the Federal Court of Justice—Germany's highest court on civil and criminal matters—officially adopted this position in a landmark decision that denied the enforcement of a California judgment awarding punitive damages.[56] Such damages, the court reasoned, contravene public policy, since under German civil justice damages serve to compensate the plaintiff, not to enrich them. Furthermore, by acting as a private-public prosecutor, the plaintiff infringes the German state's monopoly on criminal prosecution, which is safeguarded by special procedural guarantees.[57]

Other civil-law courts followed suit. In 1997, Japan's Supreme Court similarly determined that a U.S. punitive award violated Japan's public policy.[58] Italy's highest court—the Court of Cassation—made a similar determination in 2007, rejecting a million-dollar award by an Alabama court in a product liability case against an Italian manufacturer of motorcycle helmets.[59] In 2010, France's Court of Cassation ruled that punitive damages are not, per se, contrary to public policy. However, they may violate public policy and become unenforceable if they are disproportionate to the damage actually sustained and to the seriousness of the defendant's conduct.[60] EU law also cautions that punitive damages may be contrary to public policy.[61]

One could argue that the common law-civil law divergence on punitive damages is less stark than it initially appears. First, civil-law countries do vary in their approach, and some—such as Spain and Greece—may be open to the enforcement of U.S. punitive damages.[62] Second, as noted above, common-law countries also exhibit variation: in some of them punitive damages are more widely available than in others.[63] Third, punitive damages are no longer unquestioned even in the United States. Since the 1990s, significant limitations on the amount of punitive damages have been established through state and federal legislation as well as decisions of the U.S. Supreme Court, lower federal courts, and state courts.[64] Fourth, even Continental systems that repudiate the notion of punitive damages may have some penal elements in their private-law doctrines.[65] German law, for example, still denies that punitive damages form an integral part of its law of damages: "Punishment and deterrence are not yet acknowledged as legitimate general functions of damages in the German system." In reality, however, with growing frequency German courts have been awarding damages that cannot be considered purely compensatory and, in fact, come close to punitive damages. This suggests that the gap between the German and American approaches is effectively narrowing.[66]

Such trends notwithstanding, Americans and Europeans judge the fairness of punitive damages in a fundamentally different way. For Americans, awarding punitive damages in appropriate circumstances may be entirely legitimate and fair, and it can help achieve desirable social goals. For Continental lawyers, this practice confuses distinct areas of the law and is essentially unfair. In their view, punitive damages are awarded based on vague standards and give the plaintiff an unjustified windfall, while the defendant does not enjoy the necessary protections and safeguards. Hence, "[t]he chances of getting a substantial punitive damages judgment from a U.S. court recognized by any court outside the U.S. are virtually nil."[67]

Discovery

In American civil justice, discovery is a central and essential part of the pretrial phase. Indeed, for many Americans, "civil litigation without discovery is unthinkable."[68] According to one scholar, "Discovery in the United States has reached the status of a quasi-constitutional—if not an outright constitutional—right."[69] In discovery, lawyers for the parties gather the facts of the case, and they do so independently of the court and with a minimum of court supervision. It is lawyers, not judges, who decide which information to demand and which witnesses to call. Judicial intervention occurs only to adjudicate discovery disputes, that is, when attorneys reach an impasse about requested information to be exchanged.[70]

At discovery, each party may require the other party to make available for copying any document or electronically stored information that is relevant to any party's claim or defense. Information requested need not be admissible at trial to be relevant, as long as it may reasonably lead to the discovery of admissible evidence. Furthermore, while the requesting party must specify the type of documents they wish to obtain, there is no obligation to identify specific documents. This, critics argue, allows "fishing expeditions." Only three types of documents are exempt from discovery;[71] for all other documents, the default rule is disclosure. The lawyer asked to disclose must comply, unless they have a valid objection. There are few valid objections; that disclosure is burdensome is not one of them. And while courts have the authority to limit discovery through protective orders, they rarely do so.[72] In addition to documents, discovery may include depositions. Each party may take the sworn testimony upon oral examination of any person, including someone who is not a party to the lawsuit. The party's lawyer—without the prior approval of a court—has the authority to compel attendance at a deposition through a subpoena. A person who fails to comply with a subpoena may be punished with a fine or imprisonment.[73] Other tools of discovery include interrogatories (a set of questions to the other party, to be answered in writing and under oath) and physical or mental examination of parties.[74]

Liberal pretrial discovery was not always a part of U.S. civil justice. American courts initially followed the courts of England, in which pretrial discovery was nearly nonexistent. It was the 1938 Federal Rules of Civil Procedure that laid the foundation of modern-day discovery. The drafters of the rules were concerned that the absence of pretrial discovery caused a serious disadvantage to litigants, resulting in trials "by ambush" that included unfair surprises. They also believed that giving parties full knowledge of the facts before trial would alleviate power disparities between rich and poor litigants. Another expected benefit was the reduction of litigation costs. By revealing the strengths and weaknesses of each party's case early on, discovery may facilitate settlements and save valuable resources. The drafters assumed that pretrial discovery would be an efficient and self-regulating process, based on cooperation and self-interested reciprocity between the parties, which would lead to the expeditious exchange of relevant information.[75] It would therefore serve as a foundation of fair procedure.[76]

In practice, however, discovery has fallen short of these goals. Many American lawyers (and non-lawyers) are heavily critical of a process that they see as broken and dysfunctional.[77] Given their freedom to shape discovery, attorneys often abuse the process to gain advantage. They may attempt to coerce a settlement by increasing an opponent's costs through unnecessary information requests or by compelling an opponent to provide confidential, proprietary, or embarrassing information. They may engage in over-discovery or, alternatively, hide and obfuscate information. They may also request unnecessary depositions or drag out necessary ones to gain time.[78] Indeed, discovery abuse is one of the primary reasons for the congestion and delay in the U.S. judicial system. Furthermore, the discovery process is extremely expensive: by some estimates, discovery costs constitute 50–90% of a case's total litigation costs. Both the costs of discovery and the potential for abuse have risen in the age of electronic discovery, given the massive amounts of discoverable electronic material and the difficulties involved in its collection and preservation.[79]

Over the years, multiple attempts have been made to reform federal discovery rules and curb their abuse, but to limited effect.[80] Indeed, some argue that discovery's effects are incurable: the cooperative ethos underlying discovery fundamentally clashes with the oppositional character of adversarial litigation.[81] Despite the efforts to curtail its excessive scope, American discovery remains vast.[82]

Continental lawyers abhor the U.S. process of discovery for the same reasons that American lawyers consider it to be deeply flawed, dysfunctional, and prone to abuse.[83] Furthermore, the idea of discovery is alien to them: in civil-law countries there are no pretrial depositions and no pretrial evidence production. Civil-law systems have less need for extensive discovery, since they can accomplish some of its goals through other means. Consider the problem of surprise at trial—a problem that discovery aims to address. In the civil law, the problem is less severe than in the U.S. legal system. The German system, for example, can preclude surprise through its ordinary procedures: in their pleadings, the parties must identify the evidence on which they plan to rely; before taking evidence, the judge issues a formal decision stating the evidence to be taken and which disputed facts it concerns. The civil law also has less intrusive means than U.S.-style discovery for dealing with the problem of evidence necessary for one's case that the other party refuses to disclose.[84] More broadly, in the civil law gathering evidence is the primary responsibility of the judge during the main proceedings: the judge decides what evidence is needed and goes on to request documents and interrogate witnesses in person. "Digging for facts is primarily the work of the Judge."[85] A party's disclosure of information to its opponent before the main proceedings is unthinkable from this perspective.[86] Yet the civil law's discomfort with the American process of discovery goes beyond need-based considerations or different conceptions of the role of the judge. Rather, it reflects a difference in values and in the understanding of the law's function in society.

The practice of broad discovery constitutes an important component of American legal culture, which Robert Kagan labeled "adversarial legalism": "a set of legal institutions, rights, and rules that facilitate or encourage adversarial, party-dominated legal contestation."[87] Two powerful yet opposing influences fuel adversarial legalism: on the one hand, political attitudes that expect and demand broad governmental protections from serious harm, injustice, and environmental dangers—and hence an activist, powerful government; on the other hand, a sense of mistrust of concentrated power, which acts to limit and fragment political and governmental authority. Adversarial legalism mitigates this tension. In a structurally fragmented state, courts and lawsuits provide non-statist mechanisms through which individuals can demand justice from government and interest groups can pressure the government to implement ambitious public policies. In such a system, adversarial litigation becomes an essential tool for righting wrongs, curbing governmental and corporate arbitrariness, and building a just society.[88]

One of the hallmarks of adversarial legalism is litigant activism: "a style of legal contestation in which the assertion of claims, the search for controlling legal arguments, and the gathering and submission of evidence are dominated not by judges or government officials but by disputing parties or interests, acting primarily through lawyers."[89] Broad pretrial discovery serves as an important manifestation of this activism and of the attitudes that animate adversarial legalism. Tasking evidence-gathering to the parties themselves, rather than the judge, reflects a mistrust of authority and reluctance to grant power to a single person or a small group: the parties have a strong self-interest in finding information that will undermine the opponent's case as well as information that supports their own claims and defenses, and they are therefore better suited to gathering evidence than the judge. Furthermore, broad discovery is a key tool of private enforcement: it is critical when individuals employ civil litigation to enforce their rights and when interest groups seek to promote their policy goals. In areas such as product liability, the environment, and antitrust, the evidence for making a prima facie case often exists in the files and minds of the defendants. The plaintiffs therefore require extensive discovery to be able to make their case and ultimately obtain justice or change policy. In this view, the costliness of broad discovery and its oft-protracted nature are the inevitable consequences of adversarial, litigant-controlled decision-making.[90]

Civil-law countries are less inclined toward the large-scale and public-law litigation that is common in the United States. They envision a more modest view of litigation: resolution of individual disputes rather than rights enforcement or the creation of new rights and duties. Indeed, the investigation of rights violations and rights enforcement are seen as the business of state agencies, whereas the establishment of new rights comes under the mandate of the legislature—neither is a goal to be advanced through litigation. In France and Germany, such a view of the legal process inspires adherence to a bureaucratic-legalism model, which emphasizes the uniform implementation of centrally devised rules and official responsibility for fact-finding. In such a system, the litigants play a more minor role as compared to the American model, and there is no room for broad discovery: the bureaucratically recruited and embedded judge dominates evidence gathering and carries out the search for the truth.[91]

The European rejection of U.S.-style discovery also stems from an expansive notion of privacy. The differing conceptions of privacy on the two sides of the Atlantic have come to the fore in recent years with respect to online privacy and data protection: EU legislation provides more robust guarantees of data protection than does U.S. law.[92] This resulted in a series of widely publicized disputes, such as the actions of several European regulators against Google over its privacy policy.[93] The breadth of the right to privacy in Europe is among the lessons of the Holocaust. The Nazis' use of census data to identify the households of certain religious, ethnic, or other targeted groups demonstrated how seemingly innocent information could become a tool of oppression. Privacy protections also responded to the increasing size and power of welfare states in Europe. In the United States, by contrast, privacy concerns garnered less political attention.[94]

Evidence gathering requires a balance between finding the truth and protecting the privacy of litigants and non-litigants. In striking this balance, Europeans assign greater weight to the protection of privacy. A "fishing expedition"—any request that is not for a clearly identified document—is thus considered a violation of one's right to privacy. Some go as far as to argue that attempts to force one's opponent to disclose unfavorable evidence constitute a privacy violation. The U.S. legal system, by contrast, employs a narrower conception of privacy and places more emphasis on access to information as a means in the pursuit of justice.[95] As one scholar noted, "[t]he rest of the world . . . thinks U.S. lawyers, agencies, and prosecutors, start lawsuits or investigations on minimal bases, and rely on their adversaries or targets to build their cases for them," while Americans "have sometimes tended to think of the rest of the world as engaged in a massive conspiracy of concealment masquerading as privacy."[96]

Finally, Europeans find U.S. discovery troubling in yet another respect: the violation of the sovereignty of foreign countries where U.S. courts exercise long-arm discovery. In Europe, the active role of the court in the process of gathering evidence shaped the view of evidence taking as an exercise of sovereign power. In this view, evidence taking cannot occur on the territory of a foreign sovereign without that sovereign's consent: it is a formal, judicial act that must be approved by local authorities. Such approval has typically been granted through official channels—for example, based on procedures outlined in the Hague Evidence Convention, an international agreement establishing formal mechanisms for obtaining evidence abroad.[97] However, U.S. courts have often offended the European notion of sovereignty by circumventing official channels and directly ordering foreign individuals under their jurisdiction to produce evidence located abroad for inspection in the United States.[98]

Can U.S.-style discovery justify a refusal to enforce an American judgment in Europe? U.S. discovery may justify nonenforcement on public-policy grounds, but not necessarily. In its landmark 1992 decision, discussed earlier, Germany's Federal Court of Justice reasoned that mere fishing in violation of German standards did not violate German public policy. Since substantive German law contains many obligations on individuals and businesses to disclose information outside of litigation, an order to disclose based on a U.S. procedural rule would not necessarily amount to a public-policy violation. Yet in dictum the court added that discovery clearly exceeding German standards would amount to a public-policy violation and lead to nonenforcement of the foreign judgment. Discovery violating notions of sovereignty may also result in the refusal of enforcement.[99]

But nonenforcement of a foreign judgment is a measure of limited impact that may not deter U.S.-style discovery. Some countries were so alarmed about what they saw as excessive intrusion of American litigants into the affairs of their companies, as well as an infringement of their national sovereignty, that they took legislative action and established "blocking statutes" to thwart U.S. discovery.[100] The most prominent among those statutes is a 1980 French law that established a blanket prohibition on requesting, seeking, or disclosing documents or information of a commercial, financial, or technical nature for the purposes of establishing evidence in a foreign judicial procedure. Violation of these prohibitions is punishable by a six-month imprisonment or fine.[101] Despite the severity of the sanctions, French authorities rarely enforce this law,[102] and U.S. courts have generally dismissed it: they have allowed parties seeking to obtain evidence from French companies to use the discovery procedures available under the U.S. Federal Rules of Civil Procedure.[103] Yet the fact that the French legislature, as well as legislatures in other countries, established laws to stymie U.S. discovery demonstrates the gap between legal systems: a procedure that, in American eyes, promotes the fairness of the legal process is seen as highly unfair, abusive, and pernicious by others.

Jurisdiction

The issue of personal jurisdiction—whether the court holds authority over all parties to the lawsuit—has long engendered controversy between Americans and Europeans. This is a fundamental matter—jurisdictional standards determine whether a court can indeed hear and decide a case—and it figures prominently when a court is considering whether to enforce a foreign judgment.[104] As we shall see, the American-European divergence on jurisdiction reflects not only a different historical evolution, but differences in values as well as in legal thinking and style that lead Europeans to consider U.S. jurisdictional doctrines unfair.

The Continental European law of jurisdiction draws on the Roman idea of jurisdictional restraint, which reflected a notion of fairness. The Justinian maxim *actor sequitur forum rei* states that the plaintiff follows the defendant's forum.[105] Accordingly, the civil law generally requires that plaintiffs sue defendants where defendants are at home; in other words, the court at the defendant's domicile usually has jurisdiction. Yet compelling the plaintiff to sue at the defendant's home may be unfair to the plaintiff in some cases. Therefore, the civil law does recognize some additional jurisdictional bases. For example, when the plaintiff accuses the defendant of a civil wrong, they may sue in the jurisdiction where the wrong occurred; when the claim arises from a contract with the defendant, it may be brought before the court of the place of performance of the obligation in question. Overall, the civil law builds on a limited number of bright-line rules, typically enshrined in jurisdictional statues carefully crafted by the legislature.[106] The rules' specificity aims to achieve consistency and predictability, to prevent litigants from waging protracted and costly battles over jurisdiction, to avoid forum shopping, and to allow litigants to structure their affairs on the basis of relatively certain knowledge as to where jurisdiction might exist. The quest for certainty is indeed one of the hallmarks of the civil law—one which we have already encountered in the discussion of punitive damages. Legislature-made jurisdictional rules also reflect another civil-law attribute: the concern to preserve as much lawmaking power as possible in the hands of the legislature and away from the courts, limiting judicial discretion.[107] The values of certainty and limited judicial power, which undergird the civil-law approach to jurisdiction, stand in stark contrast to those embodied in the American approach to jurisdiction.[108]

The American law of personal jurisdiction is based on the common law, where judges have significant discretion in establishing and applying the law.[109] In an early landmark case, *Pennoyer v. Neff* (1878),[110] the U.S. Supreme Court elevated personal jurisdiction to a constitutional matter governed by the Fourteenth Amendment's due process clause. In that decision, the court expressed a strict territorialist view of jurisdiction, starting from the premise that every U.S. state possesses exclusive jurisdiction and sovereignty over persons and property within its territory. Yet in the 1945 case of *International Shoe v. Washington*[111] the Supreme Court departed from that approach, instead establishing a "minimum contacts" doctrine: a court acquires jurisdiction over a nonresident of the state when that nonresident has sufficient minimum contacts with that state, such that the exercise of jurisdiction over them does not offend notions of fair play and justice. This focus on minimum contacts and fairness dominates the law of personal jurisdiction in the United States to this day.[112] The minimum-contacts test applies to various jurisdictional bases, including those of most concern for Europeans: doctrines establishing "long-arm" jurisdiction over nonresident defendants—be they from another U.S. state or from abroad.

Long-arm doctrines are the product of judicial development and interpretation, and they may also be included in state legislation.[113] Three jurisdictional doctrines in particular have drawn criticism from American academics and Europeans alike.[114] First, "doing-business" jurisdiction means that a state has general jurisdiction over corporations conducting continuous and systematic business in the state. This principle seems simple enough: the defendant business has strong ties with the state and may be sued there on any cause of action. Yet the doctrine's scope is very broad: it allows a court to hear any claim brought against a defendant having regular and consistent commercial activities in the state, even if the facts of the claim are far removed from those activities.[115] Second, "tag" jurisdiction, or transient jurisdiction, allows a court to exercise jurisdiction over a nonresident defendant who is temporarily visiting the state if that defendant was properly served with process while in the state. The defendant's mere physical presence in the state, however temporary, is the foundation for the state's exercise of jurisdiction. As one critic argued, "tag jurisdiction is unjustifiable. Modern day travel takes potential litigants to many fora with which they have no connection, and in which they may remain only fleetingly."[116] Third, attachment jurisdiction allows a plaintiff that failed to acquire personal jurisdiction over the defendant to proceed against any of the defendant's property within the state, such as a house or bank account. Attachment of property within the court's jurisdiction gives the court authority over the defendant up to that property's value.[117]

In the European view, U.S. jurisdictional law—which allows all causes of action to be brought on the basis of the defendant's doing business, physical presence, or property ownership in the forum—rests on contacts that are too thin. All three doctrines confer jurisdiction on the court even in cases in which there may be no substantive connection between the actual claim and the forum state.[118] This, in European thinking, is exorbitant, arbitrary, and unfair;[119] it offends notions of due process (in the case of tag jurisdiction);[120] and it goes against the European quest for consistency and predictability in jurisdictional law:[121] an unsuspecting person or business, unaware of the possibility of a lawsuit against them before a U.S. court, might find themselves trapped in the wide net of U.S. jurisdictional policy. The European preference for clarity and predictability also leads to concerns about U.S. jurisdictional jurisprudence, which is filled with vague, open-ended, and unpredictable terms such as "traditional notions of fair play," "minimum contacts," and "reasonableness."[122] Such concepts grant courts significant discretion—in line with the American preference for flexibility and adaptability and with the relatively broad authority of the judiciary in the United States, but standing against the European preference for clarity, certainty, predictability, and limits on judicial power.[123] Instead, Europeans prefer formal jurisdictional rules that are more precise and clear-cut.[124]

The European desire for certainty and constrained judicial discretion also leads to a rejection of the common-law doctrine of *forum non conveniens*, which is well established in U.S. courts. This doctrine allows a court to decline to hear a case, which is appropriately filed under its jurisdiction, if that court is a seriously inconvenient forum for deciding the case, provided that a better-suited court is available to do so. Such a "jurisdictional calibrating device" gives judges significant discretion and requires them to conduct an ad hoc weighing of the interests at stake in the case before them. Europeans, by contrast, prefer that jurisdictional decisions be based on an *ex ante* consideration of typical interests by the legislature.[125]

From a European viewpoint, American jurisdictional schemes also raise the prospects of forum shopping. "Doing business" jurisdiction, for example, allows the plaintiff to sue the defendant in any place where the latter has extensive activities and not only in its place of incorporation or principal place of business.[126]

We have thus far emphasized European concerns about the U.S. conception of jurisdiction; however, Americans may also find the incompatibility of rules troubling. Civil law countries tend to base adjudicatory authority on the relationship between the court and the claim or the subject matter of the litigation (for example, jurisdiction can be exercised by the state where the tortious event or injury occurred). American law, by contrast, emphasizes the relationship between the court and the party over whom jurisdiction is being exercised, that is, the defendant (for example, jurisdiction where the defendant has a branch or agency). Furthermore, the U.S. emphasis on the connection between the court and the individual defendant rises to the level of a constitutional restriction on the exercise of jurisdiction, derived from the Fourteenth Amendment's due process clause. Jurisdiction based solely on the court/claim nexus would be considered a violation of due process.[127] For example, tort jurisdiction based solely on the place of the injury, with no substantial link between the defendant and the forum, would be compatible with the European notion of jurisdiction, but is inconsistent with the due process clause.[128]

This incompatible thinking about personal jurisdiction could pose an obstacle for the enforcement of foreign judgments. Typically, a court that is asked to enforce a foreign judgment will examine whether in *its* view—that is, from the perspective of the enforcing legal system—the foreign court legitimately exercised its jurisdiction over the case.[129] Given the American-European divergence, a European court might decline to enforce an American judgment if it believes that the U.S. court lacked an appropriate basis to assert jurisdiction. A survey of the reception of U.S. judgments in various countries concluded that "Most of the states surveyed have concepts of jurisdiction which are inconsistent or incompatible with U.S. concepts of long-arm jurisdiction and are not prepared to see such U.S. concepts expanded into their countries."[130] Spain, for example, will enforce a U.S. judgment if the American court applied jurisdictional rules similar to those used by Spain. It will not enforce judgments based on "exorbitant" jurisdiction, where there is no connection between the subject matter of the litigation and the commercial or other activities carried out by the defendant in that jurisdiction. Italy will similarly refuse to enforce an American judgment if jurisdiction over the defendant was based on the "minimum contacts" basis or another jurisdictional basis not recognized in Italian law.[131]

The Difficult Path to a Judgment-Enforcement Convention

Europeans' wary attitude toward foreign judgments in general, and concerns about American judgments in particular, have made it rather difficult to enforce U.S. judgments in Europe. By contrast, as explained above, American courts tend to show a much more favorable attitude toward foreign judgments. This enforcement deficit—the easy enforcement of European judgments in the United States versus the often-unwelcoming treatment of American judgments in Europe—prompted the U.S. government in 1992 to initiate a global convention on the enforcement of foreign judgments. This move constituted a significant departure from the long-held American skepticism toward treaty-making in the area of private international law and transnational litigation. Indeed, from the late nineteenth century and through much of the twentieth century the United States declined to participate in treaty negotiations or to commit to treaties in matters relating to private international law or civil procedure.[132] This reluctance stemmed from several factors: the view that private international law and civil procedure are matters of state law, which forestalls the federal government from entering into treaties that bind the states in these matters; a concern that treaties may import undesirable elements of civil-law codes into U.S. law and inhibit the organic evolution of common-law rules in response to social developments; and the advent of a unilateralist approach to transnational litigation after World War II—an approach that dismissed the constraints of international law.[133]

This view began to change in the 1970s, as the United States ratified a few multilateral transnational-litigation conventions[134] and entered into bilateral negotiations with Britain on a judgment-enforcement convention. The negotiations, held between 1976 and 1980, took into account UK concerns about the American practices of punitive and multiple damages and, more broadly, the perception that U.S. damage awards are significantly higher than those in Britain. Despite the American efforts to mitigate these concerns, negotiations broke down due to the opposition of British manufacturers and insurers.[135] A decade following this failure, the United States nonetheless came up with a much more ambitious initiative for a multilateral enforcement convention.

While the American-European gap in foreign-judgment enforcement was by no means a new phenomenon in the early 1990s, its realities and implications assumed greater prominence in the era of globalization. As the volume of cross-Atlantic commerce and attendant transnational litigation increased, it became harder to accept what some saw as a lose/lose situation for American litigants: European judgments were quickly and easily enforced in the United States, whereas American judgments were often rejected by European courts for any number of reasons. The growing number of American plaintiffs who could not collect judgments against foreign parties motivated the pursuit of a global convention to remedy this problem.[136] Such a convention, it was hoped, would level the international playing field for American litigants. It would ensure rough equality between the judgment-enforcement practices of contracting parties—an equality that would work primarily to the benefit of the United States given its generous enforcement practice. The harmonization of enforcement rules would also serve to clarify and simplify the practices and procedures of enforcement, allowing litigants to foresee the likely effect that another country would accord the judgment.[137] More broadly, a regime for coordinating the work of national courts in resolving transnational disputes would fill a gap in the legal infrastructure of the global marketplace. The free flow of judgments—the ability to enforce legal rights across borders—could serve to facilitate and encourage flows of trade and investment.[138]

In May 1992, the United States proposed that the Hague Conference on Private International Law—an international organization devoted to the unification of the rules of private international law—establish a multilateral treaty on the enforcement of foreign judgments. Five negotiating sessions in The Hague between 1996 and 1999 resulted in a preliminary draft in October 1999. The United States considered that draft unacceptable, as it suffered from "fatal defects in the approach, structure, and details of the text."[139] Consultations with industry and consumer groups, the private bar, and government litigators brought the State Department to the conclusion that the draft was not even close to being ratifiable in the United States. Before Congress, the State Department warned that "if other delegations do not begin to show more flexibility on many key provisions, we will be unable to achieve a convention that could attract sufficient support in the United States."[140] In June 2001, a diplomatic conference produced another draft, which also failed to make headway. The Hague Conference therefore decided in January 2003 to pursue a more limited convention focused on choice-of-court clauses in business-to-business contracts. In June 2005, the Convention on Choice of Court Agreements was signed. This was a much leaner version of the agreement that the United States had originally envisioned. It allows businesses that select in their contract a particular forum and win judgment in that forum to enforce that judgment in the territory of another state party. All others—noncommercial litigants, consumers, human rights claimants, and even businesses that obtain a judgment from a forum other than the one specified in their contract—are excluded from the convention. This was a far cry from the hoped-for comprehensive agreement that would have allowed American plaintiffs to enforce U.S. judgments against their opponents' foreign assets.[141] Only in 2019 did the Hague Conference adopt a fuller Convention on the Recognition and Enforcement of Foreign Judgments in Civil or Commercial Matters.

Why was it so difficult to establish a judgment-enforcement convention? Why did the early efforts, from 1996 to 2001, end in failure? At one level, this failure resulted from a simple dynamic of conflicting interests. The United States was primarily interested in securing the enforcement of its judgments in Europe; Europeans, however, sought to protect their nationals from what they perceived as an exorbitant U.S. assertion of jurisdiction as well as excessive damages awarded by U.S. courts. Indeed, a global enforcement convention would also have promoted a shared American-European interest in transnational legal certainty—an important foundation for a globalized economy. Yet, this joint interest was not enough to overcome the divergence of national interests and priorities.[142] Nor did the United States possess the bargaining power necessary to do so. According to the State Department, "[s]ince litigants from most developed countries have no substantial difficulties enforcing judgments in the United States, their governments believe they have substantial negotiating leverage over us."[143] Given the generous American approach to the enforcement of foreign judgments, and since U.S. law does not condition enforcement on reciprocity, the United States had little with which to push its European counterparts.[144] Already enjoying easy enforcement of their judgments in American courts, European countries' motivation to alter the status quo was much weaker than that of the United States.[145]

At a deeper level, the early failure to establish a full-scale enforcement convention in The Hague stemmed from deeply held, divergent attitudes concerning what is appropriate and fair in litigation. As Jeffrey Kovar, the State Department's Assistant Legal Adviser for private international law, put it, there existed "a deep-seated feeling among many other delegations that they do not wish to enforce U.S. judgments unless we make our jurisdiction practices consistent with their view of what constitutes appropriate international rules."[146] This focus on jurisdiction reflected the salience of jurisdictional standards in a decision whether or not to enforce a foreign judgment: before enforcing a foreign judgment, a court must verify that the rendering court exercised jurisdiction appropriately.[147] To facilitate foreign-judgment enforcement, agreement had to be reached on what is a permissible or impermissible basis of jurisdiction. Furthermore, the focus on appropriate jurisdictional reach in part may have masked other concerns about American litigation.[148] What Europeans really wanted was to protect their citizens and businesses from the perceived evils of the U.S. legal system, from juries through class actions to discovery.[149]

Yet agreement on jurisdictional issues proved elusive. On the one hand, Europeans were deeply uncomfortable with U.S. jurisdictional notions that they found vague and unpredictable, such as "doing business" or "minimum contacts." On the other hand, the United States could not accept certain jurisdictional grounds that lacked a substantial link between the defendant and the court. Widely applied in Europe, such grounds violate the due process clause.[150] Efforts were made, with at least partial success, to forge compromises and bridge some of the American-European divide.

Regarding jurisdiction in matters of torts and contracts, negotiators made a conscious attempt to bring together the European approach, which emphasizes the court-claim nexus, and the American approach, which emphasizes the court-defendant nexus. These efforts, however, did not result in a set of rules capable of generating a global consensus.[151]

On tag jurisdiction, which European representatives sought to eliminate, the United States was largely forthcoming, but groups interested in pursuing litigation against human rights violators, war criminals, and Holocaust profiteers did not want to forgo the possibility of suing in the United States, where tag jurisdiction may provide the only opportunity of doing so. A compromise was thus fashioned to allow the exercise of jurisdiction based only on personal service in the forum for claims of damages arising from genocide, war crimes, or other serious crimes under international law.[152]

On doing-business jurisdiction, however, American negotiators refused to yield. In the American view, there is nothing wrong with exercising jurisdiction over a defendant that conducts systematic and continuous activities within the forum state, even when the claim is unrelated to the activity. This includes defendants that are foreign companies with a permanent establishment in the United States. In European eyes, by contrast, such an exercise of jurisdiction creates uncertainty and encourages forum shopping. The American side, however, refused to include doing-business among the prohibited bases of jurisdiction.[153]

A judicial refusal to exercise jurisdiction through *forum non conveniens*—a common-law doctrine that civil-law countries reject—raised another controversy that was not fully resolved. A proposed compromise included a narrow provision for declining jurisdiction in exceptional circumstances. This provision established stricter requirements for dismissing a case, as compared to the American conception of *forum non conveniens*.[154]

Another vexing problem in the legal relations between the United States and Europe concerns the size of damages awarded by U.S. courts: non-compensatory damages—in particular, punitive damages—as well as compensatory damages that are excessive by European standards. Given that the issue of damages derailed the U.S.-UK bilateral enforcement treaty in the 1970s, American delegates recognized the need for a compromise. They accepted a provision that allows the enforcing court to reexamine the amount of damages awarded by the foreign (read: American) court and to enforce a lesser amount.[155]

In the end, however, the differences proved insurmountable, and the negotiations concluded in 2001 without a global judgment-enforcement convention. In 2012, however, the Hague Conference restarted the judgment-convention project, and the drafting of a new text began.[156] This time, the project successfully came to fruition with the adoption in July 2019 of the Convention on the Recognition and Enforcement of Foreign Judgments in Civil or Commercial Matters. What accounts for the changed outcome?

First, the Hague Conference, which used to be Eurocentric, has taken on a more global character. Asian and Latin American countries have become more actively involved, and Latin American delegations in particular have occasionally served as a counterbalance to the EU.[157] Second, thanks to the EU's work in the Area of Freedom, Security, and Justice, European law had become increasingly harmonized, creating greater consistency among European countries. EU instruments played a role in guiding the Hague negotiations.[158] Third, in a series of decisions beginning in 2011,[159] the U.S. Supreme Court had narrowed jurisdictional standards that Europeans considered exorbitant, such as doing-business jurisdiction, which made them less insistent on limiting U.S. jurisdiction.[160] Fourth, and crucially, the 2019 convention had a limited focus. The earlier, failed efforts to establish a convention had had a dual goal: to regulate how courts exercise their jurisdiction (known as "direct" jurisdiction); and to set rules for the recognition and enforcement of judgments abroad. The 2019 convention, by contrast, aimed only at the latter. It determines whether a foreign judgment qualifies for recognition and enforcement, but states remain free to determine on which grounds their own courts may, or may not, exercise jurisdiction.[161] This limited focus of the convention mitigated the American-European disagreement over jurisdiction, which had derailed the earlier efforts. While this narrower focus of the convention was the product of American insistence,[162] the United States compromised by accepting a convention provision that allows the refusal of enforcement of judgments that award punitive damages.[163]

Conclusion

This chapter has examined the dominant European *perceptions* of American civil justice. Note the emphasis on perceptions, since these are sometimes at odds with reality. Perceptions may exaggerate the differences between legal systems; or they might stick and persist without acknowledging that these differences have narrowed over time. And the present case indeed demonstrates that legal differences may shrink and that concerns about those differences should perhaps ease. Fears of trials by jury may lessen, as civil trials in the United States have become exceedingly rare, at both the federal and state levels, especially since the mid-1980s. With only a small share of cases leading to an actual trial—a phenomenon dubbed "the vanishing trial"—juries have lost much of their previous importance.[164]

We have also referred above to the increasing limitations on punitive damages, the efforts to reform discovery and rein in its abuse, and the constriction of personal jurisdiction through U.S. Supreme Court rulings. Yet these changes have made only a limited impression on the prevailing perceptions of American notions of justice as incompatible with those of Europe.

Specifically, this chapter presented three clashes between American and European conceptions of civil justice: punitive damages, discovery, and long-arm jurisdiction are all hallmarks of U.S. civil justice that Europeans abhor. In accounting for the European repudiation of U.S.-style civil litigation, one has to consider self-interest: the desire to protect citizens and businesses from having to litigate in American courts or from coming under unfavorable U.S. rules and procedures.[165] European resistance to U.S. civil justice may also stem from broader concerns about U.S. domination.[166] At their core, however, the controversies examined here reflect differing approaches to how a fair legal process should be conducted. Even more deeply, they reflect different views about the role of adjudication in society; the proper scope of judicial power; the importance of legal certainty versus flexibility; and the right balance between conflicting values, such as truth finding versus privacy. By rejecting the American views on these issues and clinging to their own understanding of what is appropriate and permissible, Europeans clearly demonstrated ethnocentric thinking: they considered their own rules, procedures, and values as the "correct" ones and rejected inconsistent American views and practices as deeply flawed and unfair. Such use of one's legal system as the metric for the assessment of foreign legal systems serves as an excellent demonstration of the idea of legal ethnocentrism that stands at the center of this book.

But the ethnocentric evaluation can work both ways: While legal system A may criticize legal system B, B may harbor its own doubts and concerns regarding A. We have seen in this chapter that while Europeans have serious qualms about American jurisdictional rules, Americans may view the European approach to jurisdiction as offending notions of due process. The following chapter examines another conflict over transnational litigation that puts the United States in the position of evaluating and criticizing foreign civil justice.

Notes

1. Bornstein and Robicheaux 2008.
2. Michaels 2006, 1006.
3. Michaels 2009.
4. Wasserstein-Fassberg 2013, chap. 4; Baumgartner 2003, 136.
5. Baumgartner 2003, 48–55; Baumgartner 2008, 184; Baumgartner 2013, 5; Wasserstein-Fassberg 2013, 254–256.
6. Baumgartner 2013, 976–977.
7. Baumgartner 2008, 184–185.
8. Baumgartner 2008, 191.
9. Juenger 1988, 7; Baumgartner 2013, 975.
10. For instance, some countries, such as Poland and Switzerland, have softened or abolished their reciprocity requirement. Baumgartner 2008, 192–193.
11. Regulation (EC) No 44/2001 on jurisdiction and the recognition and enforcement of judgments in civil and commercial matters (Brussels I Regulation) and Regulation (EU) No 1215/2012 on jurisdiction and the recognition and enforcement of judgments in civil and commercial matters (Recast Brussels Regulation).

12. Preamble of Brussels I Regulation, Recitals 2 and 6.
13. See Articles 36 and 39 of the Recast Brussels Regulation.
14. Baumgartner 2013, 970–971.
15. Dodge 2015, 2085–2086.
16. 159 U.S. 113 (1895).
17. 159 U.S. 113 (1895), 164.
18. 159 U.S. 113 (1895), 202–203, 205–206, 227–228.
19. Johnston v. Compagnie Generale Transatlantique, 152 N.E. 121 (1926); Brand 1991, 262; Bellinger and Anderson 2014, 507–508.
20. Kulzer 1968, 2.
21. Preparatory Note accompanying the 1962 Act.
22. A judgment *must not* be enforced if the foreign legal system that rendered the judgment does not meet criteria of impartiality or due process or if the foreign court lacked personal or subject-matter jurisdiction. Among the six grounds that *allow* nonenforcement are fraud in obtaining the judgment, a cause of action that is repugnant to the state's public policy, or a conflict with another judgment. 1962 Act, Sections 3 and 4. If the foreign judgment did not meet any of these invalidating criteria, an American court must make it enforceable as a U.S. judgment.
23. The 2005 model carries the title Foreign-Country Money Judgments Recognition Act. See Efrat and Newman 2018a.
24. Brand 2013, 500–502.
25. The Association of the Bar of the City of New York 2001; Baumgartner 2008.
26. Baumgartner 2013, 978–979.
27. Stürner 2001, 12.
28. Posch 2004, 374.
29. Moore 2003, 1498. See empirical debate over whether such an anti-foreigner bias of juries indeed exists: Clermont and Eisenberg 1996; Moore 2003.
30. Borchers 1998, 160; The Association of the Bar of the City of New York 2001; Stürner 2001, 12–13; Baumgartner 2008, 202; Baumgartner 2013, 978–980; Barker 2012, 8.
31. Baumgartner 2013, 979.
32. Behr 2003, 105, 109–112.
33. Owen 1994, 368–369; Gotanda 2004, 397–398; Wells 1996, 570.
34. Gotanda 2004, 421. Five U.S. states either prohibit or severely restrict the imposition of punitive damages: Nebraska, Washington, Louisiana, New Hampshire, and Massachusetts.
35. Owen 1994, 365; Gotanda 2004, 422.
36. Owen 1994, 365.
37. Owen 1994, 375–376.
38. Owen 1994, 377–378.
39. Behr 2003, 121; Owen 1994, 374–375.
40. Owen 1994, 380–381.
41. Owen 1994, 378–379; Behr 2003, 122–124.
42. Wells 1996, 565–566.
43. Koziol 2008, 751, 755–756. Wasserstein-Fassberg 2013, 7.
44. Owen 1994, 382–383.
45. Owen 1994, 382.
46. Owen 1994, 392.
47. Owen 1994, 384–385. The standards of liability for punitive damages are often defined through terms such as "malice," "recklessness," or "outrageous behavior."
48. Koziol 2008, 756; Baumgartner 2013, 992.
49. d'Aspremont 2011.
50. Merryman and Pérez-Perdomo 2007, 48.
51. Wells 1996, 561–564.
52. Wells 1996, 564–566.
53. Behr 2003, 127–128, 155.
54. Behr 2003, 129.
55. Baumgartner 2013, 994.

56. G.D.S. v. E.S., 118 BGHZ 312 (Bundesgerichtshof IX Civ. Sen. 4 June 1992). See Hay 1992.
57. Behr 2003, 157–158; Baumgartner 2008, 205–206; Liptak 2008.
58. Braslow 1999; Baumgartner 2013, 995.
59. Quarta 2008; Baumgartner 2013, 995.
60. Schlenzka & Langhorne v. Fountaine Pajot S.A., Cass. Civ. 1st, Dec. 1, 2010, no. 09-13303, Recueil Dalloz 2011, 423. See Janke and Licari 2012; Baumgartner 2013, 995–996.
61. Regulation (EC) No 864/2007 on the law applicable to non-contractual obligations (Rome II), preamble (Recital 32).
62. Berch 2010, 96–97; Janke and Licari 2012, 777n9.
63. Gotanda 2004.
64. Behr 2003, 115–120; Gotanda 2004, 422–431; Berch 2010, 62–77; Plosser 2018.
65. Berch 2010, 81–82; Baumgartner 2013, 993.
66. Behr 2003, 148.
67. Borchers 2010, 531.
68. Maxeiner 2011, 123; Beisner 2010, 554.
69. Curran 2016, 1141.
70. Maxeiner 2011, 128, 130.
71. Confidential communications between lawyer and client; certain materials related to trial preparation; and electronically stored information that is not reasonably accessible because of an undue burden or cost. Maxeiner 2011, 139.
72. Maxeiner 2011, 137–139.
73. Maxeiner 2011, 141.
74. Beckerman 2000, 514; Beisner 2010, 558. See Federal Rules of Civil Procedure 33, 35.
75. Beckerman 2000, 515; Beisner 2010, 554–557; Maxeiner 2011, 130, 153.
76. Baumgertner 2003, 83.
77. American College of Trial Lawyers 2009; Beisner 2010, 549.
78. Subrin 2009, 309; Beisner 2010, 551–552; Maxeiner 2011, 132.
79. Beisner 2010, 549, 570.
80. Beckerman 2000, 549; Beisner 2010, 563, 577.
81. Beckerman 2000, 517, 520.
82. Curran 2016, 1147.
83. Baumgartner 2008, 209.
84. Maxeiner 2011, 151–152.
85. Langbein 1985, 826–827.
86. Subrin 2009, 301; Baumgartner 2008, 208; Curran 2016, 1143.
87. Kagan 2001, 13.
88. Kagan 2001, 14–16.
89. Kagan 2001, 9.
90. Kagan 2001, 9; Subrin 2009, 309, 311.
91. Kagan 2001,11; Baumgartner 2003, 84–85; Subrin 2009, 311; Maxeiner 2011, 151; Curran 2016, 1143.
92. European Parliament 2015.
93. Streitfeld and O'Brien 2012; Satariano 2019.
94. Singleton 1999, 189–190. See generally Farrell and Newman 2019.
95. Baumgartner 2004, 1320, 135 and Baumgartner 2008, 209.
96. Lowenfeld 1986, 419–420.
97. Convention on the Taking of Evidence Abroad in Civil or Commercial Matters, 1970.
98. Stürner 2001, 14–15; Baumgartner 2003, 96–97; Born and Rutledge 2011, 970; Baumgartner 2013, 973–975.
99. Baumgartner 2013, 973–974, 982–983.
100. Born and Rutledge 2011, 972–973; Curran 2016, 1143–1144.
101. Law No. 80-538 [1978] Journal Officiel 1799, July 16, 1980, Article 1*bis*. See Born and Rutledge 2011, 972n47; Rouhette and Barda 2017.
102. The first conviction under the 1980 statute occurred in 2007. Rouhette and Barda 2017.
103. Rouhette and Barda 2017. See Societe Nationale Industrielle Aerospatiale v. U.S. District Court, 482 U.S. 522 (1987).

104. von Mehren and Trautman 1968, 1610.
105. Clermont 1999, 91.
106. Clermont 1999, 92; Baumgartner 2003, 145, 149–150; Maxeiner 2011, 64.
107. Baumgartner 2003, 150–151.
108. Silberman 2002, 328–329. The age of nationalism brought a certain deviation from the restrained European approach to jurisdiction and resulted in the formation of some new and rather exorbitant jurisdictional bases. For example, the French Civil Code grants French courts personal jurisdiction over actions brought by a plaintiff of French nationality, regardless of the defendant's identity. But this is ultimately a limited departure from the well-established European approach to jurisdiction. Baumgartner 2003, 146; and 2013, 977; Clermont 1999, 92–93.
109. Borchers 1992, 122, 132.
110. Pennoyer v. Neff, 95 U.S. 714 (1878).
111. International Shoe Co. v. Washington, 326 U.S. 310 (1945).
112. Baumgartner 2003, 133–136; van Loon 2019, 23.
113. Vedder Price n.d.; Baumgartner 2003, 175.
114. Clermont 1999, 111–115; Borchers 1992, 134–135.
115. Twitchell 2001, 173; Silberman 2002, 338–342; van Loon 2019, 23.
116. Borchers 1992, 134–135. Furthermore, in Continental systems the court's authority to adjudicate is considered to exist prior to the actual bringing of the suit; it does not arise from the service of process on the defendant. Europeans thus reject the idea of transient jurisdiction that bases the court's power to adjudicate on the delivery of process to the defendant while they are physically present in the forum state's territory. Ginsburg 1965, 90.
117. Clermont 1999, 112–113.
118. Ginsburg 1965, 98; Clermont 1999, 96, 111.
119. Ginsburg 1965, 90; Weintraub 1991, 613; Posch 2004, 368.
120. Wurmnest 2005, 170.
121. Baumgartner 2003, 150, 166; U.S. House of Representatives 2000, 23 (statement of Jeffrey D. Kovar, Assistant Legal Adviser for private international law, U.S. Department of State).
122. Borchers 1998, 160; Silberman 2002, 329; Baumgartner 2003, 176–177; Posch 2004, 372.
123. Baumgartner 2003, 179; U.S. House of Representatives 2000, 23.
124. Silberman 2002, 328.
125. Ginsburg 1965, 98; Silberman 2002, 329–330; Baumgartner 2003, 151, 179.
126. Silberman 2002, 328, 342.
127. Silberman 2000, 329–330; Brand 2002, 199–202; van Loon 2019, 23.
128. U.S. House of Representatives 2000, 23; Brand 2002, 204–205.
129. Wasserstein-Fassberg 2013, 262–263.
130. The Association of the Bar of the City of New York 2001, 384.
131. The Association of the Bar of the City of New York 2001, 387.
132. Baumagartner 2003, 22, 41–42.
133. von Mehren 1994, 273; Baumgarter 2003, 22–32.
134. The Convention on the Recognition and Enforcement of Foreign Arbitral Awards (New York Arbitration Convention)—the United States acceded in 1970; Convention on the Service Abroad of Judicial and Extrajudicial Documents in Civil or Commercial Matters (Hague Service Convention)—the United States ratified in 1967; and the Convention on the Taking of Evidence Abroad in Civil or Commercial Matters (Hague Evidence Convention)—the United States ratified in 1973. See von Mehren 1994, 273–274; Baumgartner 2003, 43–45.
135. Hay and Walker 1978; von Mehren 1994, 274; Adler and Zarychta 2006, 5.
136. Notes from NGO meeting on Hague treaty on jurisdiction and foreign judgments, October 5, 2000 (in the possession of the author); Adler and Zarychta 2006 3–4, 6.
137. U.S. House of Representatives 2000, 21; von Mehren 1994, 278–279. An enforcement convention could also prevent European courts from using exorbitant bases of jurisdiction against Americans (see note 108). von Mehren 1994, 278–279; Pfund 1998, 9; Silberman 2002, 322; Adler and Zarychta 2006, 4.
138. U.S. House of Representatives 2000, 21.

139. Letter from Jeffrey Kovar, the State Department's Assistant Legal Adviser for private international law, to J.H.A. van Loon, secretary general of the Hague Conference on Private International Law, February 22, 2000, cited in Borrás 2005, 46n12. See von Mehren 2001, 192; Brand 2002 197; Adler and Zarychta 2006, 9; van Loon 2019, 19–21.
140. U.S. House of Representatives 2000, 23. See Brand 2002, 193.
141. Adler and Zarychta 2006, 2, 10; Michaels 2006, 1009–1010.
142. Silberman 2002, 321–322; Adler and Zarychta 2006 6–7; Miller 2004, 259.
143. U.S. House of Representatives 2000, 22–23.
144. On the reciprocity requirement in U.S. foreign judgments law, see Miller 2004.
145. van Loon 2019, 20.
146. U.S. House of Representatives 2000, 22. See van Loon 2019, 20; Teitz 2019, 493.
147. Baumgartner 2003, 129–130.
148. Silberman 2002, 348.
149. Silberman 2002, 319–320.
150. U.S. House of Representatives 2000, 23; von Mehren 2001, 196; Brand 2002, 204–205.
151. Brand 2002, 203–207.
152. von Mehren 2001, 196; Silberman 2002, 345–346.
153. Silberman 2002, 338–345.
154. Silberman 2002, 346; Brand 2002, 207.
155. von Mehren 2001, 195; Silberman 2002, 327; Baumgartner 2003, 188.
156. Baumgartner 2016, 7; Teitz 2019, 499–500.
157. Teitz 2019, 497, 507–508; van Loon 2019, 22.
158. Teitz 2019, 497.
159. Goodyear Dunlop Tires Operations, S.A. v. Brown, 564 U.S. 915, 919 (2011); J. McIntyre Mach., Ltd. v. Nicastro, 131 S. Ct. 2780 (2011); Daimler AG v. Bauman, 571 U.S. 117, 122 (2014); Bristol-Myers Squibb Co. v. Superior Court of California, 137 S. Ct. 1773, 1780 (2017).
160. Teitz 2019, 498, 508.
161. van Loon 2019, 22–23. See Article 1 of the Convention on the Recognition and Enforcement of Foreign Judgments in Civil or Commercial Matters.
162. Teitz 2019, 500.
163. See Article 10 of the convention.
164. Galanter 2004; Langbein 2012.
165. Baumgartner 2003, 180.
166. Posch 2004, 367.

8

Balancing Free Speech and Reputation

A Cross-Atlantic Divide

In 2010, the U.S. Congress enacted the Securing the Protection of Our Enduring and Established Constitutional Heritage (SPEECH) Act.[1] The act's title says little about its actual content, yet it does convey an ethnocentric sentiment: this legislation seeks to defend some fundamental American values or practices—"constitutional heritage"—that are presumably under threat. What is this threat and why did Congress decide to tackle it?

Freedom of speech, which is protected by the First Amendment to the U.S. Constitution, is a sacred right in the American constitutional order. Indeed, the constitutional protection afforded to freedom of speech in the United States is perhaps the strongest protection afforded to any individual right under the Constitution, and such a robust protection is "an integral part of American culture, resulting from our own history and experience. It is an American phenomenon."[2] Viewed as a central pillar of democracy, freedom of speech generally prevails in competition with other democratic principles, such as equality, human dignity, and privacy.[3] The law of defamation presents such competition, since free speech could harm one's right to a good reputation.[4] The rules of defamation law will thus reflect a balance: greater weight assigned to the protection of reputation would mean heavier restrictions on free speech; by contrast, greater weight assigned to free speech would result in lighter restrictions on expression at the expense of reputational protection. Given the centrality of free speech in the American tradition, the United States clearly takes the latter position.

The First Amendment limits the liability of authors and publishers under state defamation law by prohibiting injunctions against defamatory statements in nearly all cases[5] and by restricting the circumstances under which a plaintiff may obtain damages for defamation. The limitation of liability has three key

Intolerant Justice. Asif Efrat, Oxford University Press. © Oxford University Press 2023.
DOI: 10.1093/oso/9780197658895.003.0008

expressions. First, the First Amendment renders non-actionable a defamatory statement of opinion that lacks a "provably false factual connotation."[6] Second, it requires *the plaintiff* to prove the falsity of the defamatory statement. It is the plaintiff that bears the burden of showing that the statements at issue were false. Third, it requires the plaintiff to prove fault, with clear and convincing evidence, by showing that the defamatory statements were published with negligence or actual malice, depending on the statement's subject matter and whether the defendant is a public figure.[7] These trial-level protections are reinforced by a unique commitment of appellate courts to conduct independent appellate review in libel cases to ensure that any decision in favor of the plaintiff does not unnecessarily intrude on free expression. This requires judges to go beyond the typical standard of appellate review of jury verdicts.[8]

As the U.S. Supreme Court stated in *New York Times v. Sullivan*, these First Amendment doctrines reflect "a profound national commitment to the principle that debate on public issues should be uninhibited, robust, and wide-open."[9] Yet such a deep commitment to an open public debate and to the freedom of speech that undergirds it is virtually unparalleled anywhere else in the world. Other democratic countries treat free speech as an important right, but one that must be balanced against other rights.[10] These countries are therefore willing to impose greater restrictions on free speech for the protection of one's reputation. As their law is more amenable to defamation suits, they may attract foreign plaintiffs who seek a favorable venue in which to prevent publication or obtain damages. More specifically, subjects of publications disseminated primarily in the United States could seek to circumvent First Amendment protections by bringing defamation suits against American authors and publishers in foreign courts. The resulting forum-shopping dynamic has come to be known as "libel tourism."

Britain used to be a particularly appealing destination for libel tourism given its plaintiff-friendly defamation law. First and foremost, British law places *on the defendant* the burden of proving the truth of the defamatory statement—in contrast to the United States, where it is the plaintiff who has to prove that the statement is false. This shift of the burden of proof greatly facilitates defamation suits and increases their prospects of success. For some defendants, especially journalists who rely on confidential sources, proving truthfulness could be an insurmountable burden.[11] Second, British law renders opinions actionable unless the defendant can successfully invoke a limited exception. Third, British law permits an injunction against the publication of defamatory material—an illegal remedy under U.S. law.[12]

A further boost to libel tourism came from British procedural law, which takes a generous approach to the exercise of jurisdiction over defendants. Whereas the Fourteenth Amendment's due process clause allows an American court to exercise personal jurisdiction over a defamation defendant only if their statement was expressly aimed at the jurisdiction in which the court sits, British law allows a court to exercise personal jurisdiction over such a defendant if their statement, wherever it was aimed, caused real or substantial harm or injury to one's reputation in Britain. British courts applied this requirement liberally, asserting jurisdiction over defendants whose books, magazines, or newspapers, though primarily distributed in the United States, reached even a few readers in Britain. As a result, British courts often heard claims where the plaintiff or defendant had a tenuous connection to Britain and where the publication in question in no way aimed at that jurisdiction. Furthermore, British courts exercised jurisdiction over American defendants whose websites, though established in the United States, were visited by persons in Britain.[13] "[O]nline content published in the U.S. and intended primarily for an American audience can be viewed anywhere around the globe, giving the English courts the thinnest of jurisdictional hooks for libel cases, but one that they have seized."[14] While British judges had discretion to dismiss cases that should be appropriately heard somewhere else—for example, by using the *forum non conveniens* doctrine—they were generally reluctant to give up jurisdiction, even when the facts of the case had almost no tie to the UK.[15]

The case of American historian Deborah Lipstadt marked the onset of libel tourism, as it exposed the transatlantic rift over free speech and the handling of libel cases.[16] In 1996, Lipstadt, an Emory University professor, was sued by British author David Irving in London for defamation after she called him a "Holocaust denier" in her book *Denying the Holocaust* (1993), which was published in the United States. Under UK law, Lipstadt bore the burden of proving that Irving had deliberately misrepresented historical evidence, and she escaped liability after successfully proving that to the UK court.[17] While this case had at least some connection to the UK—the plaintiff was British—subsequent cases were brought by plaintiffs who were *not* UK residents, but who sued there merely to exploit its plaintiff-friendly libel laws.[18] In 1997, Russian tycoon Boris Berezovsky filed suit against *Forbes* magazine in London over an article that unfavorably portrayed him under the title "Godfather of the Kremlin?"[19] *Forbes* argued that it made no sense to litigate a case involving a Russian plaintiff and a U.S.-based magazine in Britain, home to a tiny fraction of the publication's readers; but to no avail. UK courts did not relinquish their jurisdiction, and *Forbes* chose to retract the claims and settle the case rather than face trial.[20] Additional cases of libel tourism followed, typically filed by wealthy individuals or politicians against American authors, publishers, and news organizations, but sometimes against non-American defendants.[21] In fact, various American celebrities went to London to seek damages for allegedly defamatory articles published in the U.S. media. They realized their libel suits had much better prospects in a British court than in an American one.[22]

It was becoming clear that the British-American gap in the protection of free speech was being abused to the detriment of American defendants and the ground was ripe for action against libel tourism. But it took the tireless efforts of one victim of libel tourism—Rachel Ehrenfeld—to produce that remedy: federal legislation to prevent plaintiffs from circumventing First Amendment protections by bringing defamation suits against American authors and publishers in Britain. Her successful advocacy efforts demonstrate how a personal experience with abusive transnational litigation can be leveraged to trigger a political response.

In 2003, Ehrenfeld, an independent scholar, published *Funding Evil: How Terrorism is Financed and How to Stop It*. The book mentioned Khalid bin Mahfouz, a Saudi billionaire who was chief executive of the National Commercial Bank: the first bank to be established in Saudi Arabia and among the largest banks in the Arab world. In 1993 bin Mahfouz paid $225 million to settle criminal charges of bank fraud brought against him in New York.[23] Ehrenfeld's book implicated bin Mahfouz in the funding of terrorism, arguing that he had transferred some $74 million to charities that served as fronts for terrorist organizations, including al Qaeda and Hamas. Bin Mahfouz's lawyers first demanded from Ehrenfeld a public apology, a retraction, the removal of her book from circulation everywhere, and a donation to a charity chosen by bin Mahfouz. When Ehrenfeld, a New York resident, refused these demands, bin Mahfouz sued her for libel in London in 2004. Although the book was not published or marketed in Britain, the British court chose to exercise jurisdiction over the case. The basis for jurisdiction was the fact that 23 copies of the book had arrived in Britain through Internet purchases and that a chapter of the book had been available online and accessible from Britain. Ehrenfeld refused to recognize the court's jurisdiction and declined to defend herself—both because of the costs of litigating in the UK and as a principled protest against what she considered an attempt to chill her speech by suing in a country that had no connection to the case. The British court, in decisions issued in December 2004 and May 2005, entered a default judgment against Ehrenfeld and her publisher, issued an injunction and a "declaration of falsity" regarding the disputed statement, ordered Ehrenfeld to pay bin Mahfouz damages and to cover his legal fees, and required that an apology be published.[24]

Plaintiffs in libel-tourism cases often did not seek to enforce the judgments in their favor, opting to leave the judgments as swords hanging over defendants' heads.[25] Bin Mahfouz indeed did not attempt to enforce the judgment in Britain, where Ehrenfeld had no assets, but he also made no effort to enforce it in New York, where Ehrenfeld resided. Nevertheless, seeking to dispel the threat of possible enforcement,[26] Ehrenfeld filed suit against bin Mahfouz in New York to obtain a declaratory judgment barring enforcement of the British ruling. Yet the

District Court for the Southern District of New York, as well as the New York Court of Appeals, denied Ehrenfeld's request since bin Mahfouz lacked sufficient contacts with New York to come under the courts' jurisdiction.[27]

In 2008, Ehrenfeld's travails inspired the New York State Legislature to enact a law against libel tourism. Rory Lancman, the New York State Assembly member who initiated and drafted the bill, identified two primary rationales: first, the notion that a foreign lawsuit could inhibit an American from exercising their First Amendment rights offended Americans' commitment to free speech and even their sense of patriotism. Second, libel tourism posed a threat to the efforts against terrorism, since combating terrorism requires the assistance of journalists who expose terrorist networks and financiers. If journalists are not free to investigate and report about terrorists, this could cripple the efforts to root out terrorism. To emphasize the implications for terrorism, Lancman did not put "libel tourism" in the title of his proposed bill, but "libel *terrorism*." His bill was titled the "Libel Terrorism Protection Act."[28] Ehrenfeld herself advocated for the legislation, making a national-security argument to New York State lawmakers: We cannot let Saudis involved in terrorism silence us.[29]

These efforts bore fruit—fast. The New York State Legislature unanimously approved the Libel Terrorism Protection Act, and it was signed into law in May 2008—only a few months after Ehrenfeld lost her legal battle in the U.S. court system. This act requires, first, that courts not recognize foreign defamation judgments, unless the law applied by the foreign court "provided at least as much protection for freedom of speech and press in that case as would be provided by both the United States and New York constitutions." Second, the act gave New York State courts jurisdiction over persons who obtained foreign libel judgments against New York residents, provided that the publication at issue was published in New York. This was meant to allow courts to issue the kind of declaratory ruling sought by Ehrenfeld—that the foreign judgment would not be recognized in New York.[30]

As several other states passed laws modeled after the New York State legislation—establishing grounds for nonenforcement of foreign libel judgments and providing long-arm jurisdiction over foreign libel tourists[31]—Ehrenfeld began campaigning for Congressional legislation against libel tourism, together with her lawyer Daniel Kornstein. While the New York State legislation provided protection for the many authors, publishers, and news organizations situated in New York, it was important to provide similar protection to those based outside New York and to avoid a patchwork of different laws and conflicting judicial decisions across the country. A federal law was seen as a means to create a more robust, predictable protection against libel tourism.[32] The campaign that resulted in that law in 2010 provides us with an intimate look into the legislative response to a perceived abuse of transnational litigation, and it shows how victims of such abuse can motivate this response: what arguments they make to highlight the gap between the home and foreign legal systems and to convince lawmakers that this gap is harmful enough to merit political action.

Making the Case for the Law

How did advocates of federal anti-libel-tourism legislation—Ehrenfeld, representatives of authors and publishers, and sympathetic lawmakers—make their case to Congress? At the most basic level, legislation proponents had to demonstrate that Ehrenfeld's experience, which served as the primary impetus for the legislation, was not an isolated incident and that libel tourism was a broad phenomenon that threatened a significant number of authors and publishers. In her statement before the Senate, Ehrenfeld said:

> I was not the only American writer whom Mahfouz had attempted to silence . . . Mahfouz openly boasted on his website about his power to intimidate and silence his critics in the media and academia using the British libel laws and court. Among Mahfouz's victims are many familiar names [of media outlets]. . . . These media outlets and many others published retractions, corrections, and apologies to avoid legal confrontation with Mahfouz, the plaintiff friendly British laws and courts, and Mahfouz's backers in the Saudi government.[33]

Bruce Brown, a lawyer representing media companies, publishers, and journalism-advocacy organizations, similarly identified various victims of libel tourism—from *Forbes* magazine to Ukraine-based news organizations.[34] He also contrasted the fate of one libel-tourism victim—a publisher sued in a British court—to the very different fate of a publisher who enjoyed U.S. constitutional protections in an American court. In 2007, after bin Mahfouz sued, in London, two American authors who had tied him to terrorism, their publisher agreed to destroy all unsold copies of the book that had drawn bin Mahfouz's ire and apologized for the embarrassment the publication had caused. At approximately the same time, according to Brown's account, a different publisher was sued by a nonprofit group named KinderUSA over a book on Hamas. The group objected to statements in the book that linked it to the financing of terrorism. Yet shortly after filing a lawsuit against the publisher in a California court, KinderUSA withdrew the suit before the court could even hear it. Brown explained that UK law had brought the first publisher "to its knees," whereas the second publisher enjoyed the protections of the First Amendment as well as a California law that assists defendants attacked by frivolous libel suits.[35]

After demonstrating that libel tourism went beyond Ehrenfeld's case—that it affected numerous authors and publishers—legislation proponents had to make the case that libel tourism imposed serious damage on its victims. Rachel Ehrenfeld attested to the emotional costs that this practice might inflict on authors: "I spent many sleepless nights worried that Mahfouz would try to enforce the English judgment against me in New York. His deliberate nonenforcement of the judgment left it hanging over my head and my career like a sword of Damocles."[36] Ehrenfeld further claimed that libel tourism harmed her livelihood: several American publishers lost interest in publishing her work due to the London litigation.[37] Senator Patrick Leahy (D-VT) reinforced Ehrenfeld's point, noting that "Foreign libel judgments clearly impact American authors' livelihood, credibility and employment potential."[38] Another supporter of the legislation, media attorney Kurt Wimmer, suggested that authors subject to a foreign libel judgment might find it difficult to obtain future publishing contracts. Furthermore, foreign libel judgments "impose reputational harms on authors and publishers. No author or publisher wants to be tarred with the brush of a defamation judgment."[39]

Another outcome of libel tourism that legislation proponents emphasized was a chilling effect of self-censorship and decisions not to publish.[40] Rachel Ehrenfeld argued that unrestrained libel actions stopped authors from writing freely about matters of public importance and forced them to engage in self-censorship.[41] Bruce Brown suggested that the fear of substantial libel judgments in the UK has a distorting effect on what is published in the United States, stifling free speech on many important subjects.[42] In his view, libel tourism "has created a silent chilling effect that is felt by <u>any</u> author or publisher writing about controversial international subjects today. Journalists often find themselves forced to self-censor their speech to ensure not that it meets the standards for First Amendment protection, but instead so that it satisfies the much more stifling strictures of English libel law."[43] The Association of American Publishers (AAP) bemoaned the "cynical exploitation of plaintiff-friendly foreign libel laws as a weapon to intimidate and silence U.S. authors and publishers."[44] As a result, the latter may avoid taking on certain subjects, or challenging powerful interests.[45] Legislation advocates further emphasized that "Even if [libel tourists] do not attempt to enforce the foreign libel judgment in the United States, the very existence of such judgments can silence the kind of reporting that our laws are designed to encourage and protect."[46]

More broadly, legislation proponents argued that libel tourism had transformed the media landscape and created an unfavorable climate for journalists, authors, and publishers. Lawyers, as part of a new ritual, now routinely inform their clients of the calculated risks of publishing in this climate.[47] In this threatening environment, authors and publishers engage in self-censorship by "not writing about public figures known to be litigious, not engaging in investigative reporting;" and publishers choose to settle claims that would never have succeeded in U.S. courts. Given the enormous economic constraints currently faced by newspapers and magazines, they cannot incur the risks of UK litigation.[48] The Internet has aggravated the threat. "Today, any book, article, television newscast or blogpost available online, even one published exclusively in another country, can ostensibly be subject to the libel law of a foreign jurisdiction."[49] Since modern technology allows reports and publications to be read worldwide instantly, regardless of the author's intent to target a foreign market, authors and publishers run the risk of lawsuits with every book or article published. This creates a race to the bottom where "the most chilling and restrictive standards . . . will be followed."[50]

Yet the threat that libel tourism posed to authors and publishers probably would not have sufficed, in itself, to motivate Congressional legislation. The theoretical framework (Proposition 7) has posited that the activation of ethnocentric concerns may require legal differences to be framed in a way that accentuates their negative implications *for society*. Proponents of the legislation used several frames to define what it is that libel tourism imperiled and to justify action against this practice.

First, libel tourism was presented as a threat to free speech, which undermined public debate and the free circulation of information and ideas: "[T]he American people are suffering concrete and profound harm because they, their representatives, and other government policymakers rely on the free expression of information, ideas, and opinions developed by responsible journalists, academics, commentators, experts, and others for the formulation of sound public policy, including national security policy."[51] Libel tourism, it was argued, "stifle[s] the free exchange of ideas and information assured by the First Amendment"[52] and its chilling effect "deprive[s] Americans of the kind of candid commentary and uninhibited information that our laws are designed to foster and protect."[53] Since the high prevalence of foreign libel lawsuits chilled free speech and restricted both domestic and worldwide access to important information,[54] it threatened "to dramatically alter the quality of public debate both here and abroad."[55] The American press would no longer "vigorously investigate and publish news and information about the most crucial issues before the American public"; and "the rest of the world will no longer have access to the robust American investigative journalism that often is the only light being shed on despotic regimes and corrupt governments."[56] The proposed legislation was framed as an antidote that would protect the ability of American readers to obtain news and information about issues of public concern.[57]

A second frame presented libel tourism as a threat to the rights and freedom of Americans. This framing sought to turn libel tourism from an obscure problem affecting some authors and publishers to a fundamental problem of concern to Americans at large. "Foreign libel laws have become a potent weapon used by the forces of tyranny who seek to undermine our freedom;"[58] "A free society is one in which there is freedom of speech and of the press";[59] "It is no exaggeration to say that libel tourism threatens the free expression rights of all Americans."[60] These quotes all tried to convey a sense that much more than the minutiae of libel law stood at the center of the debate over libel tourism. Rather, freedom itself was at stake.

The third frame went beyond the previous two in that it turned libel tourism into an explicit us-against-them struggle and linked it to a security threat: terrorism. "We are confronted by libel tourism—a pernicious and growing phenomenon, especially after the 9/11 attacks on America—whereby wealthy and corrupt terror financiers exploit plaintiff-friendly foreign libel laws and expansive Internet jurisdiction to silence American authors and publishers."[61]

Senators Arlen Specter (R-PA) and Joe Lieberman (IN-CT) introduced one of the bills leading up to the SPEECH Act.[62] They touted the terrorism connection in an op-ed in the *Wall Street Journal* entitled "Foreign Courts Take Aim at Our Free Speech." This title has a clear us-against-them setup, and the text similarly positions terrorist sympathizers, aided by foreign courts, against Americans:

> Our Constitution is one of our greatest assets in the fight against terrorism. A free-flowing marketplace of ideas, protected by the First Amendment, enables the ideals of democracy to defeat the totalitarian vision of al Qaeda and other terrorist organizations.
>
> That free marketplace faces a threat. Individuals with alleged connections to terrorist activity are filing libel suits and winning judgments in foreign courts against American researchers who publish on these matters. These suits intimidate and even silence writers and publishers. . . .
>
> Now we are engaged in another great struggle—this time against Islamist terror—and again the enemies of freedom seek to silence free speech. Our legislation will help ensure that they do not succeed.[63]

Other contributions to the Congressional debate similarly emphasized the libel tourism-terrorism connection. "Particularly since 9/11, foreign nationals have cynically exploited foreign courts in an attempt to stifle any discussion by American journalists about the dangers of jihadist ideology and terrorist supporters."[64] As they tried to stop the reporting on Islamic terrorism and terrorist financing,[65] "[o]ne of the most powerful weapons Islamists have is the threat to use the courts to silence people who get in their way."[66] Libel tourism thus threatened both the First Amendment and U.S. national security,[67] making the legislation against this practice necessary. According to 9/11 Families for a Secure America, the proposed legislation "will have the effect of protecting not merely the First Amendment rights in America, but will by promoting exposure of terrorist financiers, provide increased security for the Nation as a whole."[68] According to the American Jewish Congress, if the law passed, citizens "will be more secure, knowing that the American market place of ideas, including discussions of terrorism, will not be distorted or constricted by wealthy foreigners using foreign courts under laws alien to our nation's fundamental values."[69] Overall, we find a strong emphasis on the national-security contribution of the proposed legislation to bolster the case for its passage.

Highlighting the Differences between American and British Libel Law

Debates on transnational litigation tend to highlight the incompatibility between the home and foreign legal systems: how the two systems differ in their norms and practices and in the underlying values. Opponents of cooperation characterize the foreign rules and procedures as unfair, arguing that they fail to meet the home country's standards and, worse, threaten to undermine those standards and put the home legal system at risk (Proposition 9). The Congressional debate over libel tourism followed this outline, drawing a sharp contrast between the "good" American law and the "bad" British law. British law was described in highly critical, even derogatory, terms, as compared to the exalted protections of the First Amendment.

Legislation proponents argued that a "deep chasm," a "stark contrast," or a "divide" separates American and British libel law,[70] with the latter providing weaker protection for free speech.[71] Libel tourism thus meant that American content was assessed "based on legal standards that are less protective of free expression than our laws."[72] The weakness of protection was manifested, first and foremost, in placing the burden of proving the truthfulness of the defamatory statement on the defendant. Rep. Steve Cohen (D-TN) characterized this feature of British law as "draconian."[73] In another difference, when a public figure brings a libel case in a U.S. court, they must prove actual malice or reckless disregard for the truth, whereas British courts have no such protections.[74] U.S. appellate courts conduct a thorough review of libel judgments, including on matters relating to the weighing of evidence; in contrast, there is no equivalent review in UK appellate tribunals.[75] While the "fair comment" exception in British law could save defendants from the burden of proving the truth of the statement at issue, this exception provides far less protection than is available under comparable

American law.[76] Another "stark difference" between the British and American systems concerned attorneys' fees,[77] and the two systems also diverged, it was argued, on the statute of limitations, jurisdiction, liability of Internet service providers, and injunctions.[78] All this—in particular, the shifting of the burden of proof to the defendant—meant that "libel laws in the U.S. and England constitute mirror images of each other . . . many identical cases would be decided differently in the two countries."[79] This resulted in "crippling libel judgments" coming from "a system 180 degrees opposite to the protections for the libel defendant at the core of the First Amendment."[80]

According to proponents of the legislation, the divergence between U.S. and UK libel law stemmed from the different balancing of the competing values at stake: the protection of one's reputation against defamation on the one hand versus free speech on the other.[81] "Other nations do not have the same high respect for their freedom of speech that we have in the United States,"[82] and their laws lack the "national commitment to robust public debate" that underlies U.S. law.[83] Indeed, "By choosing to sue American authors and publishers in countries which lack First Amendment protections for freedom of expression, foreign plaintiffs strip away rights which the Founding Fathers sought to secure, and subject American citizens to the social, cultural and religious mores of other sovereigns. Those sovereigns do not share our reverence for freedom of expression."[84] Enforcing a foreign libel judgment, in this view, would go against the core values of American law and society, and should therefore be avoided. "The U.S. interest is making sure the coercive power of our courts . . . is not mobilized to enforce judgments so antithetical to our fundamental protections"[85]—"judgments that are fundamentally at odds with our own political liberties."[86]

The emphasis on the differences between U.S. and British libel law[87] and on the conflict and incompatibility of defamation standards and judgments[88] demonstrates how opponents of cooperation on litigation seek to build support for their position: by presenting differences between legal systems as deep and irreconcilable and arguing that foreign rules and practices contradict fundamental principles and values at home. This gap between the legal systems was reinforced and dramatized through the repeated use of the terms "threat" and "danger" as well as the need to "protect" Americans. Consider the following examples: "[W]e cannot allow foreign citizens to exploit [British] courts to endanger Americans' First Amendment protected speech";[89] "We must remain vigilant to protect Americans from any foreign defamation judgments";[90] "[W]e cannot allow foreign litigants or foreign courts to tell us what can be written or published in the United States. That is a dangerous path we do not want to follow";[91] the legislation "would ensure that Americans are held to and protected by American standards";[92] libel tourism "threatens American free speech rights";[93] it "threatens the First Amendment rights of Americans to speak on matters of public concern."[94]

American Legal Imperialism?

Proponents of the legislation had to address an important dilemma: Wouldn't a refusal to enforce foreign libel judgments impose American-style free-speech protections on foreign countries? Shouldn't the United States show respect for foreign legal systems and their legal standards—the same respect it demands from the foreign systems? Some participants in the Congressional debate betrayed awareness that the U.S.'s highly restrictive approach to libel cases did not represent the only possible balance of the values at stake: both free speech and individual reputation carry much significance, and it is not surprising that different nations vary in the emphasis they give to each.[95] In fact, it was recognized that the United States was an exception in its far-reaching protection for free speech. According to Professor Linda Silberman, who provided testimony as an expert on civil procedure and conflict of laws, the kind of constitutional protection that the United States gives to speech in defamation lawsuits is not generally accepted by the rest of world, making the United States something of an outlier. Indeed, many countries give greater weight to an individual's reputation and favor plaintiffs in balancing free speech against the harm to an individual resulting from defamation.[96] Rachel Ehrenfeld noted that while Americans "take [free-speech rights] for granted and have difficulty envisioning societies in which those rights are treated as privileges, or in which those rights are provided lesser protections,"[97] many such societies do exist. Furthermore, legislation proponents acknowledged that "As a general rule, those within the family of nations ought to respect each other's court judgments,"[98] and that respect is particularly owed to "the British common law, which is the very foundation and genius of our legal system."[99] Also, as a tactical matter, in countering the problem of foreign nations imposing their libel rules on U.S. authors and publishers, Congress must be careful to avoid exposing itself to the reverse argument that its solution is imposing American rules on them.[100]

Substantively, legislation proponents offered three defenses against the possible charge of a lack of respect for foreign legal systems and their libel standards.

First, they denied that their goal was to alter foreign countries' laws. "We cannot change another country's (libel) laws, nor would we want to. We must respect their laws, as they ought to respect ours."[101] Rather, the legislation aimed to protect the U.S. legal system and American citizens from the harmful effect and encroachment of foreign laws. Nonenforcement of foreign libel judgments was thus presented as merely a defensive measure—one that does not interfere with the legal regimes of other sovereigns, but only seeks to maintain American protections for U.S. citizens, allowing them to write, publish, blog, and speak in *their* country without fear of foreign reprisals.[102] Countering the impact of libel tourism, legislation proponents argued, "is not about second-guessing foreign governments for coming to a different balance between reputational interests and freedom of speech than we have, it is about making sure that those jurisdictions do not dictate to us how we should strike this balance for ourselves."[103] According to this logic, there was no inherent contradiction between respecting the sovereign rights of other countries to enact their own laws regarding speech and protecting the First Amendment rights of Americans regarding speech that occurs in the United States.[104] Foreign countries are still entitled to strike their own balance between free speech and reputation, but "it is not in our interest to permit the balance struck in America to be upset or circumvented by foreign courts."[105] Legislation proponents insisted that the bill did *not* demonstrate American legal imperialism—"an attempt to impose our laws on the entire world"—nor was it an unwarranted departure from the deference owed other sovereigns. "The bill only prevents our courts from being enlisted in efforts to suppress speech."[106] In short, the proposed legislation was merely about the United States standing up for its free speech standards and preventing their being undermined through the exploitation of foreign courts.[107]

Legislation proponents also countered a possible charge of American legal imperialism by suggesting that American protections for free speech were in line with international standards, whereas British libel law failed to meet these standards and had drawn criticism from international bodies. Several legislation supporters referenced or cited the 2008 observations of the UN's Human Rights Committee with respect to British libel law:

> The Committee is concerned that the [UK's] practical application of the law of libel has served to discourage critical media reporting on matters of serious public interest, adversely affecting the ability of scholars and journalists to publish their work, including through the phenomenon known as "libel tourism." The advent of the internet and the international distribution of foreign media also create the danger that a State party's unduly restrictive libel law will affect freedom of expression worldwide on matters of valid public interest.[108]

The American Civil Liberties Union (ACLU), for example, argued that "the United States is justified in standing up for its progressive free speech standards which are far closer to international standards than those of Great Britain."[109] The proposed legislation, according to the ACLU, would "help the United States to stand as a beacon for the preservation of individual free speech rights and encourage other nations to adopt similarly strong standards in line with agreed-upon international norms."[110]

As a third defense against the legal-imposition critique, legislation proponents indicated that Britain's libel laws had come under attack in Britain itself and that domestic pressures for libel reform already had been building up there. This was meant to reinforce and legitimize the American criticism of libel tourism. The report of the House of Representatives' Committee on the Judiciary, for example, pointed out that the House of Lords had issued a decision that expanded the scope of protection for journalists—a decision that perhaps signaled a trend toward greater protection for the free-speech values of the First Amendment.[111] It was also noted that the House of Commons had been undertaking an inquiry into the problem of libel tourism[112] and that British members of parliament were embarrassed by the practices of UK courts:[113] "In December [2008], three influential MPs urged the government to radically reform Britain's libel laws to remedy what the Labour Party's Denis MacShane called the 'international scandal' of libel tourism that has turned British courts into a 'Soviet-style organ of censorship.' "[114] It was further argued that media entities had urged British legislators to consider removing some of the incentives for libel forum-shopping.[115]

As an aside, we should add that the domestic pressures for reform[116]—alongside the international criticism of libel tourism—brought about a revision of Britain's libel laws a few years after the passage of the SPEECH Act. The Defamation Act 2013, according to the British government, was supposed to reverse the chilling effect of libel laws on freedom of expression and legitimate debate.[117] Among the innovations of this act is a requirement of serious harm: a statement will be considered defamatory only if its publication has caused serious harm to the reputation of the plaintiff. Other innovations include defenses for operators of websites and for peer-reviewed statements in academic journals, as well as a provision against libel tourism. According to Section 9 of the act, when a libel action is brought against a person who is not a resident of the UK or the EU, the court will have jurisdiction to hear that action only if it is satisfied that England, or Wales, is clearly the most appropriate place in which to bring the case. The *New York Times*, commenting on a draft of the act, argued that it "is not nearly as protective of speech as American law," but "has the potential to bury London's deserved reputation as the world's libel capital."[118]

Outside Support for the Legislation

While Rachel Ehrenfeld's personal experience served as the primary driver of the legislation, additional actors joined her plea to curb libel tourism. One group of actors included organizations that submitted briefs in support of the legislation. The American Library Association, for example, argued that libel tourism threatened not only authors and publishers. Through its chilling effect, it also "denies the American people the right to read and to access information—another inherent First Amendment right essential to our democratic form of government."[119] The AAP explained that it "represents an industry whose very existence depends upon the unfettered exercise of free-speech and free-press rights guaranteed by the First Amendment. Libel tourism is a direct threat to those First Amendment rights."[120] The ACLU encouraged Congress to "craft legislation to protect the free speech rights of those authors and publishers entitled to such protection from the chilling effect of foreign laws that fail to conform to basic international human rights agreements."[121] The American Jewish Congress argued that "libel tourism is problematic because it so directly trenches on Americans' abilities to debate pressing issues in an informed fashion. . . . Those foreigners unhappy with our robust democracy should not be permitted to roam the world looking for a friendly venue from which to launch lawsuits intended to silence our national debates."[122] This support from major organizations was crucial in buttressing and reinforcing Ehrenfeld's case against libel tourism. According to Ehrenfeld's lawyer, who advocated for the legislation with her, "this added an element to what we've done. We were no longer just one individual challenging the law. It was showing that there was broad support from respected organizations in our society. That made a difference . . . [and] enhanced the authority of what we were saying."[123]

Lawyers play an important role in debates on transnational litigation. Lawyers may oppose cooperation on litigation for self-interested reasons: to protect their clients from foreign legal authority. Yet they may also be truly concerned about the foreign encroachment into the home legal system and the undermining of local rules and procedures that they cherish (Proposition 5). Such a dual motivation seems to have propelled a group of Washington-based media lawyers—such as Bruce Brown and Laura Handman, who testified at the hearings and submitted statements in support of the legislation.[124] These lawyers represented news and media organizations who were or could become victims of libel tourism, and in that sense had a stake in the legislation. But they also shared a deep commitment to the idea of free speech and became concerned that libel tourism was creating an end-run around the robust U.S. protections for a free press.[125]

The media itself lent support for the legislation. As we have seen in Chapter 6, media outlets may oppose cooperation on litigation on the basis of loyalty to local citizens and norms; but in the current case newspapers had a direct self-interest in legislation that aimed to fend off a threat to themselves. Op-eds supportive of the legislation were published,[126] and newspapers provided favorable coverage of the efforts to curb libel tourism. As the New York law on libel tourism was pending before the New York State Legislature, the *New York Post*, in an article titled "Rachel's Law," argued that if this bill became law, it would not only "protect our precious First Amendment freedoms in New York," but would also "attract counterterrorism scholars and journalists to our shores."[127] As the federal legislation was making its way through Congress, a *New York Times* op-ed dubbed libel tourism "a threat to America's robust free-speech traditions," and urged the United States to "ensure that other countries' pro-plaintiff libel laws do not infect this country and diminish our proud tradition of freedom of expression."[128] After the Senate passed its version of the legislation, the *New York Times* published an editorial entitled "A Victory for Writing," which explained that the law "will provide a safeguard to authors and publishers threatened with ruinous foreign judgments."[129]

Criticism and Objections

As compared to other pieces of Congressional legislation, and relative to other transnational-litigation instruments discussed in this book, the SPEECH Act enjoyed a very favorable response from lawmakers on both sides of the aisle. Both Democratic and Republican members of Congress accepted that libel tourism posed a problem that had to be addressed, and all agreed that foreign libel judgments inconsistent with the First Amendment should not be enforced by American courts. Not a single member of Congress came out on record to question the need for or logic of the legislation. Support for the bill was unanimous in both chambers of Congress.[130]

One might have expected the Department of Justice or the Department of State to oppose the legislation. As Proposition 5 suggests, and as previous chapters have shown, the justice bureaucracy tends to support cooperation on litigation as a principled commitment to the rule of law and out of concern for reciprocity. The foreign-affairs bureaucracy shares the preference for cooperation to avoid antagonizing foreign countries (Proposition 6). Both the Department of Justice and the Department of State should thus have provided little support for legislation aimed at thwarting cooperation on the enforcement of foreign judgments. Indeed, both departments expressed their lack of support by choosing to remain on the sidelines. They had little involvement in the legislative process and did not submit statements concerning the legislation, nor did they participate in the hearings. This muted response meant, however, that the departments did not actively oppose the law. It is possible that, in their view, the narrowly targeted nature of the law limited its harmful impact. Nonenforcement of British libel judgments was unlikely to imperil the broader law-enforcement cooperation between the United States and Britain, nor was it likely to jeopardize the diplomatic relations between the two countries. Furthermore, as discussed above, concerns about abusive libel judgments and calls for reform were heard in Britain itself. The American criticism of British libel law was thus unlikely to provoke an angry response in London. Indeed, besides some grumblings on the part of British libel lawyers, there was no official British protest against the American legislation.[131] The Departments of Justice and State therefore saw little need to try to block a law that threatened little damage, in their view; but they also declined to lend their support to a measure inconsistent with their preference for cooperation.

The little opposition that the legislation did face came from a very small group of legal scholars and practitioners. As it restricted the enforcement of judgments by libel plaintiffs, the legislation raised concerns among libel-plaintiff lawyers. One of them, John Walsh, submitted a statement denouncing the bill as "a flawed and unnecessary piece of legislation, generated as a reaction to a media and lobbying campaign by Rachel Ehrenfeld and her supporters which is promoting the unproven notion that 'libel tourism' is a massive threat to American constitutional values." He further warned that "the Bill exports the First Amendment with any American's published material, giving it an extra-territorial effect" and that it would disrupt "the concepts of reciprocity and mutual respect which underlie the principle of comity which is at the heart of international recognition of the judgments of other countries in the community of nations."[132]

Law professor Linda Silberman similarly criticized the bill as unnecessary, since existing U.S. law on foreign judgments allowed the nonenforcement of judgments that violate public policy, and U.S. courts already consistently invoked First Amendment values in determining whether to deny the enforcement of foreign judgments on grounds of public policy.[133] But the bill, in Silberman's view, was not only unnecessary but harmful:

> The bill may encourage U.S. courts to apply U.S. law principles without regard to context and to invoke public policy too reflexively without sufficient regard for the competing interests of other countries. The danger is then that this provision will invite "libel tourism" in reverse—where courts in the United States impose the United States view of free speech on the rest of the world regardless of the particular circumstances. The United States would then be engaging in the precise behavior of which it has been so critical.[134]

We have seen above that legislation proponents tried to rebut the "disrespect for foreign law" argument, and it gained little purchase with lawmakers. No member of Congress considered the legislation an illegitimate imposition of U.S. law and values abroad. To the extent that there was disagreement among lawmakers, this was not about the act's aim or fundamental logic but about the appropriate remedy. It was clear that the legislation should, as a minimum, prohibit the enforcement of a foreign libel judgment against an American if that judgment was inconsistent with the First Amendment. Rep. John Conyers (D-MI) highlighted this limited—but critical—remedy that can be established without interfering with foreign legal systems.[135] The denial of enforcement was thus seen as the "starting point for any federal libel tourism statute" and a "first step toward stemming the tide of libel tourism."[136]

Beyond nonenforcement, additional remedies were considered. Some libel tourists did not ask a U.S. court to enforce the judgment in their favor, choosing instead to leave it as a threat hanging over the head of the defendant. It was therefore proposed that the threat could be diffused through declaratory relief: the defendant would be able to sue the libel tourist in a U.S. court for a declaration that the foreign judgment is unenforceable and repugnant to the U.S. Constitution.[137] Others raised the option of establishing monetary remedies to increase the legislation's deterrent effect. One such remedy included the recovery of attorneys' fees for an enforcement or declaratory judgment action in a U.S. court or the recovery of attorneys' fees for the defense of the libel action in the foreign court.[138] Another possible monetary remedy involved damages: damages in the amount of the foreign judgment; damages to compensate the U.S. defendant for the harm caused by the libel action due to decreased opportunities to publish; or treble damages if the foreign plaintiff "intentionally engaged in a scheme to suppress rights under the First Amendment."[139]

Rep. Peter King (R-NY) and Senators Arlen Specter (R-PA) and Joe Lieberman (IN-CT), who introduced versions of the bill,[140] wanted aggressive legislation that would include the option of a counter-suit for damages. They expressed concern that simply prohibiting the enforcement of the foreign judgment would "not go far enough to combat the threat of libel tourism. Foreign litigants will still be allowed to file these libel lawsuits overseas with no worry of being countersued here in the U.S." Therefore, a "libel tourism bill should include punitive measures to discourage these ridiculous lawsuits from being filed in the first place."[141] Rachel Ehrenfeld similarly argued that the ability to counter-sue and obtain damages was necessary to deter libel tourists.[142]

Others, however, warned against the possible perils of allowing a counter-suit of the foreign libel tourist in an American court. According to Bruce Brown, while "it is tempting to ensure that U.S. citizens are always able to defend the attack on their First Amendment rights by hauling the foreign plaintiff into U.S. courts to answer for the affront," this risked violating the Constitutional requirement of due process: A U.S. court cannot claim jurisdiction and impose damages over individuals who have no ties to the United States other than that they have sued an American in a foreign court. "Congress must be cautious of doing precisely what makes the practice of libel tourism itself so shameful—exerting its authority over a foreigner who has few, if any, ties to the jurisdiction."[143] The legislation should thus aim to "stop libel tourists dead in their tracks, without sacrificing constitutional values."[144]

The World Press Freedom Committee—an international association of media organizations—and the AAP shared the concern about granting U.S. courts jurisdiction over foreign defendants who may not have the necessary minimum contacts with the United States.[145] The AAP also saw the idea of treble damages as problematic, since treble damages are contrary to public policy in many foreign countries and would be unenforceable there.[146] Professor Linda Silberman opposed both the cause of action for declaratory judgment and the more aggressive remedies, such as a "clawback" of damages recovered in the foreign judgment or treble damages. According to Silberman, the fact that the libel tourist sued an American in a foreign court does not land them in the U.S. jurisdictional net. Furthermore, she believed that the aggressive remedies failed to show proper respect for the American differences with other countries: Since other countries strike the balance between reputation and speech differently, the United States should go no further than refusing to enforce the foreign judgment. It should not overreach by creating other remedies.[147]

The House Judiciary Committee expressed similar misgivings regarding the more aggressive approach to libel tourism. Beyond the concern about the exercise of personal jurisdiction over a foreign libel tourist who lacks sufficient contacts with the United States, the committee was concerned that counter-suits for a declaratory judgment or damages "may represent too great an intrusion into the legal systems of other countries. Some countries might even respond in kind by authorizing suits to interfere with counter-suits in defamation cases or, more broadly, by authorizing suits to counter other types of suits in the United States to which they object. Principles of international comity counsel moderation."[148] The committee thus favored a more moderate bill, introduced by Rep. Steve Cohen, which included the remedy of nonenforcement without the option of a counter-suit in a U.S. court.[149]

Ultimately, the SPEECH Act, as passed by Congress, constituted a compromise between those who wanted a modest bill that would provide only for nonenforcement and those who advocated additional, stronger remedies. The act establishes the primary remedy of nonenforcement of a foreign libel judgment: A U.S. court will not enforce the foreign judgment unless it determines that the foreign defamation law provided at least as much protection for freedom of speech and press in that case as would be provided by the First Amendment. The foreign plaintiff seeking enforcement bears the burden of showing that. The act also establishes jurisdictional grounds for nonenforcement: a U.S. court will not enforce a foreign libel judgment unless it determines that the exercise of personal jurisdiction by the foreign court comported with the due process requirement of the U.S. Constitution. Yet the act goes beyond mere nonenforcement and does provide the remedy of a declaratory judgment: a U.S. person against whom a foreign libel judgment is entered may ask a U.S. court to declare that the judgment is repugnant to the U.S. Constitution and therefore unenforceable. Finally, in an action brought in a U.S. court to enforce a foreign defamation judgment, the act directs the court to award reasonable attorneys' fees to the party opposing enforcement if that party prevails on any of the nonenforcement grounds recognized by the act. The act, however, stops short of authorizing an action for monetary damages against foreign defamation claimants.[150] This compromise was not what legislation advocates, including Rachel Ehrenfeld, had envisioned. While they wished for legislation with stronger teeth, they agreed to compromise.[151] Ultimately, they did score a victory by getting the law passed with unanimous Congressional support.

The Puzzle of Unanimous Support

The SPEECH Act is unique among the transnational-litigation laws and agreements examined in this book. The NATO SOFA, Britain's Extradition Act, and the Australia-China extradition treaty all sought to establish cooperation on litigation, subject to certain conditions and guarantees. The SPEECH Act, by contrast, has the opposite goal of *blocking* cooperation. It did not stem from recognition of the benefits of sharing legal authority with a foreign system, but from concerns about the harm that foreign law causes to local citizens and values. As such, the SPEECH Act embodies the ethnocentric spirit that stands at the center of this book. This piece of legislation is all about protecting the home legal system from the encroachment of a foreign system that is perceived as alien and inferior. In that sense, the SPEECH Act resembles the blocking statutes enacted by different countries to stymie U.S. discovery (discussed in Chapter 7).

At the same time, the enactment of the SPEECH Act raises a puzzle. A legislative process typically involves a debate between supporters and opponents. The latter may criticize the legislation, question the need for it, and point out potential negative effects. We have seen such fierce debates over the ratification of the NATO SOFA and over issues related to extradition. By contrast, the anti-libel-tourism legislation did not meet any significant opposition and passed unanimously both in the New York State Legislature and in Congress.[152] In fact, a lawyer who advocated for the SPEECH Act suggested that its passage was "a breeze" compared to other acts of Congress.[153] While there was a minor disagreement over the remedies, lawmakers did not question the fundamental logic or desirability of the legislation. How can we explain that?

As the theoretical framework has suggested, a personal account of hardship and struggle may activate ethnocentric sentiments and evoke concerns about the exercise of foreign legal authority. The personal account turns the perils of transnational litigation from something that is remote and abstract into something tangible that one can identify and sympathize with. Rachel Ehrenfeld's story had such an effect. It personalized and dramatized the problem of libel tourism, demonstrating the hardship caused to a private individual with few resources just for seeking to publish her work.[154] The impact of the story was augmented by the identity of the libel tourist: a wealthy Arab and an alleged financier of terrorism. The contrast between the "good" and the "bad" was clear and sharp, making it easy for lawmakers to see Ehrenfeld as an in-group member who deserves protection against a "villain"—a dangerous member of the out-group. In this framing, UK libel law was not just another body of foreign law: it was a dangerous weapon used to harass, burden, and ultimately silence an American.

But provoking ethnocentric resistance to foreign law often requires more than just a personal story of hardship: the foreign legal process needs to be seen as causing harm to the home society at large. Legislation proponents thus had to convince lawmakers that libel tourism was much more than a minor legal phenomenon affecting only a handful of authors and publishers. They successfully framed libel tourism as a dual threat—both ideational and material—to the United States (consistent with Proposition 7). Ideationally, libel tourism was presented by legislation advocates as a threat to free speech—a right that enjoys almost mythical status in the American political and legal tradition as a cornerstone of democracy. Americans treat the elevated status of free speech as natural and obvious and struggle to understand how is it that foreign laws may prioritize other values or interests over free speech.[155] Libel tourism, in this view, was a foreign effort to interfere with and subvert a cherished American right: "It's like the world telling us how to handle the First Amendment."[156] Given Americans' reverence for their First Amendment rights, the idea that a foreign country would impinge upon them offended lawmakers and reinforced the us-against-them sentiment.[157]

In terms of material implications, legislation advocates managed to convince lawmakers that libel tourism threatened American security since it abetted terrorism. A measure against libel tourism, in this framing, promised to enhance American security by allowing the exposure and discussion of terrorism free from the threat of libel suits. This framing had an obvious appeal to lawmakers: "No lawmaker of either party wanted to go on the record as protecting terrorism and spiking journalists trying to expose terrorism."[158] And this appeal carried particular strength in the specific timeframe of the legislative process examined here: 2008–2010. During this period—only a few years after the attacks of September 11, 2001, and before the 2011 killing of Osama bin

Laden—the terrorist threat loomed large and anti-terrorism measures won wide support.[159] Some actors involved with the libel-tourism legislation argued that the terrorism connection clearly spoke to certain lawmakers and helped bring them on board. They also acknowledged that timing mattered: if the legislation had been proposed only a few years later, when the terrorist threat subsided, political support would probably have been harder to secure.[160]

The dual threat—to a deeply-held American value and to national security—accounts for the bipartisan support for the legislation. The free-speech concerns resonated with members of Congress on both sides of the aisle, but they carried even more influence with Democratic lawmakers committed to the protection of civil liberties and a free press. The national-security argument, by contrast, found a receptive audience among Republicans. The legislation offered "something for everyone,"[161] and members of Congress thus embraced the idea that libel tourism was an abusive and harmful practice that had to be stopped. This serves to show that legal ethnocentrism is not necessarily a partisan manner. With the correct framing, politicians from across the political spectrum may come to view foreign laws as anathema, consistent with Proposition 3.

But the broad support stemmed not only from the strong considerations *in favor* of the legislation, but also from the absence of forces working *against* it: actors expected to oppose the law had little political influence on members of Congress or chose to remain silent. Lawmakers obviously did not care much about the actors directly harmed by the legislation, namely British libel lawyers and the libel tourists who used their services. "Neither terrorists nor the UK have a constituency in the New York Legislature"[162] or in Congress. While one might have expected the Departments of State and Justice to oppose the legislation, they had little involvement in the legislative process, as discussed above. And lawyers concerned about respect for foreign laws lacked political influence, and the comity arguments they raised did not carry enough weight to thwart the legislation. Whereas relinquishing jurisdiction over American troops was necessary for America's participation in NATO, lawmakers saw little gain in respecting foreign libel judgments against U.S. authors and publishers. Comity concerns did, however, induce Congress to choose a rather moderate, proportionate remedy, without the option of counter-suing the libel tourist for damages. This moderation likely facilitated the passage of the legislation.

Conclusion

The case of libel tourism and the legislation to counter it demonstrates multiple elements in this book's theoretical framework. At the center of this case stood legal incompatibility: the difference in libel laws—and underlying values—between the United States and Britain. The Congressional debate reflected a strong sense of pride in America's cherished freedom of speech; British law, which failed to accord free speech the same weight as American law, was seen as heavily flawed. Notably, this legal conflict took place between two legal systems that are in many ways similar, both belonging to the common-law tradition. Whereas in Chapter 6 we saw that it was the UK that considered its criminal justice superior to that of the United States, in the current case it is the United States that takes pride in its more robust protection of free speech, as compared to the UK.

As for the preferences of actors, this case demonstrates lawyers' objection to cooperation on litigation on self-interested and ideational grounds. It further shows that, given the right framing, opposition to cooperation may cut across party lines and bring together politicians from the right and the left. Several elements activated lawmakers' ethnocentric sentiments: the personal story of an individual struggling under the burden of transnational litigation; the "villainous" character on the opposite side—an alleged financier of terrorism—which reinforced the us-against-them, good-versus-bad narrative; and concerns about the broader implications of legal cooperation—for free speech and an open debate and for security. This case also shows how opponents of cooperation deal with charges of legal imperialism and lack of respect for foreign laws and interests.

Finally, this case demonstrates a possible effect of noncooperation on litigation: it may motivate the foreign country to change its laws. While domestic actors in Britain demanded libel reform, an important push for that reform came from the outside: the criticism by the UN Human Rights Committee[163] and the American anger at the practice of libel tourism. The 2010 passage of the SPEECH Act signaled that the United States viewed that practice as unacceptable, and this helped pave the way for the enactment of British libel reform in 2013.[164] Of course, we would not expect legal change to occur in every instance of noncooperation on litigation. But when the criticism from outside converges with and reinforces domestic calls for reform, and when that criticism comes from the United States, legal change may indeed materialize and produce real effects on the ground: libel tourism, while not entirely gone, has subsided.[165]

Notes

1. Securing the Protection of Our Enduring and Established Constitutional Heritage (SPEECH) Act, Public Law 111–223 (2010).
2. Sedler 2006, 378–379.
3. Sedler 2006, 379.
4. Milo 2008.

5. New York Times Co. v. United States, 403 U.S. 713 (1971).
6. Milkovich v. Lorain Journal Co., 497 U.S. 1, 19–20 (1990).
7. U.S. House of Representatives 2009a, 2.
8. Bose Corp. v. Consumers Union of United States, 466 U.S. 485 (1984).
9. New York Times Co. v. Sullivan, 376 U.S. 254, 270 (1964).
10. Sedler 2006, 379.
11. Staveley-O'Carroll 2009, 257.
12. U.S. House of Representatives 2009a, 3; U.S. House of Representatives 2009b, 46–49.
13. U.S House of Representatives 2009a, 3; U.S House of Representatives 2009b, 15; U.S. Senate 2010a, 2; U.S. Senate 2010b, 47.
14. U.S House of Representatives 2009b, 15 (media lawyer Bruce Brown).
15. U.S. Senate 2010b, 47.
16. U.S. Senate 2010b, 46; author's interview with Bruce Brown, attorney at Baker & Hostetler LLP and executive director of the Reporters Committee for Freedom of the Press, March 2018, Washington, D.C.
17. Lipstadt 2005.
18. U.S. Senate 2010b, 46.
19. Klebnikov 1996.
20. U.S. Senate 2010b, 46.
21. U.S. Senate 2010b, 47.
22. U.S. House of Representatives 2009b, 75–76.
23. Martin 2009.
24. Bin Mahfouz & Others v. Ehrenfeld & Another [2005] EWHC 1156 (QB). See Staveley-O'Carroll 2009, 273–276; Bernstein 2010, 213; Taylor 2010, 191; U.S. Senate 2010b, 83.
25. U.S. Senate 2010b, 16, 129.
26. U.S. House of Representatives 2009b, 12.
27. Ehrenfeld v. bin Mahfouz, F.Supp.2d, 2006 WL 1096816 (S.D.N.Y.); Ehrenfeld v. Mahfouz, 881 N.E.2d 830 (NY, 2007). Note that both a federal court and a state court ruled on this issue. Ehrenfeld filed her lawsuit in a federal district court. After the court denied her request, she appealed to a federal appellate court, which referred the case to a state court—the New York Court of Appeals—since it involved state law. Staveley-O'Carroll 2009, 274–275; Bernstein 2010, 213.
28. Author's interview with Rory Lancman, New York, March 2018. Lancman served as a member of the New York State Assembly in 2007–2012.
29. Author's interview with Rachel Ehrenfeld, New York, March 2018.
30. Libel Terrorism Protection Act, N.Y. CPLR §§ 302(d) and 5304(b)(8); Staveley-O'Carroll 2009, 276.
31. U.S. Senate 2010a, 3–4; Staveley-O'Carroll 2009, 276–277.
32. Ehrenfeld, interview; Brown, interview; U.S. Senate 2010a, 4.
33. U.S. Senate 2010b, 84.
34. U.S. Senate 2010b, 46–47.
35. U.S. Senate 2010b, 48; Staveley-O'Carroll 2009, 267–268. The California statute is the Anti-SLAPP Law (California Code of Civil Procedure—Section 425.16).
36. U.S. Senate 2010b, 84.
37. U.S. Senate 2010b, 84.
38. U.S. Senate 2010b, 88.
39. U.S. Senate 2010b, 128.
40. U.S. Senate 2010b, 125; Staveley-O'Carroll 2009, 269.
41. U.S. House of Representatives 2009b, 13–14.
42. U.S. House of Representatives 2009b, 15.
43. U.S. House of Representatives 2009b, 23. Emphasis in the original.
44. U.S. House of Representatives 2009b, 93.
45. U.S. House of Representatives 2009b, 200.
46. U.S. House of Representatives 2009b, 93 (Association of American Publishers); U.S. Senate 2010b, 4.
47. U.S. House of Representatives 2009b, 24.

48. U.S. House of Representatives 2009b, 43, 56 (media lawyer Laura Handman).
49. U.S. House of Representatives 2009b, 55 (Laura Handman).
50. U.S. Senate 2010b, 2 (Sen. Patrick Leahy (D-VT)).
51. U.S. House of Representatives 2009b, 7 (Rep. Peter King (R-NY)).
52. U.S. Senate 2010b, 33 (American Library Association).
53. U.S. Senate 2010b, 2 (Sen. Patrick Leahy).
54. U.S. Senate 2010b, 35.
55. U.S. Senate 2010b, 2 (Sen. Patrick Leahy).
56. U.S. Senate 2010b, 129–130 (media lawyer Kurt Wimmer).
57. U.S. House of Representatives 2009b, 151.
58. U.S. House of Representatives 2009b, 12; U.S. Senate 2010b, 82 (Rachel Ehrenfeld).
59. U.S. House of Representatives 2009b, 177; U.S. Senate 2010b, 29 (ACLU).
60. U.S. Senate 2010b, 82 (Rachel Ehrenfeld).
61. U.S. House of Representatives 2009b, 12 (Rachel Ehrenfeld).
62. Free Speech Protection Act of 2009, S. 449, 111th Cong. (2009).
63. Specter and Lieberman 2008. Reprinted in U.S. House of Representatives 2009b, 37–38; U.S. Senate 2010b, 63–64. Rep. Peter King, who introduced the House version of the bill, also made the connection to terrorism. U.S. House of Representatives 2009b, 7.
64. Rivkin and Brown 2009. Reprinted in U.S. House of Representatives 2009b, 39–40; U.S. Senate 2010b, 65–66.
65. U.S. Senate 2010b, 85.
66. Washington Times Editorial 2008. Reprinted in U.S. House of Representatives 2009b, 201.
67. Rivkin and Brown 2009.
68. U.S. House of Representatives 2009b, 172.
69. U.S. House of Representatives 2009b, 122.
70. U.S. House of Representatives 2009b, 19, 21, 31 (Bruce Brown).
71. U.S. House of Representatives 2009b, 3; U.S. Senate 2010a, 2.
72. U.S. Senate 2010b, 125 (Kurt Wimmer).
73. U.S. House of Representatives 2009b, 2.
74. U.S. House of Representatives 2009b, 16.
75. U.S. House of Representatives 2009b, 19.
76. U.S. House of Representatives 2009b, 46.
77. U.S. House of Representatives 2009b, 49 (Laura Handman).
78. U.S. House of Representatives 2009b, 48.
79. U.S. House of Representatives 2009b, 46 (Laura Handman).
80. U.S. House of Representatives 2009b, 165 (Laura Handman).
81. U.S. House of Representatives 2009b, 60.
82. U.S. House of Representatives 2009b, 4 (Rep. Trent Franks (R-AZ)).
83. U.S. House of Representatives 2009b, 106 (American Jewish Congress).
84. U.S. Senate 2010b, 82 (Rachel Ehrenfeld).
85. U.S. House of Representatives 2009b, 165 (Laura Handman).
86. U.S. House of Representatives 2009b, 181 (American Jewish Congress).
87. U.S. House of Representatives 2009b, 46.
88. U.S. House of Representatives 2009b, 4, 100, 106; U.S. Senate 2010b, 28.
89. U.S. House of Representatives 2009b, 7 (Rep. Peter King).
90. U.S. House of Representatives 2009b, 4 (Rep. Trent Franks).
91. U.S. House of Representatives 2009b, 7 (Rep. Peter King).
92. Specter and Lieberman 2008.
93. U.S. Senate 2010b, 85 (Rachel Ehrenfeld).
94. U.S. House of Representatives 2009b, 5 (Rep. John Conyers Jr. (D-MI)).
95. Specter and Lieberman 2008.
96. U.S. House of Representatives 2009b, 171.
97. U.S. Senate 2010b, 86.
98. U.S. House of Representatives 2009b, 102; U.S. Senate 2010b, 30 (ACLU).
99. U.S. House of Representatives 2009b, 41 (Laura Handman).
100. U.S. House of Representatives 2009b, 135.

101. U.S. House of Representatives 2009b, 7 (Rep. Peter King).
102. U.S. Senate 2010b, 86.
103. U.S. Senate 2010b, 35, 44 (Bruce Brown).
104. U.S. House of Representatives 2009b, 7.
105. Specter and Lieberman 2008.
106. U.S. House of Representatives 2009b, 124 (American Jewish Congress), 195 (columnist Andrew C. McCarthy).
107. U.S. House of Representatives 2009b, 7; U.S. Senate 2010b, 30.
108. U.N. Human Rights Comm., Int'l Covenant on Civil and Political Rights, Consideration of Reports by States Parties Under Article 40 of the Covenant, Concluding Observations of the Comm., United Kingdom of Great Britain and Northern Ireland, ¶25, U.N. Doc. CCPR/C/GBR/CO/6 (July 30, 2008). See references in U.S. House of Representatives 2009a, 3; U.S. House of Representatives 2009b, 177; U.S. Senate 2010a, 2–3. The SPEECH Act itself cites the Human Rights Committee's finding that "in some instances the law of libel has served to discourage critical media reporting on matters of serious public interest" (§2(4)).
109. U.S. House of Representatives 2009b, 102; U.S. Senate 2010b, 30.
110. U.S. Senate 2010b, 30.
111. U.S. House of Representatives 2009a, 6–7. The referenced decision is Jameel v. Wall Street Journal Europe [2006] UKHL 44. See also U.S. House of Representatives 2009b, 47–48.
112. U.S. House of Representatives 2009a, 7.
113. U.S. House of Representatives 2009b, 82.
114. U.S. House of Representatives 2009b, 25; U.S. Senate 2010b, 51 (Bruce Brown). See also The Economist 2009 (reprinted in U.S. Senate 2010b 58–59); U.S. House of Representatives 2009b, 51.
115. U.S. House of Representatives 2009b, 160.
116. In 2009, three organizations representing writers, activists, journalists, researchers, and artists—Sense about Science, Index on Censorship, and English PEN—launched the Libel Reform Campaign, calling for a change of Britain's "unfair and repressive libel laws" (see http://archive.senseaboutscience.org/pages/launch-of-the-libel-reform-campaign.html). A report released by two of these organizations denounced "English libel law [which] imposes unnecessary and disproportionate restrictions on free speech, sending a chilling effect through the publishing and journalism sectors in the UK." The report called for bringing British libel law in line with "the interests of a modern democratic society" and removing the "international embarrassment of the UK being used as an international libel tribunal" (English PEN and Index of Censorship 2009, 2, 9). John Kampfner, CEO of Index on Censorship, brought up the laws passed by several U.S. states to block UK libel judgments and warned that "If we don't act we're at risk of becoming a global pariah" (http://archive.senseaboutscience.org/pages/launch-of-the-libel-reform-campaign.html).
117. BBC 2013.
118. New York Times Editorial 2011.
119. U.S. House of Representatives 2009b, 183.
120. U.S. House of Representatives 2009b, 93.
121. U.S. House of Representatives 2009b, 100.
122. U.S. House of Representatives 2009b, 107.
123. Author's interview with Daniel Kornstein, attorney at Emery Celli Brinckerhoff & Abady LLP, New York, March 2018.
124. U.S. House of Representatives 2009b, 15–27, 41–58; U.S. Senate 2010b, 6–7, 34–53.
125. Brown, interview; author's interview with Laura Handman, attorney at Davis Wright Tremaine LLP.
126. Abrams 2008 (reprinted in House of Representatives 2009b, 174); Specter and Lieberman 2008.
127. Abady and Silverglate 2008. Reprinted in U.S. House of Representatives 2009b, 197.
128. Cohen 2008. Reprinted in U.S. House of Representatives 2009b, 199–200.
129. New York Times Editorial 2010.
130. Author's interview with Floyd Abrams, attorney at Cahill Gordon & Reindel LLP, New York, March 2018.

131. Ehrenfeld, interview; Abrams, interview.
132. U.S. House of Representatives 2009b, 89–91.
133. U.S. House of Representatives 2009b, 64–65.
134. U.S House of Representatives 2009b, 68.
135. U.S. House of Representatives 2009b, 5.
136. U.S. Senate 2010b, 39, 51 (Bruce Brown).
137. U.S. House of Representatives 2009b, 157–158; U.S. Senate 2010b, 38–39.
138. U.S. Senate 2010b, 39.
139. S. 449, Sec. 3(d); Free Speech Protection Act of 2009, H.R. 1304, 111th Cong. (2009), Sec. 3(d). See U.S. Senate 2010b, 38; U.S. House of Representatives 2009b, 86; Taylor 2010, 207.
140. S. 449 and H.R. 1304.
141. U.S. House of Representatives 2009b, 7–9 (Rep. Peter King).
142. U.S. House of Representatives 2009b, 12.
143. U.S. Senate 2010b, 40–42.
144. Rivkin and Brown 2009.
145. U.S. House of Representatives 2009b, 86, 96.
146. U.S. House of Representatives 2009b, 97.
147. U.S. House of Representatives 2009b, 60, 70, 73, 171.
148. U.S. House of Representatives 2009a, 6; U.S. House of Representatives 2009b, 3–4.
149. H.R. 2765 (111th Cong.), introduced by Rep. Steve Cohen. See U.S. House of Representatives 2009a, 5–7.
150. See Taylor 2010, 205–208; Elbalti 2017, 253–275.
151. Ehrenfeld, interview.
152. Kornstein, interview.
153. Abrams, Interview.
154. Brown, interview.
155. Rosen 2012; Abrams, interview; Kornstein, interview.
156. Lancman, interview.
157. Lancman, Interview.
158. Kornstein, interview.
159. Tuval 2008.
160. Brown, interview; Lancman, interview; Kornstein, interview.
161. Brown, interview.
162. Lancman, interview.
163. See note 108.
164. Pfanner 2012; Brown, interview; Handman, interview.
165. Roberts 2016.

SECTION V

GENERALIZING THE FINDINGS

9

A Quantitative Look at Cooperation on Litigation

This book has argued that the prospects of cooperation between legal systems hinge on the relative evaluation of the prospective partners, in which the home legal system serves as the reference point: the prospective partner's legal institutions, standards, and procedures are compared to those of the home legal system (Proposition 2). If the foreign legal system is judged to fall below the standards of the home system, cooperation might meet resistance among home-country actors and will be more difficult to establish. In some cases, the perceived gap between the home and foreign systems will be large enough to obstruct cooperation altogether. Concerns about China's poor human rights record thwarted that country's extradition treaties with Australia and Canada, which take pride in their commitment to human rights; the early efforts to establish a convention to facilitate the enforcement of foreign judgments failed due to European concerns about American civil justice; and the U.S. Congress's sense that UK law fails to adequately protect free speech resulted in restrictions on the enforcement of British libel judgments in the United States. In other cases, the perceived gap between the home and foreign legal systems may not result in the failure of cooperation but could make the cooperative endeavor more difficult. As we have seen in Chapter 3, ratification of the NATO SOFA was ultimately achieved over stiff resistance from skeptical senators who believed that European legal systems lacked safeguards comparable to those of the U.S. Constitution.

The qualitative evidence provides ample support for the relative-evaluation proposition. This chapter takes a different tack, complementary to the case-studies in this book: rather than examine specific episodes, we look here for broad evidence of general relationship across space and time. Using large-N samples and quantitative methods, our goal is to systematically demonstrate that states tend to prefer partners whose legal system resembles their own in some fundamental way. This means that a legal gap between prospective

Intolerant Justice. Asif Efrat, Oxford University Press. © Oxford University Press 2023.
DOI: 10.1093/oso/9780197658895.003.0009

partners will reduce the likelihood of cooperation: the greater the dissimilarity in substantive legal rules or in legal procedures and institutions, the less likely are two countries to cooperate. Furthermore, we seek to verify that this negative effect of legal differences on cooperation holds in both the criminal and civil domains.

On the criminal side, we examine the signing of bilateral mutual legal assistance treaties (MLATs). The need for mutual legal assistance arises in transnational criminal cases where evidence needed for an investigation or prosecution in one country is located in another. Cooperation here means gathering evidence on behalf of the investigating/prosecuting country and sharing that evidence with that country. The provision of evidence to a foreign country to be used in an investigation or trial typically is less laden with sensitivity than the transfer of a person to stand trial through extradition. Nonetheless, sharing evidence with a foreign legal system raises concerns about appropriate treatment, similar to other transnational legal dilemmas examined in this book. In particular, evidence sharing entails a risk that the evidence provided might be leaked or be abused for political or other purposes.

On the civil side, we examine cooperation on the civil aspects of international child abduction. International parental child abduction is the removal or retention of a child outside their country of habitual residence in breach of the other parent's custody rights.[1] In simpler terms, this is a situation in which one parent takes the child to a foreign country without the knowledge or consent of the other parent—with serious consequences for both the child and the left-behind parent. In 1980, the Hague Conference on Private International Law established an agreement to tackle this problem: the Convention on the Civil Aspects of International Child Abduction (hereinafter the Hague Convention). The convention creates a mechanism for the automatic, expedited return of abducted children to their country of origin, on the assumption that this serves the best interests of the child. The convention further stipulates that the custody dispute is *not* to be decided in the country of refuge; rather, it is to be settled by the authorities of the country of origin following the child's return. This, for the country of refuge, raises concerns that echo those accompanying criminal extradition, only in a civil-dispute context: Should we send the child and the abducting parent to litigate custody before a foreign court, or based on foreign laws, that might not be fair?

The Hague Convention allows states parties to pick and choose the countries to which they are willing to return abducted children, and states can also select with whom to conclude an MLAT. In both cases, we would expect states to opt for partners similar to themselves. Similarity of substantive rules, procedures, or institutions would support the impression that the partner has a fair legal system that can be trusted to handle the exchange of evidence or to decide custody disputes in an appropriate manner.

Mutual Legal Assistance Treaties

Bilateral mutual legal assistance treaties are binding agreements that commit public officials to assisting their foreign peers in collecting and sharing legal evidence that may facilitate the investigation or prosecution of criminal offenses.[2] In a world of nation states, the investigation or prosecution of a crime may require evidence that is located in a foreign country. Without crossborder assistance, law-enforcement efforts could be derailed. The primary goal of MLATs is to facilitate the sharing of legal evidence, and these treaties typically provide for various kinds of assistance, including taking a statement or testimony from persons, effecting the production of documents or records, locating individuals, examining objects and sites, and effecting the appearance of a witness before a court of the requesting state. These different forms of assistance can be carried out by the judicial, prosecutorial, or law-enforcement personnel of the state receiving the request.[3] Underlying the spread of MLATs since the 1980s was a growing frustration with *letters rogatory*—a channel of judicial assistance that was slow and nonbinding. Using letters rogatory, a legal team from one country would make a request to a foreign court to share legal evidence. Foreign courts, however, were often reluctant to share evidence across borders or to alter their usual procedures to meet the constitutional and evidentiary requirements of other legal systems. MLATs, by contrast, establish an *obligation* to provide assistance.[4] An additional boost for the spread of MLATs came from the adoption of a UN Model Treaty on Mutual Assistance in Criminal Matters in 1990 and from the provisions on mutual legal assistance in the 1988 UN Convention against Illicit Traffic in Narcotic Drugs and Psychotropic Substances.[5]

Our dataset, described below, includes 735 bilateral MLATs signed between 1981 and 2014 by 70 countries worldwide, including all the major powers. Figure 9.1 documents the spread of these MLATs over time. As the figure shows, the number of MLATs has been steadily rising since the 1980s, with an especially precipitous increase in the 1990s.

Over time, MLATs have become a cornerstone of law-enforcement cooperation, viewed by governments as an important tool for countering the legal challenges posed by globalization and used across issue-areas, from organized crime and terrorism to regulatory matters such as securities. A 2002 U.S. Senate report described the signing of MLATs "as part of a highly successful effort to

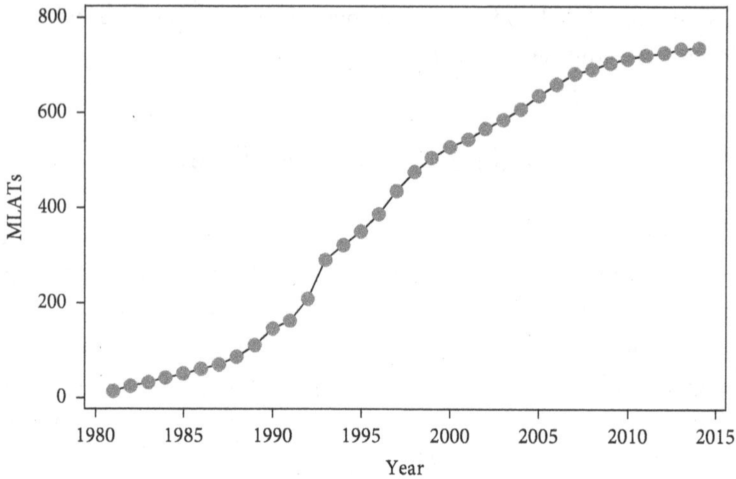

Figure 9.1 Spread of MLATs, 1981–2014.

modernize the legal tools available to law enforcement authorities in need of foreign evidence for use in criminal cases."[6] Similarly, the U.S. Department of Justice concluded that "In order to safeguard our nation and our citizens, the United States must actively and timely share critical law enforcement information with our foreign partners. United States and foreign law enforcement authorities make formal requests to each other for evidence in criminal cases through a process referred to as 'mutual legal assistance' (MLA), made often through our Mutual Legal Assistance Treaties (MLATs)."[7] The European Commission explained that "Globalisation and people's increasing mobility across the EU create new opportunities for crossborder crime. This is why mutual legal assistance and agreements on extradition are essential to stop crossborder crime."[8]

Legal-System Similarity and the Choice of MLAT Partners

MLATs present a delicate form of cooperation in which one actor provides potentially sensitive material—legal evidence—to a foreign counterpart. The provision of evidence to foreign authorities raises concerns of possible leaks or misuse that might jeopardize a country's security, commercial, or other interests. Confidential information might leak into the public domain, tarnishing the reputation of the evidence-providing authority and compromising its sources. Corrupt officials could even transfer the information to the investigative targets themselves. Furthermore, the evidence recipient might misuse the information or use it for a different purpose than the one intended by the evidence provider, raising the specter of political blowback for the latter.[9] Given these concerns, countries may require assurances that the information they provide will be handled in an appropriate manner.

Anecdotal evidence concerning the ratification of legal-assistance treaties by the United States in the late 1980s and the early 1990s demonstrates such concerns at work. Officials from the Justice Department, State Department, FBI, and CIA all made the case that legal-assistance agreements signed with Mexico, the Bahamas, and Panama represented critical tools for the United States in its effort to thwart money laundering, drug trafficking, and organized crime.[10] Senator Jesse Helms (R-NC), however, argued that corruption in these countries would result in information flowing from the government to criminal groups: "Now while the State Department has claimed that these treaties will aid efforts to prosecute drug traffickers, the fact is that in their current form a case can be made quite credibly that they may in fact benefit drug traffickers."[11] Helms's opposition became particularly potent in the case of Panama, and his concerns about the possible misuse of sensitive information significantly delayed ratification of the treaty.[12] Former Panama City Mayor Mayín Correa corroborated Helms's concerns: "I wouldn't sign an agreement to turn over information from investigations. I wouldn't have confidence in Panamanian authorities until there are radical changes."[13] Similarly, Ethan Nadelmann observes that "[B]oth the United States and many foreign states were wary of negotiating law enforcement treaties [extradition treaties and MLATs] with governments viewed as likely to use or misuse their judicial systems to punish or harass political opponents."[14]

States may gain confidence in the exchange of evidence through a careful selection of trustworthy partners. They can enter into MLATs with those countries that, in their view, are more likely to appropriately handle the evidence they receive. This book's theoretical framework (Proposition 2) suggests that in identifying trustworthy partners states will typically use their home legal system as the metric for the assessment of foreign legal systems. Foreign systems similar to the home system are more likely to be perceived as fair. As the gap between the home and foreign systems grows, the foreign system becomes a less attractive partner—one that seems unfair or dangerous.

Specifically, in assessing prospective MLAT partners, states are likely to focus on two key features of the foreign legal system. The first is judicial independence, which captures the manner in which judges are appointed and the protections they enjoy during their tenure—protections that aim to insulate them from inappropriate influence, either from outside the judiciary or from within. As such, judicial independence shapes the relationship between the judicial and executive branches and influences the legal system's ability to withstand political pressure.[15] Judicial independence may thus be used as shorthand for assessing the ability and willingness of a prospective MLAT partner to avoid the misuse of information. In particular, one would expect greater cooperation—and a higher likelihood of an MLAT being established—among legal systems that have similarly high levels of judicial independence. Countries with independent judiciaries likely consider judicial independence as a bulwark against political pressure and abuse. In their view, judicial independence may offer some assurance that information they provide will be treated responsibly and not be abused for political purposes. Countries that rank high on judicial independence will therefore seek partners whose judiciary is similarly independent, and they are less likely to turn to partners that rank low on judicial independence. An environment that ranks low on judicial independence will be viewed as riskier and less predictable—one where the responsible handling of information is in doubt. This means that we should see relatively little cooperation between countries ranking high and those ranking low on judicial independence.

While we expect to observe cooperation between countries with high levels of judicial independence, our theoretical expectation for countries sharing low levels of judicial independence is indeterminate. In these countries, the judicial system faces considerable political interference, raising the risk of violations of information-sharing commitments. Moreover, low levels of judicial independence may be correlated with judicial corruption, signaling the potential for the leaking or misuse of information.[16] Nevertheless, pairs of countries ranked low on judicial independence may accept such risks. The logic here follows Brett Ashley Leeds, who argues that autocracies cooperate with each other, as they are comfortable with partners who, like themselves, are prone to defection from international commitments.[17] That said, it is difficult to empirically identify the cause of cooperation between states with low levels of judicial independence. They may indeed find it easier to cooperate with each other; or they may simply have few alternative partners, given the tendency of states with higher levels of judicial independence to partner with each other. For our purposes, both mechanisms suggest a similar empirical pattern: a tendency of countries ranked low on judicial independence to cooperate among themselves, akin to the tendency of countries ranked high on judicial independence to cooperate among themselves. In other words, an MLAT becomes more likely among countries that have a similar level of judicial independence. As the gap in judicial independence increases, the likelihood of an MLAT diminishes.

A second indicator of similarity among potential MLAT partners is the legal tradition to which they belong: common law, civil law, or Islamic law. Lawyers immersed in their legal tradition's norms, procedures, and method of legal thinking will have greater faith in a foreign system that belongs to the same tradition. That foreign system will fundamentally resemble the home legal system in how it operates, and this resemblance fosters predictability and trust in the context of evidence sharing: it enhances the expectation that information will be used, distributed, and secured in a familiar manner, reducing the perceived risk of misuse.[18] States will thus prefer MLAT partners that belong to their own legal tradition. Countries that belong to a different legal tradition, by contrast, are less attractive partners: with different legal institutions, it is harder to trust that evidence they receive will be treated responsibly.

In summary, our analysis results in the following testable expectations:

E1: Country A and Country B are more likely to sign an MLAT as the gap in their level of judicial independence narrows, particularly among pairs that share high levels of judicial independence.

E2: Country A and Country B are more likely to sign an MLAT if they belong to the same legal tradition.

Data and Method

The first step in our empirical investigation was the collection of original data on the signing of bilateral MLATs. Such data are not centrally collected or recorded by any international agency, and the large number of treaties further complicated the data-collection task. We first identified MLATs through publicly available sources, such as UN databases, government websites, and secondary literature. Next, we emailed the relevant government ministries—typically, ministries of justice—to corroborate the publicly available sources and asked them to list all MLATs to which their country is a party.[19] Combining these sources, we were able to develop comprehensive and reliable data for 70 countries. We recognize that the sample may suffer from some reporting bias, as countries with weak bureaucratic capacity may be unable to provide data. At the same time, this sample is diverse and representative in that it includes all the major powers as well as a number of medium-sized and smaller countries, and it also covers all regions of the world. Moreover, given the dyadic nature of the data, we were often in a position to reconstruct the MLAT relationships of those countries that did not provide us with data. Overall, the dataset includes 868 MLATs, the vast majority of which—735—were signed after 1980. For reasons of data limitations on key independent and control variables, we focus our analysis on the period between 1981 and 2012. The list of countries covered in the dataset appears in Appendix A.

The dataset is in the dyad-year format. A member of each dyad is one of the 70 countries for which comprehensive MLAT data are available. This country is then coupled with all other countries in the international system to create dyads where MLATs may potentially exist. The dependent variable—MLAT signing—is coded 0 for any year in which no MLAT exists between the members of the dyad. Once an MLAT is signed, the dependent variable is coded 1, and the dyad exits the analysis.

The analysis includes two key independent variables: the gap in judicial independence between members of the dyad; and the similarity of legal tradition between them. To ensure the validity of our findings, we measure these concepts through several different indicators.

The difference in the level of judicial independence is expressed through four indicators. First, we use the judicial-independence measurement developed by Linzer and Staton (hereinafter LS).[20] This is a unified measure of judicial independence, constructed as a latent variable that draws upon eight direct and indirect indicators of judicial independence collected by various scholars. Second, we employ the judicial independence measure from the Cingranelli-Richards (CIRI) Human Rights Dataset.[21] Our third measure is the Law and Order variable from the International Country Risk Guide, which reflects the strength and impartiality of the legal system as well as the extent of the popular observance of the law. Our fourth measure is the World Bank's Rule of Law indicator, which includes judicial independence as one of its components. In fact, the concepts of judicial independence and rule of law are seen by some as overlapping.[22] For each of the four indicators, we construct a gap variable: the absolute value of the difference between the scores of the two members of the dyad.[23] This gap is expected to have a negative influence on the signing of an MLAT.

A second source of institutional similarity is a shared legal tradition, based on Mitchell and Powell[24] (hereinafter MP). This variable equals 1 if both dyad members belong to one of four legal traditions: common law, civil law, Islamic law, or mixed law.

Beyond these key variables, our models include a battery of controls. Given the literature's emphasis on regime type as a determinant of international cooperation, we control for the gap in the level of democracy between dyad members.[25] We also control for influences relating to the *need* for an MLAT. More populous countries typically face a larger volume of crime[26] and may have a greater need for evidence from abroad. The models therefore control for the size of the population in each member of the dyad.[27] The per capita Gross Domestic Product (GDP) of each member is also included in the analysis, since rich and developing countries may vary in their approach to and capacity for crime control.[28] We also control for the distance between dyad members, as the need to obtain evidence may rise with the geographic proximity between the two countries: countries close to each other experience significant crossborder exchange, with greater potential for criminal activity.[29] A more specific indicator of the demand for an MLAT would capture actual involvement in transnational crime. The indicator we use is the U.S. "Majors list": an annual presidential identification of the major drug-producing and drug-transit countries worldwide (U.S. assistance may be withheld from listed countries that fail to make substantial efforts to adhere to their counter-narcotics obligations[30]). Dyads are coded 1 if one or both members are on the Majors list, indicating significant involvement in the illegal drug trade and a need for law-enforcement cooperation.[31]

Other influences on the conclusion of MLATs concern cultural similarity between members of the dyad and the nature of their political relations. A common language indicates cultural resemblance that may facilitate cooperation.[32] As a measure of the political affinity between dyad members, we use ideal-point distance in UN General-Assembly voting. Greater distance should lower the likelihood of an MLAT being signed.[33]

Our model also takes into account two regional influences. First, although MLATs are primarily signed on a bilateral basis, several regional MLATs do exist. If members of the dyad are parties to a regional agreement, a bilateral MLAT may be unnecessary.[34] Second, studies have found that a state may choose to join a treaty if other countries in its region have done so.[35] We therefore control for the average number of MLATs in the country's region. Since each observation involves two countries, we take the lower value of this indicator for each dyad—on the assumption that the signing of an MLAT is determined by the country that has fewer MLATs in its region and is less strongly motivated to pursue such agreements.[36]

Finally, veto players—domestic actors who possess the ability to block policy change—can hinder states' entry into treaties.[37] We control for the impact of these actors through Henisz's Political Constraint index. Higher values of this index indicate greater influence of the legislative, judicial, and sub-federal authorities and diminished executive discretion. The executive that faces heavier domestic constraints will determine whether an MLAT is signed—we therefore use the higher value for each dyad.

To examine the signing of MLATs econometrically, we employ a duration model known as discrete event-history analysis. Discrete duration models use a logistic regression combined with a cubic polynomial to adjust for time dependencies.[38] This method explores the probability that a unit will experience a particular event in a period of time, given that the event has not already occurred. In the current case, we seek to estimate the probability that the event of interest—the signing of an MLAT—will occur as time elapses.

Results

Table 9.1 presents the results of five event-history models, all estimating the effects of the independent variables on the time it takes for the two members of the dyad to sign an MLAT.

Table 9.1. **Influences on the signing of MLATs**

	Model 1	*Model 2*	*Model 3*	*Model 4*	*Model 5*
Judicial-independence gap (LS)	−0.143*** (0.015)	−0.148*** (0.027)			
Judicial-independence gap (CIRI)			−0.247*** (0.071)		
Law-and-order gap				−0.212*** (0.048)	
Rule-of-law gap					−0.461*** (0.077)
Shared legal tradition (MP)	0.662*** (0.075)	0.339*** (0.101)	0.304*** (0.101)	0.223** (0.114)	0.457*** (0.135)
Democracy gap		0.01 (0.011)	−0.015* (0.009)	−0.016* (0.01)	−0.022* (0.011)
Population Country 1		0.448*** (0.03)	0.451*** (0.031)	0.473*** (0.035)	0.555*** (0.039)
Population Country 2		0.49*** (0.031)	0.494*** (0.031)	0.471*** (0.036)	0.544*** (0.04)
GDP per capita Country 1		0.301*** (0.036)	0.298*** (0.036)	0.345*** (0.042)	0.317*** (0.052)
GDP per capita Country 2		0.376*** (0.034)	0.37*** (0.034)	0.401*** (0.039)	0.403*** (0.046)
Distance		−0.766*** (0.057)	−0.773*** (0.058)	−0.604*** (0.068)	−0.792*** (0.082)
Drug Majors list		0.355*** (0.103)	0.339*** (0.104)	0.446*** (0.119)	0.398*** (0.141)
Common language		0.814*** (0.128)	0.832*** (0.129)	0.967*** (0.137)	0.889*** (0.168)
UN-voting distance		0.12* (0.066)	0.035 (0.061)	0.018 (0.067)	0.114 (0.085)
Regional MLAT		−0.791*** (0.216)	−0.807*** (0.215)	−0.999*** (0.243)	−1.194*** (0.31)
MLATs in the region		0.569*** (0.092)	0.555*** (0.087)	1.315*** (0.175)	2.185*** (0.231)

Table 9.1. **Continued**

	Model 1	*Model 2*	*Model 3*	*Model 4*	*Model 5*
Veto players		−0.695**	−1.147***	−1.337***	−2.087***
		(0.3)	(0.305)	(0.347)	(0.389)
Observations	265335	174834	167235	121623	109948
Prob>chi^2	0.00	0.00	0.00	0.00	0.00

Notes: Logit models; each model includes a cubic polynomial. * $p<0.1$; ** $p<0.05$; *** $p<0.01$. Robust standard errors in parentheses.

Model 1 is a simple model that includes only our key variables of interest: the Linzer-Staton indicator of judicial independence, and an indicator of a shared legal tradition. Consistent with *E1,* the gap in judicial independence is negatively and significantly associated with the likelihood of an MLAT being signed. *This means that an MLAT is more likely between states whose judicial-independence gap is smaller.* As the gap increases, concerns may arise about the consequences of providing information to the prospective partner. Such concerns diminish the prospects of an MLAT. Consistent with *E2*, similarity of legal tradition increases the chances of an MLAT being signed: common-law countries favor fellow common-law countries as partners; civil-law countries prefer to cooperate with other civil-law countries. These results hold in Model 2, which adds a battery of controls and shows a large substantive effect of the key covariates. In terms of odds ratio, a one-unit increase of the judicial-independence gap—on a 0–10 scale—lowers the odds of an MLAT by 14%. Put in terms of elasticity, a 1% increase of the judicial-independence gap reduces the probability of an MLAT by 0.57%. Figure 9.2 demonstrates how the predicted probability of an MLAT declines as the judicial-independence gap increases. A shared legal tradition also has a substantial impact, raising the odds of an MLAT by 40%.

Models 3–5 vary in their measurement of one of the key covariates: the quality of the legal system. Model 3 shows a negative association between the gap in the CIRI measure of judicial independence and MLAT signing. In Model 4, the gap in law and order is also negatively correlated with the likelihood of an MLAT being concluded. A one-unit increase in the gap—on a 0–6 scale—lowers the odds of an MLAT by 19%. In Model 5, the gap in the rule of law is similarly negatively correlated with the signing of MLATs. Overall, the different measures of legal-system quality yielded a consistent negative result. A shared legal tradition also exhibits a consistent effect, but a positive one—increasing the chances of an MLAT being signed in all models. Overall, these findings suggest that the hypothesized sources of institutional similarity serve as an important foundation of information exchange.

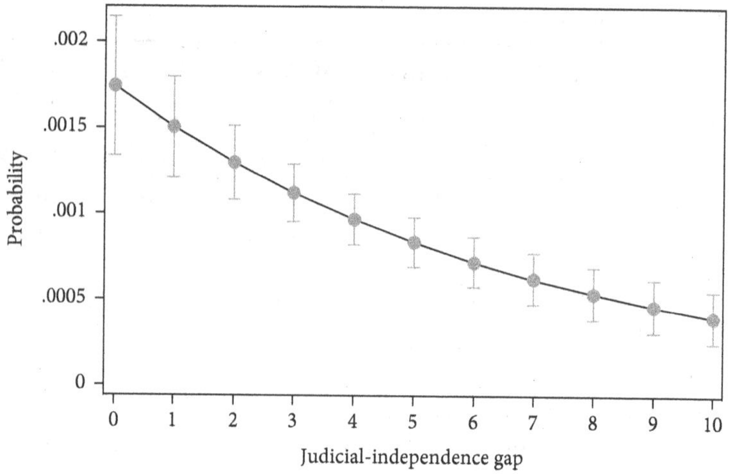

Figure 9.2 Predicted probability of an MLAT at different levels of the judicial-independence gap with 95% confidence intervals.

Compared to the large effect of judicial independence and legal tradition, the gap in the level of democracy has a weak and inconsistent effect on the signing of MLATs. In Model 2 that gap is positively signed and nonsignificant; in the other models, it is negative and only weakly significant. This indicates that regime-type similarity is too crude a basis for cooperation on the sharing of legal evidence: it says little about how legal materials will be handled by foreign authorities. Predictability in the exchange of legal information stems from more specific institutional features relating to the nature and quality of the legal system.

Other control variables generally conform to our expectations. In particular, countries separated by greater distance are less likely to conclude an MLAT, as they have less need for cooperation on criminal matters. By contrast, the likelihood of an MLAT rises if any of the dyad members has a significant involvement in the illegal drug trade, as indicated by the Majors list. As expected, a regional MLAT reduces the need for—and hence the likelihood of—a bilateral MLAT, whereas the popularity of MLATs in the region provides an incentive for further signing of MLATs. Contrary to expectations, the political affinity between the members of the dyad—indicated by distance in UN voting—does not exert a significant influence on the conclusion of MLATs. Finally, veto players diminish the likelihood of an MLAT.

In a set of robustness checks not presented here, we find that the results remain robust to the inclusion of fixed effects for year and for the first country in the dyad. The results also hold when additional controls are introduced, such as colonial relations or trade relations between the members of the dyad. All else being equal, states prefer evidence-sharing partners that are similar to themselves on two key parameters: the level of judicial independence and legal origin.

Legal-System Similarity and the Efforts against Child Abduction

International child abduction occurs when one parent takes a child to another country without the knowledge or consent of the left-behind parent. The primary victim of the abduction is the child, who suffers from the disruption of their stable routine, the loss of contact with a parent, and the necessity to adapt to a new family and social environment. Worse still, abducting parents sometimes force their children to change their appearance or their name and may tell the children that the left-behind parent is dead, does not want them, or is not trying to get them back. Overall, this experience may result in the abducted child experiencing anxiety, eating problems, nightmares, sleep disturbances, or aggressive behavior, as well as feelings of anger, fear, or guilt—sometimes with long-term effects.[39] Separated from their children, left-behind parents suffer emotional distress and hardship; they also face the financial burden of searching for the child and seeking their return.[40]

The 1980 Hague Convention on child abduction is the primary international agreement tackling this problem. Studies of the convention's operation shed additional light on the child-abduction phenomenon. In 2015, applications for the return of 2,997 children were made among 76 members of the convention; this number has increased over time (from 2,703 in 2008),[41] likely due to the growing number of marriages between individuals from different countries, soaring divorce rates, and the ease of international travel[42] (and these figures, it should be remembered, include only abductions among members of the convention; the global annual count of internationally abducted children is higher). The average age of an abducted child in 2015 was approximately 7 years. The proportion of males and females among abducted children was roughly equal,[43] but not so among the abducting parents. In the majority of reported cases—some 73%—the abducting parent was the mother.[44] In many cases, these are mothers who have lived abroad during the marriage and, after the marriage failed, wished to return to a country where they could enjoy family and support networks. Concerned that they might not be permitted to leave the country of residence with their child, these mothers took unilateral action and removed the child.[45] Fifty-eight percent of abducting parents—both fathers and mothers—chose to take the child to a country they were a national of.[46] In other cases, abducting parents took the child to another country of refuge in which they could hide or enjoy a support network, even if it was not their country of nationality. In 2015, the countries that had the largest numbers of reported incoming and outgoing abductions were the United Kingdom (649 cases), the United States (597 cases), Germany (457 cases), Mexico (306 cases), France (294 cases), Italy (243 cases), and Spain (204 cases).[47]

Abducting parents typically wish to obtain a right of custody in the country of refuge that would legalize the factual situation that they have created by removing the child. The Hague Convention's primary objective is to deter such action by restoring the pre-abduction status quo through the *prompt return of the child* to the country of origin, with the decision on custody to be made by that country's authorities. Indeed, the convention does not seek to regulate or determine the award of custody rights. It rests on the principle that custody rights should be debated before and decided by the authorities of the country where the child resided prior to the abduction.[48] The convention therefore requires the administrative or judicial authorities of the country of refuge to ensure the child's return.[49]

To bring about the return of abducted children, contracting states designate a Central Authority (typically, a unit within the ministry of justice or ministry of social affairs). In response to an incoming application for return, the Central Authority of the country of refuge is tasked with discovering the whereabouts of an abducted child; securing the voluntary return of the child; in case of failure of voluntary return, initiating or facilitating judicial proceedings aimed at obtaining the return of the child; and providing administrative arrangements to secure the child's safe return. A study of the convention's operation in 2015 shows that 57% of the applications for returning a child resulted in the child's return: in 22% of applications the return was voluntary, and in 35% the return followed a court order.[50] This means that in the majority of cases the convention achieved its primary goal of bringing about the return of the child. In another 9% of cases, the convention's mechanisms facilitated an agreement between the parents to allow the child to remain in the country of refuge or to secure a right of access to the child.[51] Given this record, the U.S. State Department considers the convention "to be one of the most effective tools available for parents or legal guardians to seek the return of their abducted children."[52]

At the same time, the convention raises the same transnational legal dilemma we have encountered throughout this book: Will the foreign country conduct a fair legal process, both procedurally and substantively? In the case of child abduction, this is, in fact, a dual question.

It applies, first, to the left-behind parent. The convention is geared toward assisting the left-behind parent in their quest: both Central Authorities and judicial authorities in the country of refuge are required to take measures to bring about the child's return. Judicial authorities are instructed to "act expeditiously in proceedings for the return of children" and to reach a decision within six weeks.[53] Subject to a few narrow exceptions, this decision should typically be an order for the return of the child.[54] Yet this mechanism may fail to function as intended if the rule of law in the country of refuge is weak: judicial authorities might be slow or inefficient; they might come under political pressure not to order a return; if they do order a return, their decisions might go unenforced; or they might exhibit bias against foreigners—an issue of particular concern for left-behind parents who are foreigners in the country of refuge. Such problems could result in a poor legal experience for the left-behind parent and in diminished prospects of a return of children from countries with a weak rule of law.

Concerns also arise with respect to courts in the child's country of origin—the courts tasked with resolving the custody dispute following the return of the child. The convention prohibits the authorities of the country of refuge from deciding on the merits of the rights of custody and further emphasizes that a decision concerning the return of the child "shall not be taken to be a determination on the merits of any custody issue."[55] Custody decisions are the purview of courts *in the country of origin*, and the abducting parent will have to litigate before them. In most cases, the abducting parent is the mother, and she may not enjoy a fair and equal legal treatment in countries that fail to guarantee women's rights and equality. The mother may not be given a full opportunity to make her case before the court, or the rules governing custody might be biased against her.[56] This suggests caution in returning children to countries where women's rights are weak. Furthermore, some abduction cases involve mothers who are fleeing domestic violence. The return of the child, accompanied by their mother, could have the unintended consequence of putting the mother at risk of renewed violence and jeopardizing the child as well.[57] This suggests even greater caution in returning children to countries with a weaker rule of law and a poor record on women's rights that are unlikely to provide adequate protections against domestic violence.

Concerns intensify given the convention's broad and diverse membership: 101 countries (as of 2022) that represent all regions of the world. The countries of Europe and the Americas constitute the majority of members, but the convention also has members in Africa, the Middle East, the Caucasus, South and East Asia, and the Pacific. This means that some members of the convention have a less-than-stellar record on the rule of law or women's rights. In addition, the Hague Convention does little to accommodate legal-difference concerns. The obligation to return the child applies regardless of any legal differences between the child's country of origin and the country of refuge, and there is no broad public-policy exception that allows nonreturn: the inclusion of such an exception in the convention was considered and rejected. The primary exceptions to return have to do not with general concerns of law or policy but with specific circumstances in which a return may not be in the child's best interests (e.g., the child is already settled in the new environment or could face physical or psychological harm if returned[58]). The convention does allow return to be refused if it is inconsistent with human rights;[59] but beyond this specific concern, no other substantive or procedural attribute of the country of origin's legal system can justify nonreturn.[60]

While the convention does not permit the refusal of child return on the grounds of low legal standards in the partner country, it does allow one not to select such countries as partners in the first place. Normally, when a country joins a multilateral treaty, legal relations are automatically established between itself and all other members of the convention. The Hague Convention, however, establishes a unique membership process that allows countries to select their treaty partners, with whom they will cooperate in the return of abducted children. More specifically, the convention distinguishes between two groups of countries. The first group consists of countries that were members of the Hague Conference on Private International Law at the time of the convention's adoption in 1980; these countries are entitled to *ratify* the convention. Most members of the convention, however, did not meet this condition for ratification and joined the convention through *accession*. The act of accession to the Hague Convention does not carry multilateral or bilateral consequences. Each country that joined the convention earlier—through ratification or accession—has to decide individually whether to engage in treaty relations with the acceding country. The same prerogative belongs to countries that ratified the convention at a later stage, even for accessions that took place before they joined the convention. The willingness to cooperate with the new member and return children to them is expressed through an acceptance of that member's accession: a formal act of depositing a declaration indicating the acceptance.[61] This means, in effect, that states do not have to cooperate with all convention members: they can pick and choose those partners that suit them.

This book's argument suggests that, in this selection process, states will assess the rule of law and protection of women's rights of prospective partners relative to themselves. They are likely to choose partners whose rule of law and protection of women's rights are at least as strong as their own. Partners with a robust rule of law are more likely to successfully and expeditiously return abducted children; partners that protect women's rights will probably treat mothers fairly in resolving custody disputes. The same cannot be expected from countries whose rule of law and/or protection of women's rights are weaker than one's own, and those are less likely to be selected as partners.

Our analysis leads to the following expectations:

E3: Country A is less likely to select Country B as a partner to the extent that Country B's rule of law is weaker than Country A's.
E4: Country A is less likely to select Country B as a partner to the extent that Country B's respect for women's rights is weaker than Country A's.

Data and Method

To examine whether legal-system similarity affects partner selection under the Hague Convention, we constructed a dataset on the acceptance of countries' accessions to the convention. The dataset is in the dyad-year format. The first country in each dyad is a country that has joined the convention by way of accession (hereinafter: acceding country). From Hungary—the first country to have acceded in 1986—through Zambia, which acceded in 2014, the dataset includes a total of 59 acceding countries. The second country in each dyad is the country that has to consider accepting the new member's accession (hereinafter: accepting country). The accepting countries have themselves acceded to or ratified the convention prior to the accession of the country in question; an accession also has to be accepted by any country that has ratified the convention at a later stage, subsequent to the accession (for example, Mexico, which acceded in 1991, had to be accepted by Venezuela, which ratified in 1996). In total, our dataset includes 3,669 dyads; an acceptance has occurred in 2,218 of them. For each dyad, coverage begins in the year when the acceding country joined the convention, or, if the accepting country is a late ratifier, in the year of subsequent ratification. Before an acceptance is made, the acceptance variable—the dependent variable in the analysis—equals zero. Once an acceptance occurs, the acceptance variable is assigned a value of 1, and the dyad then exits the analysis.

Our first explanatory variable—the gap in the rule of law—is based on the Rule of Law indicator from the World Bank's Worldwide Governance Indicators. This indicator captures several procedural dimensions of the legal system, including the speed of the judicial process and timeliness of decisions, judicial independence, enforcement of court orders, reliability of the police, and the treatment of non-nationals. The gap variable is constructed by subtracting the acceding country's rule-of-law value from the accepting country's. This difference is expected to have a negative effect on the acceptance of accessions: the weaker the acceding country's rule of law as compared to the accepting country's, the less interested the accepting country should be in establishing treaty relations with the acceding country.

The second key variable measures gender equality to capture the likely legal treatment of women in custody disputes. The indicator is the percentage of parliamentary seats held by women, which has been widely used as a crossnational measure of women's status.[62] As with the rule of law, our variable measures the gap in women's parliamentary membership between the accepting and acceding countries; it is expected to be negatively associated with accession acceptance: weaker status of women raises the concern that they might not receive fair treatment from the acceding country's authorities.

Beyond these key variables, we include a set of control variables that may shape the willingness to cooperate on child abduction. We control for the accepting and acceding countries' population and GDP per capita[63] and for the two countries' geographic distance: abductions are more likely to occur among countries close to each other, raising the need for cooperation.[64] Cooperation is also more likely among countries that generally have good political relations. We use ideal point distance in UN General-Assembly voting as an indicator of the political affinity between the acceding and accepting countries.[65] As the above analysis of MLATs has shown, countries that belong to the same legal tradition are more likely to cooperate. Thus, a shared legal tradition—common, civil, or Islamic law—can make it easier for the accepting country to cooperate with the acceding country.[66]

Beyond this set of dyadic influences, certain factors in the accepting country may affect its interest in cooperation. Since abductions typically follow a couple's separation or divorce, they might be more common as the national divorce rate rises. We thus control for the rate of divorce in the accepting country.[67] We also control for the stock of migrants residing in the accepting country. A large migrant population might raise the risk of abduction by migrants who choose to take the child to their country of origin; this increases the need for a mechanism to facilitate child return.[68] Since the decision on acceptance comes on the heels of a bureaucratic process of evaluating the acceding country, bureaucratic efficiency can speed up this process and shorten the time to an acceptance.[69] By contrast, Islam as the predominant religion in the accepting country[70] might negatively affect the acceptance of accessions. According to Sharia law, if any of the child's parents is Muslim, the child must be raised as a Muslim. But for a court in a non-Muslim country, a child born to a Muslim father and a non-Muslim mother may be entitled to be raised in the non-Muslim parent's religion.[71] This outcome would be contrary to Sharia law, leading Muslim countries to exercise greater caution in accepting accessions and committing to the return of abducted children.

To examine cooperation against child abduction under the Hague Convention, we once again employ discrete event-history modeling to estimate the probability that an event of interest—the acceptance of a newly acceding state—will occur as time elapses. Through this model—a logistic regression combined with a cubic polynomial—we seek to explain why in some dyads acceptance of the accession occurs quickly, while in others it takes longer or does not occur at all by the end point of the analysis (the year 2015).

Results

Table 9.2 presents the results of five logit models, all estimating the effects of the independent variables on the time it takes for a newly acceding state to be accepted by other convention members. Models 1 and 2 introduce, in turn, each of the key independent variables. Consistent with the theoretical expectation, Model 1 reveals a statistically significant, negative effect of the rule-of-law gap: as this gap increases, the likelihood of accepting the newly acceding state diminishes. In other words, the weaker the rule of law of the acceding country as compared to that of the accepting country, the stronger are the latter's concerns, which are manifested in a lower probability of acceptance. As Model 2 shows, a gap in women's parliamentary membership, which raises concerns regarding women's status, also reduces the likelihood of acceptance. Model 3 combines the two independent variables, and the results hold. Consistent with *E3* and *E4*, a gap in the rule of law has a negative, statistically significant effect on the probability of acceptance; so does a gap in women's parliamentary membership. The substantive effect of both variables is considerable. A one-unit increase of the rule-of-law gap—on a scale from −4.1 to 3.8—reduces the odds of acceptance by 33%. A one percentage-point increase in the gap in women's parliamentary membership lowers the odds of acceptance by 0.7%.

Overall, these statistical results provide considerable support for our theoretical expectations. They show that, far from taking acceptance lightly, accepting countries carefully scrutinize acceding countries. They wish to ensure that their treaty partners meet certain procedural and substantive standards before forging legal relations and establishing bilateral obligations.

Figures 9.3 and 9.4 plot the predicted probabilities of accession acceptance for our key indicators: gaps in the rule of law and in women's parliamentary membership. In each figure, the predicted probability is shown at different levels of the indicator, while other variables are held at their mean, based on Model 3.

Figure 9.3 shows how the gap in the rule of law affects the probability of accession acceptance. When that gap is negative, that is, when the acceding country's rule of law is stronger than that of the accepting country, the probability of accession acceptance is relatively high. The accepting country is assured that the prospective partner will handle abduction cases in a procedurally fair manner, as a strong rule of law suggests access to the legal system, relatively efficient legal proceedings, and enforcement capacity. This assurance facilitates the acceptance of the new partner: the accepting country can be reasonably

Table 9.2. **Influences on the acceptance of accessions to the Hague Convention on child abduction**

	Model 1	*Model 2*	*Model 3*	*Model 4*	*Model 5*
Rule-of-law gap	−0.386*** (0.045)		−0.394*** (0.048)		
Law-and-order gap				−0.065*** (0.025)	
Judicial-independence gap					−0.624*** (0.128)
Women's parliamentary-membership gap		−0.009*** (0.002)	−0.007*** (0.003)		
Women's political-rights gap				−0.199*** (0.061)	
Women's labor-participation gap					−0.018*** (0.004)
Acceding country's population	0.071*** (0.018)	0.054*** (0.018)	0.074*** (0.019)	0.048** (0.024)	0.052** (0.021)
Accepting country's population	0.147*** (0.016)	0.16*** (0.016)	0.152*** (0.017)	0.075*** (0.018)	0.144*** (0.017)
Acceding country's GDP per capita	−0.09** (0.038)	0.071** (0.032)	−0.138*** (0.042)	0.105*** (0.034)	0.052 (0.034)
Accepting country's GDP per capita	0.197*** (0.048)	0.177*** (0.052)	0.267*** (0.053)	0.076 (0.055)	0.153*** (0.051)
Distance	−0.178*** (0.028)	−0.166*** (0.031)	−0.167*** (0.031)	−0.143*** (0.032)	−0.142*** (0.03)
UN-voting distance	0.006 (0.036)	−0.097** (0.04)	−0.068* (0.04)	−0.015 (0.043)	−0.008 (0.039)
Shared legal tradition	0.195*** (0.058)	0.135** (0.062)	0.195*** (0.062)	0.185*** (0.066)	0.125** (0.062)
Accepting country's divorce rate	0.016** (0.007)	0.018** (0.008)	0.018** (0.008)	0.014* (0.008)	0.019** (0.008)
Migrant stock in accepting country	0.016*** (0.005)	0.005 (0.006)	0.009 (0.006)	0.014** (0.006)	0.1* (0.006)
Muslim majority in accepting country	−0.716*** (0.116)	−0.77*** (0.117)	−0.713*** (0.115)	−0.785*** (0.133)	−0.861*** (0.117)

Table 9.2. **Continued**

	Model 1	*Model 2*	*Model 3*	*Model 4*	*Model 5*
Accepting country's bureaucratic quality	0.595*** (0.076)	0.352*** (0.07)	0.651*** (0.08)	0.369*** (0.08)	0.447*** (0.074)
Number of dyads	3066	2959	2955	2125	2647
Observations	15373	14002	13968	9719	14028
Prob>chi2	0.00	0.00	0.00	0.00	0.00

Notes: Logit models; each model includes a cubic polynomial. * $p<0.1$; ** $p<0.05$; *** $p<0.01$. Robust standard errors in parentheses.

confident that the partner will indeed return abducted children. At a gap value of −2, the probability of accession acceptance is 0.19 (in the sample as a whole, only 0.092 of the observations are acceptances). This confidence in the partner, however, diminishes as the rule-of-law gap moves in the positive direction. When the acceding and accepting countries have the same level of the rule of law (gap = 0), the probability of acceptance drops to 0.097, and it continues to drop as the gap moves further in the positive direction. When the gap is positive, that is, when the acceding country's rule of law is weaker than that of the accepting country, the accepting country might doubt the prospects of child return, and this reduces the willingness for accession acceptance.

Figure 9.4 shows a similar trend for the gap in women's parliamentary membership, although the substantive impact is more modest. A negative gap—that is, a higher rate of women's political representation in the acceding country compared to the accepting country—increases the confidence that abduction cases will be treated in a substantively fair manner. As the gap moves in the positive direction—that is, as the status of women in the acceding country weakens—it raises concerns that mothers returning with children might face bias in custody proceedings. This lowers the probability of acceptance. Yet the overall impact of the variable is smaller than that of the gap in the rule of law, which means that accepting countries are more concerned about the latter.

To ensure the robustness of our results, we vary the measures of the key covariates. In Model 4 in Table 9.2, the rule of law was measured through the Law and Order indicator from the International Country Risk Guide; the indicator for women's status is the CIRI measure of women's political rights, including the right to vote, run for political office, and hold elected or appointed government positions. In Model 5, the rule-of-law measure is the judicial-independence indicator developed by Linzer and Staton; women's social and economic status was measured through the share of women in the labor force.[72] The results resemble those obtained with the original measures. The gap between the acceding and

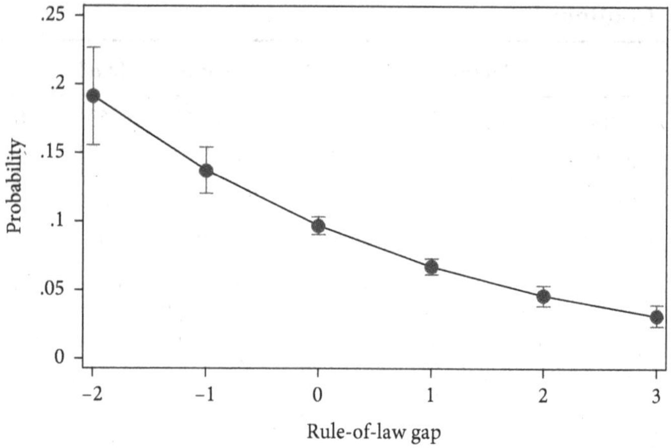

Figure 9.3 Varying gap in the rule of law: Predicted probability of accession acceptance with 95% confidence intervals.

accepting countries in law and order or judicial independence is negatively associated with the acceptance of accessions; a difference in women's political rights or labor-force participation also has a negative influence on accession acceptance.

Most of the control variables perform as expected. The size of the population in the acceding or accepting country is positively associated with the likelihood of acceptance: a larger population raises the risk of abduction and increases the need for a legal mechanism to allow for children's return. Greater geographic distance is negatively associated with acceptance, since it lowers the risk of abduction and the need for a mechanism to facilitate return. Greater distance in UN voting indicates a weaker political affinity and reduces the likelihood of accession acceptance, but in three of the five models presented it lacks statistical significance. As expected, a shared legal tradition increases the chances of acceptance. A higher divorce rate also makes acceptance more likely, as it raises the risk of abduction and the need for a mechanism to facilitate children's return. A Muslim majority, by contrast, considerably reduces the willingness to return children to foreign countries, thereby lowering the likelihood of acceptance.

In a set of robustness checks not presented here, we find that the results remain robust to the inclusion of fixed effects for year and for the first country in the dyad. The results also hold when we employ a different event-history model—a Cox proportional hazards model. Across the different measures of the key covariates and methods of estimation, the gap in the rule of law lowers the likelihood of cooperation on child abduction, as does the gap in women's status, but to a lesser extent.

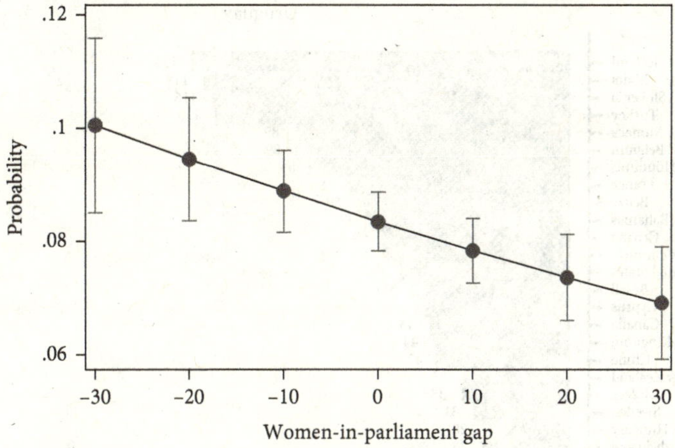

Figure 9.4 Varying gap in women's parliamentary membership: Predicted probability of accession acceptance with 95% confidence intervals.

Additional Evidence

In addition to our econometric analysis, qualitative evidence corroborates our hypothesized causal mechanism linking procedural and substantive legal standards to cooperation on child abduction. As part of the accession process, states acceding to the Hague Convention are asked to complete a standard questionnaire.[73] Importantly, several questions aim to verify the procedural fairness of new members. For example, the questionnaire asks what measures exist to ensure that applications for the return of a child will be dealt with expeditiously at first instance and on appeal; which facilities—in particular, legal aid—are available to foreign applicants to assist them in bringing their applications before the courts; and which procedures exist for the enforcement of a return order. In addition, the questionnaire reveals concerns for substantive standards in cases where the child has been returned and it falls on the local courts to decide the custody dispute: newly acceding countries are asked about their substantive legal criteria for making custody determinations and, specifically, about any differences in the legal status of mothers and fathers in custody cases. This catalogue of questions offers a first cut at the critical concerns of convention members as they assess acceding countries.

Finally, we illustrate the acceptance record of two acceding countries: Uruguay and Paraguay. We selected these two countries because they are similar in size, located in the same region, and joined the convention at approximately the same time: Paraguay in 1998 and Uruguay in 1999. The two countries, however, vary significantly on our variables of interest. In 2000, Uruguay's score on the rule of law scale was 0.53, whereas Paraguay's was −1.08. Whereas in Uruguay women

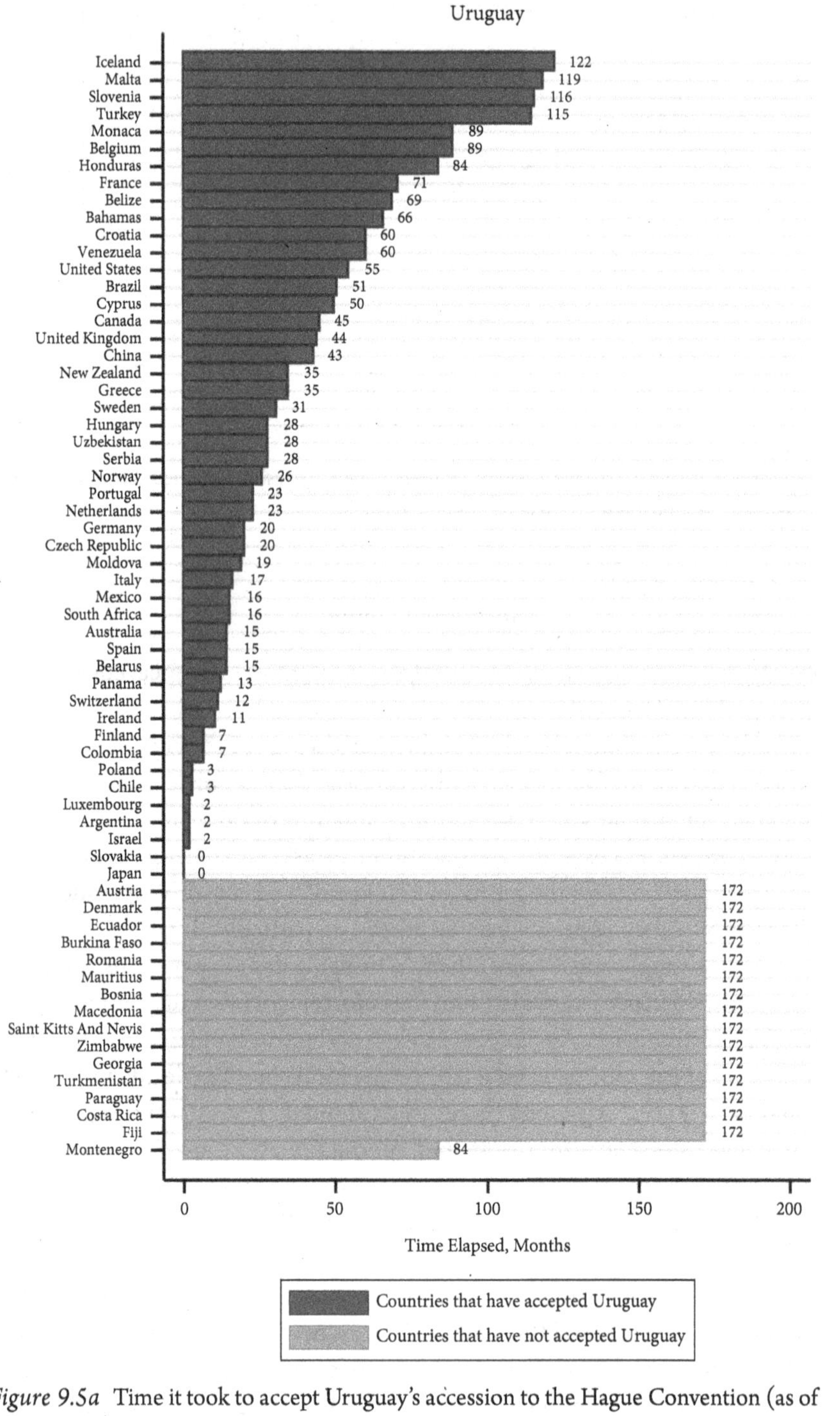

Figure 9.5a Time it took to accept Uruguay's accession to the Hague Convention (as of March 2014).

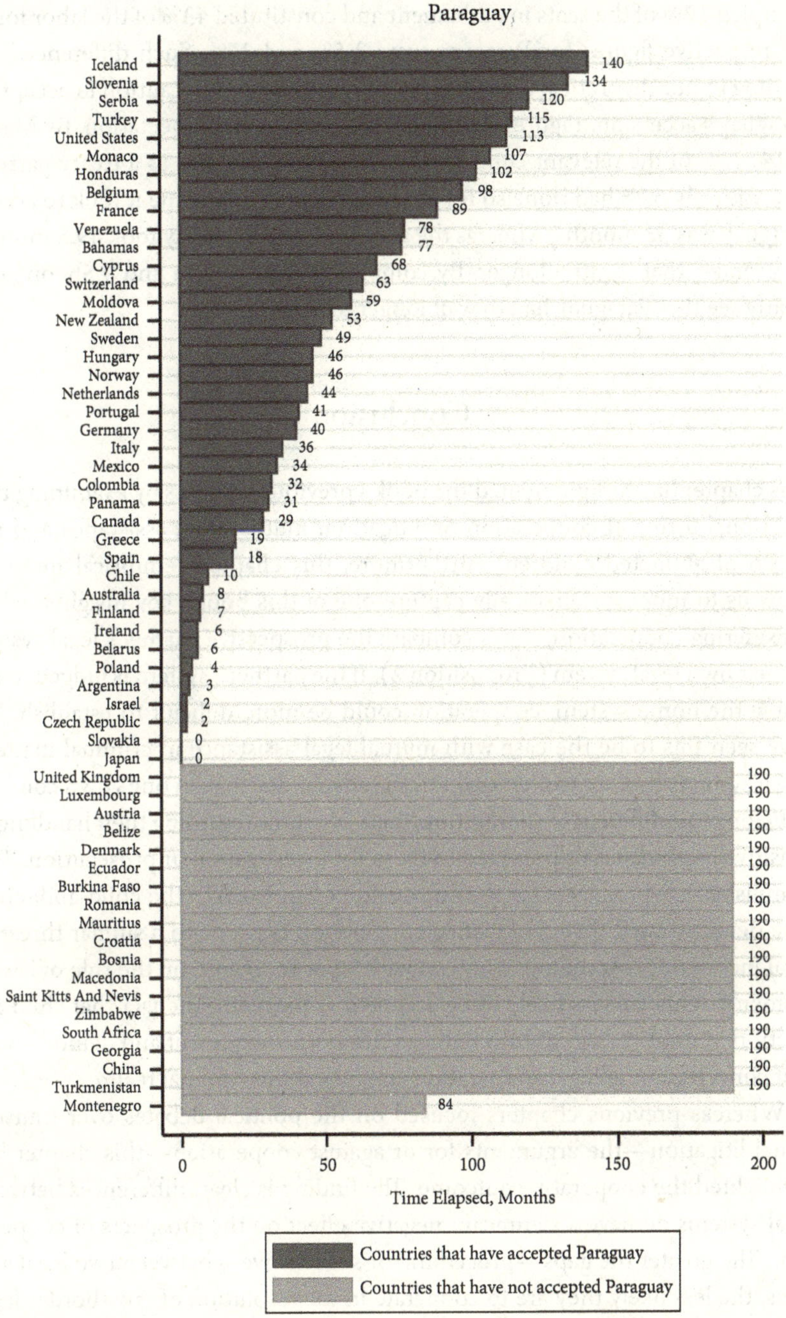

Figure 9.5b Time it took to accept Paraguay's accession to the Hague Convention (as of March 2014).

occupied 12% of the seats in parliament and constituted 43% of the labor force, the respective figures for Paraguay were 2.5% and 37%. Such differences, according to our theoretical argument, should lead to greater caution in accepting Paraguay's accession. Figures 9.5a and 9.5b confirm this expectation. By March 2014, 75% of the relevant countries had accepted Uruguay as a treaty partner, whereas only 67% had done so for Paraguay. The average time it took to accept Uruguay was 38 months, whereas the acceptance of Paraguay took 49.5 months on average, that is, 30% longer. By comparing Figures 9.5a and 9.5b, one can clearly see that Paraguay had to wait longer to be accepted.

Conclusion

This chapter has complemented the book's previous chapters by examining two additional forms of cooperation on litigation: mutual legal assistance and the return of abducted children. Furthermore, this chapter's empirical methods allow us to more systematically capture one of this book's key insights: when considering cooperation, states compare the prospective partner's legal system to their own legal system (Proposition 2). If the partner's system is judged to fall below the home system, cooperation could be more difficult to establish. We have seen this to be the case with mutual legal assistance in criminal matters. Legal systems that are weaker on judicial independence than one's own country, or belong to a different legal tradition, raise concerns regarding their handling of sensitive legal materials provided to them for investigation or prosecution. This diminishes the prospects for the conclusion of an MLAT. The child-abduction case demonstrated that civil-justice cooperation is prone to a similar threat of legal incongruity. Acceding countries with a poorer record on the rule of law or women's rights are less likely to be accepted as partners. The fact that child abduction presents a *civil* case strengthens this book's argument and demonstrates that concerns about legal cooperation go beyond the criminal realm.

Whereas previous chapters focused on the political debates over transnational litigation—the arguments for or against cooperation—this chapter has highlighted the cooperative outcome. The finding is clear: differences between legal systems do have a significant negative effect on the prospects of cooperation. The greater the gaps—procedural or substantive—between two legal systems, the less likely they are to cooperate in the resolution of crossborder legal problems. Indeed, in some cases governments manage to establish cooperation despite such gaps—the NATO SOFA is a case in point, as Chapter 3 has shown. Overall, however, the likelihood of cooperation diminishes when a prospective partner is seen as failing to meet one's standards. Legal ethnocentrism, it turns out, has real-world consequences.

Appendix A Countries included in the MLAT dataset

Algeria
Argentina
Australia
Austria
Azerbaijan
Belarus
Belgium
Belize
Brazil
Britain
Canada
Chile
China
Colombia
Croatia
Cyprus
Czech Republic
Ecuador
Egypt
Estonia
Finland
France
Georgia
Germany
Hungary
Iceland
India
Indonesia
Iraq
Ireland
Israel
Italy
Japan
Jordan
Kazakhstan
Kosovo
Latvia
Lebanon

Liechtenstein
Lithuania
Malaysia
Mexico
Moldova
Monaco
Mongolia
Morocco
Netherlands
New Zealand
Norway
Panama
Peru
Philippines
Poland
Portugal
Russia
Slovakia
Slovenia
South Africa
South Korea
Spain
Sweden
Switzerland
Thailand
Turkey
Ukraine
United States
Uruguay
Uzbekistan
Vietnam
Yemen

Notes

1. Convention on the Civil Aspects of International Child Abduction, Article 3.
2. Nadelmann 1993; Raustiala 2002; Lyman 2006.
3. Ellis and Pisani 1985, 198; Zagaris and Resnick 1997.
4. Nadelmann 1993, 331–332; Andreas and Nadelmann 2006, 141–145.
5. Bantekas and Nash 2009, 359. See Article 7 of the UN Convention against Illicit Traffic in Narcotic Drugs and Psychotropic Substances.

6. U.S. Senate 2002, 19.
7. Department of Justice 2015, 21.
8. https://ec.europa.eu/info/law/cross-border-cases/judicial-cooperation/types-judicial-cooperation/mutual-legal-assistance-and-extradition_en.
9. Nadelmann 1993, 329, 350; Yang and Maxwell 2011; D'hulster 2012.
10. U.S. Senate 1994.
11. U.S. Senate 1989.
12. Reuters 1994.
13. Otis 1993.
14. Nadelmann 1993, 351–352.
15. Ríos-Figueroa and Staton 2014; Linzer and Staton 2015.
16. Rose-Ackerman 2007.
17. Leeds 1999.
18. Mitchell and Powell 2011, 75.
19. In general, we deferred to government sources and responses in the case of any discrepancies. We then used a number of exclusion criteria. We did not include extradition treaties unless they covered both extradition and mutual legal assistance. Similarly, we did not code assistance agreements that do not focus on *legal* assistance, such as agreements on administrative assistance. Finally, we excluded nonbinding "memoranda of understanding" or "frameworks" related to mutual legal assistance. If a dyad signed multiple treaties, we coded the first instance of the relationship.
20. Linzer and Staton 2015.
21. Cingranelli, Richards, and Clay 2014.
22. Helmke and Rosenbluth 2009.
23. For the Linzer-Staton measure, we multiply the gap variable by ten to allow for easier interpretation.
24. Mitchell and Powell 2007.
25. Source: Polity IV.
26. Chang et al. 2018.
27. Source: World Bank's World Development Indicators. This variable is logged.
28. Barak 2000. Source: World Bank's World Development Indicators. This variable is logged.
29. Source: CEPII GeoDist database. This variable is logged.
30. See Storrs 2003.
31. Source: State Department's International Narcotics Control Strategy Reports and the Federal Register.
32. This variable equals 1 if dyad members have a common official language. Source: CEPII GeoDist database.
33. Bailey, Strezhnev, and Voeten 2017.
34. This variable equals 1 if dyad members are parties to a regional MLAT. Examples of regional MLATs include the European Convention on Mutual Legal Assistance in Criminal Matters and the ASEAN Treaty on Mutual Legal Assistance in Criminal Matters.
35. Simmons 2009; Bernauer et al. 2010.
36. This variable is calculated as the number of MLATs in a country's region divided by the number of countries in the region, lagged one year. Classification of countries by region is based on the State Department's categorization.
37. Haftel and Thompson 2013.
38. Carter and Signorino 2010.
39. Freeman 1998; Greif 2009; Attwood 2016, 792.
40. Greif and Hegar 1991; Spilman 2006.
41. Lowe and Stephens 2017, 3, 9.
42. Schuz 2013, 1.
43. Lowe and Stephens 2017, 9–10.
44. Lowe and Stephens 2017, 7.
45. Duncan 2000, 112; Silberman 2000.
46. Lowe and Stephens 2017, 9. About 30% of abduction cases involve more than one child. Lowe and Stephens 2017, 9.

47. Lowe and Stephens 2017, Annex 1.
48. Pérez-Vera 1981.
49. Hague Convention, Article 12.
50. Lowe and Stephens 2017, 11. Author's calculations, excluding withdrawn or pending cases.
51. Lowe and Stephens 2017, 12.
52. U.S. Department of State 2019, 4.
53. Hague Convention, Article 11.
54. Hague Convention, Articles 12–13.
55. Hague Convention, Articles 16 and 19.
56. Raday 2019.
57. Lindhorst and Edelson 2012; Yamaguchi and Lindhorst 2016.
58. Hague Convention, Articles 12, 13.
59. Hague Convention, Article 20.
60. Pérez-Vera 1981.
61. Hague Convention, Article 38. See Bruch 2000.
62. See Wängnerud 2009. Source: Inter-Parliamentary Union.
63. Source: World Bank's World Development Indicators.
64. Source: CEPII GeoDist database.
65. Source Bailey, Strezhnev, and Voeten 2017.
66. Source: La Porta, Lopez-de-Silanes, and Shleifer 2008.
67. Source: United Nations Population Division.
68. Source: World Bank World Development Indicators.
69. Regulatory Quality indicator, World Bank's Worldwide Governance Indicators.
70. Maoz and Henderson 2013.
71. Schnitzer-Reese 2004.
72. Source: World Bank's World Development Indicators.
73. The questionnaire is administered by the Hague Conference on Private International Law. http://www.hcch.net/index_en.php?act=publications.details&pid=938.

10

Conclusions and Implications

The closing pages of this book provide an opportunity to take stock of what this study has accomplished and to draw some lessons and implications.

This book has offered a unified framework for analyzing a set of transnational legal issues that are usually treated separately: from extradition through jurisdictional overlap to enforcement of foreign judgments; from tackling child abduction to mutual legal assistance. Few analysts have linked these issues which, on the surface, seem very different from each other—especially as they include both criminal and civil matters. Yet the various chapters of this book reveal the common thread connecting them: a shared political logic stemming from the human disposition of ethnocentrism. By exploring this political logic, and by analyzing the domestic political controversy surrounding transnational litigation, this book enriches the existing literature, which tends to focus on courts and their decisions in transnational cases. Much of the action in transnational litigation, this book has shown, occurs in the *political* arena. There, transnational legal issues are far from arcane, technical topics of interest to few—they raise tensions and stir heated debates involving a host of domestic actors: the government, members of parliament, the bureaucracy, the legal community, the media, NGOs, and the public.

The theoretical framework offered an outline of these debates, and the qualitative chapters largely confirmed this outline. The various debates examined here reflected concerns about legal incongruity: an incompatibility between the home and foreign legal standards or procedures. In two cases—the debates over the NATO SOFA and Britain's extradition policy—opponents of cooperation took issue with the very idea of delegating legal authority to foreign courts: they believed, respectively, that U.S. troops deserved American justice and that British citizens should receive British justice. The ethnocentric tendency to regard "the other" as inferior and threatening to oneself has certainly come through throughout the book: from the disparagement of European courts by critics of the NATO SOFA through the denunciation of China's legal system by Australians and Canadians to the labeling of British libel law as a danger to

Intolerant Justice. Asif Efrat, Oxford University Press. © Oxford University Press 2023.
DOI: 10.1093/oso/9780197658895.003.0010

Americans. Not everyone, however, subscribed to the view of foreign legal systems as a threat. Justice bureaucracies and ministries of foreign affairs and defense, seeking to reap the fruits of legal cooperation, were happy to downplay legal differences and highlight safeguards and assurances that would presumably guarantee fair treatment. But other actors resisted: the local legal community, in the Australian case, stood up to defend cherished human rights norms; the British NGOs protested the unfair treatment that, in their view, awaited those extradited to the United States or EU countries; and the media, in several of the cases, further fueled concerns about foreign justice.

There was no clear pattern as regards parliamentary criticism of cooperation on litigation: sometimes it came from the right (China case—Canada; UK extradition), sometimes from the left (foreign fighters; China case—Australia), and in some cases (NATO SOFA; SPEECH Act) it came from across the political spectrum. In the cases concerning extradition to China, it was the opposition that attacked the government for its willingness to extend cooperation; in the NATO SOFA case, the prominent Congressional critics came from the same party as the president; and the Conservative opponents of Britain's extradition policy began to air their criticism under a Labor government but persisted after their own party came to power.

While this book has emphasized concerns for a country's own citizens, who might suffer unfairness or abuse from foreign courts, the case of extradition to China demonstrates that these concerns may extend to noncitizens as well. This, in turn, leads to an important observation: legal ethnocentrism is not a simple interest-based desire to protect local citizens. Rather, it reflects a deep-seated attachment to local values and legal principles that the ethnocentric views as "the best" or "the right ones," which leads to the rejection of alternative values and principles held by foreign countries. The European concerns about American civil judgments and the American defense of the First Amendment against the threat of British libel law convey a similar impression: resistance to cooperation on litigation is not fueled only by the interests of litigants, but by pride in one's laws and legal institutions and a commitment to keeping them intact. The case of the foreign fighters, however, demonstrated the limits of that commitment. Concerns over due process and human rights were thrown out the window given the heinous nature of the crimes that ISIS members committed and the perceived security risk that they might pose upon their return.

The Cooperative Outcome

The qualitative chapters in this book centered on the political debates surrounding transnational litigation, rather than the outcome: the establishment or failure of cooperation. To understand the cooperative outcome and its variation across cases, we have to consider two additional factors: whether the government believed that the benefits of the cooperative endeavor were significant enough to pursue cooperation in the face of the ethnocentric resistance; and whether the government possessed the leverage to convince or pressure critics and assemble the necessary support for cooperation. In this concluding chapter, we can integrate these elements to account for the various cooperative outcomes.

Both judgment-enforcement chapters exhibited noncooperation: difficulties in the enforcement of American judgments in Europe and an American prohibition on the enforcement of foreign libel judgments inconsistent with the First Amendment. Both outcomes resulted from the limited benefits of cooperation, which provided little incentive to try to overcome the ethnocentric resistance. Since American courts regularly enforce judgments from Europe, European countries had no reason to renounce their skepticism of U.S. judgments and facilitate their enforcement. And the enforcement of problematic libel judgments in the United States served no vital American interest, resulting in the muted response of the Departments of Justice and State to the SPEECH Act.

In the jurisdiction and extradition cases, governments had greater interest in cooperation and a stronger motivation to try to overcome the ethnocentric resistance: the subjection of U.S. troops to foreign jurisdiction was necessary for the success of NATO and therefore for U.S. national security as well; relinquishing jurisdiction over the foreign fighters offered the "benefit" of relieving the UK of the need to repatriate and try them; for Australia, an extradition treaty offered the prospects of enhancing its relations with China; and to receive foreign assistance in its efforts against crime, the UK government had an interest in defending and preserving existing extradition arrangements.

In three of these four cases, governments possessed the political resources and leverage to overcome the objections to cooperation. The Defense, State, and Justice Departments made strong efforts to allay critics' concerns and win support for the NATO SOFA; President Eisenhower himself put pressure on senators who still hesitated through a last-minute threatening message: failure to ratify could seriously affect the security of the United States.[1] Strong public resistance to the repatriation of the foreign fighters strengthened the government's refusal to try them in the UK. And the fact that the UK extradition debate revolved around the revision of existing arrangements rather than the establishment of new ones made it easier for the government to preserve the status quo. On extradition to China, however, the Australian government failed to achieve the desired cooperative outcome as it lacked the ability to overcome parliamentary resistance and obtain the necessary support for the extradition treaty.

In summary, the qualitative chapters of this book have shown that ethnocentrism makes cooperation harder, but not impossible. A government convinced of the benefits of cooperation and possessing the necessary political leverage may be able to overcome the ethnocentric concerns and cooperate on litigation. In other cases, ethnocentrism may prevail and obstruct cooperation.

This book's quantitative chapter focused directly on the cooperative outcome and showed that ethnocentric sentiments might indeed translate into less cooperation: the larger the dyadic gap in legal norms or institutions, the less likely are two legal systems to cooperate. This empirical result is consistent with previous studies that showed how legal-system similarity facilitates cooperation.[2] Those studies, however, looked at broad characteristics of the legal system: the quality of the rule of law or the legal tradition to which the system belongs. This book, by contrast, shows that cooperation may depend on more fine-grained legal norms, procedures, and institutions: from respect for free speech through women's equality to rules of personal jurisdiction. The analysis here also goes beyond existing studies in developing the theoretical rationale underlying the tendency of similar legal systems to cooperate, and it suggests caution in identifying similar systems. To the researcher, significant similarities exist between the American and British legal systems; as Chapters 6 and 8 have shown, however, Americans and Britons would beg to differ. While Americans take pride in the stronger protection they provide for free speech, Britons believe they have higher criminal-justice standards than in the United States. The evaluation of legal similarities and differences, in other words, is in the eyes of the beholder.

We now turn to assessing the broader implications of this study under four headings. First, while this book is not about international law per se, it does offer some valuable insights for the International Law/International Relations literature. Second, while this book did not look at courts directly, we can use the concept of ethnocentrism to draw some observations on the crossborder dialogue between courts. Third, we tease out implications for debates on the changing practice of extradition. Fourth, we offer some insights for policy: How can one encourage cooperation among legal systems in the face of ethnocentric sentiments?

Implications for the Study of Law and International Relations

This book joins a large body of literature that examines the role of law and the courts in international affairs. Having emerged in the 1990s, the research program on International Law and International Relations—known as IL/IR—is extensive and diverse, but several of its common themes can be easily discerned. This literature overwhelmingly examines the establishment and design of international norms and treaties; states' commitment to and compliance with treaties;

and international courts.[3] As Christopher Whytock observes, IL/IR scholarship tends to focus on a single type of law—international law (especially public international law)—and a single type of court: international courts.[4] Indeed, IL/IR scholars recognize that international courts are not the only adjudicatory organs that matter in international politics. In particular, they acknowledge that national courts may decide cases alleging violations of international law or affecting transnational relations.[5] Yet the IL/IR scholarship has overwhelmingly focused on international courts and tribunals. From courts with a global reach, such as the World Trade Organization's (WTO) dispute settlement body and the International Criminal Court, to regional courts in Europe, Africa, and Latin America, this literature is dominated by studies of the origins, dynamics, and effects of international courts as the bodies in charge of enforcing international law.[6] National courts, by contrast, remain "an often overlooked category of adjudicators."[7] To the extent that national courts are studied, the focus is typically on their engagement with international law and their role in bringing governments to comply with international legal obligations.[8] Scholars have also looked at other interactions between the domestic legal order and the international legal system. For example, they have examined how domestic legal rules regarding treaty approval influence treaty ratification and how domestic legal traditions affect the design of international courts.[9]

Overall, scholarship on international law and international courts exhibits two key characteristics. First, it highlights vertical interactions between domestic legal systems and the international legal system. Second, the international legal system is of primary interest in this body of literature. Domestic law and domestic courts are studied not because of their intrinsic interest, but because they serve as foundations for international law and international courts.[10]

This book belongs in an emerging scholarship that puts *domestic law and domestic courts* at the center and studies their role in international affairs, independent of their relation with or impact on the international legal system.[11] As Whytock notes, domestic courts play a key function in global governance by allocating governance authority among states: they decide which country's courts will hear and decide a dispute, which country's laws will govern the transnational activity giving rise to the dispute, and which country will exercise its enforcement powers. Domestic courts also help determine the rights and obligations of transnational actors, thereby participating in the substantive regulation of transnational activity and shaping the allocation of economic and political resources.[12] The international involvement of domestic courts and domestic legal systems thus deserves to be studied in its own right.

This study contributes to our understanding of the role of domestic law and courts in world politics, and it does so with two twists. First, this book goes further than existing studies in emphasizing the interactions between domestic legal systems. The external behavior of a legal system and its willingness to cooperate depend, to a large extent, on the identity of the partner: the analysis of transnational litigation thus requires us to focus on *horizontal interactions* between domestic legal systems. This stands in contrast to the focus of the IL/IR literature on the vertical interaction between the international legal system and domestic legal systems. Second, while the dynamics analyzed in this study relate to courts, courts are not directly examined here. Judicial behavior or decisions were clearly not the phenomenon of interest across the different chapters of this book. Rather, it is the *perception and evaluation* of domestic courts and legal systems that occupied center stage. From American concerns about the courts of NATO members through the Australian view of unfairness and abuse in the Chinese legal system to European misgivings about civil justice in U.S. courts—contention over transnational litigation is fueled by how domestic courts are perceived—accurately or not—by external actors.

This book goes beyond the IL/IR literature not only in its focus on horizontal—rather than vertical—interactions between legal systems, but also in expanding the substantive issue–areas of these interactions. IL/IR scholars have focused on four primary areas: human rights, international economic law, the law relating to armed conflict, and environmental agreements.[13] This book, however, examines a set of legal-cooperation arrangements that have received little attention in IL/IR scholarship: agreements on status of forces and mutual legal assistance, extradition treaties, a judgment-enforcement convention, and the child-abduction convention. To date, these agreements have primarily been examined from a legal perspective.[14] This book has focused on the *political* contention surrounding them.

Comparative International Law

The emerging field of comparative international law seeks to identify, analyze, and explain similarities and differences in how actors in different legal systems understand, interpret, apply, and approach international law.[15] For example, a comparative analysis of international law may explain why common treaty provisions are interpreted in similar or different ways by different national courts;[16] why the executive branches in different countries put forth different interpretations of international law;[17] and why legislatures may vary in how they domesticate international legal obligations.[18]

While this book does not focus on international law per se, it does examine legal-system interaction in the framework of several bilateral or multilateral treaties, such as extradition treaties and the NATO SOFA. The analysis of these instruments here offers an important insight for international law comparativism: how states approach international legal commitments may be influenced by the *identity of the partners* toward which one applies these commitments.

The consideration of the partners' identity is often absent from comparative analyses of international law. To explain similarities and differences in how actors approach, interpret, and apply international law, analysts often look at the characteristics of states—especially state power, as great powers often have their own distinct interpretations of international law, which they may seek to advance or impose worldwide.[19] Another set of explanations focuses on domestic institutions—including courts, legislatures, executives, and regulatory agencies—and how their incentives and constraints shape the interpretation and application of international law.[20] Yet another group of explanations highlights transnational actors or processes that diffuse norms or attitudes toward international law.[21] Looking at this variety of influences, one can develop explanations for differences in national approaches to international agreements, rules, and doctrines. This, however, overlooks the fact that a country's attitude toward international norms may not be uniform. Rather, it will vary with the identity of the partner to which the norms apply, as the different chapters of this book have shown.

We have seen that U.S. policymakers felt relatively comfortable about applying the NATO SOFA to the UK, which shares significant legal similarities with the United States; by contrast, they felt apprehensive about the legal systems of civil-law countries and even more so about non-Western legal systems, such as those of the Middle East. We have seen that the UK's attitude to its extradition treaty with the United States was shaped by a lack of trust in the U.S. criminal justice system. And we have also learned that states' willingness to apply the norm of returning abducted children critically depends on the country to which the child is to be returned. This suggests a different possible interpretation of comparative international law: one focused not on the crosscountry variation in approaches to international law, but on the variation in a country's interpretation and application of international legal rules vis-à-vis different partners. Adding this dimension of comparison can enrich and add nuance to international law comparativism.

Explaining Resistance to International Law

This book offers theoretical insights that may be used for constructing a novel account of actors' resistance to international law. Most IL/IR studies offer *rationalist* explanations for states' negative behavior toward international law, that is, states' unwillingness to join international agreements, noncompliance with international agreements, or decision to exit agreements altogether. Key to those explanations are the sovereignty costs or implementation costs that international agreements entail. By entering an agreement, a government restricts its sovereignty: It surrenders control over national policies in order to adhere to the standards set by the agreement. It may also bear the costs of implementing policy changes or complying with the decisions of the international institutions overseeing the agreements.[22] Another set of explanations for the resistance to international law highlights the incompatibility between national values and the values embodied in international agreements.[23]

While the rationalist and value-based accounts no doubt carry significant explanatory power, they are ultimately unsatisfying, since they cannot account for the diversity of domestic views on international agreements. The sovereignty and implementation costs that international agreements entail are not fixed and objective: they are open to interpretation and subjective evaluation. Where one actor sees heavy restrictions on sovereignty or onerous implementation costs, another may see little reason for concern. The same applies to values. Where one believes that an international agreement diverges sharply from national values, another may identify compatibility between national and international values. Existing studies of international law, however, give us little insight into this domestic variation of views. Sovereignty and implementation costs are typically treated as country-level variables, leaving little room for the variation in the interpretation of the costs by domestic actors. Similarly, the value gap separating the country and the international agreement is typically treated as fixed in size and measured at the country level, making it difficult to explain why actors may disagree on the size and significance of that gap. As Lisa Baldez argues, "[n]ational-level variables average away the real action."[24]

Ethnocentrism offers a prism through which to get at the "real action," that is, explain why domestic actors may hold conflicting interpretations of the sovereignty/implementation costs of international agreements or of the national-international value distance. In particular, ethnocentrism can account for why some actors hold exaggerated interpretations of the costs of agreements or why they inflate the distance between national values and those embodied in international agreements. Indeed, ethnocentric actors tend to consider international law as a threat: international agreements were established by out-group actors and are enforced by out-group institutions and, as such, they may be seen as imperiling the in-group's sovereignty, interests, and values. The ethnocentric mindset, in other words, could result in an exaggerated assessment of the costs of international agreements and in a tendency to overstate the gap between the country's values and those enshrined in international agreements. Furthermore, the ethnocentric will view the values and practices of the in-group as superior to those of the international community and therefore will be skeptical of the benefit that international agreements—which reflect internationally accepted values and practices—may bring to their country. Such attitudes, of course, produce resistance toward international agreements and institutions as unnecessary at best and detrimental at worst. The result is a preference against joining agreements and institutions or against complying with them. By contrast, actors less prone to ethnocentrism will hold a more realistic assessment of the costs of international agreements or the national-international value distance. Compared to the ethnocentric, they typically hold a more favorable view of international agreements and are less likely to reject them as onerous or incompatible with national values.

Ethnocentrism can thus give us insight into why international agreements and institutions are so contentious. For example, we may explain the backlash against international courts as a result, at least in part, of ethnocentric sentiments. Since the late 1990s, international courts and tribunals—from the Inter-American Court of Human Rights through the WTO's dispute settlement mechanism to the International Criminal Court—have increasingly come under attack. States have tried to curb these courts' authority or have pulled out from their jurisdiction.[25] Erik Voeten identifies populism as an engine of such resistance to international courts. Populists are suspicious of or hostile toward courts in general, including domestic courts, as they consider them an illegitimate constraint on the will of the majority. An international court, staffed with foreign judges, will be even less legitimate in their eyes, since it does not represent the will of the people.[26] Ethnocentrism offers another promising perspective for understanding the backlash against international courts. The ethnocentric views their country as superior and rejects the authority of international institutions to pass judgment on the country's behavior or on the conduct of domestic actors.[27] For an ethnocentric, international courts belong to the out-group and, as such, pose a threat to their country. Unlike populism, ethnocentrism does not see the courts as such as a threat. An ethnocentric will believe that domestic actors, or the state itself, should be held accountable by the country's civilian or military courts. It is the exercise of *international* legal authority that seems threatening and offends the ethnocentric's sense of national superiority.

Ethnocentrism and the Transnational Dialogue among Courts

Domestic courts worldwide—typically, supreme or constitutional courts—often cite comparative or international legal materials in their decisions. Many explanations have been proposed for this phenomenon, which is known as judicial comparativism or judicial dialogue. Judges may resort to foreign law to enrich their legal knowledge and the quality of their decisions or, more cynically, to justify their ideologically desired result that lacks support in domestic law. They may also turn to foreign law when domestic jurisprudence is sparse (e.g., when the court is relatively new, or following a regime change that requires a reexamination of domestic jurisprudence) or when domestic law or jurisprudence do exist, but the court wishes to avoid or circumvent them. The use of foreign law from highly regarded courts and countries may also be a means for a court to raise its status, consolidate its legal authority, and facilitate the acceptance of its decisions among domestic audiences.[28]

Such interpretations go some way toward explaining variation among courts in the use of foreign law. For example, where popular reaction to the use of foreign law is favorable, courts may be more inclined to engage in comparativism.[29] Yet these explanations do not adequately account for the variation in the use of foreign law among judges on the same court. Furthermore, these court-focused explanations do not reveal why the practice of judicial comparativism may be domestically contentious and why it might attract fierce criticism from actors outside the judicial arena.

The debate over judicial dialogue in the United States demonstrates both the intra-court variation and the political contestation outside the court. Chapter 2 has already addressed the opposing views of U.S. Supreme Court Justices Scalia and Breyer—the former sharply opposing the use of foreign law and the latter embracing it. Other justices have also expressed their views on this issue. Joining Breyer in support of judicial dialogue, Justice Sonia Sotomayor suggested that "international law and foreign law will be very important in the discussion of how to think about the unsettled issues in our legal system," and Justice Ruth Bader Ginsburg argued that "The U.S. judicial system will be the poorer . . . if we do not both share our experience with, and learn from, legal systems with values and a commitment to democracy similar to our own." Joining Scalia, Chief Justice John Roberts has objected to the referencing of international law by U.S. courts; Justice Samuel Alito did not "think it's appropriate to look to foreign law;" and Justice Clarence Thomas argued that the Supreme Court "should not impose foreign mood, fads, or fashions on Americans."[30] As discussed in Chapter 2, the political backlash against the use of foreign law was demonstrated in the 2000s through the repeated introduction of Congressional bills aimed at banning the use of foreign law by American courts.[31] In the early 2010s, more than 30 U.S. states proposed or enacted measures against the judicial use of foreign law—triggered by concerns about the possible application of Sharia law by state courts.[32]

Martha Minow explains the resistance to judicial dialogue as "a basic concern about identity and autonomy—that we risk being taken over and losing what we are by engaging with others." Alternatively, she suggests, such resistance may reflect a belief in American exceptionalism.[33] This book offers an explanation that applies beyond the American context: an account that ties resistance to foreign law to the individual trait of ethnocentrism. Throughout this book, ethnocentric sentiments have been shown to inspire a hostile attitude toward foreign law and foreign legal institutions. Such views might hinder cooperation on the allocation of jurisdiction, extradition, and the enforcement of foreign judgments, and they may also fuel resistance to the citing of foreign legal materials in judicial rulings. From an ethnocentric point of view, foreign courts are alien and untrustworthy, and their decisions represent foreign values, circumstances, and logic—different from those of local law. Therefore, home-country courts should not base their decisions on foreign rulings. This kind of ethnocentric sentiment may find support among policymakers, publics, and judges themselves, creating a broad front against judicial comparativism, as one can see in the United States. At the same time, ethnocentric sentiments vary in their intensity: individuals may be more strongly biased against out-groups, or less so. Ethnocentrism may therefore be useful for explaining people's varying attitudes to the citation of foreign law.

Implications for the Understanding of Extradition

Extradition serves as a key mechanism of international law-enforcement cooperation. As this book has shown, the use of this tool may cause significant controversy and spark a heated domestic debate. The existing literature, however, tells us little about the domestic politics of extradition. One reason is that IR scholars have long overlooked extradition. Extradition has traditionally been studied by legal scholars, whose analysis focuses on the law of extradition rather than its politics.[34] A second, more substantive reason is that domestic politics has been seen as almost irrelevant to extradition. The surrender of criminal suspects has typically been studied as a state-to-state matter with little input from domestic publics or interest groups.[35]

Section III of this book has shown that extradition is far from an arcane, technical issue that can be analyzed in terms of unitary state interests. Indeed, it may trigger an intense domestic debate that can scuttle cooperation (Australia and Canada vis-à-vis China) or prompt a country to rethink its approach to extradition (Britain). The public, the media, NGOs, and the government's political opponents may all take issue with the commitment to sending individuals to stand criminal trial abroad. By sketching this domestic controversy, this book "normalizes" extradition into yet another matter of international cooperation shaped by domestic actors and interests. We are long accustomed to identifying the domestic considerations that motivate or constrain governments in the areas of trade or environmental cooperation;[36] extradition, it turns out, is not much different. Governments are not entirely free to engage in extradition on the basis of foreign-policy considerations; they may have to face a host of domestic actors who express serious concerns.

Chapters 5 and 6 shed light on these concerns, key among which is the threat to the human rights of the extradited person. As Chapter 5 has documented, extradition has traditionally reflected states' shared interest in fighting crime and maintaining friendly international relations, with little regard for the rights of the individual. Yet in recent decades, legal scholars argue, the pendulum has shifted toward greater protection of the individual, as manifested in the incorporation of human rights safeguards in extradition treaties and legislation and in court decisions that weigh the impact of extradition on human rights. All this, it is optimistically argued, demonstrates that human rights have come to play a significant role in matters of extradition.[37] IR scholars, by contrast, may be more skeptical in their assessment and will consider the possibility of cheap talk: while states seemingly pay greater attention to human rights in extradition as a matter of official policy, they may continue to sidestep human rights in practice.[38] Indeed, although states establish mechanisms to refuse extradition on human rights grounds, they may set a high threshold for refusal, rendering these mechanisms ineffective. In other words, states' actual conduct may still be prioritizing cooperation against crime and friendly international relations over human rights.

So how robust really is the commitment to protecting human rights in extradition? In a way, the two case-studies of extradition to China in Chapter 5 provide evidence in favor of both views: the optimistic and the skeptical. On the skeptical side, these cases show that governments still regard extradition as a tool of law enforcement that may serve to enhance relations with foreign countries; they have not fully internalized the role of human rights in extradition. Governments may be committed, as a matter of policy, to protecting the human rights of extradited persons, yet this commitment is malleable and flexible. Given the right incentives, such as the promise of better relations with a major power or trade access, governments may be willing to accept extradition partners with lower standards of justice and weaker human rights protections. A set of arguments may serve to justify such willingness: extradition partners need not have the same standards as one's own; it is better to engage with a country that violates human rights and push it to improve; assurances that the partner provides should be trusted. As we have seen, critics are quick to point out the weaknesses of such arguments, but governments may still employ them to rationalize extradition relations with human rights violators.

Our skepticism may grow even stronger when one remembers that China's pursuit of extradition treaties should have been an *easy case* for demonstrating the impact of human rights on extradition. Australia and Canada are established liberal democracies that take pride in their commitment to human rights; and the human rights abuses in China's justice system are well known and documented. Against this background, one might have expected Australia and Canada to instantly refuse an extradition treaty with China. The fact that both countries considered entering such a treaty indicates how tenuous is the status of human rights in criminal-justice cooperation.

On the more optimistic side, the Australian and Canadian cases demonstrate that while governments may have little regard for human rights in extradition, other domestic actors do expect extradition to comply with human rights norms. In both countries, the government's intention to enter into an agreement inconsistent with human rights drew fierce criticism from human rights groups, opposition politicians, lawyers, and the media. This means that extradition without due regard for human rights may be unpopular domestically, and this could give human rights their impact—so much so that a government may have to abandon its plan for an extradition treaty. The fact that, as of this writing, Australia and Canada do not have extradition treaties in force with China shows that, indeed, extradition is not immune to the impact of human rights law.[39]

However, the British experience demonstrates that concerns about extradition go beyond human rights. As Chapter 6 has shown, domestic publics, the media, and NGOs may harbor serious misgivings about the very idea of surrendering fellow citizens to be tried and punished by a foreign legal system. The support for a forum bar that would allow the refusal of extradition for an offense that took place in Britain; the pushback against the swift surrender that the European Arrest Warrant facilitates with limited grounds for refusal; and the slogan "British Justice for British People"—all these suggest deep suspicion of extradition. Rather than an important mechanism to support the rule of law, extradition has come to be seen by many in Britain as a threat; foreign courts are no longer legitimate partners in the joint fight against crossborder crime, but institutions that cannot be trusted to treat British citizens fairly. What's more, the decline of public trust in extradition is at cross-purposes to governments' push to enhance the speed and efficiency of extradition. Indeed, while in recent decades extradition law has given greater weight to human rights, some governments have been inching in the opposite direction, toward facilitating extradition and lowering protections and safeguards in the hope of better tackling the challenge of transnational crime. The simplification of extradition is manifested in the changing characterization of the process from criminal to quasi-criminal or even administrative. It is also expressed in the relaxation of the substantive and procedural conditions for extradition: the erosion of the conditions of extraditability, double criminality and specialty, and the elimination of the need for evidence.[40]

The fast-track procedure for surrender under the EAW epitomizes the trend toward easier, faster extradition.

The British case, however, shows that domestic actors may strongly object to governments' goal of facilitating extradition. Rather than support the easing of extradition, many Britons want more protections and safeguards, which would make extradition harder to execute. At this point, given the dearth of empirical work on the politics of extradition, we cannot know whether audiences in other countries harbor a similar mistrust of this mechanism, but there are good reasons to believe that they do. If such discontent has arisen in Britain—a country long committed to the idea of extradition and cooperation on crime-control—then extradition may be facing a crisis of popular confidence in other countries as well. This carries significant implications for governments' ability to establish cooperation on litigation, as the following section discusses.

Policy Implications

In a globalized world, where individuals and firms interact across borders, and where boundaries pose little obstacle to criminals, transnational litigation performs a crucial function of facilitating the enforcement of laws and legal obligations and holding actors accountable. Through cooperation on transnational litigation, offenders can be brought to justice for crimes they committed abroad, international contracts can be enforced, and abducted children may be returned to their home countries.

But not everyone thinks about cooperation on litigation in such positive terms. This book has highlighted an often-overlooked aspect of cooperation with foreign legal systems: the sensitivities it triggers and the fears and concerns it raises. We have traced these to the personal disposition of ethnocentrism, which fosters the view of foreign legal systems as inferior to the home country's legal system. This view bodes ill for the prospects of cooperation, and policymakers devising arrangements for legal cooperation would do well to remember that and tread carefully. As this book has shown, cooperation on litigation may face a domestic backlash that could weaken or disrupt the cooperative efforts. What can governments do to avoid such a backlash and build public support for cooperation with foreign legal systems? How can they establish cooperation that is reasonably smooth and depoliticized, while calming the fears of domestic actors about possible mistreatment at the hands of foreign legal authorities?

The need to obtain public support for international cooperation is, of course, not unique to the area of litigation. Governments are usually aware that public resistance might derail attempts to work with foreign partners.[41] When seeking to build popular confidence in legal-cooperation initiatives, governments may borrow from the rich experience in the area of trade, another form of international cooperation that sparks domestic controversy. Despite political contestation, however, governments have increasingly liberalized their trade policies, struck a large number of trade agreements, and delegated authority to international trade institutions.[42] The international trade regime shows that it is possible to enhance cooperation against a background of public sensitivity and concern—the same balancing act that cooperation on litigation entails. One lesson from the experience of trade concerns the importance of "selling" international agreements domestically. Leaders often highlight the economic benefits of trade liberalization for domestic constituencies, and they also tout the foreign-policy benefits of trade agreements.[43] Governments should similarly make efforts to sell the public on the importance and benefits of cooperation on legal matters. In particular, they may highlight the adverse effects of noncooperation: for instance, cybercriminals, drug traffickers, and terrorists may go unprosecuted due to the refusal of extradition; families and children may suffer tremendous emotional and psychological damage in the absence of effective cooperation over transnational family issues.[44]

A second lesson concerns two of the key principles of the trade regime: reciprocity and safeguards. States find it easier to strike trade deals when there is a rough balance between what they give to their partners and what they receive in return; the inclusion of protections against unforeseen negative effects of cooperation—such as escape clauses—also makes trade deals more palatable.[45] Similarly, to encourage public support for transnational-litigation arrangements, governments may need to demonstrate to domestic audiences that these arrangements are not one-sided but involve an exchange and give-and-take among partners. The enforcement of foreign judgments in local courts will be reciprocated through the enforcement of local judgments in foreign courts; extradition relations are similarly reciprocal. The promise of reciprocity could make it easier for domestic actors to accept the cooperative arrangement. Safeguards may have a similar effect. If cooperation on litigation is explicitly conditioned on legal fairness or respect for human rights, or if provisions to protect the interests of litigants or the public interest are in place, it may ease the minds of cooperation skeptics.

We may distill yet another lesson from the experience of two agreements examined in this book: limited scope and exclusions may contribute to the success of transnational-litigation arrangements. A global judgment-enforcement convention came to fruition in 2019 after negotiators scaled down the earlier failed efforts to focus more narrowly on enforcement, without regulating the exercise of jurisdiction. Key to the success of the NATO SOFA was the waiver option, which has allowed the majority of U.S. troops accused of crime to avoid being tried before foreign courts. One could argue that limiting the scope of cooperation, or waiving foreign jurisdiction in the majority of relevant cases, defeats the purpose. Yet it is also an acknowledgment that gaps between legal systems cannot be fully bridged, and concerns about cooperation cannot be entirely allayed. Insisting on a broader scope of cooperation or on minimizing exclusions may come at the heavy price of scuttling the cooperative efforts.

The establishment of cooperation between legal systems does not necessarily get easier with time. We saw that, in the 1950s, some members of Congress were alarmed by the prospect of U.S. troops being tried and punished by foreign courts; five decades later, many members of Congress were outraged by the mere citation of foreign law by U.S. courts.[46] In the years to come, cooperation on litigation may face growing resistance and mounting obstacles. One key reason is the changing American attitude to international agreements and institutions. The United States has led or played an important role in many initiatives for cooperation on legal matters. This book has examined several of them: the NATO SOFA; a multilateral convention on the enforcement of foreign judgments; the signing of MLATs; and the efforts against child abduction. But U.S. leadership in international cooperation has been replaced by deep mistrust of international agreements and institutions and a reluctance to accept their authority. Under the Trump administration, the United States quit the UN Human Right Council;[47] withdrew from the 2015 nuclear deal between the major powers and Iran;[48] decided to end its participation in the 2015 Paris Agreement on climate change[49] as well as in the World Health Organization;[50] considered the possibility of leaving NATO;[51] crippled the WTO's dispute settlement body;[52] and imposed sanctions on officials of the International Criminal Court for investigating whether U.S. forces had committed war crimes in Afghanistan.[53] A United States that has grown more jealous of its sovereignty and hostile to the authority of international institutions is unlikely to be interested in placing its citizens under the authority of foreign legal systems; and it is also unlikely to prod other countries to accept foreign legal authority. This absence of U.S. leadership bodes ill for the prospects of cooperation on transnational litigation.

And the United States is not alone. In Europe, right-wing populist parties have grown in power, and anti-foreign sentiments have also been heard from leaders in Turkey, Hungary, China, Brazil, India, and the Philippines.[54] "They attack liberal elites as sellouts who care more about foreigners than their fellow citizens. And they promise to put national, rather than global, interests first."[55] Such a climate of suspicion and hate toward out-groups offers an inauspicious environment for cooperation on litigation and threatens to exacerbate the political tensions surrounding the cooperative efforts. Nonetheless, this book has shown that negativity toward out-groups and concerns about foreign law do not necessarily spell doom for cooperation. A loud chorus of critics tried to scuttle the NATO SOFA before and after it entered into force, yet the agreement remained intact; the British government did not cave in to critics demanding a revision of the extradition treaty with the United States. These cases demonstrate that cooperation on litigation can sometimes endure even in the face of out-group hostility. Whether we will witness similar persistence or even progress in cooperation on litigation in the years to come remains an open question.

Notes

1. 99 Congressional Record 8779 (1953); U.S. House of Representatives 1955, 83.
2. Powell 2010; Baccini 2014.
3. For overviews of the IL/IR literature, see Hafner-Burton, Victor, and Lupu 2012; Dunoff and Pollack 2013.
4. Whytock 2018, 6.
5. Alter, Hanfer-Burton, and Helfer 2019, 453.
6. For example, Davis 2012; Jo and Simmons 2016; Alter, Helfer, and Madsen 2018.
7. Alter, Hafner-Burton, and Helfer 2019, 453.
8. Simmons 2009; Sikkink 2011; Lupu, Verdier, and Versteeg 2019.
9. Mitchell and Powell 2011; Verdier and Versteeg 2015; Efrat 2016b.
10. Whytock 2018, 7.
11. Raustiala 2009; Whytock 2011; Putnam 2016.
12. Whytock 2009a, 77, 80–81, 91–92.
13. For example, Simmons 2009; Huth, Croco, and Appel 2011; Keohane and Victor 2011; Bonnitcha, Poulsen, and Waibel 2017.
14. For example, Schuz 2013; Bassiouni 2014.
15. Roberts et al. 2018, 6.
16. McCrudden 2018; Dotan 2018.
17. Ginsburg 2018.
18. Cope and Movassagh 2018.
19. Stephan 2009; Bradford and Posner 2011.
20. Lupu 2013; Goldenziel 2018.
21. Keck and Sikkink 1998; Slaughter 2000; Goderis and Versteeg 2014.
22. Hafner-Burton, Mansfield, and Pevehouse 2015; Haftel and Thompson 2018.
23. Weiss 2003; Helfer and Voeten 2014.
24. Baldez 2011.
25. For example, Helfer and Showalter 2017; Soley and Steininger 2018; Swanson 2019.
26. Voeten 2020.
27. Simmons 2017.
28. Andenas and Fairgrieve 2015b, 12; Law 2015, 997–998.
29. Law 2015, 1002.
30. Cited in Minow 2015.
31. Seipp 2006.
32. Patel, Duss, and Toh 2013; Law 2015, 939.
33. Minow 2015.
34. Shearer 1971; Bassiouni 2014.
35. Magnuson 2012, 839.
36. For example, Kono 2006; Bryner 2008; Mansfield and Milner 2012; Marchiori, Dietz, and Tavoni 2017; Kim, Londregan, and Ratkovic 2019.
37. Dugard and Van den Wyngaert 1998; Rose 2002; Sadoff 2016, 291.
38. Pyle 2001; Posner 2014.
39. Dugart and Van Den Wyngaert 1998, 212.
40. Boister 2018b, 335. See Jansson 2020 with respect to the political-offence safeguard.
41. Minnich 2005.

42. Davis 2012; Mansfield and Milner 2012.
43. Harris 2016, 64.
44. Greif 2009.
45. Rhodes 1989; Rosendorff and Milner 2001.
46. Seipp 2006.
47. Harris 2018.
48. Landler 2018.
49. Friedman 2019.
50. Rogers and Mandavilli 2020.
51. Crowley 2020.
52. Swanson 2019.
53. Jakes and Crowley 2020.
54. See, for example, Teehankee 2016; Gettleman and Abi-Habib 2020.
55. Snyder 2019, 54.

REFERENCES

Abady, Samuel A., and Harvey Silverglate. 2008. Rachel's Law. *New York Post*, February 25.

Abrams, Floyd. 2008. Foreign Law and the First Amendment. *Wall Street Journal*, April 30.

Abramson, Jeffrey B. 2000. *We, The Jury: The Jury System and the Ideal of Democracy*. Cambridge, MA: Harvard University Press.

Adams, Brad. 2019. Japan's "Hostage Justice" System. *Japan Times*, January 11.

Adler, Matthew H., and Michele Crimaldi Zarychta. 2006. The Hague Convention on Choice of Court Agreements: The United States Joins the Judgment Enforcement Band. *Northwestern Journal of International Law & Business* 27: 1–38.

Adorno, T. W., Else Frenkel-Brunswik, Daniel J. Levinson, and R. Nevitt Sanford. 1950. *The Authoritarian Personality*. New York: Harper.

Ahmed, Azam. 2017. El Chapo, Mexican Drug Kingpin, is Extradited to U.S. *New York Times*, January 19.

Alexander, Gregory S. 1975. The Application and Avoidance of Foreign Law in the Law of Conflicts. *Northwestern University Law Review* 70: 602–638.

Allee, Todd, and Manfred Elsig. 2017. Veto Players and the Design of Preferential Trade Agreements. *Review of International Political Economy* 24(3): 538–567.

Allport, Gordon. 1954. *The Nature of Prejudice*. Reading, MA: Addison-Wesley.

Altemeyer, Bob. 1998. The Other "Authoritarian Personality." *Advances in Experimental Social Psychology* 30: 47–92.

Altemeyer, Bob. 2004. Highly Dominating, Highly Authoritarian Personalities. *Journal of Social Psychology* 144(4): 421–448.

Alter, Karen J., Emilie M. Hafner-Burton, and Laurence R. Helfer. 2019. Theorizing the Judicialization of International Relations. *International Studies Quarterly* 63(3): 449–463.

Alter, Karen J., Laurence R. Helfer, and Mikael Rask Madsen, eds. 2018. *International Court Authority*. New York: Oxford University Press.

American College of Trial Lawyers. 2009. Final Report on the Joint Project of the American College of Trial Lawyers Task Force on Discovery and the Institute for the Advancement of the American Legal System. March 11.

Amnesty International Australia. 2016. Letter to MP Luke Hartsuyker, Chair of the Joint Standing Committee on Treaties. March 24.

Andenas, Mads, and Duncan Fairgrieve, eds. 2015a. *Courts and Comparative Law*. New York: Oxford University Press.

Andenas, Mads, and Duncan Fairgrieve. 2015b. Courts and Comparative Law: In Search of a Common Language for Open Legal Systems. In *Courts and Comparative Law*, edited by Mads Andenas and Duncan Fairgrieve, 3–22. Oxford: Oxford University Press.

Andreas, Peter, and Ethan Nadelmann. 2006. *Policing the Globe: Criminalization and Crime Control in International Relations*. New York: Oxford University Press.

Andrews, Sarah, David Leblang, and Sonal Pandya. 2018. Ethnocentrism Reduces Foreign Direct Investment. *Journal of Politics* 80(2): 697–700.

Apodaca, Clair. 2006. *Understanding U.S. Human Rights Policy: A Paradoxical Legacy*. New York: Routledge.

Apodaca, Clair, and Michael Stohl. 1999. United States Human Rights Policy and Foreign Assistance. *International Studies Quarterly* 43(1): 185–198.

Appleton, Catherine, and Bent Grøver. 2007. The Pros and Cons of Life without Parole. *British Journal of Criminology* 47(4): 597–615.

Attorney-General's Department, Australia. 2016. National Interest Analysis [2016] ATNIA 6: Treaty on Extradition Between Australia and the People's Republic of China.

Attwood, Breanna. 2016. Addressing the Problem of Implementing the Hague Abduction Convention on the Civil Aspects of International Child Abduction Between the U.S. and Mexico. *Penn State Journal of Law & International Affairs* 5(2): 790–813.

Aust, Helmut Philipp, and Georg Nolte, eds. 2016. *The Interpretation of International Law by Domestic Courts: Uniformity, Diversity, Convergence*. Oxford: Oxford University Press.

Baccini, Leonardo. 2014. Cheap Talk: Transaction Costs, Quality of Institutions, and Trade Agreements. *European Journal of International Relations* 20(1): 80–117.

Bailey, Michael, Anton Strezhnev, and Erik Voeten. 2017. Estimating Dynamic State Preferences from United Nations Voting Data. *Journal of Conflict Resolution* 61(2): 430–456.

Balabanis, George, Adamantios Diamantopoulos, Rene Dentiste Mueller, and T. C. Melewar. 2001. The Impact of Nationalism, Patriotism and Internationalism on Consumer Ethnocentric Tendencies. *Journal of International Business Studies* 32(1): 157–175.

Baldez, Lisa. 2011. Why Hasn't the US Ratified the UN Women's Rights Convention? Paper presented at the Annual Meeting of the American Political Science Association, Seattle, Washington, September 1–4, 2011.

Balkin, Jack M. 2013. The American Constitution as "Our Law." *Yale Journal of Law & the Humanities* 25: 113–148.

Bang, Guri, Jon Hovi, and Detlef F. Sprinz. 2012. US Presidents and the Failure to Ratify Multilateral Environmental Agreements. *Climate Policy* 12(6): 755–763.

Bantekas, Ilias, and Susan Nash. 2009. *International Criminal Law*, 3rd ed. London: Routledge.

Barak, Gregg, ed. 2000. *Crime and Crime Control: A Global View*. Westport, CT: Greenwood Press.

Barker, Paul. 2012. Universal Civil Jurisdiction and the Extraterritorial Reach of the Alien Tort Statute: The Case of Kiobel Before the United States Supreme Court. *University of Miami International & Comparative Law Review* 20: 1–58.

Barrett, Richard. 2017. Beyond the Caliphate: Foreign Fighters and the Threat of Returnees. The Soufan Center. October.

Barton, John H., Judith L. Goldstein, Timothy E. Josling, and Richard H. Steinberg. 2006. *The Evolution of the Trade Regime: Politics, Law, and Economics of the GATT and the WTO*. Princeton, NJ: Princeton University Press.

Bassiouni, M. Cherif. 2013. *Introduction to International Criminal law*, 2nd ed. Leiden: Martinus Nijhoff.

Bassiouni, M. Cherif. 2014. *International Extradition: United States Law and Practice*, 6th ed. New York: Oxford University Press.

Bassiouni, M. Cherif, and Michael Wahid Hanna. 2006. Ceding the High Ground: The Iraqi High Criminal Court Statute and the Trial of Saddam Hussein. *Case Western Reserve Journal of International Law* 39: 21–97.

Bättig, Michèle B., and Thomas Bernauer. 2009. National Institutions and Global Public Goods: Are Democracies More Cooperative in Climate Change Policy? *International Organization* 63(2): 281–308.

Baumgartner, Samuel P. 2003. *The Proposed Hague Convention on Jurisdiction and Foreign Judgments*. Tübingen: Mohr Siebeck.

Baumgartner, Samuel P. 2004. Is Transnational Litigation Different? *University of Pennsylvania Journal of International Economic Law* 25: 1297–1393.

Baumgartner, Samuel P. 2008. How Well Do U.S. Judgments Fare in Europe? *George Washington International Law Review* 40: 173–231.

Baumgartner, Samuel P. 2013. Understanding the Obstacles to the Recognition and Enforcement of U.S. Judgments Abroad. *NYU Journal of International Law and Politics* 45: 965–1001.

Baumgartner, Samuel P. 2016. The External Dimensions of the European Law of Civil Procedure: A Transatlantic Perspective. Available at SSRN: https://ssrn.com/abstract=2742330 (accessed July 27, 2022).

BBC. 2013. Defamation Act 2013 Aims to Improve Libel Laws. *BBC News*, December 31.

BBC. 2017. British IS Fighters "Must be Killed", Minister Says. *BBC News*, October 23.

Beckerman, John S. 2000. Confronting Civil Discovery's Fatal Flaws. *Minnesota Law Review* 84: 505–587.

Bedner, Adriaan. 2010. An Elementary Approach to the Rule of Law. *Hague Journal on the Rule of Law* 2(1): 48–74.

Behr, Volker. 2003. Punitive Damages in America and German Law: Tendencies towards Approximation of Apparently Irreconcilable Concepts. *Chicago-Kent Law Review* 78: 105–161.

Beisner, John H. 2010. Discovering a Better Way: The Need for Effective Civil Litigation Reform. *Duke Law Journal* 60: 547–596.

Bellinger, John B. III, and R. Reeves Anderson. 2014. Tort Tourism: The Case for a Federal Law on Foreign Judgment Recognition. *Virginia Journal of International Law* 54(3): 501–544.

Berch, Jessica J. 2010. The Need for Enforcement of U.S. Punitive Damages Awards by the European Union. *Minnesota Journal of International Law* 19(1): 55–106.

Berger, Miriam. 2019. Here's What We Know about the ISIS Prisons Controlled by the Syrian Kurds. *Washington Post*, October 14.

Bergman, Ronen, and Oscar Lopez. 2021. Former Official Wanted by Mexico Takes Refuge in Israel. *New York Times*, July 15.

Bergmann, Eirikur. 2017. *Nordic Nationalism and Right-wing Populist Politics: Imperial Relationships and National Sentiments*. London: Palgrave Macmillan.

Bernauer, Thomas, Anna Kalbhenn, Vally Koubi, and Gabriele Spilker. 2010. A Comparison of International and Domestic Sources of Global Governance Dynamics. *British Journal of Political Science* 40(3): 509–538.

Bernstein, Ellen. 2010. Libel Tourism's Final Boarding Call. *Seton Hall Journal of Sports and Entertainment Law* 20: 205–226.

Bhattacharya, Utpal, Neal Galpin, and Bruce Haslem. 2007. The Home Court Advantage in International Corporate Litigation. *Journal of Law and Economics* 50(4): 625–659.

Bieber, Florian. 2018. Is Nationalism on the Rise? Assessing Global Trends. *Ethnopolitics* 17(5): 519–540.

Bizumic, Boris. 2019. *Ethnocentrism: Integrated Perspectives*. New York: Routledge.

Bizumic, Boris, and John Duckitt. 2012. What Is and Is Not Ethnocentrism? A Conceptual Analysis and Political Implications. *Political Psychology* 33(6): 887–909.

Blank, Thomas, and Peter Schmidt. 2003. National Identity in a United Germany: Nationalism or Patriotism? An Empirical Test with Representative Data. *Political Psychology* 24(2): 289–312.

Blanton, Shannon Lindsey. 2005. Foreign Policy in Transition? Human rights, Democracy, and U.S. Arms Exports. *International Studies Quarterly* 49(4): 647–667.

Bloom, Matthew. 2008. A Comparative Analysis of the United States's Response to Extradition Requests from China. *Yale Journal of International Law* 33: 177–214.

Boister, Neil. 2018a. *An Introduction to Transnational Criminal Law*, 2nd ed. Oxford: Oxford University Press.

Boister, Neil. 2018b. Global Simplification of Extradition: Interviews with Selected Extradition Experts in New Zealand, Canada, the US and EU. *Criminal Law Forum* 29: 327–375.

Bonnitcha, Jonathan, Lauge N. Skovgaard Poulsen, and Michael Waibel. 2017. *The Political Economy of the Investment Treaty Regime*. New York: Oxford University Press.

Booker, Christopher. 2009. EU Extradition Treaty Means British Law No Longer Protects Us. *Sunday Telegraph*, August 8.

Bookman, Pamela K. 2015. Litigation Isolationism. *Stanford Law Review* 67: 1081–1144.

Borchers, Patrick J. 1992. Comparing Personal Jurisdiction in the United States and the European Community: Lessons for American Reform. *American Journal of Comparative Law* 40(1): 121–157.

Borchers, Patrick J. 1998. A Few Little Issues for the Hague Judgments Negotiations. *Brooklyn Journal of International Law* 24(1): 157–166.

Borchers, Patrick J. 2010. Punitive Damages, Forum Shopping, and the Conflict of Laws. *Louisiana Law Review* 70: 529–555.

Born, Gary B., and Peter B. Rutledge. 2011. *International Civil Litigation in United States Courts*, 5th ed. New York: Wolters Kluwer Law & Business.

Bornstein, Brian H., and Timothy R. Robicheaux. 2008. Crisis, What Crisis? Perception and Reality in Civil Justice. In *Civil Juries and Civil Justice: Psychological and Legal Perspectives*, edited by Brian H. Bornstein, Richard L. Wiener, Robert F. Schopp, and Steven L. Willborn, 1–19. New York: Springer.

Borrás, Algería. 2005. The 1999 Preliminary Draft Hague Convention on Jurisdiction, Recognition and Enforcement of Judgments: Agreements and Disagreements. In *The Hague Preliminary Draft Convention on Jurisdiction and Judgments: Proceedings of the Round Table Held at Milan University on 15 November 2003*, edited by Fausto Pocar and Costanza Honorati, 41–72. Padova: Cedam.

Bowcott, Owen. 2020. UK Cooperation with US over Two Alleged Isis Killers Ruled Unlawful. *The Guardian*, March 25.

Boyes, Roger. 2019. We Can't Wash Our Hands of ISIS Fighters. *The Times*, August 13.

Bradford, Anu, and Eric A. Posner. 2011. Universal Exceptionalism in International Law. *Harvard International Law Journal* 52: 1–54.

Brand, Ronald A. 1991. Enforcement of Foreign Money-Judgments in the United States: In Search of Uniformity and International Acceptance. *Notre Dame Law Review* 67: 253–334.

Brand, Ronald A. 2002. Community Competence for Matters of Judicial Cooperation at the Hague Conference on Private International Law: A View from the United States. *Journal of Law & Commerce* 21: 191–208.

Brand, Ronald A. 2013. Federal Judicial Center International Litigation Guide: Recognition and Enforcement of Foreign Judgments. *University of Pittsburgh Law Review* 74: 491–549.

Braslow, Norman T. 1999. The Recognition and Enforcement of Common Law Punitive Damages in a Civil Law System: Some Reflections on the Japanese Experience. *Arizona Journal of International & Comparative Law* 16: 285–360.

Brooks, Thom. 2016. The Right to Trial by Jury. In *The Right to a Fair Trial*, edited by Thom Brooks, 83–100. New York: Routledge.

Bruch, Carol S. 2000. Religious Law, Secular Practices, and Children's Human Rights in Child Abduction Cases under the Hague Child Abduction Convention. *New York University Journal of International Law and Politics* 33: 49–58.

Bryner, Gary. 2008. Failure and Opportunity: Environmental Groups in US Climate Change Policy. *Environmental Politics* 17(2): 319–336.

Bueno de Mesquita, Bruce, Alastair Smith, Randolph M. Siverson, and James D. Morrow. 2003. *The Logic of Political Survival*. Cambridge, MA: MIT Press.

Bump, Philip. 2019. It's the Mainstream Anti-immigration Rhetoric, Not the Extreme, That's Shaping American Politics. *Washington Post*, August 13.

Bunglawala, Inayat. 2006. An Insult to Poodles. *The Guardian*, June 12.

Burns, John. F. 2009. Hacker's Extradition to U.S. More Likely. *New York Times*, July 31.

Büthe, Tim, and Walter Mattli. 2011. *The New Global Rulers: The Privatization of Regulation in the World Economy*. Princeton, NJ: Princeton University Press.

Buxbaum, Hannah L. 2009. Territory, Territoriality, and the Resolution of Jurisdictional Conflict. *American Journal of Comparative Law* 57: 631–676.

Byers, Michael. 2016. Extradition Treaty with China would be an Affront to Human Rights. *Globe and Mail*, September 30.

Byrnes, Andrew. 2016. Letter to MP Stuart Robert, Chair of the Joint Standing Committee on Treaties. November 25.

Calder, Kent E. 2007. *Embattled Garrisons: Comparative Base Politics and American Globalism.* Princeton, NJ: Princeton University Press.

Callick, Rowan. 2017. Australia's Extradition Treaty with China a Done Deal. *The Australian*, March 4.

Callimachi, Rukmini. 2014. Militant Group Says It Killed American Journalist in Syria. *New York Times*, August 19.

Caplan, Gerald. 2016. No "Sunny Ways" for Canadian Extradited to France, So How Fair Will China Be? *Globe and Mail*, October 12.

Carothers, Thomas. 2006. The Backlash against Democracy Promotion. *Foreign Affairs* 85(2): 55–68.

Carpenter, R. Charli, Sirin Duygulu, Alexander H. Montgomery, and Anna Rapp. 2014. Explaining the Advocacy Agenda: Insights from the Human Security Network. *International Organization* 68(2): 449–470.

Carter, David B., and Curtis S. Signorino. 2010. Back to the Future: Modeling Time Dependence in Binary Data. *Political Analysis* 18(3): 271–292.

Casciani, Dominic. 2018. Was 2017 the Worst Year for UK Terrorism? *BBC News*, January 3.

Cassel, Pär Kristoffer. 2012. *Grounds of Judgment: Extraterritoriality and Imperial Power in Nineteenth-Century China and Japan.* New York: Oxford University Press.

Cave, Damien. 2017. Australian Vote on Extradition Treaty with China is Canceled. *New York Times*, March 28.

Cave, Damien. 2019. Australia's China Challenge. *New York Times*, May 20.

Center for Security Policy. 2010. *Shariah: The Threat to America.* An Exercise in Competitive Analysis. Report of Team B II. Washington, DC: Center for Security Policy.

Center for Security Policy. 2011. Shariah Law and American State Courts: An Assessment of State Appellate Court Cases. Occasional Paper Series. May.

Cha, Jiyoung. 2010. Comparison and Analysis of Korea and Japan Status of Forces Agreements and their Implications for Iraq's SOFA. *Cardozo Journal of International and Comparative Law* 18: 487–525.

Chandler, Charles R., and Yung-mei Tsai. 2001. Social Factors Influencing Immigration Attitudes: An Analysis of Data from the General Social Survey. *Social Science Journal* 38(2): 177–188.

Chang, Yu Sang, SungSup Brian Choi, Jinsoo Lee, and Won Chang Chin. 2013. Population Size vs. Number of Crimes: Is the Relationship Super-linear? *International Journal of Information Systems and Social Change* 9(1): 26–39.

Chase, Steven, and Robert Fife. 2016. Justin Trudeau Defends Extradition Treaty Talks with China. *Globe and Mail*, September 21.

Chase, Steven, Robert Fife, and Nathan Vanderklippe. 2017. Former CSIS Directors Question Canada's Pursuit of Extradition Treaty with China. *Globe and Mail*, March 28.

Chilton, Adam S., and Christopher A. Whytock. 2015. Foreign Sovereign Immunity and Comparative Institutional Competence. *University of Pennsylvania Law Review* 163(2): 411–486.

China Daily. 2006. China Widens Net for Fugitive Fraudsters. *China Daily*, April 29.

Cho, Erin. 1998. Caught in Confucius' Shadow: The Struggle for Women's Legal Equality in South Korea. *Columbia Journal of Asian Law* 12: 125–189.

Choo, Sabrina. 2018. Circumventing the China Extradition Conundrum: Relying on Deportation to Return Chinese Fugitives. *NYU Journal of International Law & Politics* 50: 1361–1415.

Choudhry, Sujit. 2013. Living Originalism in India: Our Law and Comparative Constitutional Law. *Yale Journal of Law & the Humanities* 25: 1–22.

Christensen, Darin, and Jeremy M. Weinstein. 2013. Defunding Dissent: Restrictions on Aid to NGOs. *Journal of Democracy* 24(2): 77–91.

Chulov, Michael. 2019. The Rise and Fall of the ISIS "Caliphate." *The Guardian*, March 23.

Cingranelli, David L., David L. Richards, and K. Chad Clay. 2014. The CIRI Human Rights Dataset. Available at http://www.humanrightsdata.com/. Version 2014.04.14. (accessed July 27, 2022).

Civic, Melanne Andromecca. 1995. Comparative Analysis of International and Chinese Human Rights Law: Universality Versus Cultural Relativism. *Buffalo Journal of International Law* 2: 285–322.

Clark, Andrew, and Claire Truscott. 2007. Natwest Three Plead Guilty to $7.3m Enron-linked Transatlantic Fraud. *The Guardian*, November 29.

Clarke, Donald C. 2006. Lost in Translation? Corporate Legal Transplants in China. GWU Law School Public Law Research Paper No. 213.

Clermont, Kevin M. 1999. Jurisdictional Salvation and the Hague Treaty. *Cornell Law Review* 85: 89–133.

Clermont, Kevin M., and Theodore Eisenberg. 1996. Xenophilia in American Courts. *Harvard Law Review* 109: 1120–1143.

Clermont, Kevin M., and Theodore Eisenberg. 2007. Xenophilia or Xenophobia in U.S. Courts? Before and after 9/11. *Journal of Empirical Legal Studies* 4(2): 441–464.

Clermont, Kevin M., and Emily Sherwin. 2002. A Comparative View of Standards of Proof. *American Journal of Comparative Law* 50: 243–275.

Cohen, Adam. 2008. "Libel Tourism": When Freedom of Speech Takes a Holiday. *New York Times*, September 14.

Cole, David. 2003. Are Foreign Nationals Entitled to the Same Constitutional Rights as Citizens? *Thomas Jefferson Law Review* 25: 367–388.

Coles, Anita. 2009. Extradition without Justice. *The Guardian*, July 16.

Collier, Jane F. 1994. Intertwined Histories: Islamic Law and Western Imperialism. *Law & Society Review* 28(2): 395–408.

Connell, John. 2011. *Medical Tourism*. Wallingford, Oxfordshire: CAB International.

Cook, Joana, and Gina Vale. 2018. From Daesh to "Diaspora": Tracing the Women and Minors of Islamic State. International Center for the Study of Radicalisation, King's College London.

Cooley, Alexander. 2008. *Base Politics: Democratic Change and the U.S. Military Overseas*. Ithaca, NY: Cornell University Press.

Cope, Kevin L., and Hooman Movassagh. 2018. National Legislatures: The Foundations of Comparative International Law. In *Comparative International Law*, edited by Anthea Roberts, Paul B. Stephan, Pierre-Hugues Verdier, and Mila Versteeg, 271–291. New York: Oxford University Press.

Cotterrell, Roger. 2012. What is Transnational Law? *Law & Social Inquiry* 37(2): 500–524.

Courea, Eleni, and Steven Swinford. 2019. Diehard ISIS Prisoners Must Stay in Syria, Says Defence Secretary Ben Wallace. *The Times*, October 2.

Cowell, Alan, and John F. Burns. 2012. Britain Refuses to Extradite Computer Hacker Sought in U.S. *New York Times*, October 16.

Crabtree, Charles, and Michael J. Nelson. 2017. New Evidence for a Positive Relationship between de facto Judicial Independence and State Respect for Empowerment Rights. *International studies Quarterly* 61(1): 210–224.

Creery, Jennifer. 2019. China Extradition Law Should be Handled with Extreme Caution Says Hong Kong Trade Group. *Hong Kong Free Press*, March 31.

Crépeau, François, and Estibalitz Jimenez. 2004. Foreigners and the Right to Justice in the Aftermath of 9/11. *International Journal of Law and Psychiatry* 27: 609–626.

Crowley, Michael. 2020. Allies and Former U.S. Officials Fear Trump Could Seek NATO Exit in a Second Term. *New York Times*, September 3.

Curran, Vivian Grosswald. 2016. United States Discovery and Foreign Blocking Statutes. *Louisiana Law Review* 76: 1141–1149.

Curry, Andrew. 2015. Here Are the Ancient Sites ISIS Has Damaged and Destroyed. *National Geographic*, September 1.

Cutler, A. Claire, and Thomas Dietz, eds. 2017. *The Politics of Private Transnational Governance by Contract*. New York: Routledge.

d'Aspremont, Jean. 2011. *Formalism and the Sources of International Law: A Theory of the Ascertainment of Legal Rules*. Oxford: Oxford University Press.

Davis, Christina L. 2012. *Why Adjudicate? Enforcing Trade Rules in the WTO*. Princeton, NJ: Princeton University Press, 2012.

Dean, Arthur H. 1953. The Bricker Amendment and Authority over Foreign Affairs. *Foreign Affairs* 32(1): 1–19.

Dearden, Lizzie. 2019. Only One in 10 Jihadis Returning from Syria Prosecuted, Figures Reveal. *The Independent*, February 21.

Deen–Racsmany, Zsuzsanna. 2004. A New Passport to Immunity? Non-Extradition of Naturalized Citizens versus Criminal Justice. *Journal of International Criminal Justice* 2(3): 761–784.

de Felipe, Miguel Beltrán, and Adán Nieto Martín. 2012. Post 9/11 Trends in International Judicial Cooperation: Human Rights as a Constraint on Extradition in Death Penalty Cases. *Journal of International Criminal Justice* 10(3): 581–604.

de Figueiredo, Rui J. P., and Zachary Elkins. 2003. Are Patriots Bigots? An Inquiry into the Vices of In-Group Pride. *American Journal of Political Science* 47(1): 171–188.

Del-Bove, Marion Charret, and Laurence Francoz-Terminal. 2015. How Common is the Common Law? Some Differences and Similarities in British and American Superior Court Decisions. *Revista Alicantina de Estudios Ingleses* 28: 59–82.

Demleitner, Nora V. 1999. Combating Legal Ethnocentrism: Comparative Law Sets Boundaries. *Arizona State Law Journal* 31: 737–762.

Department of Defense. 2017. Base Structure Report: Fiscal Year 2017 Baseline. Available at https://www.acq.osd.mil/eie/Downloads/BSI/Base%20Structure%20Report%20FY17.pdf (accessed February 23, 2022).

Department of Foreign Affairs and Trade [Australia]. n.d. Australia and Human Rights: An Overview. 4th ed.

Department of Foreign Affairs and Trade [Australia]. 2018. Australia's Strategy for Abolition of the Death Penalty. June.

Department of Justice. Criminal Division. 2015. FY 2016 President's Budget. Available at https://www.justice.gov/sites/default/files/jmd/pages/attachments/2015/02/02/10._criminal_division_crm.pdf (accessed July 27, 2022).

Desch, Michael C. 1992. Bases for the Future: U.S. Military Interests in the Post-Cold War Third World. *Security Studies* 2(2): 201–224.

D'Hulster, Katia. 2012. Cross-border Banking Supervision: Incentive Conflicts in Supervisory Information Sharing between Home and Host Supervisors. *Journal of Banking Regulation* 13: 300–319.

Diamond, Larry, and Orville Schell. 2019. *China's Influence and American Interests: Promoting Constructive Vigilance*. Rev. ed. Stanford, CA: Hoover Institution Press.

Dodd, Vikram, and Jessica Elgot. 2018. Javid Accused of Assuming "Power of Life and Death" over Isis Suspects. *The Guardian*, July 24.

Dodge, William S. 2015. International Comity in American Law. *Columbia Law Review* 115: 2071–2142.

Doebbler, Curtis F. J. 2007. An Intentionally Unfair Trial. *Journal of International Criminal Justice* 5(2): 264–271.

Dollard, John. 1937. *Caste and Class in a Southern Town*. New Haven, CT: Yale University Press.

Dotan, Shai. 2018. Comparative Views on the Right to Vote in International Law: The Case of Prisoners' Disenfranchisement. In *Comparative International Law*, edited by Anthea Roberts,

Paul B. Stephan, Pierre-Hugues Verdier, and Mila Versteeg, 379–395. New York: Oxford University Press.

Drezner, Daniel W. 2001. Globalization and Policy Convergence. *International Studies Review* 3(1): 53–78.

Drury, Ian. 2009. An Affront to British Justice: Cameron Attacks McKinnon Hypocrites. *Daily Mail*, July 19.

Duckitt, John. 2000. Culture, Personality, and Prejudice. In *Political Psychology: Cultural and Crosscultural Foundations*, edited by Stanley A. Renshon and John Duckitt, 89–107. New York: New York University Press.

Dugard, John, and Christine Van den Wyngaert. 1998. Reconciling Extradition with Human Rights. *American Journal of International Law* 92(2): 187–212.

Duhaime, Christine. 2016. An Extradition Treaty with China Sends a Message about Corruption. *Globe and Mail*, September 26.

Duncan, William. 2000. Action in Support of the Hague Child Abduction Convention: A View from the Permanent Bureau. *New York University Journal of International Law and Politics* 33: 103–123.

Dunoff, Jeffrey L., and Mark A. Pollack. 2013. International Law and International Relations: Introducing an Interdisciplinary Dialogue. In *Interdisciplinary Perspectives on International Law and International Relations: The State of the Art*, edited by Jeffrey L. Dunoff and Mark A. Pollack, 3–32. New York: Cambridge University Press.

Dustmann, Christian, and Ian P. Preston. 2007. Racial and Economic Factors in Attitudes to Immigration. *BE Journal of Economic Analysis & Policy* 7(1): Art. 62.

Dziedzic, Stephen. 2016. Parliamentary Committee Recommends Extraditing Criminals to China Despite Human Rights Concerns. *ABC News*, December 16.

Edwards, Tim. 2012. Extradited Businessman Tappin to Appear in US Court Today. *The Week*, February 27.

Efrat, Asif. 2012. *Governing Guns, Preventing Plunder: International Cooperation against Illicit Trade*. New York: Oxford University Press.

Efrat, Asif. 2016a. Promoting Trade through Private Law: Explaining International Legal Harmonization. *Review of International Organizations* 11: 311–336.

Efrat, Asif. 2016b. Legal Traditions and Nonbinding Commitments: Evidence from the United Nations' Model Commercial Legislation. *International Studies Quarterly* 60(4): 624–635.

Efrat, Asif. 2019. Assessing Mutual Trust among EU Members: Evidence from the European Arrest Warrant. *Journal of European Public Policy* 26(5): 656–675.

Efrat, Asif. 2022a. Facing U.S. Extraterritorial Pressure: American Troops in Foreign Courts during the Cold War. *Journal of Politics* 84(1): 242–257.

Efrat, Asif. 2022b. Troop Crime in Peacetime: Criminality and Accountability of U.S. Troops Worldwide during the Cold War. *Armed Forces & Society*. https://doi.org/10.1177/0095327X211011578.

Efrat, Asif, and Abraham L. Newman. 2016. Deciding to Defer: The Importance of Fairness in Resolving Transnational Jurisdictional Conflicts. *International Organization* 70(2): 409–441.

Efrat, Asif, and Abraham L. Newman. 2018a. Cultural Intolerance and Aversion to Foreign Judgments in the American States. *Asian Journal of Law and Economics* 9(2): 1–15.

Efrat, Asif, and Abraham L. Newman. 2018b. Divulging Data: Domestic Determinants of International Information Sharing. *Review of International Organizations* 13(3): 395–419.

Efrat, Asif, and Abraham L. Newman. 2020. Intolerant Justice: Ethnocentrism and Transnational-Litigation Frameworks. *Review of International Organizations* 15(1): 271–299.

Egan, John W. 2006. The Future of Criminal Jurisdiction over the Deployed American Soldier. *Emory International Law Review* 20: 291–343.

Ekins, Richard, Patrick Hennessey, Khalid Mahmood MP, and Tom Tugendhat MP. 2018. Aiding the Enemy: How and Why to Restore the Law of Treason. Policy Exchange.

Elbalti, Béligh. 2017. Reciprocity and the Recognition and Enforcement of Foreign Judgments: A Lot of Bark but Not Much Bite. *Journal of Private International Law* 13(1): 184–218.

El Deeb, Sarah, and Matthew Lee. 2019. US Calls for Repatriation of Foreign Fighters Held in Syria. *Associated Press*, February 4.

Elgot, Jessica. 2017. British Isis Fighters Should be Hunted Down and Killed, Says Defence Secretary. *The Guardian*, December 8.

Elkins, Zachary, Andrew T. Guzman, and Beth A. Simmons. 2006. Competing for Capital: The Diffusion of Bilateral Investment Treaties, 1960–2000. *International organization* 60(4): 811–846.

Ellis, Alan, and Robert L. Pisani. 1985. The United States Treaties on Mutual Assistance in Criminal Matters: A Comparative Analysis. *The International Lawyer* 19(1): 189–223.

Emmerson, Ben, Andrew Ashworth, and Alison Macdonald. 2012. *Human Rights and Criminal Justice*, 3rd ed. London: Sweet & Maxwell.

Engel, Christoph. 2009. Preponderance of Evidence versus *Intime Conviction*: A Behavioral Perspective on a Conflict between American and Continental European Law. *Vermont Law Review* 33: 435–467.

English PEN and Index on Censorship. 2009. Free Speech is Not for Sale: The Impact of British Libel Law on Freedom of Expression.

Erickson, Jennifer L. 2013. Market Imperative Meets Normative Power: Human Rights and European Arms Transfer Policy. *European Journal of International Relations* 19(2): 209–234.

Erickson, Richard J. 1994. Status of Forces Agreements: A Sharing of Sovereign Prerogative. *Air Force Law Review* 37: 137–153.

European Commission. 2020. Replies to Questionnaire on Quantitative Information on the Practical Operation of the European Arrest Warrant—Year 2018. Brussels. July 2. SWD(2020) 127 final.

European Parliament. 2015. A Comparison between US and EU Data Protection Legislation for Law Enforcement. Study for the LIBE Committee. Available at https://www.europarl.europa.eu/thinktank/en/document.html?reference=IPOL_STU(2015)536459 (accessed February 23, 2022).

Fariss, Christopher J. 2014. Respect for Human Rights has Improved Over Time: Modeling the Changing Standard of Accountability. *American Political Science Review* 108(2): 297–318.

Fariss, Christopher J. 2018. The Changing Standard of Accountability and the Positive Relationship between Human Rights Treaty Ratification and Compliance. *British Journal of Political Science* 48(1): 239–271.

Farmer, Lindsay. 2013. Territorial Jurisdiction and Criminalization. *University of Toronto Law Journal* 63(2): 225–246.

Farrell, Henry, and Abraham L. Newman. 2019. *Of Privacy and Power: The Transatlantic Struggle over Freedom and Security*. Princeton, NJ: Princeton University Press.

Feldman, Stanley. 2003. Enforcing Social Conformity: A Theory of Authoritarianism. *Political Psychology* 24(1): 41–74.

Feller, S. Z. 1975. The Scope of Reciprocity in Extradition. *Israel Law Review* 10(4): 427–455.

Fife, Robert. 2016. Ottawa to Negotiate Extradition Treaty with China. *Globe and Mail*, September 20.

Finnemore, Martha, and Kathryn Sikkink. 1998. International Norm Dynamics and Political Change. *International organization* 52(4): 887–917.

Finnemore, Martha, and Stephen J. Toope. 2001. Alternatives to "Legalization": Richer Views of Law and Politics. *International Organization* 55(3): 743–758.

Fisher, Lucy. 2019. Theresa May Rejects Donald Trump's Call to Take Back and Try ISIS Fighters. *The Times*, February 19.

Flynn, Jonathan T. 2012. No Need to Maximize: Reforming Foreign Criminal Jurisdiction Practice under the U.S.-Japan Status of Forces Agreement. *Military Law Review* 212: 1–69.

Ford, Robert. 2011. Acceptable and Unacceptable Immigrants: How Opposition to Immigration in Britain is Affected by Migrants' Region of Origin. *Journal of Ethnic and Migration Studies* 37(7): 1017–1037.

Fredericks, Bob. 2019. Trump, Macron Trade Jabs over Captured ISIS Fighters. *New York Post*, December 3.

Freeman, Marilyn. 1998. The Effects and Consequences of International Child Abduction. *Family Law Quarterly* 32(3): 603–621.

Frey, Linda S., and Marsha L. Frey. 1999. *The History of Diplomatic Immunity*. Columbus: Ohio State University Press.

Friedman, Lisa. 2019. Trump Serves Notice to Quit Paris Climate Agreement. *New York Times*, November 4.

Fuhrmann, Matthew. 2012. *Atomic Assistance: How "Atoms for Peace" Programs Cause Nuclear Insecurity*. Ithaca, NY: Cornell University Press.

Fung, Timothy KF, Wenjie Yan, and Heather Akin. 2018. In the Eye of the Beholder: How News Media Exposure and Audience Schema Affect the Image of the United States among the Chinese Public. *International Journal of Public Opinion Research* 30(3): 443–472.

Funk, Michelle, Alberto Minoletti, Natalie Drew, Jacob Taylor, and Benedetto Saraceno. 2006. Advocacy for Mental Health: Roles for Consumer and Family Organizations and Governments. *Health Promotion International* 21(1): 70–75.

Galanter, Marc. 2004. The Vanishing Trial: An Examination of Trials and Related Matters in Federal and State Courts. *Journal of Empirical Legal Studies* 1(3): 459–570.

Gao, Rijie Ernie. 2009. Between a Rock and a Hard Place: Tensions Between the US–ROK Status of Forces Agreement and the Duty to Ensure Individual Rights Under the ICCPR. *Fordham International Law Journal* 33: 585–647.

Garland, David. 2012. *Peculiar Institution: America's Death Penalty in an Age of Abolition*. Cambridge, MA: Harvard University Press.

Gelter, Martin, and Mathias M. Siems. 2014. Citations to Foreign Courts: Illegitimate and Superfluous, or Unavoidable? Evidence from Europe. *American Journal of Comparative Law* 62: 35–86.

Gettleman, Jeffrey, and Maria Abi-Habib. 2020. In India, Modi's Policies Have Lit a Fuse. *New York Times*, March 1.

Gher, Jaime M. 2002. Status of Forces Agreements: Tools to Further Effective Foreign Policy and Lessons to Be Learned from the United States–Japan Agreement. *University of San Francisco Law Review* 37: 227.

Gilligan, Michael J. 1997. *Empowering Exporters: Reciprocity, Delegation, and Collective Action in American Trade Policy*. Ann Arbor: University of Michigan Press.

Ginosar, Avshalom. 2015. Understanding Patriotic Journalism: Culture, Ideology and Professional Behavior. *Journal of Media Ethics* 30(4): 289–301.

Ginsburg, Ruth B. 1965. The Competent Court in Private International Law: Some Observations on Current Views in the United States. *Rutgers Law Review* 20: 89–100.

Ginsburg, Tom. 2018. Objections to Treaty Reservations: A Comparative Approach to Decentralized Interpretation. In *Comparative International Law*, edited by Anthea Roberts, Paul B. Stephan, Pierre-Hugues Verdier, and Mila Versteeg, 231–250. New York: Oxford University Press.

Globe and Mail Editorial. 2016. China Wants an Extradition Treaty. Ottawa Should Say No. *Globe and Mail*, September 20.

Goderis, Benedikt, and Mila Versteeg. 2014. The Diffusion of Constitutional Rights. *International Review of Law and Economics* 39: 1–19.

Goldenziel, Jill I. 2018. When Law Migrates: Refugees in Comparative International Law. In *Comparative International Law*, edited by Anthea Roberts, Paul B. Stephan, Pierre-Hugues Verdier, and Mila Versteeg, 397–418. New York: Oxford University Press.

Goldman, Adam, Eric Schmitt, and Charlie Savage. 2018. Britain Presses U.S. to Avoid Death Penalty for ISIS Suspects. *New York Times*, February 28.

Gollust, Sarah E., Laura Attanasio, Amanda Dempsey, Allison M. Benson, and Erika Franklin Fowler. 2013. Political and News Media Factors Shaping Public Awareness of the HPV Vaccine. *Women's Health Issues* 23(3): e143–e151.

Goodwin-Gill, Guy S., and Hélène Lambert, eds. 2010. *The Limits of Transnational Law: Refugee Law, Policy Harmonization and Judicial Dialogue in the European Union*. New York: Cambridge University Press.

Gotanda, John Y. 2004. Punitive Damages: A Comparative Analysis. *Columbia Journal of Transnational Law* 42: 391–444.

Government Accountability Office. 2006. Human Trafficking: Better Data, Strategy, and Reporting Needed to Enhance U.S. Anti-trafficking Efforts Abroad. GAO–06–825.

Government of Canada. 2020. *Canada's Approach to Advancing Human Rights*. Available at https://www.international.gc.ca/world-monde/issues_development-enjeux_developpement/human_rights-droits_homme/advancing_rights-promouvoir_droits.aspx?lang=eng (accessed February 23, 2022).

Green, Jessica F. 2013. *Rethinking Private Authority: Agents and Entrepreneurs in Global Environmental Governance*. Princeton, NJ: Princeton University Press.

Greif, Geoffrey L. 2009. The Long-term Aftermath of Child Abduction: Two Case Studies and Implications for Family Therapy. *American Journal of Family Therapy* 37(4): 273–286.

Greif, Geoffrey L., and Rebecca L. Hegar. 1991. Parents Whose Children are Abducted by the Other Parent: Implications for Treatment. *American Journal of Family Therapy* 19(3): 215–225.

Gresh, Geoffrey F. 2015. *Gulf Security and the U.S. Military: Regime Survival and the Politics of Basing*. Stanford, CA: Stanford University Press.

Grierson, Jamie, Jennifer Rankin, and Lisa O'Carroll. 2020. UK to Withdraw from European Arrest Warrant. *The Guardian*, February 27.

Griffiths, James, Helen Regan, and Eric Cheung. 2019. Hong Kong Extradition Bill: Hundreds of Thousands Join Third Huge Protest in a Week. *CNN*, June 17.

Grover, Sonja. 2005. Advocacy by Children as a Causal Factor in Promoting Resilience. *Childhood* 12(4): 527–538.

Gurowicz, Amy. 2006. Looking Outward: International Legal Norms and Foreigner Rights in Japan. In *Local Citizenship in Recent Countries of Immigration: Japan in Comparative Perspective*, edited by Takeyuki Tsuda, 153–170. Lanham, MD: Lexington Books.

Hafner-Burton, Emilie M., Edward D. Mansfield, and Jon C. W. Pevehouse. 2015. Human Rights Institutions, Sovereignty Costs and Democratization. *British Journal of Political Science* 45(1): 1–27.

Hafner-Burton, Emilie M., David G. Victor, and Yonatan Lupu. 2012. Political Science Research on International Law: The State of the Field. *American Journal of International Law* 106(1): 47–97.

Haftel, Yoram Z., and Alexander Thompson. 2013. Delayed Ratification: The Domestic Fate of Bilateral Investment Treaties. *International Organization* 67(2): 355–387.

Haftel, Yoram Z., and Alexander Thompson. 2018. When Do States Renegotiate Investment Agreements? The Impact of Arbitration. *Review of International Organizations* 13(1): 25–48.

Hagan, Teresa L., and Heidi S. Donovan. 2013. Self-advocacy and Cancer: A Concept Analysis. *Journal of Advanced Nursing* 69(10): 2348–2359.

Hainmueller, Jens, and Dominik Hangartner. 2013. Who Gets a Swiss Passport? A Natural Experiment in Immigrant Discrimination. *American Political Science Review* 107(1): 159–187.

Hainmueller, Jens, and Michael J. Hiscox. 2010. Attitudes toward Highly Skilled and Low-skilled Immigration: Evidence from a Survey Experiment. *American Political Science Review* 104(1): 61–84.

Hainmueller, Jens, Michael J. Hiscox, and Yotam Margalit. 2015. Do Concerns about Labor Market Competition Shape Attitudes toward Immigration? New Evidence. *Journal of International Economics* 97(1): 193–207.

Hall, Nina, Hans Peter Schmitz, J. Michael Dedmon. 2020. Transnational Advocacy and NGOs in the Digital Era: New Forms of Networked Power. *International Studies Quarterly* 64(1): 159–167.

Hall, Richard. 2020. British "Isis Members" to be Put on Trial in Syria as Kurds Plan Special Court for Foreign Fighters. *The Independent*, February 6.

Hamilton, Fiona, and John Simpson. 2018. 200 Isis Fighters who Came from UK Cannot Return. *The Times*, February 17.

Hammel, Andrew. 2010. *Ending the Death Penalty: The European Experience in Global Perspective*. London: Palgrave Macmillan.

Harris, Gardiner. 2018. Trump Administration Withdraws U.S. From U.N. Human Rights Council. *New York Times*, June 19.

Harris, Jennifer M. 2016. America, Europe and the Necessary Geopolitics of Trade. *Survival* 58(6): 63–92.

Hay, Peter. 1992. The Recognition and Enforcement of American Money-Judgments in Germany: The 1992 Decision of the German Supreme Court. *American Journal of Comparative Law* 40: 729–750.

Hay, Peter, and Robert J. Walker. 1978. The Proposed U.S.-U.K. Recognition-of-Judgments Convention: Another Perspective. *Virginia Journal of International Law* 18: 753–768.

He, Baogang, and Hannah Murphy. 2007. The Role of International Non-Governmental Organisations in Constructing Global Social Contracts: Global Social Justice at the WTO? *International Affairs* 83(4): 707–727.

Helfer, Laurence R., and Anne E. Showalter. 2017. Opposing International Justice: Kenya's Integrated Backlash Strategy Against the ICC. *International Criminal Law Review* 17(1): 1–46.

Helfer, Laurence R., and Erik Voeten. 2014. International Courts as Agents of Legal Change: Evidence from LGBT Rights in Europe. *International Organization* 68(1): 77–110.

Hello, Evelyn, Peer Scheepers, and Peter Sleegers. 2006. Why the More Educated are Less Inclined to Keep Ethnic Distance: An Empirical Test of Four Explanations. *Ethnic and Racial Studies* 29(5): 959–985.

Helmke, Gretchen, and Frances Rosenbluth. 2009. Regimes and the Rule of Law: Judicial Independence in Comparative Perspective. *Annual Review of Political Science* 12: 345–366.

Hensel, Paul R., and Sara McLaughlin Mitchell. 2005. Issue Indivisibility and Territorial Claims. *GeoJournal* 64(4): 275–285.

Hernández, Javier C. 2020. Harsh Penalties, Vaguely Defined Crimes: Hong Kong's Security Law Explained. *New York Times*, June 30.

Hertel, Shareen, Lyle Scruggs, and C. Patrick Heidkamp. 2009. Human Rights and Public Opinion: From Attitudes to Action. *Political Science Quarterly* 124(3): 443–459.

Hillebrecht, Courtney. 2014. *Domestic Politics and International Human Rights Tribunals: The Problem of Compliance*. New York: Cambridge University Press.

Hirschl, Ran. 2008. The Judicialization of Mega–Politics and the Rise of Political Courts. *Annual Review of Political Science* 11: 93–118.

Hoffman, Adam, and Marta Furlan. 2020. Challenges Posed by Returning Foreign Fighters. Program on Extremism, George Washington University. March.

Home Affairs Committee. House of Commons. 2002. *Extradition Bill. HC 138*. December 5. London: The Stationary Office.

Home Affairs Committee. House of Commons. 2012. *The US–UK Extradition Treaty*. Vol. I. HC 644. March 30. London: The Stationary Office.

Home Affairs Committee. House of Commons. 2013. *Pre–Lisbon Treaty EU Police and Criminal Justice Measures: The UK's Opt–in Decision*. HC 615. October 31. London: The Stationary Office.

Home Office. 2011. A Review of the United Kingdom's Extradition Arrangements. Presented 30 September. Available at https://assets.publishing.service.gov.uk/government/uploads/system/uploads/attachment_data/file/117673/extradition-review.pdf (accessed February 23, 2022).

Home Office. 2012. UK Extradition Arrangements: Evidence Given to the Review Panel. Available at https://www.gov.uk/government/publications/uk-extradition-arrangements-evidence-given-to-the-review-panel (accessed February 23, 2022).

Hong Kong Bar Association. 2019. Observations of the Hong Kong Bar Association on the Fugitive Offenders and Mutual Legal Assistance in Criminal Matters Legislation (Amendment) Bill

2019. Available at https://www.hkcnews.com/article/19529/bar_association-fugitives_bill-19529/observations-of-the-hong-kong-bar-association-on-the-fugitive-offenders-and-mutual-legal-assistance-in-criminal-matters-legislation-amendment-bill-2019 (accessed February 23, 2022).

Hood, Roger, and Carolyn Hoyle. 2015. *The Death Penalty: A Worldwide Perspective*, 5th ed. Oxford: Oxford University Press.

HOPE not hate. 2019. State of Hate 2019: People vs the Elite?

Horowitz, Donald L. 1977. *The Courts and Social Policy*. Washington, DC: Brookings Institution Press.

Hughes, Caitlin Elizabeth, Kari Lancaster, and Bridget Spicer. 2011. How Do Australian News Media Depict Illicit Drug Issues? An Analysis of Print Media Reporting across and between Illicit Drugs, 2003–2008. *International Journal of Drug Policy* 22(4): 285–291.

Human Rights Watch. 2013. Iraq: A Broken Justice System. January 31. Available at https://www.hrw.org/news/2013/01/31/iraq-broken-justice-system (accessed February 23, 2022).

Human Rights Watch. 2019. Call to Eliminate Japan's "Hostage Justice" System by Japanese Legal Professionals. April 10. Available at https://www.hrw.org/news/2019/04/10/call-eliminate-japans-hostage-justice-system-japanese-legal-professionals (accessed July 27, 2022).

Huth, Paul K., Sarah E. Croco, and Benjamin J. Appel. 2011. Does International Law Promote the Peaceful Settlement of International Disputes? Evidence from the Study of Territorial Conflicts since 1945. *American Political Science Review* 105(2): 415–436.

ICC. 2015. Statement of the Prosecutor of the International Criminal Court, Fatou Bensouda, on the Alleged Crimes Committed by ISIS. April 8. Available at https://www.icc-cpi.int/Pages/item.aspx?name=otp-stat-08-04-2015-1 (accessed February 23, 2022).

Illuminati, Giulio. 2013. Transnational Inquiries in Criminal Matters and Respect for Fair Trial Guarantees. In *Transnational Inquiries and the Protection of Fundamental Rights in Criminal Proceedings*, edited by Stefano Ruggeri, 15–24. Heidelberg: Springer.

International Bar Association. 2008. Report of the Task Force on Extraterritorial Jurisdiction. Available at https://www.ibanet.org/MediaHandler?id=ECF39839-A217-4B3D-8106-DAB716B34F1E (accessed February 23, 2022).

International Security Advisory Board. 2015. Report on Status of Forces Agreements. January 16. Available at https://2009-2017.state.gov/t/avc/isab/236234.htm (accessed February 23, 2022).

Israeli, Zipi, and Elisheva Rosman-Stollman. 2015. Men and Boys: Representations of Israeli Combat Soldiers in the Media. *Israel Law Review* 30(1): 66–85.

Ives, Mike, and Tiffany May. 2019. Hong Kong Residents Block Roads to Protest Extradition Bill. *New York Times*, June 11.

Jacobsohn, Gary Jeffrey. 2010. *Constitutional Identity*. Cambridge, MA: Harvard University Press.

Jacobson, Stephen. 2002. Law and Nationalism in Nineteenth-Century Europe: The Case of Catalonia in Comparative Perspective. *Law and History Review* 20(2): 307–347.

Jakes, Lara, and Michael Crowley. 2020. U.S. to Penalize War Crimes Investigators Looking into American Troops. *New York Times*, June 11.

Janke, Benjamin West, and François-Xavier Licari. 2012. Enforcing Punitive Damage Awards in France after *Fountaine Pajot*. *American Journal of Comparative Law* 60(3): 775–804.

Janssens, Christine. 2013. *The Principle of Mutual Recognition in EU Law*. Oxford: Oxford University Press.

Jansson, Julia. 2020. *Terrorism, Criminal Law and Politics: The Decline of the Political Offence Exception to Extradition*. New York: Routledge.

Jenkins, Brian Michael. 2019. Options for Dealing with Islamic State Foreign Fighters Currently Detained in Syria. *CTS Sentinel* 12(5): 11–23.

Jensen, Nathan M., and Edmund J. Malesky. 2018. Nonstate Actors and Compliance with International Agreements: An Empirical Analysis of the OECD Anti-Bribery Convention. *International Organization* 72(1): 33–69.

Jiménez-Guerrero, José Felipe, Juan Carlos Gázquez-Abad, and Emilia del Carmen Linares-Agüera. 2014. Using Standard CETSCALE and Other Adapted Versions of the Scale for Measuring Consumers' Ethnocentric Tendencies: An Analysis of Dimensionality. *Business Research Quarterly* 17(3): 174–190.

Jo, Hyeran, and Beth A. Simmons. 2016. Can the International Criminal Court Deter Atrocity? *International Organization* 70(3): 443–475.

Joint Committee on Human Rights. House of Lords and House of Commons. 2011a. *Human Rights Implications of UK Extradition Policy*. HL Paper 156; HC 767. June 22. London: The Stationary Office.

Joint Committee on Human Rights. House of Lords and House of Commons. 2011b. Human Rights Implications of UK Extradition Policy: Written Evidence.

Joint Standing Committee on Treaties, Parliament of Australia. 2016a. *Official Committee Hansard*. Canberra. May 2.

Joint Standing Committee on Treaties, Parliament of Australia. 2016b. *Official Committee Hansard*. Canberra. November 24.

Joint Standing Committee on Treaties, Parliament of Australia. 2016c. *Report 167 on China Extradition Treaty*. Canberra. December.

Joint Standing Committee on Treaties, Parliament of Australia. 2016d. *Report 167 on China Extradition Treaty. Dissenting Report by Labor Members*. Available at https://www.aph.gov.au/Parliamentary_Business/Committees/Joint/Treaties/Extradition-China/Report_167/section?id=committees%2Freportjnt%2F024024%2F24319 (accessed February 23, 2022).

Jonakait, Randolph N. 2003. *The American Jury System*. New Haven, CT: Yale University Press.

Jones, Stephen H., and Amy Unsworth. 2022. The Dinner Table Prejudice: Islamophobia in Contemporary Britain. University of Birmingham. Available at https://www.birmingham.ac.uk/documents/college-artslaw/ptr/90172-univ73-islamophobia-in-the-uk-report-final.pdf (accessed February 23, 2022).

Juenger, Friedrich K. 1988. The Recognition of Money Judgments in Civil and Commercial Matters. *American Journal of Comparative Law* 36: 1–39.

Jung, Youngjin, and Jun-Shik Hwang. 2003. Where Does Inequality Come From? An Analysis of the Korea–United States Status of Forces Agreement. *American University International Law Review* 18: 1103–1144.

Justice Centre Hong Kong. 2019. Submissions on Cooperation between Hong Kong and Other Places on Judicial Assistance in Criminal Matters. March.

Kaczmarek, Sarah C., and Abraham L. Newman. 2011. The Long Arm of the Law: Extraterritoriality and the National Implementation of Foreign Bribery Legislation. *International Organization* 65(4): 745–770.

Kagan, Robert A. 2001. *Adversarial Legalism: The American Way of Law*. Cambridge, MA: Harvard University Press.

Kahneman, Daniel, Jack L. Knetsch, and Richard H. Thaler. 1990. Experimental Tests of the Endowment Effect and the Coase Theorem. *Journal of Political Economy* 98(6): 1325–1348.

Kahneman, Daniel, Jack L. Knetsch, and Richard H. Thaler. 1991. Anomalies: The Endowment Effect, Loss Aversion, and Status Quo Bias. *Journal of Economic Perspectives* 5(1): 193–206.

Kam, Cindy D., and Donald R. Kinder. 2012. Ethnocentrism as a Short-Term Force in the 2008 American Presidential Election. *American Journal of Political Science* 56(2): 326–340.

Kawato, Yuko. 2015. *Protests against U.S. Military Base Policy in Asia: Persuasion and Its Limits*. Stanford, CA: Stanford University Press.

Kayaoglu, Turan. 2010. *Legal Imperialism: Sovereignty and Extraterritoriality in Japan, the Ottoman Empire, and China*. New York: Cambridge University Press.

Keck, Margaret E., and Kathryn Sikkink. 1998. *Activists beyond Borders: Advocacy Networks in International Politics*. Ithaca, NY: Cornell University Press.

Kelley, Judith. 2007. Who Keeps International Commitments and Why? The International Criminal Court and Bilateral Nonsurrender Agreements. *American Political Science Review* 101(3): 573–589.

Kendall, Wesley, and Joseph M. Siracusa. 2013. *The Death Penalty and U.S. Diplomacy: How Foreign Nations and International Organizations Influence U.S. Policy*. Lanham, MD: Rowman & Littlefield.

Keohane, Robert O. 1984. *After Hegemony: Cooperation and Discord in the World Political Economy*. Princeton, NJ: Princeton university press.

Keohane, Robert O. 1986. Reciprocity in International Relations. *International Organization* 40(1): 1–27.

Keohane, Robert O., and David G. Victor. 2011. The Regime Complex for Climate Change. *Perspectives on Politics* 9(1): 7–23.

Kim, In Song, John Londregan, and Marc Ratkovic. 2019. The Effects of Political Institutions on the Extensive and Intensive Margins of Trade. *International Organization* 73(4): 755–792.

Kinder, Donald, and Cindy Kam. 2009. *Us against Them: Ethnocentric Foundations of American Opinion*. Chicago: University of Chicago Press.

King, Archibald. 1942. Jurisdiction over Friendly Foreign Armed Forces. *American Journal of International Law* 36(4): 539–567.

Klebnikov, Paul. 1996. Godfather of the Kremlin? *Forbes*, December 30.

Klein, Milton M. 1995. Mythologizing the U.S. Constitution. *Soundings: An Interdisciplinary Journal* 78(1): 169–178.

Kleinfeld, Joshua. 2016. Two Cultures of Punishment. *Stanford Law Review* 68: 933–1036.

Koh, Harold Hongju. 2008. *Transnational Litigation in United States Courts*. New York: Foundation Press.

Kollewijn, Roeland Duco. 1951. Conflicts of Western and Non-western Law. *International Law Quarterly* 4(3): 307–325.

Konitzer, Tobias B., Shanto Iyengar, Nicholas A. Valentino, Stuart Soroka, and Raymond M. Duch. 2019. Ethnocentrism versus Group-specific Stereotyping in Immigration Opinion: Cross-national Evidence on the Distinctiveness of Immigrant Groups. *Journal of Ethnic and Migration Studies* 45(7): 1051–1074.

Kono, Daniel Y. 2006. Optimal Obfuscation: Democracy and Trade Policy Transparency. *American Political Science Review* 100(3): 369–384.

Koremenos, Barbara. 2001. Loosening the Ties That Bind: A Learning Model of Agreement Flexibility. *International Organization* 55(2): 289–325.

Koremenos, Barbara. 2005. Contracting around International Uncertainty. *American Political Science Review* 99(4): 549–565.

Koziol, Helmut. 2008. *Punitive Damages: A European Perspective. Louisiana Law Review* 68: 741–764.

Kraft, Dina. 1999. Sheinbein Sentenced to 24 Years. *Washington Post*, October 24.

Kulzer, Barbara. 1968. Recognition of Foreign Country Judgments in New York: The Uniform Foreign Money-Judgment Recognition Act. *Buffalo Law Review* 18: 1–51.

Kuo, Lily. 2020. China Halts Hong Kong Extradition Treaties with Canada, Australia and UK. *The Guardian*, July 28.

Kupfer, Matthew. 2016. Trudeau Says Canada has "Extremely High Standards" for Extradition Treaty with China. *CBC News*, September 21.

Lai, Brian, and Dan Reiter. 2000. Democracy, Political Similarity, and International Alliances, 1816–1992. *Journal of Conflict Resolution* 44(2): 203–227.

Lam, Jeffie. 2019. Extradition Agreement with Mainland China Would Damage Hong Kong's "Safe Reputation" for Business, AmCham Says. *South China Morning Post*, March 6.

Landler, Mark. 2018. Trump Abandons Iran Nuclear Deal He Long Scorned. *New York Times*, May 8.

Langbein, John H. 1985. The German Advantage in Civil Procedure. *University of Chicago Law Review* 52(4): 823–866.

Langbein, John H. 2012. The Disappearance of Civil Trial in the United States. *Yale Law Journal* 122: 522–572.

La Porta, Rafael, Florencio Lopez-de-Silanes, and Andrei Shleifer. 2008. The Economic Consequences of Legal Origins. *Journal of Economic Literature* 46(2): 285–332.

Laurenceson, James, and Michael Zhou. 2019. Small Grey Rhinos: Understanding Australia's Economic Dependence on China. Australia–China Relations Institute, University of Technology Sydney. May 22. Available at https://www.australiachinarelations.org/content/small-grey-rhinos-understanding-australia%E2%80%99s-economic-dependence-china (accessed February 23, 2022).

Law Council of Australia. 2016. Treaty on Extradition between Australia and the People's Republic of China. March 24. Available at https://www.lawcouncil.asn.au/resources/submissions/treaty-on-extradition-between-australia-and-the-peoples-republic-of-china (accessed February 23, 2022).

Law, David S. 2015. Judicial Comparativism and Judicial Diplomacy. *University of Pennsylvania Law Review* 163(4): 927–1036.

Law Society of Hong Kong. Fugitive Offenders and Mutual Legal Assistance in Criminal Matters Legislation (Amendment) Bill 2019: Submission. June 5.

Lee, Yoon-Ho Alex. 2003. Criminal Jurisdiction under the U.S.-Korea Status of Forces Agreement: Problems to Proposals. *Journal of Transnational Law & Policy* 13: 213–249.

Leeds, Brett Ashley. 1999. Domestic Political Institutions, Credible Commitments, and International Cooperation. *American Journal of Political Science* 43(4): 979–1002.

Leeds, Brett Ashley, Michaela Mattes, and Jeremy S. Vogel. 2009. Interests, Institutions, and the Reliability of International Commitments. *American Journal of Political Science* 53(2): 461–476.

Lempert, Richard. 2015. The American Jury System: A Synthetic Overview. *Chicago-Kent Law Review* 90: 825–859.

Lennox, Tom. 2017. Extradition Treaty with China is a Bad Deal for Justice. *The Australian*, January 26.

Lepper, Seven J. 1994. A Primer on Foreign Criminal Jurisdiction. *Air Force Law Review* 37: 169–189.

Levie, Howard S. 1958. The NATO Status of Forces Agreement: Legal Safeguards for American Servicemen. *American Bar Association Journal* 44(4): 322–326.

Levin, Dan. 2016. Canada Agrees to Talks on Extradition Treaty with China. *New York Times*, September 20.

Levine, Robert A., and Donald T. Campbell. 1972. *Ethnocentrism: Theories of Conflict, Ethnic Attitudes, and Group Behavior*. New York: Wiley.

Lindhorst, Tarin, and Jeffrey L. Edelson. 2012. *Battered Women, Their Children, and International Law: The Unintended Consequences of the Hague Child Abduction Convention*. Boston: Northeastern University Press.

Linzer, Drew A., and Jeffrey K. Staton. 2015. A Global Measure of Judicial Independence, 1948–2012. *Journal of Law and Courts* 3(2): 223–256.

Lipkowitz, Noah E. 2019. Why Countries Diverge over Extradition Treaties with China: The Executive Power to Extradite in Common and Civil Law Countries. *Virginia Journal of International Law* 59: 440–501.

Lipstadt, Deborah E. 2005. *History on Trial: My Day in Court with David Irving*. New York: Ecco.

Liptak, Adam. 2008. Courts Outside U.S. Wary of Punitive Damages. *New York Times*, March 26.

Lowe, Nigel, and Victoria Stephens. 2017. A Statistical Analysis of Applications Made in 2015 Under the Hague Convention of 25 October 1980 on the Civil Aspects of International Child Abduction—Global Report. Available at https://www.hcch.net/en/publications-and-studies/details4/?pid=6598&dtid=32 (accessed February 23, 2022).

Lowenfeld, Andreas F. 1986. Some Reflections on Transnational Discovery. *Journal of Comparative Business and Capital Market Law* 8: 419–443.

Lowenfeld, Andreas F. 2002. International Litigation and Arbitration, 2nd ed. St. Paul, MN: West Group.

Lupu, Yonatan. 2013. Best Evidence: The Role of Information in Domestic Judicial Enforcement of International Human Rights Agreements. *International Organization* 67(3): 469–503.

Lupu, Yonatan. 2015. Legislative Veto Players and the Effects of International Human Rights Agreements. *American Journal of Political Science* 59(3): 578–594.

Lupu, Yonatan, Pierre-Hugues Verdier, and Mila Versteeg. 2019. The Strength of Weak Review: National Courts, Interpretive Canons, and Human Rights Treaties. *International Studies Quarterly* 63(3): 507–520.

Lutz, Robert E. 2007. *A Lawyer's Handbook for Enforcing Foreign Judgments in the United States and Abroad*. New York: Cambridge University Press.

Lyman, Robert Neale. 2006. Compulsory Process in a Globalized Era: Defendant Access to Mutual Legal Assistance Treaties. *Virginia Journal of International Law* 47: 261–293.

Madsen, Mikael Rask. 2016. The Challenging Authority of the European Court of Human Rights: From Cold War Legal Diplomacy to the Brighton Declaration and Backlash. *Law and Contemporary Problems* 79(1): 141–178.

Magnuson, William. 2012. The Domestic Politics of International Extradition. *Virginia Journal of International Law* 52(4): 839–901.

Maher, Shiraz. 2019. The Case of Shamima Begum Shows There are No Easy Choices for the West as Isis Collapses. *New Statesman*, February 2014.

Manicom, James, and Andrew O'Neil. 2012. China's Rise and Middle Power Democracies: Canada and Australia Compared. *International Relations of the Asia–Pacific* 12(2): 199–228.

Mansfield, Edward D., and Helen V. Milner. 2012. *Votes, Vetoes, and the Political Economy of International Trade Agreements*. Princeton, NJ: Princeton University Press.

Mansfield, Edward D., Helen V. Milner, and Jon Pevehouse. 2007. Vetoing Cooperation: The Impact of Veto Players on International Trade Agreements. *British Journal of Political Science* 37(3): 403–432.

Mansfield, Edward D., Helen V. Milner, and B. Peter Rosendorff. 2002. Why Democracies Cooperate More: Electoral Control and International Trade Agreements. *International Organization* 56(3): 477–513.

Mansfield, Edward D., and Diana C. Mutz. 2009. Support for Free Trade: Self-Interest, Sociotropic Politics, and Out-Group Anxiety. *International Organization* 63(3): 425–457.

Mansfield, Edward D., and Diana C. Mutz. 2013. US versus Them: Mass Attitudes toward Offshore Outsourcing. *World Politics* 65(4): 571–608.

Maoz, Zeev, and Errol A. Henderson. 2013. The World Religion Dataset, 1945–2010: Logic, Estimates, and Trends. *International Interactions* 39(3): 265–291.

Marchiori, Carmen, Simon Dietz, and Alessandro Tavoni. 2017. Domestic Politics and the Formation of International Environmental Agreements. *Journal of Environmental Economics and Management* 81: 115–131.

Margalit, Yotam. 2012. Lost in Globalization: International Economic Integration and the Sources of Popular Discontent. *International Studies Quarterly* 56(3): 484–500.

Markesinis, Basil, and Jörg Fedtke. 2006. *Judicial Recourse to Foreign Law: A New Source of Inspiration?* New York: Routledge.

Martin, Douglas. 2009. Khalid bin Mahfouz, Saudi Banker, Dies at 60. *New York Times*, August 27.

Martin, Lisa L. 2000. *Democratic Commitments: Legislatures and International Cooperation*. Princeton, NJ: Princeton University Press.

Mason, R. Chuck. 2012. Status of Forces Agreement (SOFA): What Is It, and How Has It Been Utilized? *Congressional Research Service*, March 15.

Mason, Rowena. 2019. Trump is Right, UK Must Take Back Isis Fighters—Ex-British Army Chief. *The Guardian*, February 17.

Mathias, Matthew D. 2013. The Sacralization of the Individual: Human Rights and the Abolition of the Death Penalty. *American Journal of Sociology* 118(5): 1246–1283.

Mattli, Walter. 2001. Private Justice in a Global Economy: From Litigation to Arbitration. *International Organization* 55(4): 919–947.

Mattli, Walter, and Thomas Dietz. 2014. *International Arbitration and Global Governance: Contending Theories and Evidence*. Oxford: Oxford University Press.

Mauther, Menachem. 2011. Three Approaches to Law and Culture. *Cornell Law Review* 96: 839–867.

Maxeiner, James R. 2011. *Failures of American Civil Justice in International Perspective*. New York: Cambridge University Press.

Mayda, Anna Maria. 2006. Who Is against Immigration? A Cross-country Investigation of Individual Attitudes toward Immigrants. *Review of Economics and Statistics* 88(3): 510–530.

Mayda, Anna Maria, and Dani Rodrik. 2005. Why Are Some People (and Countries) More Protectionist than Others? *European Economic Review* 49(6): 1393–1430.

McCaffrey, Stephen C., and Thomas O. Main. 2010. *Transnational Litigation in Comparative Perspective: Theory and Application*. New York: Oxford University Press.

McClean, David. 2012. *International Co-Operation in Civil and Criminal Matters*, 3rd ed. Oxford: Oxford University Press.

McCrudden, Christopher. 2018. CEDAW in National Courts: A Case Study in Operationalizing Comparative International Law Analysis in a Human Rights Context. In *Comparative International Law*, edited by Anthea Roberts, Paul B. Stephan, Pierre-Hugues Verdier, and Mila Versteeg, 459–500. New York: Oxford University Press.

McFarland, Sam, and Melissa Mathews. 2005. Who Cares about Human Rights? *Political Psychology* 26(3): 365–385.

McKenzie, John C. 1958. What is Truth? A Defense of the Jury System. *American Bar Association Journal* 44(1): 51–54, 76.

Meeusen, Cecil, Thomas de Vroome, and Marc Hooghe. 2013. How Does Education have an Impact on Ethnocentrism? A Structural Equation Analysis of Cognitive, Occupational Status and Network Mechanisms. *International Journal of Intercultural Relations* 37(5): 507–522.

Merryman, John Henry, and Rogelio Pérez-Perdomo. 2007. *The Civil Law Tradition: An Introduction to the Legal Systems of Europe and Latin America*, 3rd ed. Stanford, CA: Stanford: Stanford University Press.

Mezey, Naomi. 2001. Law as Culture. *Yale Journal of Law & the Humanities* 13: 35–67.

Michaels, Ralf. 2006. Two Paradigms of Jurisdiction. *Michigan Journal of International Law* 27: 1003–1069.

Michaels, Ralf. 2009. Recognition and Enforcement of Foreign Judgments. In *Max Planck Encyclopedia of Public International Law*, edited by Rüdiger Wolfrum. New York: Oxford University Press.

Michaels, Ralf. 2012. Code vs. Code: Nationalist and Internationalist Images of the Code Civil in the French Resistance to a European Codification. *European Review of Contract Law* 8: 277–295.

Miller, Jerome G. 1996. *Search and Destroy: African-American Males in the Criminal Justice System*. New York: Cambridge University Press.

Miller, Katherine R. 2004. Playground Politics: Assessing the Wisdom of Writing a Reciprocity Requirement into U.S. International Recognition and Enforcement Law. *Georgetown Journal of International Law* 35: 239–318.

Miller, Steven V. 2020. Economic Anxiety or Ethnocentrism? An Evaluation of Attitudes toward Immigration in the U.S. from 1992 to 2017. *Social Science Journal*. https://doi.org/10.1080/03623319.2020.1782638.

Milo, Dario. 2008. *Defamation and Freedom of Speech*. Oxford: Oxford University Press.

Minnich, Daniel J. 2005. Veto Players, Electoral Incentives and International Commitments: The Impact of Domestic Institutions on Intergovernmental Organization Membership. *European Journal of Political Research* 44(2): 295–325.

Minow, Martha. 2015. The Controversial Status of International and Comparative Law in the United States. In *Courts and Comparative Law*, edited by Mads Andenas and Duncan Fairgrieve, 513–551. Oxford: Oxford University Press.

Mirabella, Julia Grace. 2012. Scales of Justice: Assessing Italian Criminal Procedure through the Amanda Knox Trial. *Boston University International Law Journal* 30: 229–260.

Mitchell, Sara McLaughlin, and Emilia Justyna Powell. 2007. The International Court of Justice and the World's Three Legal Systems. *Journal of Politics* 69(2): 397–415.

Mitchell, Sara McLaughlin, and Emilia Justyna Powell. 2011. *Domestic Law Goes Global: Legal Traditions and International Courts*. Cambridge: Cambridge University Press.

Møller, Jørgen, and Svend-Erik Skaaning. 2012. Systematizing Thin and Thick Conceptions of the Rule of Law. *Justice System Journal* 33(2): 136–153.

Møller, Jørgen, and Svend-Erik Skaaning. 2014. *The Rule of Law: Definitions, Measures, Patterns and Causes*. London: Palgrave MacMillan.

Moore, Kimberly A. 2003. Xenophobia in American Courts. *Northwestern University Law Review* 97(4): 1497–1550.

Morrow, James D. 2007. When Do States Follow the Laws of War? *American Political Science Review* 101(3): 559–572.

Mudde, Cas. 1995. Right-wing Extremism Analyzed: A Comparative Analysis of the Ideologies of Three Alleged Right-wing Extremist Parties (NPD, NDP, CP'86). *European Journal of Political Research* 27(2): 203–224.

Mude, Torque. 2017. Demystifying the International Criminal Court (ICC) Target Africa Political Rhetoric. *Open Journal of Political Science* 7(1): 178–188.

Müller, Amrei. 2017. *Judicial Dialogue and Human Rights*. New York: Cambridge University Press.

Murdie, Amanda M., and David R. Davis. 2012. Shaming and Blaming: Using Events Data to Assess the Impact of Human Rights INGOs. *International Studies Quarterly* 56(1): 1–16.

Murphy, Hannah. 2010. *The Making of International Trade Policy: NGOs, Agenda-setting and the WTO*. Cheltenham, UK: Edward Elgar.

Murphy, Katherine. 2017a. Government Withdraws China Extradition Treaty after Party Revolt. *The Guardian*, March 27.

Murphy, Katherine. 2017b. Australia "Committed to" China Extradition Treaty, but Opposition Has Heard Nothing. *The Guardian*, April 24.

Murray, Craig, Kary Parry, Piers Robinson, and Peter Goddard. 2008. Reporting Dissent in Wartime: British Press, the Anti-War Movement, and the 2003 Iraq War. *European Journal of Communication* 23(1): 7–27.

Mutz, Diana C., and Eunji Kim. 2017. The Impact of In-group Favoritism on Trade Preferences. *International Organization* 71(4): 827–850.

Nadelmann, Ethan A. 1993. *Cops across Borders: The Internationalization of U.S. Criminal Law Enforcement*. University Park: Penn State Press.

Neuberg, Steven L., and Jason T. Newsom. 1993. Personal Need for Structure: Individual Differences in the Desire for Simpler Structure. *Journal of Personality and Social Psychology* 65(1): 113–131.

New York Times Editorial. 2010. A Victory for Writing. *New York Times*, July 22.

New York Times Editorial. 2011. Libel Tourism, R.I.P.? *New York Times*, March 22.

Nielsen, Richard A., and Beth A. Simmons. 2015. Rewards for Ratification: Payoffs for Participating in the International Human Rights Regime? *International Studies Quarterly* 59(2): 197–208.

Nomi, Yoshihisa. 2006. The CISG from the Asian Perspective. In *Celebrating Success: 25 Years United Nations Convention on Contracts for the International Sale of Goods*, 169–177. Singapore: Singapore International Arbitration Center.

Nossiter, Adam, Aurelien Breeden, and Katrin Bennhold. 2015. Three Teams of Coordinated Attackers Carried Out Assault on Paris, Officials Say; Hollande Blames ISIS. *New York Times*, November 14.

Novak, Andrew. 2020. *Transnational Human Rights Litigation: Challenging the Death Penalty and Criminalization of Homosexuality in the Commonwealth*. Cham, Switzerland: Springer.

OECD. 2019. *Education at a Glance 2019: OECD Indicators*. Paris: OECD Publishing. https://doi.org/10.1787/f8d7880d-en.

Ogletree, Charles J., and Austin Sarat, eds. 2012. *Life without Parole: America's New Death Penalty?* New York: NYU Press.

Onishi, Norimitsu, and Elian Peltier. 2019. Turkey's Deportations Force Europe to Face Its ISIS Militants. *New York Times*, November 17.

O'Reilly Ciaran. 2008. Primetime Patriotism: News Media and the Securitization of Iraq. *Journal of Politics and Law* 1(3): 66–72.

Ortega, Francesc, and Javier G. Polavieja. 2012. Labor-market Exposure as a Determinant of Attitudes toward Immigration. *Labour Economics* 19(3): 298–311.

Otis, John. 1993. After Months of Cajoling and Arm-twisting by the United . . . . *UPI*, December 6.

Owen, David G. 1994. A Punitive Damages Overview: Functions, Problems and Reform. *Villanova Law Review* 39(3): 363–413.

Patel, Faiza, Matthew Duss, and Amos Toh. 2013. Foreign Law Bans: Legal Uncertainties and Practical Problems. Center for American Progress and Brennan Center for Justice. May.

Patterson, Malcolm. 2017. The Folly of an Australian-China Extradition Treaty. *Sydney Morning Herald*, January 5.

Pearson, Allison. 2012. Gary McKinnon: A Harmless Oddball's Triumph over Torment. *Daily Telegraph*, October 17.

Peltier, Elian. 2020. U.S. Refuses Extradition in Fatal Crash, Prompting Anger in U.K. *New York Times*, January 24.

Pérez-Vera, Elisa. 1981. Explanatory Report on the 1980 Hague Child Abduction Convention. Hague Conference on Private International Law. Available at http://www.hcch.net/index_en.php?act=publications.details&pid=2779 (accessed February 23, 2022).

Peters, Margaret E. 2019. Immigration and International Law. *International Studies Quarterly* 63(2): 281–295.

Peterson, Timothy M., Amanda Murdie, and Victor Asal. 2018. Human Rights, NGO Shaming and the Exports of Abusive States. *British Journal of Political Science* 48(3): 767–786.

Pfanner, Eric. 2012. Britain to Seek Curbs to "Libel Tourism." *New York Times*, May 9.

Pfund, Peter H. 1998. The Project of the Hague Conference on Private International Law to Prepare a Convention on Jurisdiction and the Recognition/Enforcement of Judgments in Civil and Commercial Matters. *Brooklyn Journal of International Law* 24: 7–15.

Pimentel, David, and Brian Anderson. 2013. Judicial Independence in Postconflict Iraq: Establishing the Rule of Law in an Islamic Constitutional Democracy. *George Washington International Law Review* 46: 29–54.

Plachta, Michael. 1999. (Non-)extradition of Nationals: A Neverending Story? *Emory International Law Review* 13: 77–159.

Plachta, Michael. 2003. European Arrest Warrant: Revolution in Extradition? *European Journal of Crime, Criminal Law and Criminal Justice* 11(2): 178–194.

Pletcher, David M. 2003. The United States and Extraterritoriality. *Diplomatic History* 27(3): 405–407.

Ploscowe, Morris. 1945. Jury Trial in France. *Minnesota Law Review* 29: 376–387.

Plosser, W. McDonald. 2018. United States: Sky's The Limit? A 50-State Survey of Damages Caps and the Collateral Source Rule. December 11. Available at http://www.mondaq.com/unitedstates/x/762574/Insurance/Skys+The+Limit+A+50State+Survey+Of+Damages+Caps+And+The+Collateral+Source+Rule (accessed February 23, 2022).

Posch, Willibald. 2004. Resolving Business Disputes through Litigation or Other Alternatives: The Effects of Jurisdictional Rules and Recognition Practice. *Houston Journal of International Law* 26: 363–383.

Posen, Barry R. 2003. Command of the Commons: The Military Foundation of U.S. Hegemony. *International Security* 28(1): 5–46.

Posner, Eric A. 2013. Human Rights, the Laws of War, and Reciprocity. *Law & Ethics of Human Rights* 6(2): 147–171.

Posner, Eric A. 2014. *The Twilight of Human Rights Law*. New York: Oxford University Press.

Powell, Emilia Justyna. 2010. Negotiating Military Alliances: Legal Systems and Alliance Formation. *International Interactions* 36(1): 28–59.

Powell, Emilia Justyna. 2015. Islamic Law States and Peaceful Resolution of Territorial Disputes. *International Organization* 69(4): 777–807.

Powell, Emilia Justyna. 2020. *International Law and Islamic Law: Peaceful Resolution of Disputes*. New York: Oxford University Press.

Powell, Emilia Justyna, and Jeffrey K. Staton. 2009. Domestic Judicial Institutions and Human Rights Treaty Violation. *International Studies Quarterly* 53(1): 149–174.

Prince, Rosa. 2009. Hundreds of Britons will be Extradited for Minor Crimes under New Rules. *The Telegraph*, August 17.

Putnam, Tonya L. 2009. Courts without Borders: Domestic Sources of U.S. Extraterritoriality in the Regulatory Sphere. *International Organization* 63(3): 459–490.

Putnam, Tonya L. 2016. *Courts without Borders: Law, Politics, and U.S. Extraterritoriality*. New York: Cambridge University Press.

Pyle, Christopher H. 2001. *Extradition, Politics, and Human Rights*. Philadelphia, PA: Temple University Press, 2001.

Quarta, Francesco. 2008. Recognition and Enforcement of U.S. Punitive Damages Awards in Continental Europe: The Italian Supreme Court's Veto. *Hastings International & Comparative Law Review* 31: 753–782.

Quffa, Wedad Andrada. 2016. A Review of the History of Gender Equality in The United States of America. *Social Sciences and Education Research Review* 3(2): 143–149.

Quintanilla, Marcus S., and Christopher A. Whytock. 2012. The New Multipolarity in Transnational Litigation: Foreign Courts, Foreign Judgments, and Foreign Law. *Southwestern Journal of International Law* 18: 31–49.

Quintard-Morénas, François. 2010. The Presumption of Innocence in the French and Anglo-American Legal Traditions. *American Journal of Comparative Law* 58: 107–149.

Raday, Frances. 2019. Gender Equality and Women's Rights in the Context of Child Custody and Child Maintenance: An International and Comparative Analysis. UN Women Discussion Paper No. 30. July.

Rakoff, Jed S. 2014. Why Innocent People Plead Guilty. *The New York Review of Books*, November 20.

Ramzy, Austin. 2020. Australia Halts Hong Kong Extradition Agreement and Extends Visas. *New York Times*, July 9.

Ramzy, Austin, and Elaine Yu. 2019. Hong Kong's Leader, Carrie Lam, to Withdraw Extradition Bill That Ignited Protests. *New York Times*, September 4.

Raustiala, Kal. 2002. The Architecture of International Cooperation: Transgovernmental Networks and the Future of International Law. *Virginia Journal of International Law* 43: 1–92.

Raustiala, Kal. 2009. *Does the Constitution Follow the Flag? The Evolution of Territoriality in American Law*. New York: Oxford University Press.

Reuters. 1994. Panama Official to Press U.S. on Drug Treaty. *Reuters News*, March 22.

Rho, Sungmin, and Michael Tomz. 2017. Why Don't Trade Preferences Reflect Economic Self-Interest? *International Organization* 71(S1): S85–S108.

Rhodes, Carolyn. 1989. Reciprocity in Trade: The Utility of a Bargaining Strategy. *International Organization* 43(2): 273–299.

Riordan, Primrose. 2017. Chongyi Feng: Extradition Treaty with China Would be a Fatal Mistake. *The Australian*, April 3.

Ríos-Figueroa, Julio, and Jeffrey K. Staton. 2014. An Evaluation of Cross-National Measures of Judicial Independence. *Journal of Law, Economics, and Organization* 30(1): 104–137.

Rivkin, David B. Jr., and Bruce D. Brown. 2009. "Libel Tourism" Threatens Free Speech. *Wall Street Journal*, January 10.

Roberts, Anthea, Paul B. Stephan, Pierre-Hugues Verdier, and Mila Versteeg. 2018. Conceptualizing Comparative International Law. In *Comparative International Law*, edited by Anthea Roberts,

Paul B. Stephan, Pierre-Hugues Verdier, and Mila Versteeg, 3–31. New York: Oxford University Press.

Roberts, Jeff John. 2016. Privacy Laws Pose New Threat to Free Speech. *Fortune*, January 19.

Rogers, Katie, and Apoorva Mandavilli. 2020. Trump Administration Signals Formal Withdrawal from W.H.O. *New York Times*, July 7.

Rosas, Allan. 2007. The European Court of Justice in Context: Forms and Patterns of Judicial Dialogue. *European Journal of Legal Studies* 1(2): 121–136.

Rose, Thomas. 2002. A Delicate Balance: Extradition, Sovereignty, and Individual Rights in the United States and Canada. *Yale Journal of International Law* 27: 193–215.

Rose-Ackerman, Susan. 2007. Judicial Independence and Corruption. In *Global Corruption Report 2007: Corruption in Judicial Systems*, edited by Transparency International, 15–24. New York: Cambridge University Press.

Rosen, Mark D. 2012. The SPEECH Act's Unfortunate Parochialism: Of Libel Tourism and Legitimate Pluralism. *Virginia Journal of International Law* 53: 99–126.

Rosenberg, Gerald N. 2008. *The Hollow Hope: Can Courts Bring about Social Change?*, 2nd ed. Chicago: University of Chicago Press.

Rosenblatt, Paul C. 1964. Origins and Effects of Group Ethnocentrism and Nationalism. *Journal of Conflict Resolution* 8(2): 131–146.

Rosendorff, Peter B., and Helen V. Milner. 2001. The Optimal Design of International Trade Institutions: Uncertainty and Escape. *International Organization* 55(4): 829–857.

Rouhette, Thomas, and Ela Barda. 2017. The French Blocking Statute and Cross-Border Discovery. *Defense Counsel Journal* 84(3): 1–19.

Rozenberg, Joshua. 2012. Gary McKinnon: Theresa May Had No Choice but to Use Human Rights Grounds. *The Guardian*, October 16.

Rubin, Alissa J. 2019a. France Hands ISIS Suspects to Iraq, Which Sentences Them to Hang. *New York Times*, May 29.

Rubin, Alissa J. 2019b. French ISIS Supporters on Death Row in Iraq Ask for Mercy. *New York Times*, June 3.

Rubin, Alissa J., Aurelien Breeden, and Anita Raghavan. 2016. Strikes Claimed by ISIS Shut Brussels and Shake European Security. *New York Times*, March 22.

Russell, Andrew. 2016. Canada-China Extradition Treaty: Here's What You Need to Know. *Global News*, September 21. Available at https://globalnews.ca/news/2953881/canada–china–extradition–treaty–heres–what–you–need–to–know (accessed February 23, 2022).

Ryngaert, Cedric. 2015. *Jurisdiction in International Law*, 2nd ed. Oxford: Oxford University Press.

Sabbagh, Dan. 2019. Thirty Britons Believed to be among Isis Fighters Held in Syria. *The Guardian*, December 6.

Sabbagh, Dan. 2020. Syrian Kurds to Put Isis Fighters from Dozens of Countries on Trial. *The Guardian*, February 6.

Sadoff, David A. 2016. *Bringing International Fugitives to Justice: Extradition and Its Alternatives*. New York: Cambridge University Press.

Sampei, Yuki, and Midori Aoyagi-Usui. 2009. Mass–media Coverage, Its Influence on Public Awareness of Climate-Change Issues, and Implications for Japan's National Campaign to Reduce Greenhouse Gas Emissions. *Global Environmental Change* 19(2): 203–212.

Sandholtz, Wayne, Yining Bei, and Kayla Caldwell. 2018. Backlash and International Human Rights Courts. In *Contracting Human Rights: Crisis, Accountability, and Opportunity*, edited by Alyson Brysk and Michal Stohl, 159–178. Cheltenham: Edward Elgar.

Santora, Marc. 2019. Poland Bashes Immigrants, but Quietly Takes Christian Ones. *New York Times*, March 26.

Sarat, Austin, and Thomas R. Kearns. 1998. The Cultural Lives of Law. In *Law in the Domains of Culture*, edited by Austin Sarat and Thomas R. Kearns, 1–20. Ann Arbor: University of Michigan Press.

Satariano, Adam. 2019. Google is Fined $57 Million Under Europe's Data Privacy Law. *New York Times*, January 21.

Savage, Charlie. 2020. British Give U.S. Evidence Against ISIS "Beatles," Clearing Way for Trial. *New York Times*, September 22.

Savage, Charlie, and Adam Goldman. 2019. British Officials Worried About Angering Trump over ISIS Captives. *New York Times*, January 18.

Savage, Charlie, and Adam Goldman. 2020. Citing Death Penalty, U.K. Court Blocks Giving Evidence on ISIS "Beatles" to U.S. *New York Times*, March 25.

Savitsky, Douglas. 2012. Is Plea Bargaining a Rational Choice? Plea Bargaining as an Engine of Racial Stratification and Overcrowding in the United States Prison System. *Rationality and Society* 24(2): 131–167.

Scalia, Antonin, and Stephen Breyer. 2005. A Conversation between U.S. Supreme Court Justices. *International Journal of Constitutional Law* 3: 519–525.

Scheve, Kenneth F., and Matthew J. Slaughter. 2001a. Labor Market Competition and Individual Preferences over Immigration Policy. *Review of Economics and Statistics* 83(1): 133–145.

Scheve, Kenneth F., and Matthew J. Slaughter. 2001b. What Determines Individual Trade-Policy Preferences? *Journal of International Economics* 54(2): 267–292.

Schleutker, Elina. 2019. Discrimination against Religious Minorities. *Journal of Church and State* 61(2): 282–307.

Schmidt, Sebastian. 2014. Foreign Military Presence and the Changing Practice of Sovereignty: A Pragmatist Explanation of Norm Change. *American Political Science Review* 108(4): 817–829.

Schnitzer-Reese, Ericka A. 2004. International Child Abduction to non-Hague Convention Countries: The Need for an International Family Court. *Northwestern Journal of International Human Rights* 2(1): 2–19.

Schraer, Rachel. 2018. Does the Treason Act Need Updating? *BBC News*, July 25.

Schuz, Rhona. 2013. *The Hague Child Abduction Convention: A Critical Analysis*. Oxford: Hart.

Seamark, Michael, James Slack, and Rebecca Evans. 2012. Gary McKinnon "Tearful with Joy" after Top Prosecutor Confirms the Computer Hacker will Face No Further Criminal Action. *Daily Mail*, December 14.

Sedler, Robert A. 2006. An Essay on Freedom of Speech: The United States versus the Rest of the World. *Michigan State Law Review* 2006: 377–384.

Seidman, Ann, and Robert B. Seidman. 2006. Law in Aid of Development: Hasty Legal Transplants and the Fatal Race. *Journal of Comparative Law* 1: 282–320.

Seipp, David J. 2006. Our Law, Their Law, History, and the Citation of Foreign Law. *Boston University Law Review* 86: 1417–1446.

Select Committee on Extradition Law. House of Lords. 2015a. *Extradition: UK Law and Practice*. HL Paper 126. March 10. London: The Stationary Office.

Select Committee on Extradition Law. House of Lords. 2015b. Oral and Written Evidence.

Shaffer, Gregory. 2013. Transnational Legal Ordering and State Change. In *Transnational Legal Ordering and State Change*, edited by Gregory Shaffer, 1–22. New York: Cambridge University Press.

Shearer, Ivan Anthony. 1971. *Extradition in International Law*. Manchester: Manchester University Press.

Sherif, Muzafer. 1966. *In Common Predicament: Social Psychology of Intergroup Conflict and Cooperation*. Boston: Houghton Mifflin.

Shimp, Terence A., and Subhash Sharma. 1987. Consumer Ethnocentrism: Construction and Validation of the CETSCALE. *Journal of Marketing Research* 24(3): 280–289.

Sieff, Kevin, Arelis R. Hernández, and Gabriela Martinez. 2019. In Ecuador, Assange's Expulsion Reflects Desire for Better Relations with the U.S. *Washington Post*, April 12.

Sikkink, Kathryn. 2011. *The Justice Cascade: How Human Rights Prosecutions Are Changing World Politics*. New York: W.W. Norton.

Sil, Rudra, and Peter J. Katzenstein. 2010. Analytic Eclecticism in the Study of World Politics: Reconfiguring Problems and Mechanisms across Research Traditions. *Perspectives on Politics* 8(2): 411–431.

Silberman, Linda. 2000. Hague Child Abduction Convention Turns Twenty: Gender Politics and Other Issues. *New York University Journal of International Law and Politics* 33: 221–250.

Silberman, Linda. 2002. Comparative Jurisdiction in the International Context: Will the Proposed Hague Judgements Convention be Stalled? *DePaul Law Review* 52: 319–350.

Silbey, Susan S. 1992. Making a Place for Cultural Analyses of Law. *Law & Social Inquiry* 17(1): 39–48.

Simmons, Alan J. 2017. Domestic Attitudes towards International Jurisdiction over Human Rights Violations. *Human Rights Review* 18(3): 321–345.

Simmons, Beth A. 2009. *Mobilizing for Human Rights: International Law in Domestic Politics.* New York: Cambridge University Press.

Simmons, Beth A., Paulette Lloyd, and Brandon M. Stewart. 2018. The Global Diffusion of Law: Transnational Crime and the Case of Human Trafficking. *International organization* 72(2): 249–281.

Singleton, Solveig. 1999. Privacy and Human Rights: Comparing the United States to Europe. CATO Institute. Available at https://www.cato.org/white-paper/privacy-human-rights-comparing-united-states-europe (accessed February 23, 2022).

Sissons, Miranda, and Ari S. Bassin. 2007. Was the *Dujail* Trial Fair? *Journal of International Criminal Justice* 5(2): 272–286.

Siverson, Randolph M., and Juliann Emmons. 1991. Birds of a Feather: Democratic Political Systems and Alliance Choices in the Twentieth Century. *Journal of Conflict Resolution* 35(2): 285–306.

Slack, James, and Michael Seamark. 2009. Twice as Many Suspects are Extradited to U.S. (Is That fair to Gary McKinnon?). *Daily Mail,* December 10.

Slaughter, Anne-Marie. 2000. Judicial Globalization. *Virginia Journal of International Law* 40: 1103–1124.

Smith, Matthew. 2020. Two Thirds of Americans Support Anne Sacoolas Extradition. January 28. Available at https://yougov.co.uk/topics/politics/articles-reports/2020/01/28/two-thirds-americans-support-anne-sacoolas-extradi (accessed February 23, 2022).

Smyth, Jamie. 2016. Australia Poised to Sign Extradition Treaty with China. *Financial Times,* December 22.

Sniderman, Paul M., Pierangelo Peri, Thomas Piazza, and Daniele Albertazzi. 2000. *The Outsider: Prejudice and Politics in Italy.* Princeton, NJ: Princeton University Press.

Snyder, Jack. 2019. The Broken Bargain: How Nationalism Came Back. *Foreign Affairs* 98(2): 54–60.

Soley, Ximena, and Silvia Steininger. 2018. Parting Ways or Lashing Back? Withdrawals, Backlash and the Inter-American Court of Human Rights. *International Journal of Law in Context* 14(2): 237–257.

Specter, Arlen, and Joe Lieberman. 2008. Foreign Courts Take Aim at Our Free Speech. *Wall Street Journal,* July 14.

Spencer, Richard. 2019. UK Resists Attempts to Return Isis Fighters. *The Times,* November 16.

Sperti, Angioletta. 2013. United States of America: First Cautious Attempts of Judicial Use of Foreign Precedents in the Supreme Court's Jurisprudence. In *The Use of Foreign Precedents by Constitutional Judges,* edited by Tania Groppi and Marie-Claire Ponthoreau, 393–410. Oxford: Hart Publishing.

Spilman, Sarah K. 2006. Child Abduction, Parents' Distress, and Social Support. *Violence and Victims* 21(2): 149–165.

Spohn, Cassia. 2015. Race, Crime, and Punishment in the Twentieth and Twenty-first Centuries. *Crime and Justice* 44(1): 49–97.

Ssenyonjo, Manisuli. 2018. State Withdrawal Notifications from the Rome Statute of the International Criminal Court: South Africa, Burundi and the Gambia. *Criminal Law Forum* 29(1): 63–119.

Staveley-O'Carroll, Sarah. 2009. Libel Tourism Laws: Spoiling the Holiday and Saving the First Amendment? *NYU Journal of Law & Liberty* 4: 252–292.

Stenner, Karen. 2005. *The Authoritarian Dynamic*. New York: Cambridge University Press.

Stephan, Paul B. 2009. Symmetry and Selectivity: What Happens in International Law When the World Changes. *Chicago Journal of International Law* 10: 91–123.

Stephan, Walter G., and Cookie White Stephan. 1984. The Role of Ignorance in Intergroup Relations. In *Groups in Contact: The Psychology of Desegregation*, edited by Norman Miller and Marilynn. B. Brewer, 229–255. Orlando, FL: Academic Press.

Stephen, Krasner. 1999. *Sovereignty: Organized Hypocrisy*. Princeton, NJ: Princeton University Press.

Stephens, Hugh. 2016. Why an Extradition Treaty with China is a Good Idea. October 12. Available at https://www.asiapacific.ca/op-eds/why-extradition-treaty-china-good-idea (accessed February 23, 2022).

Stolzenberg, Lisa, Stewart J. D'Alessio, and David Eitle. 2013. Race and Cumulative Discrimination in the Prosecution of Criminal Defendants. *Race and Justice* 3(4): 275–299.

Stone, Timothy D. 2006. U.S.-Japan SOFA: A Necessary Document Worth Preserving. *Naval Law Review* 53: 229–258.

Storrs, Larry K. 2003. Drug Certification/Designation Procedures for Illicit Narcotics Producing and Transit Countries. Congressional Research Service Report. September 22.

Streitfeld, David, and Kevin J. O'Brien. 2012. Google Privacy Inquiries Get Little Cooperation. *New York Times*, May 22.

Stuntz, William J. 2011. *The Collapse of American Criminal Justice*. Cambridge, MA: Harvard University Press.

Stürner, Rolf. 2001. *Why are Europeans Afraid to Litigate in the United States?* Roma: Centro di studi e ricerche di diritto comparato e straniero.

Subrin, Stephen N. 2009. Discovery in Global Perspective: Are We Nuts? *DePaul Law Review* 52: 299–318.

Sumner, William Graham. [1906] 2008. *Folkways: A Study of the Sociological Importance of Usages, Manners, Customs, Mores, and Morals*. A Project Gutenberg eBook.

Swanson, Ana. 2019. Trump Cripples the W.T.O. as Trade War Rages. *New York Times*, December 8.

Tajfel, Henri, and John C. Turner. 1979. An Integrative Theory of Intergroup Conflict. In *The Social Psychology of Intergroup Relations*, edited by William G. Austin and Stephen Worchel, 33–47. Monterey, CA: Brooks/Cole.

Tajfel, Henri, and John C. Turner. 1986. The Social Identity Theory of Intergroup Behavior. In *Psychology of Intergroup Relations*, edited by William G. Austin and Stephen Worchel, 7–24. Chicago: Nelson-Hall.

Tamanaha, Brian Z. 2004. *On the Rule of Law: History, Politics, Theory*. New York: Cambridge University Press.

Tankard, Margaret E., and Elizabeth Levy Paluck. 2017. The Effect of a Supreme Court Decision Regarding Gay Marriage on Social Norms and Personal Attitudes. *Psychological Science* 28(9): 1334–1344.

Tayler, Letta. 2016. Foreign Terrorist Fighter Laws: Human Rights Rollbacks under UN Security Council Resolution 2178. *International Community Law Review* 18: 455–482.

Taylor, Daniel C. 2010. Libel Tourism: Protecting Authors and Preserving Comity. *Georgetown Law Journal* 99: 189–226.

Taylor, Stuart. 2008. Outside the Outsiders: Media Representations of Drug Use. *Probation Journal* 55(4): 369–387.

Teehankee, Julio C. 2016. Duterte's Resurgent Nationalism in the Philippines: A Discursive Institutionalist Analysis. *Journal of Current Southeast Asian Affairs* 35(3): 69–89.

Teitz, Louise Ellen. 1996. *Transnational Litigation*. Charlottesville, VA: Michie.

Teitz, Louise Ellen. 2019. Another Hague Judgments Convention? Bucking the Past to Provide for the Future. *Duke Journal of Comparative & International Law* 29: 491–511.

Thaler, Richard. 1980. Toward a Positive Theory of Consumer Choice. *Journal of Economic Behavior & Organization* 1(1): 39–60.

Thayer, Carlyle A. 2011. China's Rise and the Passing of U.S. Primacy: Australia Debates Its Future. *Asia Policy* 12: 20–26.

The Association of the Bar of the City of New York. 2001. Survey on Foreign Recognition of U.S. Money Judgments. *The Record* 56(3): 380–410.

The Economist. 2009. Writ Large: Are English Courts Stifling Free Speech Around the World? *The Economist*, January 8.

The Star Editorial. 2016. Extradition Treaty with China is a Dangerous Proposition. *The Star*, September 22.

The Times. 2018. Lawyers Slam Sajid Javid over ISIS "Beatles" Extradition Plan. *The Times*, July 23.

The Times. 2019. The Times View on British Citizens Held in Syria: Bring Them Back. *The Times*, October 1.

Toft, Monica Duffy. 2014. Territory and War. 2014. *Journal of Peace Research* 51(2): 185–198.

Tonry, Michael H. 2011. *Punishing Race: A Continuing American Dilemma*. New York: Oxford University Press.

Toobin, Jeffrey. 2008. *The Nine: Inside the Secret World of the Supreme Court*. New York: Anchor Books.

Tow, William T., and H. D. P. Envall. 2015. Australia Debates American Primacy in Asia. In *United States Engagement in the Asia Pacific: Perspectives from Asia*, edited by Yoichiro Sato and See Seng Tan, 297–323. Amherst, NY: Cambria Press.

Tremonti, Anna Maria. 2016. *The Current*. September 22. Transcript available at https://www.cbc.ca/radio/thecurrent/the-current-for-september-22-2016-1.3773673/september-22-2016-full-episode-transcript-1.3774619#segment1 (accessed July 27, 2022).

Trevaskes, Susan. 2012. *The Death Penalty in Contemporary China*. New York: Palgrave MacMillan.

Turner, John C. 1981. The Experimental Social Psychology of Intergroup Behaviour. In *Intergroup Behaviour*, edited by John C. Turner and Howard Giles, 66–101. Oxford: Basil Blackwell.

Turner, John C., Michael A. Hogg, Penelope J. Oakes, Stephen D. Reicher, and Margaret S. Wetherell. 1987. *Rediscovering the Social Group: A Self-categorization Theory*. Oxford: Basil Blackwell.

Tuval, Yogev. 2008. Anti-Terrorism Legislation in Britain and the U.S. after 9/11. The Israel Democracy Institute. September 10. Available at https://en.idi.org.il/articles/6936 (accessed February 23, 2022).

Twitchell, Mary. 2001. Why We Keep Doing Business with Doing-Business Jurisdiction. *University of Chicago Legal Forum* 2001: 171–214.

Ugelvik, Thomas. 2017. The Incarceration of Foreigners in European Prisons. In *The Routledge Handbook on Crime and International Migration*, edited by Sharon Pickering and Julie Ham, 137–150. New York: Routledge.

UNAMI (United Nations Assistance Mission for Iraq) and OHCHR (Office of the United Nations High Commissioner for Human Rights). 2020. Human Rights in the Administration of Justice in Iraq: Trials under the Anti-terrorism Laws and Implications for Justice, Accountability and Social Cohesion in the Afterman of ISIL. January. Baghdad.

UNDP and UNODC. 2016. International Cooperation: The Pacific's Implementation of Chapter IV of the UN Convention against Corruption. Available at https://www.unodc.org/documents/corruption/Publications/2016/Pacifics_Implementation_of_UNCAC_Chapter_IV.pdf (accessed February 23, 2022).

U.S. Department of State. 2019. Annual Report on International Child Abduction. April. Available at https://travel.state.gov/content/dam/NEWIPCAAssets/pdfs/2019%20Report.pdf (accessed February 23, 2022).

Usherwood, Simon, and Nick Startin. 2013. Euroscepticism as a Persistent Phenomenon. *Journal of Common Market Studies* 51(1): 1–16.

U.S. House of Representatives. 1955. Hearings before the Committee on Foreign Affairs on H. J. Res. 309 and Similar Measures Providing for the Revision of the Status of Forces Agreement. Part 1. 84th Cong, 1st sess. July 13, 14, 19, 20, 21, and 26.

U.S. House of Representatives. 1957. Report of the Committee on Foreign Affairs on H. J. Res. 16 Providing for the Revision of the Status of Forces Agreement. House Report No. 678. 85th Cong., 1st sess. July 1.

U.S. House of Representatives. 2000. Internet and Federal Courts: Issues and Obstacles. Hearing before the Subcommittee on Courts and Intellectual Property of the Committee on the Judiciary. 106th Cong., 2nd sess. June 29.

U.S. House of Representatives. Committee on the Judiciary. 2009a. Recognition of Foreign Defamation Judgments. Report 111–154 [To accompany H.R. 2765]. 111th Cong., 1st sess. June 15.

U.S. House of Representatives. 2009b. Libel Tourism. Hearing before the Subcommittee on Commercial and Administrative Law of the Committee on the Judiciary. 111th Cong., 1st sess. February 12.

U.S. President. 1952. Message from the President of the United States Transmitting a Certified Copy of an Agreement between the Parties to the North Atlantic Treaty Regarding the Status of Their Forces, Signed at London on June 19, 1951. 82nd Cong., 2nd sess. June 16.

U.S. Senate. 1953a. Hearings before the Committee on Foreign Relations on Status of the North Atlantic Treaty Organization, Armed Forces, and Military Headquarters. 83rd Cong., 1st sess. April 7–8.

U.S. Senate. Committee on Foreign Relations. 1953b. Agreements Relating to the Status of the North Atlantic Treaty Organization, Armed Forces, and Military Headquarters. Executive Report No. 1. 83rd Cong., 1st sess. April 28.

U.S. Senate. 1953c. Supplementary Hearing before the Committee on Foreign Relations on Status of Forces of the North Atlantic Treaty. 83rd Cong., 1st sess. June 24.

U.S. Senate. 1953d. Hearing Held before the Committee on Foreign Relations on Agreement Regarding Status of Forces of Parties of the North Atlantic Treaty. Executive Session. July 2.

U.S. Senate. 1955a. Operation of Article VII, NATO Status of Forces Treaty: Report of the Committee on Armed Services. 84th Cong., 1st sess. July 29.

U.S. Senate. 1955b. Operation of Article VII, NATO Status of Forces Treaty: Hearings before a Subcommittee of the Committee on Armed Services, 84th Cong. March 29, 31, and June 21.

U.S. Senate. 1958. Operation of Article VII, NATO Status of Forces Treaty: Report of the Committee on Armed Services, Made by Its Subcommittee on the Operation of Article VII of the NATO Status of Forces Agreement. 85th Cong., 2nd sess. August 23.

U.S. Senate. 1968. Operation of Article VII, NATO Status of Forces Treaty: Report of the Committee on Armed Services, Made by Its Subcommittee on the Operation of Article VII of the NATO Status of Forces Agreement. 90th Cong., 2nd sess. October 9.

U.S. Senate. 1989. Hearing on Mutual Legal Assistance before the U.S. Senate Subcommittee on Terrorism, Narcotics and International Operations. April 18. Transcript available with the author.

U.S. Senate. 1994. Recent Developments in Transnational Crime Affecting US Law Enforcement and Foreign Policy; Mutual Legal Assistance Treaty in Criminal Matters with Panama, Treaty Doc. 102–15; And 1994 International Narcotics Control Strategy Report. Hearings before the Subcommittee on Terrorism, Narcotics, and International Operations of the Committee on Foreign Relations. 103rd Cong., 2nd sess. April 20 and 21.

U.S. Senate. Committee on Foreign Relations. 2002. Mutual Legal Assistance Treaties with Belize, India, Ireland, and Liechtenstein. Exec. Rpt. 107–115. 107th Cong., 2nd sess. October 17.

U.S. Senate. Committee on the Judiciary. 2010a. Securing the Protection of Our Enduring and Established Constitutional Heritage ("SPEECH") Act. Report 111–224 [To accompany H.R. 2765]. 111th Cong., 2nd sess. July 19.

U.S. Senate. 2010b. Are Foreign Libel Lawsuits Chilling Americans' First Amendment Rights? Hearing before the Committee on the Judiciary. 111th Cong., 2nd sess. February 23.

Valentino, Nicholas A., Ted Brader, and Ashley E. Jardina. 2013. Immigration Opposition among U.S. Whites: Ethnocentrism or Media Priming of Attitudes about Latinos? *Political Psychology* 34(2): 149–166.

Vanderklippe, Nathan. 2016. China's Fox Hunt in Canada Strains Trust that an Extradition Treaty is Possible. *Globe and Mail*, September 23.

Vanderklippe, Nathan. 2017. McCallum: Canada "a Long, Long" Way from China Extradition Deal. *Globe and Mail*, April 3.

van Loon, Hans. 2019. Towards a Global Hague Convention on the Recognition and Enforcement of Judgments in Civil or Commercial Matters. Collection of Papers, Faculty of Niš no. 82: 15–36.

Vedder Price. n.d. Long-Arm Statutes: A Fifty-State Survey. Available at http://euro.ecom.cmu.edu/program/law/08-732/Jurisdiction/LongArmSurvey.pdf (accessed February 23, 2022).

Verdier, Pierre-Hugues, and Mila Versteeg. 2015. International Law in National Legal Systems: An Empirical Investigation. *American Journal of International Law* 109(3): 514–533.

Verdier, Pierre-Hugues, and Erik Voeten. 2015. How Does Customary International Law Change? The Case of State Immunity. *International Studies Quarterly* 59(2): 209–222.

Verlegh, Peeter W. J. 2007. Home Country Bias in Product Evaluation: The Complementary Roles of Economic and Socio-Psychological Motives. *Journal of International Business Studies* 38(3): 361–373.

Versteeg, Mila, and Tom Ginsburg. 2017. Measuring the Rule of Law: A Comparison of Indicators. *Law & Social Inquiry* 42(1): 100–137.

Voetelink, Joop. 2015. *Status of Forces: Criminal Jurisdiction over Military Personnel Abroad*. The Hague: Asser Press.

Voeten, Erik. 2020. Populism and Backlashes against International Courts. *Perspectives on Politics* 18(2): 407–422.

Volokh, Eugene. 2014. Religious Law (Especially Islamic Law) in American Courts. *Oklahoma Law Review* 66(3): 431–458.

von Mehren, Arthur T. 1994. Recognition and Enforcement of Foreign Judgments: A New Approach for the Hague Conference? *Law and Contemporary Problems* 57(3): 271–287.

von Mehren, Arthur T. 2001. Drafting a Convention on International Jurisdiction and the Effects of Foreign Judgments Acceptable World-Wide: Can the Hague Conference Project Succeed? *American Journal of Comparative Law* 49: 191–202.

von Mehren, Arthur T., and Donald T. Trautman.1968. Recognition of Foreign Adjudications: A Survey and a Suggested Approach. *Harvard Law Review* 81: 1601–1696.

Wallach, Laurie R. 1986. Intercircuit Conflicts and the Enforcement of Extracircuit Judgments. *Yale Law Journal* 95(7): 1500–1521.

Wängnerud, Lena. 2009. Women in Parliaments: Descriptive and Substantive Representation. *Annual Review of Political Science* 12: 51–69.

Washington Times Editorial. 2008. A Victory for Free Speech. *Washington Times*, May 11.

Wasserstein-Fassberg, Celia. 2013. *Private International Law*, vol. I. Jerusalem: Nevo.

Waters, Melissa A. 2005. Mediating Norms and Identity: The Role of Transnational Judicial Dialogue in Creating and Enforcing International Law. *Georgetown Law Journal* 93: 487–574.

Weber, Steve. 1991. *Cooperation and Discord in U.S-Soviet Arms Control*. Princeton, NJ: Princeton University Press.

Wee, Sui-Lee. 2011. China Hails Canada Decision to Extradite Fugitive. *Reuters*, July 22.

Wee, Sui-Lee. 2014. Corrupt Chinese Hiding in Western Nations Elude Beijing's "Fox Hunt." *Reuters*, August 27.

Weintraub, Russell J. 1991. An Objective Basis for Rejecting Transient Jurisdiction. *Rutgers Law Journal* 22: 611–626.

Weiss, Anita M. 2003. Interpreting Islam and Women's Rights: Implementing CEDAW in Pakistan. *International Sociology* 18(3): 581–601.

Weissbrodt, David. 2014. International Fair Trial Guarantees. In *The Oxford Handbook of International Law in Armed Conflict*, edited by Andrew Clapham and Paola Gaeta, 410–440. Oxford: Oxford University Press.

Wells, Michael. 1996. Punitive Damages for Constitutional Torts. *Louisiana Law Review* 56: 841–872.

Wen, Philip. 2016. Federal Government Poised to Ignore Protests and Ratify Extradition Treaty with China. *Sydney Morning Herald*, December 16.

Wexler, Ian. 2008. Comfortable SOFA: The Need for an Equitable Foreign Criminal Jurisdiction Agreement with Iraq. *Naval Law Review* 56: 43–86.

Whitman, James Q. 2003. *Harsh Justice: Criminal Punishment and the Widening Divide between America and Europe*. New York: Oxford University Press.

Whytock, Christopher A. 2009a. Domestic Courts and Global Governance. *Tulane Law Review* 84: 67–123.

Whytock, Christopher A. 2009b. Myth or Mess? International Choice of Law in Action. *New York University Law Review* 84: 719–790.

Whytock, Christopher A. 2011. The Evolving Forum Shopping System. *Cornell Law Review* 96: 481–584.

Whytock, Christopher A. 2018. From International Law and International Relations to Law and World Politics. Legal Studies Research Paper Series No. 2018–29, University of California, Irvine.

Williams, Christopher J., and Martijn Schoonvelde. 2018. It Takes Three: How Mass Media Coverage Conditions Public Responsiveness to Policy Outputs in the United States. *Social Science Quarterly* 99(5): 1627–1636.

Wingfield-Hayes, Rupert. 2019. Carlos Ghosn and Japan's "Hostage Justice" System. *BBC News*, February 14.

Wodak, Ruth. 2015. *The Politics of Fear: What Right-wing Populist Discourses Mean*. London: Sage.

Wurmnest, Wolfgang. 2005. Recognition and Enforcement of U.S. Money Judgments in Germany. *Berkeley Journal of International Law* 23: 175–200.

Yamaguchi, Sawako, and Taryn Lindhorst. 2016. Domestic Violence and the Implementation of the Hague Convention on the Civil Aspects of International Child Abduction: Japan and U.S. Policy. *Journal of International Women's Studies* 17(4): 16–30.

Yang, Tung-Mou, and Terrence A. Maxwell. 2011. Information-Sharing in Public Organizations: A Literature Review of Interpersonal, Intra–Organizational and Inter-Organizational Success Factors. *Government Information Quarterly* 28(2): 164–175.

Yeo, Andrew I. 2011. *Activists, Alliances, and Anti-U.S. Base Protests*. New York: Cambridge University Press.

Zagaris, Bruce, and Jessica Resnick. 1997. The Mexico–U.S. Mutual Legal Assistance in Criminal Matters Treaty: Another Step toward the Harmonization of International Law Enforcement. *Arizona Journal of International and Comparative Law* 14: 1–96.

Zeugner-Roth, Katharina Petra, Vesna Žabkar, and Adamantios Diamantopoulos. 2015. Consumer Ethnocentrism, National Identity, and Consumer Cosmopolitanism as Drivers of Consumer Behavior: A Social Identity Theory Perspective. *Journal of International Marketing* 23(2): 25–54.

Zhao, Minxing. 2016. The Death Penalty in China and Its Impact on Sino-Canadian Criminal Justice Cooperation. In *Facing China as a New Global Superpower*, edited by Huhua Cao and Jeremy Paltiel, 109–124. New York: Springer.

INDEX

For the benefit of digital users, indexed terms that span two pages (e.g., 52–53) may, on occasion, appear on only one of those pages.
Tables and figures are indicated by *t* and *f* following the page number